This work is an original and critical analysis of Sikh literature from a feminist perspective. It begins with Gurū Nānak's vision of Transcendent Reality and concludes with the mystical journey of Rāṇī Rāj Kaur, the heroine of a modern Punjabi epic. The eight chapters of the book approach the Sikh vision of the Transcendent from historical, scriptural, symbolic, mythological, romantic, existential, ethical, and mystical perspectives. Each of these discloses the centrality of the woman, and shows convincingly that Sikh Gurūs and poets did not want the feminine principle to serve merely as a figure of speech or literary device; it was intended rather to pervade the whole life of the Sikhs. The book bolsters the claim that literary symbols should be translated into social and political realities, and in so doing puts a valuable feminist interpretation on a religious tradition which has remained relatively unexplored in scholarly literature.

# THE FEMININE PRINCIPLE IN THE SIKH VISION OF THE TRANSCENDENT

CAMBRIDGE STUDIES IN RELIGIOUS TRADITIONS

Edited by John Clayton (University of Lancaster), Steven Collins (University of Chicago) and Nicholas de Lange (University of Cambridge)

1. *Religion and the individual: A Jewish perspective*
   Louis Jacobs
2. *The body divine: the symbol of the body in the works of Teilhard de Chardin and Rāmānuja*
   Anne Hunt Overzee
3. *The feminine principle in the Sikh vision of the Transcendent*
   Nikky-Guninder Kaur Singh

# THE FEMININE PRINCIPLE IN THE SIKH VISION OF THE TRANSCENDENT

NIKKY-GUNINDER KAUR SINGH

*Department of Religious Studies, Colby College*

CAMBRIDGE
UNIVERSITY PRESS

Published by the Press Syndicate of the University of Cambridge
The Pitt Building, Trumpington Street, Cambridge CB2 1RP
40 West 20th Street, New York, NY 10011–4211, USA
10 Stamford Road, Oakleigh, Melbourne 3166, Australia



First published 1993

Printed in Great Britain at the University Press, Cambridge

*A catalogue record for this book is available from the British Library*

*Library of Congress cataloguing in publication data*

Singh, Nikky-Guninder Kaur
The feminine principle in the Sikh vision of the Transcendent /
Nikky-Guninder Kaur Singh.
p. cm. – (Cambridge studies in religious traditions: 3)
Includes bibliographical references.
ISBN 0 521 43287 1
1. Women in Sikhism. 2. Feminism – Religious aspects – Sikhism.
3. Sikhism – Doctrines. 4. Femininity (philosophy). I. Title.
II. Series.
BL2018.5.W65S56 1993
294.6′2′082 – dc20 92–25828 CIP

ISBN 0 521 43287 1 hardback



UP

*In memory of my grandmother, Roop Kaur*

# *Contents*

# *Preface*

*The feminine principle in the Sikh vision of the Transcendent* is the outcome of many years of reverie and research, and I could never succeed in acknowledging everyone for their input into it. From my grandmother, who gave me an image of what a Sikh woman could be, to my current students at Colby College, who make me recast and recreate my ideas with their provocative queries and comments, there are many, many conscious and unconscious contributors to whom I owe my thanks.

I spent several years of my childhood with my grandmother and was nurtured on her stories about life. Lying next to her on the terrace of our ancestral home under the starry skies I would keep asking Bībījī (for this is how we referred to my grandmother) to narrate to me incidents of my favorite protagonist, her maternal aunt – the strong and courageous woman who was afraid of nothing, not even of snakes. This tall and beautiful woman with big dark eyes as big as a triangle (Bībījī would join her two thumbs to make the base of a triangle formed by her index fingers) governed her own farm, and with her intelligence and kindness won the affection of all, including that of robbers and cobras. Each night I would stay up late hearing from my dainty grandmother's lips the daring episodes of her maternal aunt. With my mother, of course, it was different: she would read to me stories of Cinderella and Little Red Riding Hood, and I enjoyed them immensely. I especially enjoyed seeing their lovely pictures – one did not encounter their blonde hair and blue eyes in my part of the world. The convent school that my parents sent me to in the Punjab, and then Stuart Hall in Virginia, and later again Wellesley College continued to feed my imagination with many more figures like Cinderella. But somehow the image of Bībījī's maternal aunt had been impressed too deeply ever to be forgotten.

From my mother I received an aesthetic appreciation of Sikh

sacred literature. I would wake up in the morning to her melodious recitation of the Sikh scripture. I was too young to know what the verses meant, but their beautiful rhythms and melodies were to reverberate in my being for many a year to come. It was my father who ever so gently launched me on the academic search for my literary heritage. His devotion to the Sikh scholarly world was inspiring. He always encouraged me to interpret the sacred text for myself and to discover its meaning from my own perspective. And when I began to approach it from the feminist stance I had learned in America, he welcomed my new readings with an enchanted enthusiasm.

Apart from my childhood mentors, I wish to thank my teachers, colleagues, and students. I especially thank Debra Campbell, Yeager Hudson, Bill Mahan, Seyyed Hossein Nasr, Nancy Paxton, Annemarie Schimmel, my brother, Nripinder Singh, Giani Gurcharan Singhji, and my husband Harry Walker for reading drafts of my work and giving me valuable suggestions. I thank Grace Von Tobel, who typed the entire manuscript and created a special font for transliterating the Gurmukhī alphabet. I am very grateful to Colby College for granting me a pretenure sabbatical which enabled me to complete my research for this book at Brown University and in India. I warmly thank my gracious hosts at the Bhāī Vīr Singh Sadan in New Delhi and the Punjabi University in Patiala. Finally, I wish to extend my very deep thanks to my editor at Cambridge University Press, Mr. Alex Wright, for his endorsement of a project that has meant so much to me.

*Colby College, Waterville, Maine* NIKKY SINGH

# *Introduction*

As far back as I can remember, the characterization of girls and women in my society was a source of constant ambivalence and thus always fascinated me. The Sikh household into which I was born was part of a Punjabi society that brought together diverse traditions in which the status of women was as dubious as it was crucial. I saw them exalted, and I saw them downgraded. Over the years those feelings developed into a search for an explanation of this paradox. I came to the United States to finish my secondary education at an all-girls' high school in Virginia and then went on to study religion, philosophy, and literature at a liberal arts college for women. And yet, I returned every summer to my own home in India and saw once again the paradox of a society in which one woman could be exalted to the prime-ministership and another murdered with impunity for her dowry. Graduate school catalyzed my queries and perplexities. But it was the sessions on Women and Religion at the American Academy of Religion in 1984 that marked a turning point in my life. To hear and be in the midst of women like Mary Daly, Rosemary Ruether, Elisabeth Schüssler Fiorenza, Carol Christ, Judith Plaskow, Naomi Goldenberg – this for me was a moment of enlightenment and empowerment. I wished to turn to my own literature and discover its import from my female point of view. Thereafter the exploration of the feminine dimension in Sikh sacred and secular literature became the dominant motif in my research. These thealogians – for this is how feminist scholars of religion would accurately be described – had launched me onto recovering the rightful position of the feminine principle in my own tradition.

For me, and many other women, western feminists are the ones who inspired us to examine the feminine condition *vis-à-vis* our religio-cultural milieu. They have spurred women around the globe to explore both the presence and the absence of the feminine in our metaphysical, ethical, and ritual systems. Even in the East, several texts and autobiographies that have emerged from India, Pakistan, Egypt, Iran, in the last decade alone attest to the sensitive guidance provided by western feminists. And yet, although Third World women have excitedly picked up this new wave of western feminism, they find that their own experience has been excluded by the leaders whom they so greatly admire. After all of the significant advances made over the last decade, the understanding of women's experience has remained essentially circumscribed in its contexts. To find today that the leaders of the feminist avant-garde pay no attention to the response these selfsame articulations elicited within groups in some other parts of the world is especially regrettable.

Among women in the East, there is naturally the feeling of being let down, but a substantial group of women in the West has also been omitted. We must not forget after all that there is a large presence of eastern women in the West. Caught between two distinct cultures – maintaining their traditions, while trying to fit in with modern society – these eastern women face some very complex problems. Their multi-dimensional and polytheological–polythe*a*logical worldview is constantly challenged by the western, monotheological one, creating an intense psycho-religious inner tension. There is, then, an urgency that their Angst be shared, their voices be heard.

Even such a work as the substantial anthology of feminist spirituality *Weaving the Visions* is not as inclusive as it claims to be, although it does address a wide range of women's experiences in a variety of methodologies, voices, and forms of expression. In their introduction, co-editors Judith Plaskow and Carol Christ acknowledge that, in their first volume, *Womanspirit Rising*, published a decade earlier, women's experience only stood for "white, middle-class women's experience." They also admit that in exploring women's heritage, it focused on the Christian past, with brief forays into Gnosticism and goddess religions.[1] They realized that they had used "women" in an exclusivist manner just as patriarchal thinkers so often say "human" when they are only talking about males. Their second volume attempts to break away from both abstractionism and exclusivity, and echoes the voices of Jewish, Native American, African-American and lesbian women who express themselves palpably in discursive, non-linear, meditative, and poetic forms. Alas, the experience of women from the Middle East, South Asia, and the Far East is still absent.

The western feminists inspired me to follow their example and helped me to recognize that a feminist consciousness ought to be extended to eastern cultures. The task of reevaluating my tradition was a deeply personal act of self-discovery, but it was also a very necessary one to fill a major hiatus in the world of feminist writings. The feminine principle in the Sikh vision of the Transcendent will add a rich and colorful pattern to the visions woven by western feminists. Within the Sikh scriptural corpus the feminine principle is especially significant, and furthermore in the writings of the Sikh Gurūs, pride of place is given both to the female person and to the female psyche. *Ikk Oaṅ Kār* (One Being Is) is the core representation of the Sikh faith: the numeral 1 (Ikk or One) celebrates the existence of That which is beyond gender, space, time, and causality, and refers directly to the Ultimate Reality, to Being Itself. Yet this One is sensuously addressed and cherished in the Sikh holy writ as mother and father, sister and brother – thus as both male and female.

Focusing on the feminine dimension, we discover that Sikh literature is replete with rich feminine symbols and imagery. The Gurū Granth, the Sikh scripture, refers to the ontological ground of all existence as *mātā*, the Mother; to the divine spark within all creatures as *joti*, the light; to the soul longing to unite with the Transcendent One as *suhāgan*, the beautiful young bride; to the benevolent glance coming from the Divine as the feminine *nadar*, grace. Later Sikh writings both in poetry and in prose also evoke feminine models to portray physical and mental strength, spiritual awakening, existential Angst, ethical values, and mystical union. Thus Sikh literature continuously provides us with a multivalent and complex feminine imagery; the variety presents a host of options through which we can see who we are and what we might hope to become.

Modern western feminists have made us aware of the widespread negative effects of the exclusion of the feminine experience from Jewish and Christian scriptures. Carol Christ formulated western women's problem over a decade ago in the following words:

> Her word [Mary's] never became flesh and dwelt among us. Perhaps no one ever asked her what she was thinking. Perhaps she never heard stories which could give her words for her own experience. Perhaps the man who wrote the gospel narrative simply could not imagine what it felt like to be in her position. Whatever the reason, her experience and the experience of other women have not shaped the sacred stories of the Bible.[9]

Carol Christ's words still haunt us. Western women have inherited a worldview wherein "the daughters do not exist" and the images and symbols of sons and males are predominant.[3] In "Transcendental Etude," Adrienne Rich laments the estrangement women suffer from themselves and from other members of modern western societies because of the omission of feminine expression. Christine Downing has poignantly expressed the need for female images:

> We are starved for images which recognize the sacredness of the feminine and the complexity, richness, and nurturing power of female energy. We hunger for images of human creativity and love inspired by the capacity of female bodies to give birth and nourish, for images of how humankind participates in the natural world suggested by reflection on the correspondences between menstrual rhythms and the moon's waking and waning.[4]

Ironically, Sikh literary heritage abounds in precisely the kinds of images for which western feminist critics yearn so painfully. We see her in many roles: as the Mother, as the bride figure, as Durgā riding her lion fearlessly, as the maiden weaving, as Sundarī galloping in the jungles, as the unknown Punjabi woman walking solitarily to the lake, as the ambrosial Word that comes from the other world, as Rāṇī Rāj Kaur going through her mystical experience . . . In one mode or the other, *she* expresses the sacredness and honor bestowed upon woman and indicates the multivalency and richness of her power. No negative associations belittle her. Instead of being a hindrance, she is the paradigmatic figure who opens the way towards the Divine.

Through the varied and vivid imagery is expressed joyful affirmation of the feminine as a category of being with essential values and strength. The denigration of the female body "expressed in many cultural and religious taboos surrounding menstruation and childbirth" is absent from the Sikh worldview.[5] There is nothing inferior or abhorrent about the sexuality or sensuality of the bride. Gurū Nānak openly chides those who attribute pollution to women because of menstruation. "How can we call her polluted from whom the noblest of the world are born?" he asks.[6] In another passage in the Gurū Granth, Gurū Nānak reprimands his contemporaries for barring menstruating women from religious worship: "Pollution lies in the heart and not in the stained garment."[7] Female activities and accoutrements are assigned a high value, even a transcendent value: necklaces, ribbons, jewels, clothes, and cosmetics, and feminine activities such as stitching, dressing, or applying make-up are all imbued with spiritual significance.

The feminine principle in the Sikh vision of the Transcendent presents a holistic way of imagining and experiencing sacred power that can itself be a mode of empowerment. Such symbolism fits in snugly with the objectives of modern feminists who both recognize that female and male images perpetuate modes of domination and power-over and seek "ways to imagine sacred power as present in the whole complex web of life, not as power-taker but as empowerer."[8] The multitude of structurally united meanings present in the female figure manifest the unity of mind, body, and spirit; of social hierarchies; of transcendent and this-worldly; of cosmos and individual; of the self and others; of religion and art. The representation of the feminine in the Sikh tradition is an especially useful source for contemporary feminist thealogies since it enables us to rethink and restructure traditional ideas. As Marion Ronan has affirmed, "A central task of feminist spirituality is experiencing, expressing and bringing about the connectedness of creation, a connectedness seriously endangered by patriarchal polarization and phallocentrism."[9]

Many feminists join in condemning this dualistic antithesis which lies at the heart of the patriarchal vision of reality. The alienation of the masculine from the feminine is discerned to be the root of all dualities out of which emerge all other forms of alienation, for example, the split of the mind from the body, the separation of the subjective self from the objective world, the subjective retreat of the individual from the social community. Rosemary Ruether traces the roots of this bi-partite structure in which nature is subordinated to the spirit back to the apocalyptic–Platonic religious heritage of classical Christianity. Her argument can be heard in these powerful words:

> a static, devouring, death-dealing matter is imaged, with horror, as extinguishing the free flight of transcendence consciousness. The dualism of nature and transcendence, matter and spirit as female against male is basic to male theology. Feminist theology must fundamentally reject this dualism of nature and spirit. It must reject both sides of the dualism: both the image of mother–matter–matrix as 'static immanence'; and as the ontological foundation of existing, oppressive social systems and also the concept of spirit and transcendence as rootless, antinatural, originating in an 'other world' beyond the cosmos, ever repudiating and fleeing from nature, body, and the visible world.[10]

In Sikh literature, on the other hand, whether as Mother or bride or Durgā or Suṅdarī, the woman is portrayed as the center, interlinking many realms. Such a representation symbolically discloses varied images of how humankind can – and does – participate in the varied connecting spheres of the family, society, nature, cosmos, and the Transcendent.

Furthermore, in the Sikh vision of the Transcendent that Singular Reality, totally beyond, is to be revisioned within the very self. In the West one comes across many feminists who have rejected the Ideal notion of a white male god sitting up there. This insight has been brought forth in a passionate statement by Alice Walker which has become justly famous. In *The Color Purple*, Celie writes to her sister Nettie and in the letter she quotes Shug: "God is inside you and inside everybody else. You come into the world with God. But only them that search for it inside find it. And sometimes it just manifest itself even if you are not looking, or don't know what you looking for."[11] Shug's revisioning and redefining of God as the spirit within her and everyone else finds a parallel in a verse in the Sikh scripture: "sabh mahi joti joti hai soi – there is a light in all and that light is It."[12] That the transcendent reality remains within all beings was an enlightenment for a contemporary black southern woman in the USA. That was also the revelation Gurū Nānak, the first Sikh Gurū, brought to men and women in fifteenth-century India.

The Sikh vision of the Transcendent is derived from the Gurū Granth, the Sikh scripture. Its manifestation in secular literature – especially that manifestation which seeks to recapture and reinterpret the elements composing the ideality – is a vital topic to study in the context of the Sikh understanding of the Ultimate Reality. My primary objective, then, is to analyze the feminine dimension in the Sikh vision of the Transcendent One in both sacred and secular literature. I will be sifting through the more representative creations of the Sikh literary imagination and aesthetic sensibility in order to identify the status allocated to that component. To understand how the Sikh tradition has cherished the feminine principle, we must apprehend its significance in Sikh scripture and metaphysics as well as in Sikh literature and aesthetics.

My study, I hope, will accomplish a second, albeit ancillary, objective. Modern scholarship has posited Kabīr, the medieval Indian devotional poet, as a precursor of the Sikh faith,[13] and many have averred (see, for example, S. M. Ikram[14]) that Gurū Nānak was a follower of Kabīr. Historians are hard put to it to determine the extent to which Kabīr influenced the thought of Nānak or even to authenticate a time and place at which the two met (if they ever did!). Kabīr, as some scholars have pointed out, was rather contemptuous of and derogatory towards women.[15] Gurū Nānak certainly did not share that perspective, so to what extent can he be considered as a "follower" of Kabīr? Do not such constructs – Kabīr as master, Nānak as follower – in fact undermine the divine revelation that Gurū Nānak received independently? This line of argument implicates the entire debate surrounding what has been termed "the origin of Sikhism." I find it necessary to seek to extricate the Sikh enterprise from the usual presumption which, in identifying its origins, declares that Sikhism is a "cross between Hinduism and Islam."[16] The scriptures and the Sikh Gurūs, my study claims, have a *raison d'être* all their own. The celebration of the feminine principle within the Sikh tradition not merely acknowledges this principle as a significant component of Sikh identity but also gives us a measure of the autonomy of Sikh identity.

As far as methodology is concerned, I will use a hermeneutic approach to the literary texts. The remembrance and recognition of the feminine principle in the Sikh literary sensibility demands an analysis of the vocabulary, imagery, and themes articulated by seers and composers themselves. I consider the principles of "epochē" (bracketing out all presuppositions), "eidetic vision" (seeing things in themselves), and "critical corporate self-consciousness" to be universal academic virtues to which I would, of course, attempt to adhere stringently. In searching out a base for studying the Sikh vision of the Transcendent, I have become sensitive to the views of some contemporary scholars who have expressed methodological concerns in a more inclusive manner. Gaston Bachelard's method of "Poetics" in particular has impressed me as one that follows these three hermeneutic principles and reveals an exceptional sensitivity to language. He is especially conscious of the subordination of the feminine in literary discourse: "Vocabulary, it seems, is partial; it gives a privileged place to the masculine while treating the feminine very often as a derived or subordinate gender."[17] Bachelard's goal is to reawaken our appetite for language and our taste in words, and his method is "to lay bare the feminine depths in the words themselves."[18]

Without wishing to sound trivial or sacrilegious, I quote the final passages from his introduction to *The Poetics of Reverie*:

> But it is not sufficient to receive; one must welcome. One must say with the pedagogue and the dietician in the same voice, "assimilate." In order to do that, we are advised not to swallow too large a bite. We are told to divide each difficulty into as many parts as possible, the better to solve them. Yes, chew well, drink a little at a time, savor poems line by line. All these precepts are well and good. But one precept orders them. One first needs a good desire to eat, drink, and read. One must want to read a lot, read more, always read.
>
> Thus in the morning, before the books piled high on my table, to the god of reading, I say my prayer of the devouring reader: "Give us this day our daily hunger . . ."[19]

Bachelard's approach promises to be very relevant to the present study. While embracing many principles of phenomenology, Bachelard does not adhere exclusively to this system for its own sake. In fact, his approach avoids the dangers inherent in the preoccupation with "methodology" *per se*. In his lecture on "Methodology and the Study of Religion: Some Misgivings," Wilfred Cantwell Smith states that "methodology is the massive red herring of modern scholarship, the most significant obstacle to intellectual progress, the chief distraction from rational understanding of the world."[20] Smith is absolutely right in saying this. There is today an overemphasis on the *how* – on the methodology, on finding the right (right being defined as scientifically objective) approach – which diverts us from the actual content, thereby giving precedence to the *method* used in studying a particular subject over the *actual* study of it. This danger is short-circuited by Bachelard: a brief but ardent prayer – and off he goes to his books. In emulation, I propose not to waste time armoring myself with a methodological coat-of-arms.

Bachelard's approach is also attractive in that it seems to be in harmony with the Sikh perspective on learning and knowledge. In fact, the very genesis of the Sikh faith is traced to Gurū Nānak's (the first prophet) *drinking* of a cup of ambrosia of the Divine Name. And the Sikh holy writ concludes by inviting all readers to savor fully the Divine Word:

> thālu vici tini vastū paīo
> satu saṅtokhu vīcāro . . .
> je ko khāvai je ko bhuṅcai
> tis kā hoi udhāro.[21]

> On the platter lie arranged three delicacies:
> Truth, contentment, and contemplation . . .
> S/he who eats them, s/he who savors them
> Obtains liberation.

In this passage, which constitutes the epilogue to the Gurū Granth, the scripture itself is perceived as a delicious platter, containing the epistemological values of truth, contentment, and contemplation. Through the centuries, Sikhs have derived constant nourishment from the Divine Word. Bachelard's analogy with physical appetite and savoring is sustained throughout Sikhism. The French literary critic enables us to recognize the integral connection between aesthetics and epistemology in Sikhism, and he entices us to look at the texts closely. Hungry and thirsty, we approach with a wholesome appetite rather than with a fastidious intent to test and sample but never quite enjoy.

The Sikh scriptures, certain transitional writings of the Sikhs, and modern Sikh secular literature will form the core of the present work. These writings span almost five centuries of Sikh literature, from the utterances vouchsafed to Gurū Nānak (1469–1539) to the works of the modern Sikh poet and scholar Bhāī Vīr Singh (1872–1957). The parameters of my study may appear extensive, but this breadth is necessary to obtain a clear understanding of the subject as pursued through the different phases of Sikh literary history. The focus, however, will remain on the feminine principle, and my course will be well marked. The scope of the study will be further restricted by limiting the choice of authors and works to such as will for obvious reasons be necessary. The criterion for selection in both cases will be their capacity to illumine the theme of the feminine principle. The abundant materials at hand point to the significance of that theme.

The book falls into eight chapters. Each approaches the Sikh vision of the Transcendent from a different perspective: historical, scriptural, symbolic, mythological, romantic, existential, ethical, and mystical. Throughout, the leitmotif is the unearthing of the feminine principle.

In the first chapter, "The Primal Paradox: seeing the Transcendent," I shall look into the historical origins of the Sikh religion – focusing on the revelation bequeathed to Gurū Nānak. As recorded in the *Purātan Janamsākhī*, Gurū Nānak received *bāṇī*, the Divine Word – feminine in gender – from the Transcendent One Itself. More than five centuries later, the Sikhs today observe their faith vividly through *bāṇī*. Icons and images form no part of Sikh sacred space. It is the *bāṇī* alone – wherever and whenever seen, heard, or recited – that makes their space and time sacred. The Sikh community's ideals, institutions, and rituals continue to derive their meaning from it. Chapter 1 then addresses issues such as these: What constitutes the phenomenon of seeing? How can the Transcendent One be seen so palpably, so sensuously through the Word? What is the significance of the feminine in the divine–human encounter?

Taking up the problem of religious language, Chapter 2, "Mother: the Infinite Matrix," will explore the analogical ontology of the feminine principle. In Sikh literature itself, male and female principles play an equally important role in the process of analogy, but in Sikh studies up until now, the male principle has tended to dominate. Clearly, a more holistic comprehension of the Singular Reality is required in order to do justice to the Sikh vision of the Transcendent, and it is precisely this holistic perspective that is provided by the term *mātā*, Mother, and other images and concepts that are born of her. The analogical relationship between the Transcendent and the Female shows that she embodies what the Reality uniquely is. Mother, the Infinite Matrix, and the Transcendent Reality are linked together by common attributes. She is *joti* or light, the spirit informing all – the She within us all whom Ntozake Shange found and loved fiercely. She is *kudarati*, creation itself, the intimation of the Transcendent One – the *saguna* form of the totally *nirguṇa*. She is *nadar*, the benevolent glance from beyond. She is the "Eternal Feminine who draws us onward."

Fundamental to Sikh scripture, the Gurū Granth, is the image of the bride with whom the Sikh Gurūs, beginning with Gurū Nānak, identified themselves and expressed through her voice the ardor of their hearts. In Chapter 3, "The bride seeks her Groom," I explore the intricate and vibrant network of the physical, psychological, and spiritual realms woven by the young bride who is essentially embodied, passionate, relational, communal, and religious. This chapter will focus on the way in which the symbol of the bride presents a holistic pattern of imagining and experiencing the sacred that can be a mode of empowerment. How does the bridal symbol expand women's heritage? How does Gurū Nānak's symbol – so distant in time and space – nourish diversity? These are vital questions that must be addressed.

Gurū Gobind Singh, the last of the ten Gurūs or prophet-teachers of the Sikh faith, succeeded to the spiritual seat of Gurū Nānak in AD 1675. The fusion of the devotional and the martial was the most important feature of the philosophy of Gurū Gobind Singh and of his career as a spiritual leader and harbinger of a revolutionary impulse. From this transitional stage of Sikh literature, I will be analyzing his Braj and Punjabi compositions where Durgā is the central character. Gurū Gobind Singh chose her and employed the poetic medium to impart a new orientation to the minds of a people given to passivity and riven with inequalities. Interestingly, from amongst the traditionally accounted 330 million gods and goddesses, it is the invincible Durgā, the autonomous Hindu goddess (for she is not a consort), who captures the imagination of the Sikh prophet. Drawing upon the writings of feminists such as Bella Debrida and Merlin Stone, I will assess Gurū Gobind Singh's aesthetic portrayal of the Hindu goddess. Further concerns are addressed in this fourth chapter: How does the main transitional figure in Sikh history use the feminine principle to convey the "masculine" virtues of courage and justice? What is the function of this Hindu myth? How and why is the metaphor of Durgā's sword introduced into the Sikh envisioning of the Transcendent One? What meaning does this metaphor have today as Sikhs all over the world recite their daily supplications, which begin with a remembrance of the goddess's weapon?

The works of the major twentieth-century writer Bhāī Vīr Singh also abound with feminine symbols illustrating the feminine principle. He celebrates women by making them the principal characters in his novels and poetry. Popular in every sense of the word, his works are required reading at high schools and universities in the Punjab. Yet his insights regarding the feminine are glossed over and ignored by the very culture which reveres him. He is the paradigm of one who has been greatly admired but completely misunderstood in his powerful portrayal of life in all its modes.

My fifth chapter is "The maiden weaves: garlands of songs and waves." As the title suggests, it strains the capacity of language to express the polarities of the romantic: proximity and distance, infinitesimal and infinite, human and divine, male and female, past and future, empty and full. Human language explodes in its effort to communicate with the Transcendent One – so near, so far! It is the young woman who fearlessly expresses the scriptural emotion of love. Like the bride figure in the Gurū Granth, Bhāī Vīr Singh's heroine restates the primacy of the feminine consciousness in the search for the Transcendent One. While tracing the connections between the scripture of the Sikhs and the poetry of Bhāī Vīr Singh, I will explore two further questions: What is the relationship between the text and the hermeneute? Why is the poetic syntax so central to the Sikh enterprise?

"Jivan Kī Hai" ("What is Life?"), written in 1922, is one of Bhāī Vīr Singh's earlier poems. Its sole character is a woman who wrestles deeply with the fundamental question: "What is Life?" She sees herself separate and standing apart from nature – the lake and the other beautiful objects around her. Unable to tranquilize herself and escape the radicalness of her human condition, she keeps questioning herself and her surroundings painfully. This mood of Angst, however, leads the woman to a very significant disclosure which is but a vivid and poignant illustration of the quintessential statement of Sikh philosophy: *Ikk Oaṅ Kār*. After five visits to a beautiful lake, the woman has the vision of the Singular and Transcendent Reality. I shall attempt in Chapter 6 to see how Bhāī Vīr Singh's protagonist reiterates the Sikh existential standpoint.

*Suṅdarī*, the first novel in the Punjabi language (published in 1898), illustrates the lived ethical ideals of the Sikh religion and especially its injunctions against social injustices and religious corruption. Suṅdarī, the heroine after whom the novel is named, struggles for justice and peace, a struggle carried on far from "home and hearth" – in forests. The ideal of womanhood in India is that of wife and mother. Sītā, Savitrī, and Satī are the classical examples of the paradigmatic Indian woman. As a woman with a broken-off engagement, fighting boldly with men, Suṅdarī must have come across as a unique ethical paradigm! She is the incarnation of all that is best in Sikh life and tradition, yet she does not remain a remote paragon of excellence or a distant goddess. Chapter 7 then analyzes the character of Suṅdarī living out in her life truths and morals enshrined in the Sikh faith, particularly her embodiment of the Sikh moral imperative: *kirat karnī vaṇḍ chhakṇā te nām japṇā* – working, sharing your earnings with others, and reciting the Divine Name.

In the epic *Rāṇā Sūrat Singh*, Bhāī Vīr Singh depicts the spiritual odyssey of Rāṇī Rāj Kaur, the young widow of the king. Starting out from her palace where she sits forlornly, Rāṇī Rāj Kaur ascends through the spiritual levels described in the Gurū Granth as the *Gyān Khaṇḍ*, *Saram Khaṇḍ*, *Karam Khaṇḍ*, and *Sac Khaṇḍ* – the realms of Knowledge, Aesthetics, Grace, and Truth. After her mystical experience, the agonized and shattered young widow is transformed into an energetic administrator who intelligently and justly performs her queenly duties. The final chapter explores how the Rāṇī's voyage empirically renders the metaphysical structure of spiritual ascension enunciated in Sikh scripture. In examining the mystical dimensions of the Sikh tradition, I shall use the four characteristics of mysticism recorded by William James in his *Varieties of Religious Experience*, namely ineffability, noetic quality, transiency, and passivity.

The Sikh tradition, as such, has remained relatively unexplored. Even the most eminent students of the history of religion generally regard the Sikh faith as sectarian in character, and therefore inconsequential in comparison to what is considered "its parent religion, Hinduism." Some years ago, Mark Juergensmeyer attended to this question and presented his study in an aptly chosen title: "The Forgotten Tradition: Sikhism in the Study of World Religions."[22] He advanced the thesis that Sikh religion has suffered neglect in academic circles because it does not meet the usual definitions of a "religious tradition." He also notes that matters Sikh have been omitted from the thematic studies of Eliade, van der Leeuw, Wach, and others belonging to the history of religions school. In such writings, Sikh religious experience – myths about Gurūs, the sacred scriptures, *gurbānī* worship – never appears.[23] Even within general texts on the religion and civilization of India, Sikh studies, Juergensmeyer contends, fall victim to two prejudices. The first prejudice is that against the modern period. A book on Indian philosophy is a book on ancient Indian philosophy. The thrust of scholarship is on antiquity. With the persistence of such classicist tendencies, Sikhism, a relatively modern phenomenon, finds no place. The second prejudice which faces Sikh studies in the literature on Indian studies is the prejudice against regionalism. The Sikh religion is not only relatively modern, but is almost exclusively Punjabi. Scholarship on Indian civilization thus ignores the regionally specific culture of the Sikhs.[24] More than two decades have gone by, but Juergensmeyer's lament has elicited no significant response.

Stephen Dunning has also reflected upon the neglect of this "virtually unknown faith in the West." In his article "The Sikh Religion: An Examination of Some of the Western Studies," he states that a major barrier to the study of the Sikh religion is that a wide variety of languages has been used in the Gurū Granth. Many upcoming scholars are put off by the fact that they would have to study these languages before they could approach this tradition meaningfully.[25]

My study aims to initiate new research that will contribute in a fundamental manner to the small body of literature that does exist on Sikh studies. Biographies of the Sikh Gurūs and major poets are widely available; so too are a variety of polemical tracts and sociological studies treating separate aspects of Sikh belief and social organization. The present study – tracing the continuity of the feminine aspect of the Transcendent from Gurū Nānak to modern literature – will constitute a fresh orientation which is radically independent but at the same time contributes to the slender critical corpus accumulating ever so slowly in Sikh studies.

The Sikh tradition provides a striking instance in the history of religion of a faith that acknowledges the significance of the feminine component within human existence. Yet, this fact has suffered neglect at the hands of academicians, Sikh and others. The feminine principle in Sikh literature is a great resource for uplifting women's psyche, but needs to be rediscovered. A few modern feminist writers have noticed that the Sikh religion advocates equality among men and women. Theodora Foster Carroll, for instance, is impressed with Nānak's advocacy of women's rights: "Anyone from any caste or class was welcome, and females came nearer to achieving religious and social equality through Sikhism than through the other vying religions of the region . . . Nānak consistently praised women, denounced their oppression, strongly rejected suggestions made by his followers that women were evil or unworthy, and refused to make additions to the Adi Granth that would have reviled women."[26] For the most part, however, even when it has been noticed, Gurū Nānak's distinctive contribution has remained unexplored. Feminist thealogians, especially Asianists such as Rita Gross, who have produced some very perceptive studies on the Hindu goddess, have disregarded the striking feminine symbolism pervading Sikh literature.

In spite of its presence in literature, a recognition and validation of female symbolism has been neglected in the Punjab itself. I recall my grandmother requesting a male member of the family to recite to her the appropriate verses from the *Bārah Māh* text on the first day of the month, for it would be inauspicious for her to hear the dawning month announced by feminine lips! During menstruation, women are cautioned against walking amid flowers and crops, lest they cast a shadow of blight upon the land!! In Sikh hermeneutic and exegetical work, the importance of the feminine dimension is generally glossed over. The commentators, interpreters, and translators of Sikh scripture have primarily elaborated the masculine principle; the feminine – so powerful and eloquent – has been overlooked. Often the exegetes have succumbed to the patriarchal worldview and reversed the symbol's meaning. For instance, while explaining one of Gurū Nānak's hymns in his book *Gurū Nānak Bāṇī Prākaś*, Taran Singh proceeds to overturn the symbol,[27] and renders the hymn in masculine terms. This offends the text where it is the woman who speaks and the mood and imagination are feminine. Gurū Nānak in particular, and the Gurū Granth as a whole, attest to how the Transcendent can be apprehended most sensitively and aesthetically through the feminine experience. My own research will, I hope, invite further academic scrutiny both of the tradition itself and of issues pertaining to the role of women within its historical development.

By arriving at a meaningful awareness of the vision of the Transcendent espoused by that community's mentor-preceptors, we can construct the ideal female character; women should be encouraged to acknowledge that ideal. By analyzing the secular literature we can see the diverse articulations on that ideal; by searching through the material we can reconstruct the original message. More significantly, to many of us the ideal of the equality of the sexes to which Gurū Nānak beckoned the people in the fifteenth century could serve as a model, and Gurū Nānak could be seen as an early champion of issues so unequivocally arresting in our own day and age. The breaking of icons – be they visual or aural – in the depiction of Being was Gurū Nānak's own *modus operandi*. His *bāṇī* (revealed word), uttered some five centuries ago during an exceptionally trying religio-political situation, is replete with phrase and imagery that could give a new meaning, a new direction, a new authenticity to our own cause of equality chartered only in recent decades in the West.

CHAPTER I

# *The Primal Paradox: seeing the Transcendent*

bāṇī gurū gurū hai bāṇī
vicu bāṇī amrit sare.

*bāṇī* is the Gurū, the Gurū *bāṇī*
Within *bāṇī* lie all elixirs.

The genesis of the Sikh religion can be traced to Gurū Nānak's seeing of the Transcendent. That epiphanic moment in Sikh history discloses what I would term a the*a*logical vision. It anticipates modern feminist concerns about the reconciliation of polarities which shatter the binary oppositions manipulated by the theological vision of ultimate reality; it proscribes all forms of idolatry; it generates a new ideal with a strong commitment to social change; and its inspired poetic syntax promotes a shift from an androcentric to a feminist construction of the cosmos in a new and liberating relationship between the human and the divine. In turn, a reseeing of Gurū Nānak's vision could be a mode of empowerment for many of us of the "Second Sex."

Gurū Nānak was born in AD 1469 at Talvaṇḍī, a small village about fifty miles southwest of Lahore in the Punjab. The Punjab was then part of the Lodi empire, and the formative years of Nānak's life coincided with the relatively stable period of Bāhlol Khān (1451–88).[1] Nānak's father, Kalyān Cand (Kālū, for short), belonged to the Bedī clan of the Kśatriyas. As the village accountant, he kept rent records of the estate of the local Muslim landlord, Rāi Bulār.

The birth and life stories of Gurū Nānak coming down the generations form a distinctive genre called Janamsākhīs. They are short narratives written in the Punjabi language (which uses the Gurmukhī script), and they represent the earliest extant models of prose in that language. They are stories (*sākhīs*) of the birth (*janam*) and life of Gurū Nānak (1469–1539), the first prophet-mentor of the

Sikh religion. The earliest Janamsākhīs were written towards the end of the sixteenth century, and have come down through the years in a variety of renditions such as the Bālā, Miharbān, Ādī, and Purātan Janamsākhīs.[2] They underscore the importance and uniqueness of Gurū Nānak's birth and life in terms of the personal loyalties and proclivities of their authors.

Despite this diversity, the Janamsākhis maintain one common strand: the portrayal of Gurū Nānak's life through an idiom and style reminiscent of allegory and myth. One could, for instance, see a host of striking similarities between some of these narratives and those found in Otto Rank's book *The Myth of the Birth of the Hero*. In their central concern and luminous descriptions, the accounts of Nānak's life have a great deal in common with those of Christ, Buddha, and Kṛṣṇa.[3] According to the Janamsākhī accounts, prodigies attended the illustrious advent. In the spirit of the birth narratives in the gospels, light flashed across the mud-built room in which the birth took place. The gifted and wise both in the celestial and in the terrestrial regions rejoiced in the momentous event and stood in obeisance to the exalted spirit which had adopted bodily vesture in fulfillment of the Divine Will. Daultāṅ, the Muslim midwife, reported that there were many children born under her care, but none so extraordinary as baby Nānak.

The family priest, Paṇḍit Hardyāl, came to cast the horoscope and told the happy parents that their son would sit under a canopy. He prophesied about the child's mission:

> Both Hindus and Muslims will pay him reverence. His name will become current on earth and in heaven. The ocean will give way to him; so will the earth and the skies. He will worship and acknowledge but the One Formless Lord and teach others to do so . . . Every creature he will consider as God's very own creation.[4]

While growing up in Talvaṇḍī, the child Nānak was considered to be a favorite of both Hindus and Muslims. A quotation from the *Miharbān Janamsākhī* shows how followers of both religions admired him:

> A Hindu chancing to pass by would involuntarily exclaim, "Great is Gobind the Lord! Such a small child and yet he speaks so auspiciously. His words are as immaculate as he is handsome. He is the image of God Himself!" And if a Muslim saw him, he would remark with equal enthusiasm, "Wonderful is Thy creation, Merciful Master! How good-looking is the child, how polite his speech! Talking to him brings one such satisfaction. He is a noble one blessed by Almighty Allah Himself."[5]

Geographically as well as culturally, the boy Nānak grew up between Hindus and Muslims. At the age of eleven he refused to undergo the [*upanāyana* ceremony and take the sacred thread of the Hindu upper caste to which he belonged. The story notes how Nānak condemned social divisions from his very childhood. We are told that he spent most of the time outside, tending the family herd of cattle, conversing with wayfaring Sādhūs and Sūfis, and devoting his time to solitude and inward communion. Later, at the invitation of his sister Nānakī and her husband Jai Rām, he moved to Sultānpur, where he worked in the Muslim Nawāb's *modikhānā* (grain stores).

At Sultānpur, Nānak had a vision of a totally formless and transcendent Being, a vision which launched him on his mission, a vision which formed the foundations of the Sikh religion. Seeing the Transcendent, which we refer to as the Primal Paradox of the Sikh religion, is vividly described in *sākhī* no. 10 in the *Purātan Janamsākhī*. As the name implies, *Purātan* (meaning "old," in Punjabi) is considered to be the oldest version of the extant Janamsākhī accounts. It can be found in the edition prepared by Bhāī Vīr Singh and published as *Purātan Janamsākhī* in 1926.[6] In spite of its size and the large number of *sākhīs* it contains, the standard title for the text remains in the singular. The fragile Colebrooke manuscript formed the primary text for Bhāī Vīr Singh – its missing lines being supplied from the Hāfizābād manuscript.[7] The particular *sākhī* describing Gurū Nānak's revelatory experience has been designated as "Beiṅ Pravesh" – entry into the river Beiṅ.

It is said that while staying in the home of his sister Nānakī in Sultānpur, Nānak would daily bathe in the river Beiṅ. One morning, he did not return home after his ablutions and everyone believed he had drowned. But Nānak reappeared on the bank of the Beiṅ on the third day. According to the *Purātan Janamsākhī*, the interval was spent in communion with the Supreme Being:

> As the Primal Being willed, Nānak, the devotee, was ushered into the Divine Presence. Then a cup filled with *amrit* (nectar) was given him with the command, "Nānak, this is the cup of Name-adoration. Drink it . . . I am with you and I do bless and exalt you. Whoever remembers you will have my favor. Go, rejoice, in My Name and teach others to do so . . . I have bestowed upon you the gift of My Name. Let this be your calling." Nānak offered his salutations and stood up.

Nānak celebrated the favor through a song of praise:

Were my age to be extended by millions of years
and I could make air my food and drink,
Were I to seal myself in a cave and ceaselessly to meditate
without seeing the sun or the moon and without any sleep,
Even then I would not be able to measure Your greatness,
nor signify the glory of Your Name!
The Formless One is the eternal, irreplaceable truth,
Do not try to describe That by hearsay.
If it pleases It, in Its grace It will reveal Itself.
Were I to be shredded and ground like grain in a mill,
Were I to be burnt in a fire and reduced to ashes,
Even then I would not be able to measure Your greatness,
nor signify the glory of Your Name!
Were I to fly like a bird beyond the skies,
Were I to vanish from human gaze at will,
and could live without food and drink,
Even then I would not be able to measure Your greatness,
nor signify the glory of Your Name!
Had there been ton upon ton of paper, says Nānak,
and had I absorbed the wisdom of volumes beyond count,
If I had a supply of inexhaustible ink and I could
write with the speed of the wind,
Even then I would still not be able to measure Your greatness,
nor signify the glory of Your Name![8]

Thereupon, the Voice spoke: "Nānak, you discern My will." Nānak recited the *Japu*, which constituted the core of his doctrine and which became the opening text of the Sikh scripture.

The Voice was heard again: "Who is just in your eyes, Nānak, shall be so in Mine. Whoever receives your grace shall abide in Mine. My name is the Supreme God; your name is the divine Gurū." Gurū Nānak then bowed in gratitude and was given the robe of honor. A sonorous melody in the Rāga Dhanāsarī rang forth:

The skies are the platter; sun and moon, lamps; stars, the pearls.
The breeze is the incense;
Entire verdure, a bouquet of flowers.
What an *āratī*! . . .
There is a light in all and that light is That One.
From Its light, all are illumined.
Through the Gurū the light becomes visible.
What pleases You, becomes Your *āratī*!
Like the bumble-bee, day and night I long for your lotus-feet.
Pleads Nānak, grant the thirsty bird, the nectar of Your Name.[9]

Gurū Nānak remained in unbroken silence after his reappearance.

When he spoke the following day, the first words he uttered were: "There is no Hindu; there is no Musalmān."

This marks a coalescence of significant elements that constitute Nānak's seeing of the Transcendent One, a seeing which I interpret as a thealogical vision. They are closely connected, but I shall attempt to identify four of them – and endeavor to do so without violating their essential integrity.

## I

As he is ushered into the Divine Presence, Nānak has a profound insight into the existence as well as into the nature of the Transcendent Reality; his experience manifests a connectedness which thealogians across the continents yearn for. We find that he does not see It, but only hears Its voice and drinks from the ambrosial cup of Its Name. The hearing of the command, the holding of the cup, the savoring of the nectar of Its Name – these together constitute the fullness of his vision of the Infinite One. Drinking the ambrosia signifies the sapiential quality of knowledge received from the Divine. It is an utterly simple yet a most viable and highly penetrating portrayal of Gurū Nānak's encounter with the Transcendent Reality. He does not see any being at all and yet acquires insight into the very ground of Being. To recall Santayana (*The Sense of Beauty*), sight is perception par excellence:

> Sight is a method of presenting psychically what is practically absent; and as the essence of the thing is its existence in our absence, the thing is spontaneously conceived in terms of sight.[10]

Gurū Nānak thus sees or has *darśana* (which literally means "seeing" from the root *drś*, "to see") of Reality. This seeing provides him with a spontaneous recognition of absolute knowledge. Seeing and knowing in the intrinsic sense are one: *darśana* in Sanskrit denotes both seeing and philosophic speculation. Similarly, the Sanskrit root *vid*, meaning "to know," is etymologically related to the Latin *videre* = to see, and to the Greek *oida* = to know, and even to the English *wit* (that natural talent of the medieval *wit*-ches, who were slandered for their superior gifts).[11] Several of Gurū Nānak's hymns bear witness to such a "seeing" of the Transcendent as the source of Knowledge and stand in fundamental opposition to insights gained through doubt (Descartes) and intense inquiry (the Upaniṣads). To quote Gurū Nānak from the Gurū Granth:

> jah jah dekhā tah tah soi.[12]
> To whichever direction I turn my eyes, there It is.
>
> jah dekhā tah rahiā samāi.[13]
> Wheresoever I see, there It pervades.
>
> jah dekhau tah ekaṅkāru.[14]
> Wherever I see, there is the Singular Reality.
>
> jah dekhā tah ekau tūṅ.[15]
> Wheresoever I see, there are You.
>
> mūrakh hoe na akhī sūjhai.[16]
> Ignorant is s/he who sees not Reality with her/his own eyes.

In all of these instances, the emphasis is upon seeing the Infinite through the eyes. No arguments or proofs – ontological, cosmological, moral, or teleological – will do; the Primal Paradox is the certitude of seeing That which is totally beyond the physical world. Rudolph Arnheim's equation of eyesight with insight finds a remarkable parallel in Gurū Nānak's equation of *dekhai* with *sujhai*.[17] *Dekhai* is the faculty of seeing and corresponds with Arnheim's term "eyesight." Yet, *dekhai* or eyesight is, metaphysically speaking, identical with the category of *sujhai* – realization or discovery; literally, being endowed with insight into phenomena as they intrinsically are. Senses and rationality are not pitted against each other; on the contrary, they include each other.

We may note that these two faculties of physical seeing and intellectual insight have been lucidly elaborated in Hindu scriptures as well. The Kaṭha Upaniṣad, for example, contains a highly philosophical dialogue between Yama, the god of death, and young Naciketas, who desires to obtain knowledge of the ontological base of the universe. Through the parable of the chariot, Lord Yama explains to Naciketas the various layers of the "self." The intrinsic self (*ātman*) is compared to the owner of a chariot (*rathin*). The body, the human physique, corresponds to the chariot (*ratha*). The five senses (*indriyāni*) – eyesight being one of them – are represented by the horses. The horses in turn are controlled by the reins (*pragraha*) which stand for *manas* or mind. But the reins are held by the charioteer (*sārathi*), which in this episode is called *buddhi* or consciousness, the faculty of discrimination. And the horses go nowhere but where the charioteer desires.[18] Thus, in this classical text as well, eyesight – the power to see – and insight, the power to discriminate or realize, are ultimately the same.

In the *Bhagavad Gītā*, too, we see something quite similar. Arjuna's charioteer is Lord Kṛṣṇa, who at the outset drives the chariot – with the horses under his control – into the middle of the battlefield of Kurukśetra, where Arjuna sees all his kinsmen in the two armies. However, his divine charioteer, Lord Kṛṣṇa, through psychological, sociological, and philosophical arguments provides Arjuna with insight into the real nature of the universe, the microcosmic form of which is the undying, immortal, and invincible *ātman*.[19] Sight and insight are thus seen as convergent phenomena.

There is, however, one major difference. In the *Bhagavad Gītā*, Kṛṣṇa, the blue-black, lotus-eyed god, assumes a physical form and plays an active role in the unfolding of the human drama. Later Kṛṣṇa manifests his universal form to Arjuna, beholding which the Pāṇḍu brother begins to tremble. Says Arjuna:

> Thy great form, of many mouths and eyes,
> O Great-armed one, of many arms, thighs and feet
> Of many bellies, terrible with many tusks –
> Seeing it the worlds tremble, and I too.[20]

The Janamsākhī account of Nānak's vision of the Transcendent, in contrast, does not postulate such a physical presence or vision of Ultimate Reality. The Transcendent does not exist in any perceivable form. Nānak does not see the Divine Being in "form" – whether it be physical or cosmic (as does Arjuna); rather, he experiences the presence of the Formless One. Moreover, there is not even a hint as to the spatial placement of Being; Nānak is simply ushered into the Divine Presence. This paradigmatic process of envisioning the utterly formless became fundamental to the Sikh tradition. In the *Japu*, Gurū Nānak states: "thāpiā na jāe kītā na hoe āpe āpi nirañjanu soe[21] – It cannot be installed in any temple, It cannot be fashioned in any form. The Immaculate One is self-existent." Later he adds that "It has no form, no feature, no color; of the three qualities It is independent – rūpu na rekh na raṅgu kichhu trihu gun te prabh bhinn."[22] Throughout there is an absolute rejection of any gender qualifications. We discern that male images do not manipulate Nānak's perception of the Transcendent.

Since the unity of aesthetics and ontology underlies such a process of envisioning the Transcendent, I would like to advance "aesthet-icontology" as a technical term through which Gurū Nānak's own emphases can be better understood. I use this compound to underscore the integral unity of aesthetics and ontology so central to Gurū Nānak's perception. To use the two terms independently would fail to do justice to his vision. While *aesthetic* evokes the immediacy and directness of Gurū Nānak's vision, *ontology* brings out the is-ness, the substance of it. What is most significant is that Gurū Nānak's process reveals for us a the*a*logical vision. The notion that transcendence is "rootless, antinatural, originating in an 'other world,' beyond the cosmos, ever repudiating and fleeing from nature, body, and the visible world" is clearly rejected in Gurū Nānak's most physical and sensual seeing."[23] Rosemary Ruether, Mary Daly, Carol Christ, and other feminists in the West have been plagued by the divisions residing in the patriarchal theological construction of Reality. Ruether, for instance, argues that the male monotheistic vision of God splits Reality into a dualism of the superior transcendent spirit and the inferior and dependent physical nature: "Bodiless ego or spirit is seen as primary, existing before the cosmos. The physical world is made as an artifact by transcendent, disembodied mind or generated through some process of devolution from spirit to matter."[24] In this bi-partite framework, the sensual and material dimension is not only subordinated to the mind and spirit, but also given a negative identity.

Such chasms and hierarchies are omnipresent in western philosophy. For example, Baumgarten designates aesthetics as the science of sensuous knowledge the object of which is beauty – in contrast with logic, the object of which is truth.[25] In fact, most western thinkers tend to divide philosophy into logic, ethics, and aesthetics, the goals of which are separately the true, the good, and the beautiful. A person's thinking is then determined by the truth, his or her character and behavior by the good, and his or her feelings by the beautiful. We may recall Kierkegaard's distinction amongst the three realms – that of aesthetics, ethics, and religion – with the aesthetic at the bottom rung. On the contrary, we find that Gurū Nānak's unified "aestheticontological" experience bypasses all divisions and hierarchies, and manifests the co-existence of sensuous knowledge (hearing of the divine command, holding the cup of name-adoration, drinking it) and absolute Truth (insight into the Singular Reality). Ethics would be but its natural co-product.

2

A second element which emerges from Nānak's Primal Paradox is the utter unicity of the Transcendent Reality, proscribing all forms of idolatry. Gurū Nānak simultaneously sees, comprehends, and rejoices in the formlessness and singularity of the Ultimate Reality. This totally aestheticontological experience induces his verbalization of Ultimate Reality which has come down in Sikh philosophy as the Mūl Mantra. Its beginning – *Ikk Oaṅ Kār* – is a clear assertion and celebration of the One formless ontological ground of all that exists. In the configuration of ੴ (1 Be-ing Is), three modes of knowledge have been used to signify the is-ness of the One Absolute: numerical, alphabetical, and geometrical. The number '1' is the primary number. 'ਓ' is the alpha of the Gurmukhī script. '⌒' is the geometrical arch. Although '੧' and 'ੳ' are the beginning of the mathematical and verbal languages, the arch is at once without beginning or end. Here, then, is succinctly present Gurū Nānak's vision of the Transcendent: the '1' is the beginning of all, and yet the commencement or cessation of Its condition cannot be comprehended. The Ultimate Reality symbolized in the numeral One is beyond gender and causality, It is spaceless and timeless. In his commentary on the *Japu*, Bhāī Vīr Singh calls It *bīj mantra* – the root formula.[26]

Nānak's Primal Paradox inheres with the rejection of the doctrine of *avtārvād*. In a hymn in the Gurū Granth, too, Gurū Nānak says: "Nānak nirbhau nirankāru hori kete rām ravāl[27] – in comparison with the Fearless, Formless One, innumerable deities are as dust." Or: "koti bisan kīne avatār koti brahmanḍ jāke dhramsāl koti maheś upāi samāe[28] – millions of Viṣṇus has It created, millions of universes has It spawned, millions of Śivas has It raised and assimilated." Denounced here is the primacy of the varied traditional male deities. Denounced here is the all-preserving and all-nurturing Viṣṇu; denounced, too, is Śiva, god of death and destruction, even though he also holds the drum of creation and his phallus remains the supreme symbol of potency and generation. For Nānak, however, both Viṣṇu and Śiva and, implicitly, the other deities are all mutable and finite. It must have been a revolutionary step thus to discard centuries-old symbols of male dominance and power. Stripping away all gender characterizations, Nānak posits the reality as *sati* (Truth). Our myth contains the scriptural statement "ādi sacu jugādu sacu, hai bhī sacu nānak hosī bhī sacu – Truth it was, Truth it ever was, Truth it is and, says Nānak, Truth it shall be." The Transcendent is envisioned as real and immutable throughout time – past, present, or future. The Janamsākhī account provides us with hints of Nānak's exorcism of an internalized father God in his various manifestations and incarnations, an exorcism which is the starting point of Mary Daly's metapatriarchal journey.[29]

In his attempt to shatter, exorcise, and blot out the traditional icons and images, Nānak named the Transcendent as numeral "One." His successors followed his example, and we find the Gurū Granth replete with the numerical symbol:

sāhibu merā eko hai
eko hai bhāī eko hai.[30]

My lord is One,
One It is, yes One only.

ekam ekankāru nirālā
amaru ajonī jāti na jālā.[31]

One, One Being exists uniquely –
Eternal, unborn, without any caste or limitation.

ham kichu nāhī ekai ohi
āgai pāchai eko soī.[32]

We are naught, only That One is;
Ahead and/or behind remains That One.

gahir gabhīru athāhu apāru agaṇatu tūṅ
nānak vartai ikku ikko ikku tūṅ.[33]

Deep, fathomless, infinite, innumerable are You,
Says Nānak, only One, One alone, sustains all.

āpe paṭī kalam āpi upari lekhu bhi tūṅ
eko kahiai nānakā dūjā kāhe ku?[34]

You Yourself are the slate, You the pen, and You are the writing upon it as well,
Says Nānak, proclaim but the One, why call any other?

"One" is the essential way of presenting the total singularity and unity of Ultimate Reality. Masculine identity is here denied as the norm for imaging the Transcendent. Gurū Nānak's seeing of the

Transcendent as the numeral One reveals a significant repatterning of that theological mold which has the male in the center and the female as but subordinate and auxiliary to him.

Gurū Nānak's apprehension of Ultimate Reality as absolute Oneness is radically divergent from that of the Sants in medieval India, though some scholars feel that the great Sant Kabīr was his spiritual teacher. Even if we were to compare Gurū Nānak and Kabīr's apprehension of Ultimate Reality for a moment, we would discover how immense a difference lies between the two. Unlike Gurū Nānak, who celebrates the Transcendent as utter unicity, Kabīr perceives That as void. Charlotte Vaudeville's excellent study of Kabīr shows that the Sant referred to Ultimate Reality as "the Void" (*sunya*), which she traces to Tantric Buddhism.[35] Vaudeville writes, "Kabīr sometimes adopts a monotheistic stance, but in many of his *sākhī* and *pads*, he adopts a nihilistic attitude and his utterances come nearer to the teaching of Siddhas and Nāths of yore, who were the propagators of the Tantric Yoga later taught by the Shaiva Nāth Yogis."[36] So certain and assured is Gurū Nānak in proclaiming the existence of the Oneness of Ultimate Reality that nihilism just does not enter his vocabulary. Both our *sākhī* and the Gurū Granth provide ample testimony to the vision of absolute and eternal Reality. *Ikk*, the One – never *sunya* – pervades Gurū Nānak's worldview.

But this Oneness is not governed by the principle of an abstract and mathematical formula; it is not, so to say, a monistic principle or a purely conceptual idea. The symbol of the *Ikk* (1) maintains a subjectivity and an existential quality which, for Paul Tillich[37] and Mircea Eliade,[38] are intrinsic to symbols. We discover in Sikh literature – be it the prose of the Janamsākhī or the poetry of Gurū Granth – a personal encounter with That One. After all, That One is physically seen, not just mentally conceived. This is an authentic human situation. The juxtaposition of the Absolute and Infinite One to the second-person *tuṅ* (a familiar form of the word "you," like the French *tu*), exemplified in many of the lines above, presents a very informal and intimate relationship between one and the One. The "I–Thou" encounter put forth by Buber is reminiscent of the communion envisaged by Gurū Nānak between the individual and the Divine.[39] A verse from the Gurū Granth highlights the nexus between the absolute Truth and the different individuals: "sati sarūpu ridai jini māniā karan karāvan tini mūlu pachhāniā[40] – those who know the True form to reside within their hearts, they recognize the root (*mūla*) of the doer and creator of all." The True One, Timeless, Transcendent, and the Creator of all, exists within the very heart! The *Ikk Oaṅ Kār* is therefore not a concept in and of itself, and it does not call for a formulation of dogmas, doctrines, and categories usually systematized in patriarchal theology; rather it is a revelation of a living reality to be *in*wardly seen. The object of Gurū Nānak's vision is the subject within the very self, a process to be "recognized" – *pachhāniā*.

3

The third element that arises from Nānak's Primal Paradox is his commitment to social change and justice. Some years ago, Mary E. Hunt clearly articulated that feminist theology assumes a base of praxis aimed at social change and that feminist theology never stands alone, but always in the good company of practical ethics: "No action–reflection model will be adequate that does not put real life questions to the fore."[41] Against the horizon of total Oneness, Gurū Nānak proclaims: "There is no Hindu; there is no Musalmān." Thereafter the utter unicity of the Transcendent One is practically translated into Gurū Nānak's espousal of the equality of all humankind, of all castes, sexes, races, and religions. Our *sākhī* thus underscores the existential dimension of Gurū Nānak's cognition of the Transcendent. The priority of action or praxis is considered by feminists to be in sharp contrast to the patriarchal methodology, which, to quote Mary E. Hunt again, "begins with philosophically-based theology and with luck, gives way to ethics, and only much later, if ever, to concrete work for justice."[42]

It is said that for a whole day after his emergence from the river Beiṅ, Gurū Nānak sat silently in deep meditation. This liminal stage is indicative of the profundity of the experience that preceded it. Perhaps that is when he was engaged in his intense hermeneutic process and tried to reflect upon the meaning of what he had seen. Gurū Nānak's first words after the crucial spiritual encounter clearly indicate that, for him, the Transcendent One was an existential phenomenon.

These words of his from the *Purātan Janamsākhī* are often misunderstood. In saying "There is no Hindu; there is no Musalmān," Gurū Nānak was not making a value judgment about the religious life of the Hindus and Muslims of his day, nor was he refuting these or, by implication, any other religious designations such as Jain, Buddhist, Jew, or Christian. He was, in fact, pointing towards the oneness of society: the Oneness of the Transcendent being translated into the oneness of humanity. Neither does the statement aim at religious uniformity or a reduction of the pluralistic variety of Hinduism, Islam, and other beliefs into a single religion. He is not asking people to abandon their faith and adopt another. The words simply stress the fundamental, common truth that Gurū Nānak saw underlying the diverse faiths and systems of belief. The vision of the Transcendent disclosed to him the commonness and oneness of his fellow-beings – men and women – which was to become the ethical paradigm for him and for his followers. "This was a simple announcement, and yet a significant one in the context of India of his day. To a society torn by conflict, he brought a vision of common humanity – a vision which transcended all barriers of creed and caste, race and country."[43]

The vision of the Transcendent marks the beginning of Gurū Nānak's mission. The gift of the Divine Name is bestowed upon him and he is called upon to share the revelation he has been vouchsafed. The *sākhī* concretely depicts Gurū Nānak as being bestowed with the robe (*siropāo*) from the heavenly court. Upon receiving his commission, Gurū Nānak bows in humility. The *sākhī* account specifically marks out his special métier. Nānak becomes the Gurū,[44] and in this new role he transmits the light of wisdom to his followers: "gur sākhī joti pargaṭu hoi – via the Gurū, the Light, the ontological basis of all, becomes visible."[45] Nānak is thus charged to deliver the message bequeathed to him through the vision, a message which essentially entails discerning and rejoicing in the infinite and singular reality beyond the fragmented parts and particles. Our myth expresses his being vouchsafed a very special dispensation. As he enters upon the momentous phase of articulating the message, Gurū Nānak utters a hymn of simple gratefulness: "A humble bard was I without occupation; Praise be to the One who has called me to work." Through this scriptural hymn the Janamsākhī narration of the crucial encounter is confirmed. Something new came on the horizon. For twenty-four years thereafter Gurū Nānak traveled throughout India and beyond spreading the Divine Word. He was accompanied during most of his travels by his Muslim companion Mardānā, who played on the *rabāb* (a kind of rebeck) as Gurū

Nānak recited praises of the One. Wherever Gurū Nānak went, men and women were attracted by the directness of his manner and the simplicity of his words. Many were won by his liberal and universal teaching. A new way of life opened up for them. Those who accepted him as their "Gurū" and followed his teachings came to be known as Sikhs – from the Sanskrit *śiśya*, and Pali *sekha*, meaning a learner or disciple.[46]

The dress he wore as he set out on his preaching tours combined elements of Hindu and Muslim wear, a mixture which was symbolic of his common message for all peoples. Recognizing and accepting the religious plurality amidst which he lived, he freely mixed with the exponents of different traditions. Throughout his lifetime, he continued to point towards the common element of humanness which, to his way of thinking, transcended all racial, societal, and gender barriers. The basic commonness, the oneness of humanity was a reality for him, and this is what he wished people of all faiths to perceive and cherish. During his extensive travels (*udāsīs* or preaching odysseys) throughout India, he visited places of worship belonging to various religious traditions – temples, mosques, vihāras, and khānaqāhs – and attended their fairs and festivals. He thereby acknowledged the presence and entity of the different religious faiths. The "gracious, spacious, moving processes of diverse being and diverse becoming" which is a central element of feminist thealogizing seems to be reflected in Gurū Nānak's attitude to life and living as well. In the Sikh scripture we come across evidence of his having met with Hindu Yogis, Muslim Sufis, and Buddhist Nāthas. When he met Muslims, he adjured them to be faithful to the teaching of their faith; when he met Hindus, he urged them to abide by the tenets of their own tradition. The essential and eternal truth which lay beyond all externals and particularisms was the core of Gurū Nānak's vision of the Transcendent One.

At the end of his travels, Gurū Nānak settled in Kartārpur. This was a village he had himself founded on the right bank of the river Rāvī. Here a community of disciples grew up and established the very cornerstone of Sikh life and living. It was not a monastic order of any kind, but consisted of men and women actively engaged in everyday different occupations in life – while being devoted to the teaching of Gurū Nānak. A notable feature, especially pertinent to the theme of Nānak's thealogical vision, was the complete equality men and women enjoyed in this new community. In his book *Sikh*

*Religion and Philosophy*, Nirmal Kumar Jain reflects upon the Gurū's radical perception of the status of women:

> The attitude of a race towards its women is expressive of their psychological state. Woman who was once a companion in the spiritual journey had come to be known as a positive hindrance and an immediate danger in this racial attitude. It was an outer symptom of cowardice, escape and falsehood.[47]

Further on, Jain makes the following remark:

> The Gurūs have tried to build a road for men and women on which both could walk hand in hand. It [Sikhism] is for this reason a very revolutionary creed, for most of the religions in practice have created a gulf between the two.[48]

The paving of a road on which both men and women could walk as equals had its genesis in the community of Sikhs initiated at Kartārpur. In her introduction to *Woman in the Sacred Scriptures of Hinduism*, Mildreth Pinkham also notes that "In Sikhism the Hindu degradation of woman was repudiated as she was held in higher regard."[49] From the very beginning of the tradition, Gurū Nānak took special care to give women a position of equality with men in matters religious as well as mundane. One of his hymns contains a categorical statement on this theme – and one strikingly modern in concept. He says:

> Of woman are we born, of woman conceived,
> To woman engaged, to woman married.
> Woman we befriend, by woman do civilizations continue.
> When a woman dies, a woman is sought for.
> It is through woman that order is maintained.
> Then why call her inferior from whom
> all great ones are born?
> Woman is born of woman;
> None is born but of woman.
> The One, who is Eternal, alone is unborn.
> Says Nānak, that tongue alone is blessed
> that utters the praise of the One.
> Such alone will be acceptable at the Court of the True One.[50]

Gurū Nānak chooses the term *bhaṇḍu* for woman, which literally means "a vessel." He sees her as a cornucopia from which all creation pours forth. His was a new positive attitude towards woman, who had long been relegated to a low place in social life and mythicized as the agent of sin and evil. The extraordinary import of

Gurū Nānak's social restructuring has been admired by present-day scholars. G. S. Randhawa makes the following comment on the above hymn:

> If anything, the woman needs greater attention than her counterpart. All this may not seem revolutionary now, but in the social milieu in which Gurū Nānak preached and functioned, it was like rousing to fuller opportunities in life, one-half of the society who had for ages been denied.[51]

A woman scholar, Upinder Jit Kaur, bestows similar praise on Gurū Nānak's respect for women:

> Guru Nanak, the founder of the Sikh faith, raised his voice for justice to women and provided the scriptural basis for equality which was not to be found in the scriptures of other India born religions. It is to be noted that he pleaded the cause of women and strove for their liberation in the fifteenth century, whereas the women's emancipation movement in Europe started much later, in the eighteenth and the nineteenth centuries. In an age when the inferiority of women was taken for granted and female infanticide and the customs of *purdah* and *sati* were commonly practised, the Guru spoke out against them with a voice of reason and sanity.[52]

In his verse, Gurū Nānak tries to raise the position of women and equates them with men. They are not to be considered inferior in any manner. He sees them as active partners in furthering goodwill, general happiness, and the collective moral values of society. Married life, *grihasta*, is celebrated to restore to woman her due place and status as an equal in life. Celibacy and asceticism, which by implication negate this equality, are denied. At the Court of the True One, there will be no distinctions made on the grounds of sex or creed. Those who repeat the praise of the One will prove acceptable. That tongue alone will be blessed that utters words of devotion, be it man's or woman's.

At Kartārpur, men and women sat together in *saṅgat*, holy congregation, to recite praises of the Divine. They sat together again, irrespective of differences of high and low, of caste and creed, to eat a common meal in the Gurū kā Laṅgar or community refectory. The institution of *laṅgar* established by Gurū Nānak was a potent factor in fostering the values of equality, fellowship, and humility, and in affirming a new and dynamic sense of "familyhood."

A key element in this process of restructuring religious and social life was the spirit of *sevā*, or self-giving service. Corporal works of charity and mutual help were undertaken voluntarily and zealously, and considered to be a peculiarly pious duty.[53] In the *langar*, the disciples – men and women – engaged themselves in one task or another. Rosemary Ruether, in *Sexism and God-Talk*, makes a significant remark about our modern sexist society: women are in charge of essential work, whereas men are in charge of leisure; for instance, women cook; men barbecue.[54] But in this first "Sikh" society taking shape at Kartārpur, both men and women took equal part in essential tasks: both drew water from the well, both reaped and ground corn, both cooked food in the kitchen, and both cleaned dishes. The food was eaten in common by all, sitting in rows together as equals irrespective of sex, caste, or rank. The practice continues to this day wherever Sikhs congregate in prayer.

Could we go as far as to call Nānak a feminist? In *Philosophy and Feminist Thinking*, Jean Grimshaw writes that "for any viewpoint to count as feminist, it must believe that women have been oppressed and unjustly treated and that something needs to be done about this."[55] Now Gurū Nānak loudly raised his voice against the disabilities to which women were subject, and he tried to break the "edifice of patriarchy." When Mary Daly lists all the infrastructures of this edifice – "from buddhism and hinduism to islam, judaism, christianity, to secular derivatives such as freudianism, jungianism, marxism, and maoism" – the Sikh religion is not mentioned.[56] Although this absence is perhaps accidental, it is flattering for the Sikhs that their religion does not conform to that patriarchal edifice. For my part, I find some affinity between Mary Daly and Gurū Nānak. In *Gyn-Ecology*, for instance, Mary Daly has powerfully shown us the planetary oppression of women in the sado-ritual syndromes of Indian *satī*, African genital mutilation, Chinese foot-binding, European witchburnings, and American gynecology. Although neither in such a radical mode nor from such a global perspective, Nānak was himself aware of and made his contemporaries aware of the enormity of customs like *satī*, confinement of women after childbirth, and *purdah* prevalent in his milieu. And like Mary Daly, he traced the root of such "sado-ritual syndromes" to an obsession with purity. In many of his verses Nānak condemns the false notion of pollution. For instance, a hymn in the measure Āsā reads:

> If pollution attaches to birth, then pollution is everywhere (for birth is universal).
> Cow-dung [used as fuel] and firewood breed maggots;

> Not one grain of corn is without life;
> Water itself is a living substance, imparting life to all vegetation.
> How can we then believe in pollution, when pollution inheres within staples?
> Says Nānak, pollution is not washed away by purificatory rituals;
> Pollution is removed by true knowledge alone.[57]

Gurū Nānak rejected the prevalent superstition that a woman who gave birth to a child remained polluted for a number of days – forty as was commonly believed – and that the home in which the birth took place was similarly polluted. Even in Japan and China, pollution was associated with childbirth. Japanese literature dating back to the *Kojiki* mentions the segregation of women into parturition huts.[58] Even up till the early part of the twentieth century, the Chinese regarded the sight of pregnant women as offensive, and their visit to temples as most irreverent.[59] Gurū Nānak, on the other hand, asserts that pollution lies in the heart and mind of the person and not in the cosmic natural process of birth. Clearly he wanted to remove the false notion that women were unclean. Women's subjugation and oppression were central concerns in the message ensuing from Gurū Nānak's revelatory experience in the river Beiṅ, and they confirm his thealogical vision. His insights had a practical effect on women in the sixteenth-century Punjab and can still be used to promote the full enfranchisement of women. Today with the continuance of oppression of women – maybe more psychological than physical, but nevertheless equally if not more mutilating – it might be valuable to remember Gurū Nānak's thealogical vision and emulate his manner of speech and protest.

4

Finally, the fourth major characteristic of the Primal Paradox is that it validates feelings and emotions – it is the basis for the Sikh poetic syntax. Western feminists have shown the contrast between the abstract, intellectual, patriarchal theology and the feminist thealogy which is "the reawakening of sensitivity to the forgotten dimensions, to the spheres of the senses, the psyche, the body, the imagination."[60] Gurū Nānak's Primal Paradox ushers in the feminist thealogical reawakening of sensitivity. The revitalization of the senses, the psyche, the body, the imagination is inaugurated by Gurū Nānak through poetry.

Our Janamsākhī account illustrates Gurū Nānak's poetic savoring of the enchanting paradox: we hear Nānak reiterating the greatness and infinity of the Being and the glory of Its name. The resounding melody in the *sākhī* is: "I would still not be able to measure Your greatness nor signify the glory of Your Name." In the song of praise he states that the Formless One is the eternal, irreplaceable Truth which cannot ever be described. The impulse to describe the Ineffable, to recognize the Unfathomable, engenders awe and wonder. In recapitulating these overwhelming sentiments, this Janamsākhī account resonates with Rudolph Otto's characterization of the Wholly Other as "mysterium," "tremendum," and "fascinans."[61] We find Gurū Nānak resorting from image to image, symbol to symbol, without, as he admits, being able to capture either Its intensity or Its infinity.

Poetry became the sole medium of his expression. In *Gurū Nānak and Origins of the Sikh Faith*, Harbans Singh comments upon the significance of Gurū Nānak's poetic mode: "All of Gurū Nānak's teaching is set forth in verse. His genius was best expressed in the poetical attitude. No other way would have been adequate to the range and depth of his mood – his fervent longing for the Infinite, his joy and wonder at the beauty and vastness of His creation . . . His compositions reveal an abounding imagination and a subtle aesthetic sensitivity."[62] Our Janamsākhī anecdote represents Nānak celebrating the Divine favor through a song of praise; song was to be the medium of his divine inspiration ever after. He revelled in calling himself a poet: "sāsu māsu sabhu jīo tumārā tū mai kharā piārā nānaku sāiru eva kahatu hai sace parvadgārā[63] – to you belong my breath, to you my flesh; says the poet Nānak, you the True One are my Beloved."

Gurū Nānak's exultation and celebration in seeing the Transcendent become the starting point of the Sikh scripture, the Gurū Granth. Poetry thus became the mode of Sikh sacred literature as a whole. Gurū Nānak's Primal Paradox expresses the joyous note at the heart of Sikhism, a note which cannot be accounted for by those who maintain that Gurū Nānak was "a follower of Kabīr" or "a reinterpreter of the Sant tradition." Several scholars have pointed out that the beauty and power of Kabīr's verse emerges from his acute consciousness of the brevity of life. As Charlotte Vaudeville says, "the hovering presence of death (*kāl*)" gives "to the warnings of Kabīr their tragic intensity."[64] On the contrary, the Janamsākhī account and the Gurū Granth verses bear witness to a sensibility which exults in the human condition. In direct contrast to Kabīr's "tragic intensity," Gurū Nānak's is a "joyous intensity." The presence of death, the evanescence of life – these are clearly admitted, but they do not constitute the predominant leitmotif of Gurū Nānak's poetry.

The project of creating a book that would proclaim the Word of Divine Truth started with Gurū Nānak himself, though the Granth was actually compiled by Gurū Arjan (Nānak V). The Sikh historian and theologian Bhāī Gurdās (1551–1636) tells us that Gurū Nānak carried a *pothī* (manuscript) under his arm.[65] Chapter 56 of the *Purātan Janamsākhī* also records that, before the end came, Gurū Nānak bequeathed his word recorded in a *pothī* to Gurū Aṅgad (Nānak II).[66] To quote Nripinder Singh, "It was he [Gurū Nānak] who celebrated and consecrated the item by making his *pothī* the oil and mantle for the anointing of a successor, a successor who, in turn, composed more hymns, commissioned more *pothīs* for a growing body of disciples already attuned to the words of their First prophet-mentor."[67] Following the example of Gurū Nānak, Gurū Aṅgad (Nānak II) added his own writings to the *pothī* received from Nānak I and passed it on to the third Gurū. Soon after there arose schismatic groups which started composing hymns and making them current under the name of Nānak. The problem of the "counterfeit" word became especially acute during Gurū Arjan's time. Since Gurū Rām Dās (Nānak IV) had bypassed his two older sons and appointed the third Arjan to the Gurūship, Pirthī Cand, the eldest, was estranged from him. He and his gifted son Miharbān began to compose poetry under the name of Nānak. It was in response to such compositions that Gurū Arjan (Nānak V) began to codify the sayings of the Gurūs into an authorized volume.[68] He wished to affix his seal of approval on the sacred Word and preserve it in its authentic form for posterity.

Gurū Arjan called upon Bhāī Gurdās for help in this great work. Messages were sent to Sikhs to gather the hymns of the preceding Gurūs. Bābā Mohan, son of Gurū Amar Dās (Nānak III), possessed a collection of *pothīs* of the Gurūs' hymns, inherited from his father. But, as the Sikh tradition says, he refused to see anybody who came to ask for these. Bhāī Gurdās traveled all the way to Goiṅdvāl, where Bābā Mohan lived; Bābā Mohan turned him away. Bhāī Buddhā, one of the oldest Sikhs from Gurū Nānak's days, was similarly refused. At last, Gurū Arjan went himself. Seating himself on the street below the balcony of Bābā Mohan's lodgings, he started serenading him on the *tamburā*. Bābā Mohan was deeply touched at this gesture of the Gurū. He fled down the stairs and presented the Gurū with the *pothīs*. Such reverence was bestowed upon the Word that the *pothīs* were placed on a palanquin bedecked with precious stones and carried by the Sikhs on their shoulders, while Gurū Arjan walked behind barefoot.

Gurū Arjan marked out a picturesque spot on the outskirts of Amritsar, where he and Bhāī Gurdās set to work on the sacred volume.[69] This monumental task demanded great physical endurance and intellectual discipline. Gurū Arjan had to select the poetic utterances of the four preceding Gurūs as well as songs and hymns by saints and Sūfīs from amongst a continually increasing body of literature. Additionally, what was genuine had to be sifted from what was spurious. Being a superb poet and possessing an extraordinary mystical insight, Gurū Arjan carried out the work of compiler and editor with exactness and enthusiasm. The Gurmukhī script was used for transcription. Once the material was selected, it was assigned to appropriate *rāgas* or musical measures and arranged in a definite structure. First came *padas* (stanzas) by the Gurūs in the order of their succession. Then came *chhands*, *vārs* and other poetic forms in a set order. The compositions of the Gurūs in each *rāga* were followed by those of Bhaktas and Sūfīs in the same format.[70] The poetry of love and devotion was to be approached with reverent wonder; it could not be pried into with mere intellect. The poetry of the Sikhs empowered by the *rāgas* in turn became the instrument for stimulating the senses and the mind into intuiting the Transcendent One.

The completion of the Granth was celebrated with much jubilation. In *Gurbilās Chhevīn Pātshāhī*, the festivity has been compared with that of a wedding.[71] In thanksgiving, *karāhprasād* (the consecrated food of the Sikhs) was prepared and a very large number of Sikhs came to see the sacred poetic text. Thrilled at the very sight of it, they bowed in veneration. The Holy Volume was brought for installation to the Harimandir Sāhib – the Golden Temple of the present day. While Bhāī Buddhā, the elderly and venerable Sikh devotee, carried the Granth on his head, Gurū Arjan walked behind waving the *caṅvar* (whisk) in homage over it. Musicians recited verses from the sacred text. On August 16, 1604, the Book was ceremoniously installed in the inner sanctuary of the Harimandir Sāhib. Bhāī Buddhā opened the Granth with reverence to obtain from it the divine command (*hukm*); Gurū Arjan stood in attendance behind. At dusk, the Granth was taken to a specially built chamber. There it was placed on a pedestal while Gurū Arjan slept on the floor by its side out of reverence. Such was the veneration shown to the Granth by the Gurūs themselves. The original copy of the sacred book prepared under the care of Gurū Arjan is preserved to this day by some of his descendants at Kartārpur.

Gurū Gobind Singh, the tenth and last Sikh Gurū, ended personal Gurūship and installed the Granth as Gurū. Before he passed away in 1708, Gurū Gobind Singh apotheosized the volume and made it the Gurū Eternal for the Sikhs. A contemporary Sikh document, *Bhatt Vahī Talaudā Parganah Jīnd*, describes the event in detail:

> Gurū Gobind Singh, the Tenth Prophet, son of Gurū Tegh Bahādur, grandson of Gurū Hargobind, great-grandson of Gurū Arjan, of the family of Gurū Rām Dās, Surajbaṅsī Gosal clan, Sodhī Khatrī, resident of Anandpur, parganah Kahlūr, now at Naṅder, in the Godāvarī country, in the Deccan, asked Bhāī Dayā Singh, on Wednesday, October 6, 1708, to fetch Sri Granth Sāhib. In obedience to his orders, Dayā Singh brought the Granth Sāhib. The Gurū placed before it five paise and a coconut and bowed his head before it. He said to the congregation, "It is my commandment: Own Sri Granth Jī in my place. Whosoever acknowledges it thus will obtain her/his reward. The Gurū will rescue that Sikh. Know this as the truth."[72]

Several other old Sikh documents also state that the succession was passed on by Gurū Gobind Singh to the Gurū Granth. According to Harbans Singh this was the most significant development in the history of the community. Henceforth it was for the Sikhs the perpetual authority, spiritual as well as historical.[73]

It is the poetry of this book which forms the centre of Sikh life, and at the core of it is Nānak's joy in seeing the Transcendent. As Nānak rejoices, words come with their own speedy meter and cadence. His language is poetically dynamic. The Primal Paradox incites him to project the inexpressible One into poetry, and spontaneously a powerful and joyous dynamism is produced with a wealth of alliteration, assonance, consonance, symmetry, and various other artistic devices. The style itself sets Sant Kabīr and Gurū Nānak radically apart. Linda Hess, in a very engaging essay entitled "Kabīr's Rough Rhetoric," analyzes his style thus: "Kabīr pounds away with questions, prods with riddles, stirs with challenges, shocks with insults, disorients with verbal feints. It seems that if one read him responsively one could hardly help getting red in the face, jumping around, squirming, searching, getting embarrassed, or shouting back."[74] Hess effectively makes the point that the reader or listener is central in Kabīr's didactics. "Nearly everyone in North India is familiar with the formula *kahai Kabira suno bhai sadho* – Kabir says listen brother sadhu! ... It is Kabīr's trademark."[75] She also draws the comparison between Kabīr's use of rhetorical devices as teaching aids with "the Zen koan – a problem the student can't solve and can't escape, a matrix of verbal impossibilities."[76] These kinds of rhetorical and pedagogical techniques are alien to Gurū Nānak's style. Whether we look at the Janamsākhī account or passages from the Gurū Granth, there is no pounding with questions or prodding with riddles. Rather, *visamāda*, the mode of supreme wonder, the seeing of the Infinite One, is what the Gurū intensely experiences and, as he utters that paradox, he incites – through a naturally spontaneous poetry, not through rhetorical devices – his listeners and readers to attain to the same state. The passage from the Āratī contained in our *sākhī* is a prime instance of poetry which expresses and evokes the numinous. The conscious cultivation of persuasiveness dominating a reformer's style is absent in Gurū Nānak. In the Gurū Granth, Gurū Nānak's Primal Paradox is evoked, "we are intoxicated with wonder, and struck with this wonder we sing the Divine praises."[77] In the same tone, Gurū Arjan says, "sun samādhi anhat tahu nād kahanu na jāi acraj bismād – listen to the melody ringing day and night within the self, ineffable is the marvel!"[78] So overwhelming is the glimpse of infinity that the individual ego is shattered and one begins to praise its source. The quest to get closer and closer to That which is the source of the awe and wonder is aroused. Joyously singing Its praises is a natural corollary.

The poetic syntax of the Granth substantiates the Sikh thealogical vision in four interconnected ways. Firstly, feelings, emotions, imagination, and reason are fully validated in the Primal Paradox. "But reason, or the intellect, is not merely logical reason; it involves an exceedingly more profound – and more obscure – life, which is revealed to us in proportion as we endeavor to penetrate the hidden recesses of poetic activity."[79] Patriarchal thought sets up an opposition between spontaneity, celebration, and feelings on the one hand, and cerebral, rational, and very balanced deliberations on the other. It denigrates the former and patronizes the latter. True poetry, however, unites all human faculties and thus promotes a shift from an androcentric to a feminist construction of the cosmos. The poetic mode is crucial for the expression of the essentially thealogical vision of the Sikhs, a vision which shares in the immediacy and universality of poetry.

Such a poetic synthesis is at the heart of our *Janamsākhī*. It presents the holistic panorama of Gurū Nānak – one in which the terrestrial, celestial, and atmospheric worlds are not split asunder but integrated into a harmonious unity. After Nānak is given the robe of honor, the hymn known in the Gurū Granth as the *Āratī* springs forth. At the opening of it, we hear the Gurū marveling at the entire cosmos making its worship to the Ultimate One: "gagan mai thālu ravi caṅdu dīpak bane tārikā maṇḍal janak motī dhūpu malānlo pavanu cavaro kare sagal banrāi phūlaṅt jotī kaisī āratī hoi – The skies are the platter; sun and moon, lamps; stars, the pearls. The breeze is the incense; entire verdure, a bouquet of flowers. What an *āratī*!" Here Nānak in gratitude is making an offering to the Transcendent through the entire cosmos. In his imaginative leap the vast skies become a platter, upon which the moon and the sun are placed like lamps and the stars – beaded together? – as tiny pearls. A few roses are not picked up to please the divinity; rather, all of vegetation – organically growing together – is presented to the Transcendent One. The breeze blowing from and in all directions becomes the fragrant incense. While many scholars have looked into this passage by Guru Nanak as a repudiation of extraneous ritual, I don't think they have discerned the full poetic import of Nānak's panorama in which the triple-tiered structure of the cosmos is shattered and instead a rich singular "platter" is created. Without any divisions, parts, and particles, all of the cosmos is imbued with holiness; music and the visual processes are also synthesized in Nānak's homage to the Transcendent One.

Indeed Nānak's seeing is to be interpreted as a thealogical vision because it affirms a profound connection with all life and reflects a reverent attitude towards divinity and nature. Over the years feminists have cautioned us about the nuclear and ecological crises that threaten our planet. In "Rethinking Theology and Nature," Carol Christ says poignantly: "To poison rivers and seas and the ground on which we stand so that we can have televisions and air-conditioning, to engage in wars of conquest in order to exploit other people's labor and take the resources of their land, is to forget that we are all connected in the web of life."[80] Nānak's integrated "platter" (the metaphor is present both in our *Janamsākhī* account and the Gurū Granth) poetically endorses such modern feminist concerns.

Secondly, through poetry the dialectic between the finite and the Infinite is constantly maintained, giving equal ontological status to both men and women. What we notice in Nānak's vision is that each and every form is informed by the Formless in a marvelous dialectic of the particular and the universal, the physical and the metaphysical, the secular and the Divine. In Plato, the pure ideas are divorced and distanced from the particular, from everyday phenomena. For example, only the is-ness, the essence, the formlessness of the rose is real; the particular roses – those that can be seen, smelled, and touched – are but mutable, temporary, and unreal. From Gurū Nānak's perspective, the universal is seen in the particular; the universal highlights the particular; form is Formless and vice versa. It is important that the dialectic is ever alive; otherwise, Gurū Nānak's vision would be misperceived. The Transcendent is not understood as actually residing within, or encapsulated inside a form, for then it would become substantialized, reified, reduced to finitude. The Transcendent is everywhere without being contained in anything as such. Gurū Nānak's is not a pantheistic vision; the Ultimate never becomes immanent – It is transcendent, and transcendent It remains. His vision is a dynamic and joyous one in which a fluid connection between the particulars and the universal is maintained and the entire world pulsates with divine potentiality, every atom vibrating with ultimate possibility. Through the process of seeing, the particular is constantly thrust into the beyond, towards the universal. Both women and men would be equal participants in such a process.

In Gurū Nānak's vision of the Transcendent we can discern a striking similarity with the impulse towards movement and process in the conception and perception of "God" initiated by contemporary feminist thealogians. For instance, Mary Daly in *Beyond God the Father* proposed a shift in the image of God from a static, fixed, and reified noun to a moving and dynamic verb "Be-ing."[81] As Beverly Wildung Harrison clarifies for us, Mary Daly urged that a God understood as stasis and fixity should have no place in feminist theism, and "that out of women's experience the sacred is better imaged in terms of process and movement."[82] In Gurū Nānak's "see*ing*" the Transcendent, we observe a rejection of reifications and fixtures; instead, it resonates with the thealogical insistence on movement and dynamism.

In the process, Gurū Nānak gives primacy to the personal experience of seeing, for paradoxically the Universal One has to be experienced fully by each particular human being. The particularity of an experience has been very aptly expressed by Gadamer in the language of western secular philosophy: "The experience has a definite immediacy which eludes every opinion about its meaning. Everything that is experienced is experienced by oneself."[83] The "oneself" includes both men and women. Women and men are *equally equipped* for the seeing of the Infinite. In the opening of her 75th Anniversary Lecture at the Annual Meeting of the American Academy of Religion in 1984, Ruether stated that "Patriarchal theology is the kind of theology we have had in the past, a theology defined not only without the participation of women, but to exclude the participation of women."[84] That the Primal Paradox is authenticated in its reexperience by Sikh men and women here and now attests to Gurū Nānak's thealogical vision.

Heidegger's understanding of poetry is helpful in grasping the importance of the poetic mode initiated in the Primal Paradox of the Sikh religion. Quoting the poet Hölderlin, "Poetically Man Dwells," Heidegger makes the point that human existence rests and builds upon poetry: "Language itself is poetry in the essential sense."[85] For Heidegger, "Poetry . . . is not an aimless imagining of whimsicalities and not a flight of mere notions and fancies into the realm of the unreal. What poetry, as illuminating projection, unfolds of unconcealedness and projects ahead into the design of the figure, is the Open which poetry lets happen, and indeed in such a way that only now, in the midst of beings the Open brings being to shine and ring out."[86] Vivid visual and aural images have been used to describe the nature of poetry: it is the disclosure of truth, a disclosure which clearly shines and rings, a disclosure which takes place here and now, but which is only a beginning – a leap forward! What we conclude from Heidegger's words here is that the very arch in the configuration of the *Ikk Oaṅ Kār* at the outset of the Gurū Granth projects the individual here and now – woman and man – into the open, into a non-ending beginning . . .

Thirdly, the poetic context illustrates the inclusivist approach of the Sikh religion. Acceptance of plurality and diversity and a multi-paradigmatic view of the world is central to feminist thealogy. I am especially aware of the concerns of Asian-American women like Rita Nakashima Brock who ardently seek "an inclusive, pluralistic monotheism, with room for a diversity of ways to speak about the sacred dimension of life."[87] In fact, the term "thealogies" is much more common in feminist parlance than the singular, "thealogy." Now looking at the Gurū Granth, an inevitable question arises: Why did Gurū Arjan include in the holy text compositions of Hindu and Muslim saints and mystics with the poetic utterances of the Sikh Gurūs themselves? Scholars given to stressing the syncretic aspect of Sikh faith find in this approach further evidence to buttress their claims.[88] Sikh Gurūs, they claim, wished to present the faith as a compound product. But this, I argue, does not do justice to the Primal Paradox of the Sikh tradition or to the message communicated by the Gurūs and cherished throughout the Sikh heritage. By including the poetry of the Hindu and Muslim saints and mystics from different social levels and castes in the Granth, Gurū Arjan was continuing the tradition established by Gurū Nānak: he was denouncing the religious and social divisions and prejudices inherent in his milieu. Whatever was in congruence with Gurū Nānak's vision of the Transcendent, be it Hindu or Muslim, high caste or low, Gurū Arjan included it in the Gurū Granth. He did not aim at a blend of Hindu-Muslim ideas, for that would deny the rich distinctions; what he did seek was a vertical expansion of the spiritual consciousness commonly shared – something most prized by Gurū Nānak himself. What governed Gurū Arjan's choice was not a random mixing of concepts and doctrines from prevalent religious traditions; rather, it was his penetrating insight into the Beyond. Like his predecessors, Gurū Arjan believed that knowledge of the Transcendent is attained neither through servitude to a god of the Hindu pantheon (*sevai gusaīā*) nor through worship of Allah (*sevai Allah*). It is received, rather, through an active recognition of, and participation in, the Divine Will. In Rāg Rāmkalī, he says:

> koī bolai rām rām koī khudāi
> koī sevai gusaīā koī allāhi . . .
> kahu nānak jini hukmu pachhāta
> prabh sāhib kā tini bhedu jātā.[89]

> Some address Rām, some Khudā,
> Some worship Gosāīn, some Allah . . .

Says Nānak, those who recognize the Divine Will
It is they who know the secret of the Transcendent One.

The theological motifs current in medieval India and upheld through worship of male paradigms such as Rām and Khudā are in the Sikh poetic text replaced by the primacy of the individual experience – be it the experience of a Hindu, a Muslim, or a Sikh. Plainly, Gurū Arjan did not seek to mix the Hindu and Islamic traditions. He had, in the manner of his mentor, Gurū Nānak, recognized a new and different way – a more holistic way – of understanding the Transcendent One. By including the poetic utterances of Hindus and Muslims he was emulating and translating into practice Gurū Nānak's words, "There is no Hindu; there is no Musalmān." Such a bridging of the gap between theory and practice is, as we have seen, the goal of feminist thealogians.

Poetry in the Sikh heritage functions as both the medium and the source of divine revelation. A fourth way, then, in which the poetic syntax substantiates the Sikh thealogical vision is by intimating the feminine principle in the seeing of the Transcendent. As a medium of divine revelation, poetry conjoins the male and female principles in the Sikh tradition. My point is that the Sikh Gurūs, who were all male, understood their poetic utterances as feminine. *Bāṇī*, grammatically feminine, is the general designation for the sacred poetry. It is then identified with the male Gurūs. For instance, in the words of Gurū Rām Dās (Nānak IV):

bāṇı guru gurū hai bāṇī
vici bāṇī amritu sāre.[90]

Bāṇī is the Gurū, the Gurū Bāṇī,
Within Bāṇī are contained all elixirs.

The communication and the revelation are thus identical. They were perceived to be a single entity by the Sikh Gurūs and are not differentiated by those who profess the faith. The communicators were all males; their revelation, the feminine principle, takes equal rank with them.

Our *Janamsākhī* narration underscored the point that the source of Gurū Nānak's poetic and artistic outpouring was the Transcendent One. In the Gurū Granth, too, Gurū Nānak is recorded as saying: "jaisī mai āve khasam kī bāṇī taisaṛā karī giānu ve lālo[91] – as comes to me the Husband's word that is how I deliver it, Oh Lālo." In this verse, Gurū Nānak is telling his companion, Lālo, that just as the *bāṇī* comes to him, so does he speak forth. The process is immediate and instantaneous. The Gurū is merely the medium for expression of that which lies yonder. He is not a receptacle where the words get lodged in a state of incipiency to be further refined later on. In other hymns he declares:

> tā mai kahiā kahaṇu jā tujhai kahāiā[92]
>
> I spoke only because the One made me to speak.
>
> hau āpahu boli na jāṇdā
> mai kahiā sabhu hukmāo jīo.[93]
>
> I know not how to utter;
> I communicated only the command from above.

This view of revelation is best comprehended through the term "inspiration," which literally means "breathing into." The "breathing into" by the Divine Source is not mediated through any conscious or conceptual constructs. It is an immediate experience: *Bāṇī* bursts forth, intuitively and spontaneously, from the Gurūs' lips. The fourth Gurū, Gurū Rām Dās, explained his experience as follows:

> satigur kī bāṇī sati sati kar jāṇhau gursikhu
> hari kartā āpi muhhu kaḍhāi.[94]
>
> Truth, Truth is the Word of the true Gurū,
> know it as the truth, O Sikhs,
> For the Creator Itself makes me speak so!

The fifth, Gurū Arjan, expressed it in this way:

> agam agocaru sacu sāhibu merā
> nānaku bolai bolāiā terā.[95]
>
> Unfathomable, Ineffable, Truth is my Ruler,
> Nānak voices what You wish to be voiced.

This was the Gurūs' testimony that whatever they are uttering and even the manner in which they are uttering it comes from Beyond. The source – as betokened in the words of Gurū Nānak and as cherished in the Sikh tradition – is the Transcendent One.

But we also find another identification: an identification between *bāṇī* and the Transcendent Itself:

> vāhu vāhu bāṇī niraṅkār hai
> tisu jevaḍu avaru na koi.[96]

Hail, hail, the *bāṇī*,
*bāṇī* which is the Formless One Itself.
There is none other, nothing else to be reckoned equal to it.

"Vāhu vāhu bāṇī niraṅkār hai – *bāṇī* is the Formless One!" The alpha point of the Sikh vision of the Transcendent is Gurū Nānak's seeing of *niraṅkār*, the Formless One; the omega point for the Sikhs is the reseeing of that Primal Paradox in the form of the *bāṇī*. The word *bāṇī*, we noted, is a feminine noun: it imparts primacy to the feminine principle within the totality which we have termed the "Primal Paradox." It is through *bāṇī* that the Gurūs' vision was transmitted and preserved: Gurū Arjan gave *baṇī* the form of Granth and Gurū Gobind Singh, the last of the Sikh spiritual teachers, put the seal of finality on *bāṇī* when he institutionalized it as Gurū, proclaiming the holy book, Gurū Granth, his successor. Since then, *bāṇī*, as recorded in the Gurū Granth, has been the singular object of devotion for the Sikhs, their singular religious reference. From the day of its compilation, the Gurū Granth has exerted a profound power in Sikh life. "Gurū Granth jī mānio pargaṭ gurāṅ kī deh – acknowledge the Gurū Granth as body visible of the Gurūs"[97] – is recited by the Sikhs daily in their morning and evening supplications. The feminine dimension is also affirmed in the Sikhs' perception and conception of the poetic text as a substitute for the Farthest One: "pothī parmesaru kā thānu[98] – know the book in the place of the Ultimate One" (*pothī*, meaning book, is again a feminine noun).

Departing from male-dominated images and symbols, the Sikh poetic text in the form of *bāṇī*, *pothī*, or Gurū Granth sheds new light on the past and suggests new possibilities for the future. Beginning with Gurū Nānak's epiphanic moment, it has become over the years the sole image and icon of the tradition, and, as such, resolves the antithesis put forward by Victor Zuckerkandl that one "attains the inwardness of life by hearing and its outwardness by seeing."[99] For, the Sikhs cherish not only hearing but also seeing their sacred poetry. In times of uncertainty and difficulty, or of joy and auspiciousness, *saptah* (seven-day), *akhaṇḍ* (non-stop for forty-eight hours), *sampat* (one particular hymn repeated after each hymn), and *khullā* (not limited in time or manner) recitations of the holy text are prescribed modes for religious observance. Both men and women can read and recite and take equal part in the ceremonies. For the Sikhs, the physical presence and the metaphysical content of their sublime poetry have constituted the twin regulative principles of their psyche and conduct. The poetic text for the Sikhs is the continuing authority, spiritual as well as historical. Through this sacred poetry they have been able to observe their faith more fully, more vividly. "From it [the Gurū Granth] the community's ideals, institutions, and rituals have derived their meaning."[100] All rites of passage and ceremonies relating to birth, initiation, marriage, and death take place with the sound and sight of this text. "Dhur kī bāṇī āī tini sagalī cint miṭāī[101] – the soothing word came from the Beyond, putting an end to all suffering."

Our fifth and final way in which the poetic syntax substantiates the Sikh thealogical vision is that the Sikh poetic context promotes women's authentic religious self-actualization and self-transcendence. Gurū Nānak's seeing of the Transcendent can be interpreted as a liberating and emancipating phenomenon for the Second Sex, for it sets up a crucial precedent: the importance of direct and unmediated religious experience within the tradition. Just as there were no barriers between the one here and the One There in his encounter with the Divine as recorded in the *Purātan Janamsākhī*, so there are no structures mediating between the one here and the One There in a reseeing of that Transcendent. There are no priests, no commentators, no rituals, no philosophical doctrines, no societal or gender hierarchies that stand in between a person and the sacred poetry. Authority – that of the *paṇḍit* in Hinduism, of the *'ulama* in Islam, of the rabbi in Judaism – that would interpret for the person his or her duty, has no place in the direct poetic encounter. Western thealogians have agonized over the stolid male block between women and God. In the Jewish and Christian worlds, women do not find a direct access to the Divine; it is a male experience and mentality which have to be translated or transferred onto them. In the words of Rosemary Ruether:

> Male monotheism reinforces the social hierarchy of patriarchal rule through its religious system in a way that was not the case with the paired images of God and Goddess. God is modeled after the patriarchal ruling class and is seen as addressing this class of males directly, adopting them as his "sons." They are his representatives, the responsible partners of the covenant with him. Women as wives now become symbolically repressed as the dependent servant class. Wives, along with children and servants, represent those ruled over and owned by the patriarchal class. They relate to man as he relates to God. A symbolic hierarchy is set up: God–male–female. Women no longer stand in direct relation to God; they are connected to God secondarily, through the male.[102]

In the Sikh tradition, only the veil of ignorance or one's ego stands in the way between the one here and the One There. The poetry of the Gurū Granth, then, is that dynamism which tears the veil and thrusts one forward into recognizing That One. The poetic syntax unfolds Sikhism as a religion of aesthetics, a religion that heightens the senses and the mind – it is the route to the Transcendent One, but no more than a route. "Religion is a means and not the end. If we make it the end in itself we become idolatrous," wrote Radhakrishnan.[103] The poetry of the Sikhs is a channel towards that Infinite One; the more it stirs, the closer becomes the destination. The basis of the Sikh community, then, is the poetic sensation received through the medium of the Gurū Granth with its genesis in Gurū Nānak's experience of the Primal Paradox. From the time of Gurū Nānak, *saṅgats* (Sikh congregations) met and recited the sacred songs. The hearing or reciting of *bāṇī* – being stirred by its rhythm – is shared by the *saṅgats* of the past and the present (and, perhaps, also the future); it is felt across the continents. That shared experience constitutes the Sikh Paṅth or community. The joyous savoring of each moment and every space is accomplished through the poetic syntax. According to the Gurū Granth, "tahā baikunṭhu jaha kīrtanu terā[104] – where there is the recitation and hearing of the divine word, that indeed is paradise." Gurū Arjan in his *Sukhmanī* has said, "singing the divine praises, all pollution disappears, the poison of ego is bid riddance."[105] The poetic syntax provides stability for the flickering psyche, enabling the flight from the conscious to the unconscious and into the Transcendent. The direct experience which forms the core of Sikhism is induced solely by the poetic mode. It spells out that all are *equally* equipped in their search for the Transcendent One: there is no hierarchy between the reciter and the listener, the musician and the hearer, the interpreter and the reader. The mind and the senses, matter and spirit are together impelled onwards. The Primal Paradox engenders a context which would empower women to resolve the problems that feminists from Simone de Beauvoir to Rosemary Ruether have identified as arising out of dualistic worldviews. All kinds of binary oppositions and antitheses pivotal to the androcentric vision of reality are overcome and overtaken by the holistic and direct aesthetic experience of Sikhism as attested by Gurū Nānak.

CHAPTER 2

# *Mother: the Infinite Matrix*

bhaṇḍau hī bhaṇḍu ūpajai
bhaṇḍai bājh na koi.

Of woman are all born
Without woman none should exist

As we may recall, Gurū Nānak's Mūl Mantra precedes the *Japu*. The *Purātan Janamsākhī* records that the *Japu* was the first expression of Gurū Nānak's vision of the Transcendent articulated in the Divine Presence. The *Japu* is the opening text in the Gurū Granth, and it has become the morning prayer for the Sikhs. The Mūl Mantra or the Creed Essential at the outset of the *Japu* begins with the celebration of *Ikk Oaṅ Kār* – the singular metaphysical ground of all that exists. We observed that the Mūl Mantra of the Sikh religion went on, characterizing that One as Truth, Creator of all, without fear, without enmity, timeless, unborn, without causality, and One Who can be known through the grace of the Gurū alone. The Mūl Mantra is epigrammatic in style, without the use of any conjunctions or prepositions. It has been read and interpreted in various ways. W. H. McLeod comments:

In itself, however, the statement conveys relatively little. To a devout Sikh it imparts a wealth of meaning, but only because he has behind him an understanding of what the individual words mean.[1]

The rich metaphysical import of this crucial statement is not, however, as esoteric as McLeod would have it. To grasp the import of the Mūl Mantra, it is not absolutely necessary to have been brought up with "devoutness" or "understanding of individual words."

The language of the Mūl Mantra transcends the dichotomy of gender, its rhythm has a startling speed, all characteristics of the metaphysical reality are portrayed as physical – these aspects of the

Mantra are remarkable in themselves. It is the total *nirguṇa* (*nir* = without; *guṇa* = qualities) that is here envisioned through qualities as *saguṇa* (*sa* = with; *guṇa* = qualities), but these very qualities only further refine its *nirguṇa* aspect! What can the "devout" bring into its meaning? With what kind of understanding of the words need one armor oneself? Their spontaneity and immediacy direct one towards envisioning the Being. If and when the words are taken individually, the dynamism of the statement is missed. The Mūl Mantra conveys the core of the Sikh vision of the Transcendent, for it becomes a means whereby one can reenvision the Being as seen by Gurū Nānak. It does not seem to hold on to any latent concepts that would hinder the mind in deciphering their meaning; on the contrary, via the speedy spelling out of the *nirguṇa* and *saguṇa* characteristics, a momentum is created which impels the mind and senses together into a direct encounter between the individual and the Transcendent. How, then, could its "meaning" be limited "to the devout" alone?

The *śloka* or finale to the *Japu* is, on the other hand, full of vibrant and concrete images. Structurally, the *śloka* is crucial to the theme. It carries the Nānakian insight forward. It reads:

> Air is the Gurū, water the Father,
> The great earth, the Mother of all.
> Day and night are the female and male nurses,
> With the entire creation playing in their lap.

Apparently, there seems to be in the *śloka* a contradiction between the Singular One of the Mūl Mantra and the several elements – air, water, earth; between the Beyond-gender Absolute and Mother and Father, female and male nurses; between the spaceless, timeless, birthless, non-dual reality and a creation playing in the lap of duality – of day and night. But these two statements, the Mūl Mantra and the *śloka*, in fact fulfill each other. As Gurū Arjan (Nānak V) says in a hymn in the Granth, "ikkasu te hoio ananta nānak ekasu mahi samāe jīo[2] – from the One issue myriads and into the One they are ultimately assimilated." Unity becomes plurality, and plurality eventually becomes unity. The Kantian dictum about totality being plurality regarded as unity echoes the same truth. It is the Oneness of Be-ing which is fundamental to Sikh thought, and which, as we noticed in Chapter 1 also, is stressed in the Gurū Granth throughout. "Sadā sadā tūn eku hai[3] – always, always you alone are the One Reality." "Asti ek digari kuī ek tuī ek tuī[4] – only the One is, there is none other; only You, You only." The words of the latter verse are repeated by Gurū Nānak in three different hymns. In the first line he emphatically announces the unicity of Be-ing using Persian words – *asti y ek*, i.e. the One is; *digar kuī*, i.e. none other. Twice in Punjabi he repeats, *ek tuī, ek tuī*, i.e. only you, you only are the Reality. The use of the term *tuī* is to be especially noted here. It is the familiar, the most intimate and direct form of address (equivalent to the French *tu*), and it is the only way in which one may address the Being beyond. One example out of many clearly indicates how naturally Gurū Nānak used this familiar form when speaking to the Ultimate Being. The Ultimate Truth is "tisu binu dūjā avaru na koi – Besides It, there is none other,"[5] but when he wishes to make a variation on its form by addressing the Ultimate Truth directly, he automatically uses the familiar *tuī*, "tujh binu dūjā nāhī koi – besides you there is none other."[6]

Through verse after verse, hymn after hymn, the basic principle of the Mūl Mantra – the Oneness of the Transcendent Being – is proclaimed in the Gurū Granth. That the One subsumes all has been variously put forth:

> āpe dhartī dhaulu akāsaṅ.[7]
>
> The Being Itself is the Earth, the bull or support
> underneath the Earth, and the skies above.
>
> āpe pauṇu pāṇī baisaṅtaru
> āpe mel milāī he.[8]
>
> The Being Itself is the air, the water, the fire,
> It Itself is the uniter of all.
>
> pauṇ pāṇī agnī asrūpu
> eko bhavaru bhavai tihu loi.[9]
>
> The Being Itself is the form of the air,
> the water, the fire,
> The One pervades all the three worlds.

The pluralities, the specification of the gender, water as the father and Earth as the Mother, the creation playing in the lap of female and male nurses of day and night, and various other images in the *śloka* of the *Japu* are only a physical way of comprehending the metaphysical totality as defined in the Mūl Mantra. The vivid feminine and masculine imagery of the epilogue does not distract or distort the Transcendent nature of the One enumerated in the Mūl Mantra;

rather, it emphasizes the transcendence of the Transcendent One, suggesting that the Transcendent is essentially unfathomable and cannot be adequately designated in any singular way. The varied imagery but reveals the relativity of all images in the depiction of the Transcendent One and in turn opens up a range of possibilities for experiencing That One.

What we do notice in the epilogue to the *Japu* is the presence of equivalent female and male images. One gender is not appropriated over the other, and the feminine principle in the Sikh vision of the Transcendent finds an equal expression with that of the masculine. The line that concerns us most is the second one:

> mātā dharti mahatu.
> The Great Earth is the Mother of all.

Now this line is pregnant with meaning, and it offers a wealth of significance for all cultures. Ironically it is the specific female figure along with her feminine qualities that have been neglected by the Sikh patriarchs in their paternal elaborations. In the various commentaries on the *Japu* the female gender and the feminine characteristics in the imagery of the Transcendent have somehow remained unattended to. I shall specifically refer to Gurbachan Singh Talib's translation. His work is a very fine English version of this central Sikh text, with a detailed commentary. Since it first appeared, it has continued to enjoy immense popularity with Sikh scholars. However, the author fails to take notice of the feminine image in the *śloka*. Commenting upon the words *mata dharti mahatu*, Talib says:

> Mahat is great, vast. The concept of the Earth as mother is so well-known that it need not be explained further. In most languages of the world and in imaginative expression the Earth is spoken of as the Mother, from whose womb all life comes, and whose resources sustain it.[10]

The issue is bypassed with the statement, "The concept of the Earth as mother is so well-known [*sic*] that it need not be explained further." To us this "concept" of Earth as the Mother is a most important and complex one. The Earth as Mother may be a universal expression found everywhere and at all times, but that makes its explication even more necessary. Our new horizon darkened by the tragedies of pollution, global waste, and alienation from our environment both natural and social makes the task of reinterpreting this ubiquitous symbol even more urgent than ever.

The Sikh tradition does not, of course, believe in worshiping the Earth as a goddess, but it does honor the maternal nature of our planet. It only acknowledges one supreme reality, but that Transcendent One is as much female as male. Unfortunately, this has not been recognized in spite of the fact that the Sikh scripture clearly celebrates the feminine aspect of the Divine. The Gurū Granth affirms: "āpe purakhu āpe hī nārī – It itself is man; It itself is *woman*."[11] In the original Punjabi the gender of the One is not differentiated, but the translators, interpreters, and commentators have invariably referred to the One as "He" and kept the male image at the center of their discussions. This "sexism" has affected other religious traditions as well and has been seen as a cause of the decline of religion.[12] Logically, it does not matter how the One is understood in human terms: Be-ing is totally transcendent and beyond all categories. Our point is that in the Sikh tradition, wherein both female and male dimensions run parallel, commentators and interpreters have relied only on the male principle in comprehending Reality. Thealogians in the West have pointed out how this exclusivism denotes a trend towards idolatry. Sallie McFague, for example, says, "since all agents are either male or female, either pronoun and both pronouns can and should be used. If we use only the male pronoun, we fall into idolatry, forgetting that God is beyond male and female."[13] Some years ago Rosemary Ruether forcefully stated, "It is idolatrous to make males more 'like God' than females."[14] Even some men, such as John Cobb, realize this androcentric preoccupation: "Historically, whatever God's true nature and identity may be, God has been experienced, conceived, and spoken of as masculine."[15] Across the continents and through the centuries, the feminine dimension of Ultimate Reality has been either curtailed or completely ignored. Our *śloka* illustrates the equivalency of the two genders; it does not emphasize any particular image, nor does it dwell with an idolatrous fixation on anyone or anything particular. Since a lot of importance has already been imparted to male symbols, I will explore how powerful and significant the female figure in Sikh literature is. In fact, there is a sense of the primacy of the female nurse over the male, for *dāī* (female nurse) precedes the *dāiā* (male). The male thus appears to be her consort rather than the other way around. Regrettably, it has been more usual in sacred art and literature for women to be shown as merely the consorts of the male. The millions of Hindu goddesses (with the exception of Durgā and Kālī) are imaged as consorts to the gods. The *śloka* imagery is radically different from this norm. My objective is to analyze the rich imagery relating to the Mother in Sikh scripture and thereby counterbalance the male exegesis. Whenever one image is isolated and prized over the rest, there is an implicit reversion to idolatry. To continue the one-sided androcentric hermeneutics would surely be a distortion of Gurū Nanāk's seeing of the Transcendent One.

I will therefore proceed to analyze in some detail the very verse ignored by Sikh scholars – "mātā dharti mahat." Clearly, it is a celebration of "Mother," the Infinite Matrix. This chapter will explore the theme of Mother in both her female gender and her feminine dimension in the context of the Sikh tradition. While "female" refers to her gender, her biological being, "feminine" refers to qualities conventionally associated with women.[16] Both, I maintain, are essential to comprehending the full import of the maternal Reality in Sikh sacred literature.

The "Mother" engenders several questions: How does Nānak's image of the Mother *form* the Infinite Matrix? How would this female image then *inform* our worldview? How would that in turn *transform* our ethical values towards our neighbors and our planet? How would our ethical ideals enable us to *perform* in our everyday interactions? How would those relationships *conform* to the values of our sisters in the West? While these issues constitute the backdrop of the chapter, the theme of Mother as the Infinite Matrix will be explored in terms of the following three categories.

ONTOLOGICAL
EPISTEMOLOGICAL
SOTERIOLOGICAL

Under this threefold rubric, we shall analyze the images pertaining to Mother employed in the Sikh scripture. We come across images such as *garbha* (womb), *joti* (light), *kudarati* (nature), *mati* (wisdom), and *nadar* (grace). Images are valuable, for they integrate the intellectual component with aesthetic, axiological, and emotional components. Beatrice Bruteau defines "image" in the following manner. It

> is not an element of the intellect only, that is, not just an idea. It does not belong exclusively to the domain of the emotions; it is not simply a feeling. It is not to be restricted to the perceptive or aesthetic realm as if it were only

a form and an appreciative response. Nor is it merely an axiological entity. It is a figure in our consciousness to which each of these faculties has made its appropriate contribution. It is an aesthetic form which embodies an idea and a value in which we have a significant amount of feeling invested.[17]

We shall attempt to unlock the intellectual and visual significance of our images. Our approach will be an integration of the verbal and visual processes.[18] In analyzing words and ideas such as *garbha*, *joti*, *nadar*, we shall not confine ourselves to a solely intellectual apprehension; rather we shall try to *see* those categories as images and, in the process, experience them as holistic entities. Only through such an integrated mode of inquiry can we discern the true import of the feminine principle in the Sikh vision of the Transcendent.

### ONTOLOGICAL

Questions as regards the origin of the self, the universe, the very being of the person and of the cosmos are raised several times in Sikh scriptural texts. Three characteristic instances of such questioning from the Granth are found in the following verses:

jāto jāi kahā te āvai
kah upajai kah jāi samāvai[19]

Where does one come from and where does one go to?
Where is the origin from? Into what the mergence?

kat kī māī bāpu kat kerā
kidū thāvhu ham āe[29]

Who is our Mother? Who the Father?
Where have we come from?

kavaṇu su velā vakhtu kavaṇu
kavaṇ thithi kavaṇu vāru
kavaṇi si rutī māhu kavaṇu
jitu hoā ākāru[21]

What was the time, what the hour
what was the date, what the day?
What was the season, what the month
when the cosmos came into being?

The inquiries contained in the above verses relate to the origin and destiny of the human being as well as to the genesis of the cosmos. It is noteworthy that the female predominates in the Sikh perception of the cosmogony. In the second citation, the origin of the human being is traced primarily to the female. "Who is our Mother?" (*kat kī māī*) precedes "Who the Father?" (*bāpu kat kerā*).

Equality between women and men is one of the basic postulates of the Sikh faith. This is derived from the Sikh view of creation, according to which the entire cosmos came into being all at once as willed by the Transcendent One. In the *Japu*, Gurū Nānak says, "kītā pasāu eko kavāu – by one Word was the whole expanse created."[22] It is not like the cosmos, natural and societal, that issues forth sequentially from the Primal Puruśa or Cosmic Man of Vedic conception. When he speaks of the creation of humanity, Gurū Nānak says, "nāri purakh sirjīai – woman and man are created [by the One]."[23] We find that the word *nārī* (woman) here again takes precedence over *purakh* (man). In the Sikh understanding of the being and the becoming of the universe, woman is assigned no secondary place. In fact, the Mother image pervading the Gurū Granth makes one rethink Simone de Beauvoir's famous answer to her own question "what is a woman?": "She is defined and differentiated with reference to man and not he with reference to her; she is the incidental, the inessential as opposed to the essential. He is the Subject, he is the Absolute – she is the Other."[24] We shall see that De Beauvoir's statement is not universally valid, as we proceed to analyze the image of the Mother as the Infinite Matrix. We shall examine its presence in Sikh ontology from the (a) physical, (b) spiritual, and (c) cosmological standpoints.

### *Physical*

We may begin this line of inquiry by referring to a line from the Gurū Granth: "mā kī raktu pitā bidu dhārā – from mother's blood and father's semen is created the human form."[25] Here priority is given to *mā kī raktu* (mother's blood). So also in *Vār Jaitsrī*: "raktu bindu kari nimiā – from blood and semen is one created."[26] Mentioned first is *raktu* (mother's blood) and then *bindu* (semen). Modern feminists such as Penelope Washbourn[27] and Judy Grahn[28] and psychologists such as Judith Bardwick[29] refer to the degrading of menstruation in our culture. It is considered a private, shameful process, equated with being ill or weak. The concern of these spokeswomen is that the disdain for this natural feminine phenomenon by our society has led to the lowering of the status of women. To quote Judy Grahn: "The status and social control women have had has fallen with the fall of menstruation."[30] Far from being disdained, menstrual bleeding is acknowledged in Sikh thought as an essential, natural process. Life itself begins with it. In fact, Gurū Nānak, reprimands those who stigmatize as polluted the garment stained with menstrual blood.[31] "Mother" is again accorded importance in Gurū Nānak's utterance, "mili māt pitā piṇḍ kamāiā[32] – from the union of the mother and father one received the body." The Sikh scripture is not reticent in regard to birth imagery: female body, flesh, the natural female processes are fully affirmed.

In the woman's womb resides the embryo. Images of *garbha* (womb) and *agni* (heat and warmth) have been used interchangeably in the Gurū Granth, both underscoring the principle that sustains the fetus for nine months. Such images boldly affirm the glory of womanhood – something at the heart of all contemporary feminist thinking in religion. In a hymn in *Rāg Āsā*, Gurū Nānak reiterates twice how by the Divine Will life initiates in the womb:

> pahilai pahrai raiṇi kai vaṇjāriā mitrā
> hukmi paiā garbhāsi . . .
> kahu nānak prāṇī pahilai pahrai hukmi paiā garbhāsi.[33]
>
> In the first stage of life, o friend,
> you by the Divine Will lodged in the womb . . .
> Says Nānak, in the first stage of life, the creature
> by the Divine Will lodged in the womb.

In another hymn, the word *garbha* is substituted by the *agni* which generates life: "agni bimb jal bhītar nipje[34] – in the warmth [of mother's womb] are we inseminated." Conception and birth are from women. In *Āsā kī Vār* Gurū Nānak says: "bhaṇḍi jamīai bhaṇḍi nimīai[35] – Of woman are we born, of woman conceived." In the Sikh worldview the female is thus crucial to the origin of life. She is the matrix out of which everything that is originates and evolves.

The distinction between the creation of the universe as an intellectual-aesthetic act and its creation as a physical event is a major one for feminists in the Jewish and Christian world. In her very persuasive book, *Models of God: Theology for an Ecological, Nuclear Age*, Sallie McFague writes that in the western monotheistic religions, God is distanced from his creation. The picture that has emerged from the Genesis account of creation is one in which God fashions the world, "either intellectually by word (a creation of the mind) or aesthetically by craft (a creation of the hands), but in either case out of what is totally different from God, and in a manner that places humanity above nature, spirit above body."[36] The Sikh scriptural statements seem to share her feminist emphasis that the mother *bodies* forth her child. For, in the process of giving birth, the most intimate and organic connection between mother and offspring is expressed. There is no hierarchy between them in this natural relationship. Furthermore, the process of giving birth expresses the unique bond of the mother with her offspring, which no artist could ever have with his or her creation. The physical acts of gestation and giving birth, which constitute the basis of the model of God as Mother suggested by McFague, find a vivid validation in the Sikh sacred text.

Nurturing and sustenance depend upon women, too. Again, there are telling images in the Gurū Granth depicting the mother in this role. She is the source of the primal experiences of the newly born child.

> pahilai piāri laggā thaṇ dudhi
> dūjai māi bāp kī sudhi.[37]
>
> The child's first attraction is to the mother's breastmilk.
> Second, to the recognition of the mother and the father.
>
> pahilai pahirai . . . khīr pīai.[38]
>
> At the first stage of its existence, the child takes to the [mother's] milk.

These verses indicate the physical and psychological reliance of the child upon the mother. The child's first attraction is for the mother's breast (*thaṇ dudhi*). This is its primal psychological experience, which then leads on to a recognition of the mother and the father. From the breastmilk (*dudhi* or *khīr*) it derives its physical sustenance as well. Mother's breast is the first reality the child encounters, and this is the starting point of its physical and psychological development after birth. The breast image in Gurū Nānak's verses is a striking example of the honor the female body and the feminine principle receive in the Sikh *Weltanschauung*. We find that the feminine images rediscovered by contemporary Jewish scholars in their retranslating and reimaging of Hebraic words are quite explicitly present in Gurū Nānak's literary repertoire. In order to recover new meaning, Lynn Gottlieb transforms *Shaddai* from "the Almighty" to "my breasts."[39] The energizing female vitality retrieved by her, a modern Rabbi, is openly expressed by Gurū Nānak.

The imagery of conception, gestation, giving birth, and lactation is unambiguously and powerfully present in the Gurū Granth. What we have recovered from the Sikh images so far is not some vague Mother-Earth symbol but a firm understanding that validates femaleness. The Sikh validation of the female comes across to me as something unique in the history of religions and something that only contemporary feminist thealogians are seeking. For although Sikhism is of Indian origin, it does not share the fascination for female sexuality that its immediate neighboring traditions like Hinduism and Buddhism do. The Mother is not represented as a tantalizing figure – overly voluptuous with exaggerated erotic overtones. In Hinduism, Pārvatī's sexuality is accepted and in fact magnificently amplified so long as she lodges in the distant Mt. Kailasha; in the everyday household, however, sexuality is a hidden and repressed matter. Hindu *mandirs* and Buddhist *stupas* depict the female most ornately in myriads of forms – the goddesses, the *yakshīs*, the *apsarās*. Many a time, these figures merely embellish gateways, their significance remaining ambiguous. Is the lush female to be left behind in the profane world or is she some*body* who is going to be ushering the devotee into the sacred? Feminine images farther from India but still eastern do not display this overwhelming fascination for her sexuality. However, their validation of her is also different from that of Sikhism. For example, in the classic Chinese text *Tao Tê Ching*, the paradox of *wu wei* (actionless activity, the goal of the sage)[40] is illustrated through the lowlying, humble, "female" valley, and the female passively lying beneath the male. One would have to admit that there is sexual imagery in this Chinese text, though this is denied by Holmes Welch.[41] The female in this profound work remains an idealized version, used to illustrate the concept of *wu wei*. On the contrary, in the Sikh perspective, she *exists* as a person upon whom depend creation and nurturing. The structure of her body is prized. She is accorded value as a woman, as an individual – neither as a goddess to be worshiped in some hidden sanctuary nor as a temptress to be left behind. Nor is her sexuality feared in Sikhism as it would be in western religions. Rather, it is accepted as essential to life.

Now some western feminists have been attracted to the "basically metaphorical" motherhood of the Hindu goddesses. In the goddess's freedom from literal mothering, women sense a welcome alternative to the traditional role of housewife and diaper-changer. According to Rita Gross, the conspicuous absence of literal mother-and-child icons amongst Hindu female deities is balanced by the omnipresence of a metaphorical creative motherhood, which enables women to participate in the goddess's life-giving potential.[42] However, if we look a bit closer, the great metaphor in fact abstracts women and places them on a Platonic pedestal. The mother who is central to the Hindu *Weltanschauung* is not a real mother but an idealized version of the mother as virgin – an image we find again in the Christian notion of the Virgin Birth. The Mother in the Sikh tradition is revered because she is a Mother – one who has gone through the natural processes of conception, gestation, giving birth, and lactation – and not because she is a Virgin. Sikh scripture makes a simple but powerful statement about the Mother which calls out to contemporary feminists. The verses from the Gurū Granth undergird through the poetic mode what Sallie McFague has expressed in a superbly articulated argument:

> There is simply no other imagery available to us that has this power for expressing the interdependence and interrelatedness of all life with its ground. All of us, female and male, have the womb as our first home, all of us are born from the bodies of our mothers, all of us are fed by our mothers. What better imagery could there be for expressing the most basic reality of existence: that we live and move and have our being in God?[43]

### *Spiritual*

As the "spiritual" principle, the female images the One Transcendent within the individual. The term used most frequently in Sikh scripture for the spirit within the body is *joti* (or *nūr* at times), meaning light. *Joti* is grammatically feminine; *joti* is metaphysically the feminine dimension of the numeral One. Light has been a crucial concept in the religious heritage of humankind. It is used to describe the Godhead, God's creation or the state of highest spiritual experience. This image is found in various traditions:

Hindu:

> Lead me from the unreal to the real,
> From Darkness lead me to Light.[44]

Jewish:

> Lift up the light of thy countenance upon us, O Lord![45]

Buddhist:

> Hold firm to the truth as a lamp and refuge.[46]

Christian:

> God is light; in him there is no darkness at all.[47]

Islamic:

> God is the light of the heavens and the earth.[48]

Shinto:

> She lights the far corners of Heaven and Earth – the great Kami of the Sun.[49]

And Sikh:

> There is a light in all and that light is the Ultimate One.[50]

It is in its aspect as light – as *joti* – that we shall now explore the role of the feminine principle in the Sikh vision of the Transcendent. This dimension of the feminine principle raises three important issues: What is the nature of *joti*? How can the Transcendent remain transcendent if the One Light is immanent in all? What meaning does this ontological base have for society?

We shall first examine the feminine nature of *joti* and its relation to the Transcendent. *Joti* (light) has been strikingly – and aptly – used as an image for the Transcendent Reality, for the nature of light is manifestation. Light is being, just as its absence, darkness, is nothingness. "There is nothing that is more without need of being defined than light."[51] *Joti*, constituting the feminine demension of the Transcendent, is no ordinary light. Its ineffability and noetic quality have been beautifully rendered by Gurū Nānak:

> jhilmili jhilkai candu na tārā
> sūraj kiraṇi na bijuli gaiṇārā
> akathī kathau cihanu nahī koī.[52]

> It is brilliantly dazzling,
> yet it is neither the moon nor the stars,
> Neither the sun-ray, nor the lightning in the skies.
> Words cannot describe it, nor can any sign or symbol.

*Joti* is thus totally transcendent: it is not the radiance from the moon, the stars, or the sun, or the flash of lightning. In this case, light has no form, and it never becomes an attribute of anything other than itself. It subsists by itself.

This image of *joti* from Sikh scripture corresponds to Suhrāwardī's perception of *Nūr al-anwār* and the Upaniṣadic-Gitic perception of *Jyotiśām jyotī*. Both *Nūr al-anwār* and *Jyotiśām jyotī* signify the light of lights, the ontological ground of the universe. In both philosophies, the light of lights has a direct symbol in every domain: the sun in the skies, the fire in the elements, and *al-nūr al-ıspahbadī* (Ishrāqi) or *ātman* (Hindu) within the individual. The cosmos in both cases is constituted by the gradation of light, elucidated in the *tashkīk al-dhāti* and *guṇā* theories within Ishrāqi and Hindu schools of thought, respectively.[53] We may not find *Nūr al-anwār* and *Jyotiśām Jyoti* mentioned directly in Sikh scripture or the theories pertaining to the gradation of light elaborated in Sikh thought, yet they acknowledge that light is paramount. *Joti* is accepted as the source of all energy and every being – everything depends upon it. A verse in the Gurū Granth reminds us of the ontological base of our existence; we exist only because of the *joti* placed in our bodies by the One:

> e sarirā meriā hari tum mahi joti rakhī
> tā tū jag mahi āiā.[54]
>
> O my body, the One put *joti* (light) inside you,
> Only then did you come into this world.

That *joti* pervades the body is reiterated in another hymn of Gurū Nānak as well:

> jis dā jio prāṇu hai
> aṅtari joti apārā.[55]
>
> The One who has given life and breath
> Has placed in the body Its *joti* (light) infinite.

Another hymn by Gurū Nānak traces the sequence in which the cosmos developed: from the One Truth emanated air, from which came water, from which originated the three worlds. *Joti* is what permeates all creation:

> sāce te pavanā bhaiā pavanai te jalu hoi
> jal te tribhavaṇu sājiā ghaṭi ghaṭi joti samoe.[56]
>
> From the Truth eternal came air and from the air came water,
> From the water were created the three worlds, with *joti* (light) permeating all.

*Joti*, as the feminine dimension of the Transcendent, is also conceived as ultimate beauty:

> candu sūraju dui joti sarūpu
> jotī antari brahmu anūpu.[57]
>
> The sun and the moon are the embodiment of *joti* (light),
> But within *joti* is the One of incomparable beauty.

*Joti* is the medium of envisioning ultimate beauty. The perception of the aesthetic aspect of the Transcendent Reality is made possible through the feminine principle. The verse cited above presents an enchanting phenomenon: the cosmos is made up of *joti*, which in turn is made up of the beautiful One. A perfect unity of the Universe is implied here.

Totally immaterial and insubstantial in itself, *joti* is the ground of all existence. It is the spirit pervading the universe; it is the manifestation of the Divine. It marks the principle of harmony underlying creation. The phenomenon is poetically described by the Islamic philosopher Muhammad Iqbal: "The universe, in one word, is a petrified desire; a crystallized longing after light."[58]

We have discovered that the nature of *joti* is all-pervasive, but we must now ask how the Transcendent can remain transcendent if *joti* is immanent in all. The Infinite Light (*joti apāru*) is indeed in all creatures; at the same time, it is beyond creation. The Infinite Light does not exhaust itself by generating and sustaining creation. A unique relationship exists between the One There and the one here in the world: all creation is from the Creator, yet it cannot be identified with It. The One pervades all, but all are not One, for the One transcends all. The closeness between the two realms – the Creator and Its creation – is established through *joti*, the feminine principle. This relationship becomes further meaningful through the longing of the individual to unite with that Infinite Matrix from which it originated, to which it belongs. According to the Gurū Granth, most of us remain oblivious to the divine light within us. This condition is portrayed through an eloquent simile – that of a deer which, ignorant of the musk within its own body, runs frantically in the jungle searching for it. "The perennial light is within us all," says a verse; "it's only the enlightened ones who recognize this" (*ghaṭi ghaṭi joti nirantarī būjhai gurmati sāru*).[59]

*Joti* is therefore both all-pervasive and transcendent, and this single ontological base has enormous significance for human society.

A popular couplet from the Granth brings out the social implications latent in this conception of the Transcendent:

> avāl allāh nūru upāiā kudrati ke sabh bande
> ek nūr te sabhu jagu upjiā kaun bhale ko mande?[60]
>
> Allah first created Its light; and from it were all made,
> From that One Light came the whole cosmos,
> whom shall we then declare good, whom bad?

From One Light (*ek nūr*) has originated the entire cosmos. One Light is beyond all and yet simultaneously within all. Three dimensions of the One Light can here be discerned: Light Itself, the source; radiated light, the channel; and created light, we and our cosmos. Through light a continuous relationship is thus sustained. This concept of harmony between man, woman, and the cosmos is echoed in the words of our modern feminist thealogian, Rosemary Ruether: "The 'Brotherhood of Man' needs to be widened to embrace not only women but also the whole community of life."[61]

It is because creation emanates from the One Source, *ek nūr*, that the Sikh tradition upholds the equality and unity of humankind. When from One Light all are born, who can be called good, who bad, who high, who low? The equality of all humankind, irrespective of sex, caste, or creed, is the foundation of Sikh ethics. "False," said Gurū Nānak, "is caste and false the titled fame. The One Supreme sustains all."[62] And this is a belief he repeats again and again: "Neither caste nor position will be recognized hereafter. They alone will be pronounced good whose merit is reckoned worthy of honor."[63] "Neither caste nor birth will be inquired . . . as you act so will be your caste and your status."[64] Equally categorical was Gurū Nānak in affirming the equality of the sexes. He declares that in no case should woman be called inferior.[65] The same Light informs man and woman. Gurū Nānak even says that "a simpleton is not to be considered inferior to a wise one, for the light within them is the same – *mūrakhu siāṇā eku hai ek joti dui nāu*."[66] A thoroughly egalitarian and liberating structure emerges out of the Transcendent Light's being the spirit in us all. Shattered are all caste structures; shattered are all racial and gender monopolies. The ground is set for a just social, political, and economic world in which oppressive and hierarchical systems would not find any solid base.

The Sikh understanding of *joti*, the feminine principle of the Transcendent, residing within all initiates the search of the individual, man and woman, for his or her origin. It provides both men and women with the spiritual goal, with the right and opportunity to exclaim with Ntozake Shange:

> i found god in myself
> & i loved her
> i loved her fiercely.[67]

*Cosmological*

The word *kudarati* (*qudrat* in Arabic) has been frequently used in Sikh scripture in the sense of all that is created, and like *joti*, the term *kudarati* is grammatically feminine. Literally, *kudarati* in Punjabi means "nature," but in the Sikh conception, it is the feminine manifestation of the Transcendent. Where *joti* was the Divine Spirit informing creation, *kudarati* is creation itself. To quote from the Gurū Granth:

> kudarati disai kudarati suṇīai kudarati bhau sukh sāru
> kudarati pātālī ākāsī kudarati sarab ākāru
> kudarati veda purāṇa katebā kudarati sarab vīcāru
> kudarati khāṇā pīṇā painaṇu kudarati sarab piāru.[68]

> What we see is the One's *kudarati*, what we hear is the One's *kudarati*, *kudarati* is at the core of happiness and fear,
> The skies, the nether regions and all that is visible is the One's *kudarati*,
> The Vedas, the Purāṇās, the Qur'ān, indeed all revelation is *kudarati*,
> Eating, drinking, dressing up is *kudarati*, so is all love *kudarati*.

All that exists materially – Earth, skies, nether regions; all that is experience – the psychological states of joy, love and fear; the revealed word of the Hindus and Muslims – the Vedas, Purāṇas and the Qur'ān; all that is done – the practical activities like eating, drinking, and dressing; everything is the One's *kudarati*. The passage discloses an inclusivist approach towards other faiths. Hindu and Muslim scriptures are not set aside or excluded; rather they are seen as a revelation of the One Indivisible Reality. All matter, all thought, all emotion, all action comprise *kudarati*.

*Kudarati* is thus the *saguṇa* form of the *nirguṇa* Transcendent. For it is through her that the One is seen (*kudarati disai*) and heard (*kudarati suṇiai*). Gurū Arjan (Nānak V) reiterates the same concept: "tū sabh mahi vartahi āpi kudarat dekhāvahī[69] – the One is in all, so does *kudarati* reflect it." The causative form *dekhāvahī* of the root *dṛś* indicates how through *kudarati* we are made to see the One. A verse in Gurū Arjan's *Sukhmanī* reads:

> nirgunu āpi sargunu bhī ohī
> kalā dhāri jini sagalī mohī.[70]

> *Nirguṇa* is the One, *Saguṇa (Sarguṇa)* is It too,
> By taking on form, It has allured all.

In *saguṇa* form, the One becomes the cause of alluring human beings. No longer does it remain completely unknown. Instead, it becomes a fascinating enigma, the One which we can know – or, at least, hope to know. We can then so regulate ourselves as finally to unlock the enigma, to realize the One. This regulation in Sikh terminology is called *sādhanā*, again a feminine term. Thus *sādhanā* is a positive conception of the noumenal world where the individual seeks to know the unknown through the faculty of intelligence rather than sense experience. The Transcendent in Its *saguṇa* form becomes apprehensible, realizable. However, we should not conclude that this form is being installed as an idol. Idolatry or incarnation is not accepted in the Sikh tradition. In the *Japu*, Gurū Nānak emphatically rejects such a possibility:

> thāpiā na jāi kītā na hoi
> āpe āpi niraṅjanu soi[71]

> It cannot be installed as an idol,
> Its likeness cannot be made,
> Of Its own, It manifests Itself.

It is through *kudarati* that the Divine is manifested, not through any human-made idol or form. The One in its *saguṇa* aspect inheres in the entire cosmos.

Yet, the Transcendent still remains transcendent: the *saguṇa* is not inclusive of the *nirguṇa*. The One is manifested in everything – in substance, in thought, in emotion, and in action; the One is not totally embraced in Its *saguṇa* manifestation, nor does It fail to maintain Its transcendence with regard to Its multiple qualities. A verse in the Gurū Granth cherishes the *nirguṇa* dwelling in Its *Kudarati*, yet proclaims Its utter incomprehensibility, Its infinity – "balihārī kudarati vasiā terā aṅtu na jāī lakhiā."[72] As *saguṇa*, the Transcendent can be envisioned in *kudarati*, but as *nirguṇa*, It is still infinitely far beyond, Its vastness and greatness being incomprehensible. The One thus remains uniquely a blend of qualities and non-qualities. In a hymn in *Kīrtan Sohilā*, Gurū Nānak expresses his wonder at this phenomenon:

> sahas tav nain nan nain hahi tohi kau
> sahas mūrati nanā ek tohī
> sahas pad bimal nan ek pad gaṅdh binu
> sahas tav gandh iv calat mohī.[73]

> You have a thousand eyes, yet without eyes you are,
> You have a thousand forms, yet without form you are,
> You have a thousand feet, yet without feet you are,
> You have a thousand fragrances, yet without fragrance you are,
> Thoroughly enchanted am I.

Through the repetition of "thousand," Gurū Nānak attempts to visualize the One; but by juxtaposing the words "thousand" and "without," he proclaims Its immensity and magnificence, which are beyond all description.

From our discussion one conclusion emerges clearly: *kudarati* is crucial to the Sikh perception of the Transcendent. We can see its overall importance both for the Transcendent Creator Itself and for Its manifested creation.

The One, true, eternal, immutable Transcendent. But without Its *kudarati*, the Transcendent would remain a totally "Hidden Treasure"! In Its absoluteness, the One transcends all qualities and qualifications; without Its *kudarati* the One would remain unknown and unknowable, forever a mystery, the mystery of mysteries, the most indeterminate of all indeterminates. It would be everything in Itself, but it is only in Its manifestation – Its feminine projection – that a multi-faceted cosmos comes into being, proclaiming, according to the Sikh view, Its existence. Through the material and substantial formation, along with the subtleties of thought and emotion, the One is recognized and sought after. The challenge begins with *kudarati*. She gives the cosmos an inkling of its transcendent source, and thereafter the quest begins. Perhaps we could interpret Goethe's aphoristic finale to *Faust* – "The Eternal Feminine draws us onward" – as *kudarati*, who, by providing tantalizing hints of the One, urges us onward to see and to know the One.

The significance of the feminine principle from the point of view of the Divine finds two rather interesting crosscultural parallels. The first is from Hindu philosophy – the feminine principle "i" which seems to be intrinsic to Sanskrit etymology as well as to Hindu art. Lord Śiva – the all-powerful creator, preserver, and destroyer – without the "i" is *śava*, literally meaning corpse. It is thus the feminine "i" which provides him with *śakti*, her power and energy. That may be a reason why Hindu divinities, such as Viṣṇu, Śiva, and Kṛṣṇa, are generally seen with their female consorts – Laxmī, Pārvatī, and Rādhā. In a visual presentation, a painting from the Kāṅgṛā school entitled *Śava–Śiva*,[71] we see two male figures, one lying on top of the other. The bottom one is that of Śava (without "i"), literally a corpse. Śava lies with his eyes closed and his arms lying listlessly on the ground. Above him is Śiva on the verge of coming to life because on Śiva stands Kālī – the black, female goddess of death. Kālī holds the scissors that snap off life in one hand, a begging-bowl in another, a sword in the third; the fourth hand is in *abhāya mudrā* – a symbolic gesture suggesting nurturing and grace; she wears a skirt of severed arms and from her ears dangle skulls. But she dances triumphantly over Śava, and with the touch of her feet the male body starts getting energized, coming to life, becoming Śiva. Without the female, the god of death is but dead.

The second parallel is from D. H. Lawrence's "The Man Who Died," a symbolic extension of the resurrection of Christ. In the story the man from inside a carved hole in the rock wakes up after a long sleep and starts moving around numbly and coldly, in a death-like state. In Sanskrit his listless and lifeless self would indeed be *śava*. Some time later, this man is drawn on to have a sexual union with the priestess of Isis – very much reminiscent of Kālī touching Śava. This physical process leads to his coming to life, to his "resurrection."

These two instances – in their own and separate ways – highlight the importance of the feminine principle. They are thus relevant to our own theme as well. The female principle – *kudarati* – is, as we have observed, crucial to our apprehension of the Transcendent. She is essential to Its simultaneous revelation and concealment. Without her, in fact, there would not even be a Mystery or an Unknown! She provides intimations of the Transcendent One.

*Kudarati* is also vital for the modern feminist conception of society as the offspring of the "Mother." Through the Transcendent–*Kudarati* relationship, the Sikh tradition provides a striking precedent for this type of society idealized by feminist thealogians such as Ruether, Bruteau, and McFague. For the feminists, the "Mother" image (instead of male Lord or God), because of the creativity of motherhood, promotes growth and independence.

> If God is conceived as Mother, Her own creativity is in no way in conflict with the creativity of Her children. They cannot "usurp" her prerogatives, because it is precisely Her intention that they should be *creative*. They are not separate from Her; they are Her creativity in the finite world. By the same token, they would express their creativity in unionist ways . . . Their justice would move toward healing and renewing life rather than toward punishment. They would not take advantage of the non-human world but would regard it too as the offspring of the Mother with Whom they hold life in common.[75]

The crux of the mother–child relationship is harmony: it is a state where there is no opposition, no conflict, no suggestion of fear, or possibility of hostility. Gurū Nānak does not equate the Transcendent One with the Mother alone (for the One is both Mother and Father, Sister and Brother . . .), yet he sees perfect harmony between the Transcendence of the One and Its manifestation – *kudarati*. This harmony between the Transcendent and *kudarati* provides a thealogical foundation for our society in which the Divine, humanity, and nature are linked together rather than tiered into hierarchical levels with humans in the middle distorting and oppressing the life-support system.

The cosmos originates from the Infinite Matrix; it is a spontaneous unfolding and blooming of the Infinite, of which it is the finite form. There is no hypothetical or contingent relation between the Transcendent and Its *kudarati*: they are one, totally non-dualistic. The life-energy circulating amongst the beings of the world is communicated by each to all within the comprehensive Oneness of the Metaphysical Reality. The result is the healing and harmonious mother–child relationship. Just as a mother would care about her child, attentively watch over him or her, and think about his or her needs and requirements, "the Transcendent ponders over Its *kudarati* and sustains it – kudarati bīcāre dhāran dhāre."[76]

Based on the Infinite Matrix of the Mother, Sikh ontology reverberates with the ethical objectives of contemporary feminists: the concern with justice, based on care and pertaining to our present lives. Jewish and Christian thinkers inform us that in the Mother model of theology, a future "kingdom" of God is not awaited, nor is its justice concerned with condemning in the future.[77] The love embodied in the Mother extends now into our immediate families, into our primary communities, and into other species. She in whom are united the ingredients of life and of life's continuity – blood, water, breath, sex, and food[78] – is *care*fully involved in positively creating a just and harmonious family. Since the whole community – of humans and nature – constitutes her family, she does not favor humans over nature, nor does she favor the immediate advantage of the dominant class, race, and sex. Our Mother, the Infinite Matrix, provides us with a deep ecological sensitivity important in our nuclear age. She paves the way towards "a new synthesis, a new creation in which human nature and nonhuman nature become friends in the creating of a livable and sustainable cosmos."[79] The Mother image offers a profound lesson in relativity, a lesson which has been put forth artistically by Carol Christ: "we are no more valuable to the life of the universe than a field flowering in the color purple, than rivers flowing, than a crab picking its way across the sand – and no less."[80] By truly recognizing the import of the Mother as Infinite Matrix in Sikh scripture, our consciousness could be transformed and raised towards all our other *family* members. The glorious outcome has been described graphically by yet another eminent western thealogian:

> We would no longer see a world we named and ruled, or like the artist God, made: mothers and fathers to the world do not rule or fashion it. Our positive role in creation is as preservers, those who pass life along and who care for all forms of life so they may prosper. Our role as preservers is a very high calling, our peculiar calling as human beings, the calling implied in the model as mother.[81]

## EPISTEMOLOGICAL

> mātā mati pitā santokh.[82]
> Mother is wisdom; father, contentment.

The identification of *mati*, wisdom, with the mother, the female, in the above line by Gurū Nānak seems to me to be the quintessential characteristic of Sikh epistemology. But scholars and commentators have not paid sufficient attention to this. This aspect of Sikhism has suffered neglect in the western traditions as well. Lately, however, some modern thinkers such as Leonard Swidler have examined the idea of "wisdom as feminine" in their own traditions. For example, in his articles entitled "God, Father and Mother" and "God the Father: Masculine, God the Son: Masculine, God the Holy Spirit:

Feminine,"[83] Swidler shows that wisdom is conceived as feminine in the Jewish and Christian traditions, both grammatically (Hokmah in Hebrew and Sophia in Greek) and in its depiction in the wisdom literature of the Hebrew Bible, that is, as a woman. Like Rosemary Ruether, Swidler reminds us that in Hebrew both the adjective and verb reflect the feminine gender of the word:

> All of this makes the Hebrew reader of the pertinent passages constantly aware of the feminine quality of divine Wisdom, *Hokmah.* In the biblical books of Proverbs, Job, Baruch, Ecclesiasticus (Sirach), and Wisdom, there are many examples of wisdom, Hokmah, as a personified, feminine dimension of God. It is really a depiction of God facing humanity, creation.[84]

In the same way, in *Knowledge and the Sacred*, Seyyed Hossein Nasr points to the Virgin Mary as a symbol of wisdom.[85]

In the Sikh instance, *bāṇī* is the medium of divine revelation: amrit *bāṇī* tat vakhāṇī – ambrosial Word (*amrit bāṇī*) brings one face to face with the One (*tat vakhāṇī*). Now, whereas *bāṇī* is a vision of the Transcendent, *mati*, I would say, is the process, the channel for envisioning the Transcendent. Since *mati* is the individual's cognitive faculty of seeing the Beyond, it denotes not only wisdom, but also the mind, intelligence, and consciousness that make the vision possible. In this context, *mati* is the inevitable but ineffable juncture between the "eyesight" and "insight." This medium has four striking feminine aspects: (a) as beauty, (b) as clarity, (c) as churning of butter, and (d) as sister.

## *Mati as beauty*

The Sikh scripture provides a fundamental connection between *mati* and *saca*:

> saca kī mati sadā nautan.[86]
> Wisdom once imbibed from Truth remains perennially fresh.

Wisdom is thus understood to have been derived from Truth Itself – an emanation from the Transcendent One. The source of It is here viewed as eternally fresh (*nautan*). The image of "freshness" suggests a natural beauty and grace which imply that *mati* functions at the level of both mind and body. The above verse presents *mati* as a radiant and lively female who is intrinsically and immanently related with the *saca*, the Transcendent Truth.

In Sikh sacred texts, the term *mati* is associated with the quality of beauty, and the literary images representing it are imbued with feminine characteristics. To quote from the *Japu*:

> mati vici ratan jawāhar māṇik.[87]
> Wisdom comprises jewels, gems and pearls.

*Mati* is beheld as a treasury of precious stones. Jewels (*ratan*), gems (*jawāhar*), and pearls (*māṇik*) conjure up images of luster and beauty. Worn primarily by women, jewels, gems, and pearls evoke the female world. The nexus between wisdom and woman is metaphorically established.

Philosophers and poets from different cultures have been attracted to the relation between the feminine dimension of beauty and wisdom or knowledge. In the *Symposium*, Diotima explains to Socrates that the highest form of knowledge is utmost beauty. For the Upaniṣadic seers, Umā, the extremely beautiful female – *bahuśobhamānām umām* – is the personification of wisdom,[88] the dispeller of darkness and ignorance. The beautiful daughter of the Himalayas – Umā – has been a constant source of inspiration for the Hindu sages. "Wisdom is the most beautiful of all beautiful things."[89] Again, for the entire Suhrāwardian school – the Ishrāqi or Illuminationist movement – the goal of wisdom is perceived in the splendid beauty of the rising sun. The root meaning of Ishrāq is the first moment of light appearing in the geographical East. Wisdom appeared to many Muslim sages in the celestial form of Fātimah, the Prophet's daughter. Ibn 'Arabi is said to have written his *Tarjumān al-ashwāq*, one of his most powerful works on gnosis, upon beholding the beautiful face of a young Persian woman walking around the Ka'bah.[90] Likewise, the central goddess of China, Kuan Yin, and that of Japan, Amaterasu, combine both beauty and wisdom. In the chapter "Beauty and Truth" from his book *Christian and Oriental Philosophy of Art*, Ananda Coomaraswamy reflects on the theme of beauty and wisdom. He cites theologians and philosophers such as St. Thomas Aquinas, St. Bonaventura, and Ulrich of Strasburg in an effort to establish that the two are closely related. The chapter opens:

> It is affirmed that "beauty relates to the cognitive faculty" (St. Thomas Aquinas, *Sum. Theol.*, I, 5, 4 *ad.* 1) being the cause of knowledge, for, "since knowledge is by assimilation, and similitude is with respect to form, beauty properly belongs to the nature of a formal cause" (ib.). Again, St. Thomas

endorses the definition of beauty as a cause; in *Sum. Theol.*, III, 88, 3, he says that "God is the cause of all things by his knowledge" and this again emphasizes the connection of beauty with wisdom. "It is knowledge that makes the work beautiful" (St. Bonaventura, *De reductione artium ad theologiam*, 13). It is of course, by its quality of lucidity of illumination (*claritas*), which Ulrich of Strassburg explains as the "shining of the formal light upon what is formed or proportioned," that beauty is identified with intelligibility: brilliance of expression being unthinkable apart from perspicacity. Vagueness of any sort, as being a privation of due form, is necessarily a defect of beauty.[91]

This "inextricable bond between knowledge and beauty" is also the thesis of a contemporary thinker, Seyyed Hossein Nasr.[92] Notwithstanding St. Thomas Aquinas' delimitation of God in the pronoun "his," the feminine character of wisdom – through beauty – is recognizable in western as well as in eastern thought.

## *Mati as clarity*

*Mati* is integrally connected with *joti*, for the ultimate source of both is the Transcendent Itself. As Gurū Nānak says, "The creator who contemplates Its creation is the imparter of wisdom – nānak jini kari dekhiā devai mati sāī."[93] Without light or illumination there can be no wisdom. How can the Transcendent be seen without light? Light here is not any physical phenomenon, but illumination and perspicacity – and ultimately wisdom. In the transition from eyesight to insight, wisdom that is clear and illuminating is essential. That is how the Transcendent is known and seen – without any doubt or any dark, nebulous veiling. Darkness is equivalent to ignorance, the opposite of wisdom and light.

Essentially, light is knowledge, the clear and lucid apprehension of the One Be-ing. "Sā mati pūrī jitu hari gun gāvai[94] – that wisdom is perfect which leads one to recite the praises of the One." In this verse Gurū Arjan (Nānak V) affirms that it is only the wise one who perceives and celebrates the existence of the Transcendent. In the melodies which celebrate such a realization, *mati* functions as the musical instrument (*vājā*).[95] *Mati* thereby acquires yet another distinctive characteristic: it becomes the vehicle of joyous cognizance. The sonorous element joins with the visual – the *joti*, the light.

In Hindu and Islamic thought also wisdom is conceived in terms of light. According to the Qur'ān, the Prophet Muhammad was sent by God "as a light-giving lamp."[96] In Sūrāh XIV it is stated: "And we sent Moses with our signs – Bring forth thy people from the shadows to the Light." In the words of the Prophet, "Knowledge is light" (*al'ilmu nūrun*).

In the Vedas, the light sought after is intrinsically wisdom:

> O Brhaspati, put us in possession of the bright substance which excels in worth that of the outsider; which procures brilliant light, and is resourceful among men, which shines powerfully, O Thou That art born of the cosmic law.[97]

Light – *nūr* and *joti* – in the Islamic and Hindu contexts, as well as in Sikh literature, does not remain abstract or allegorical; it is understood as vision, as the seeing of Ultimate Reality, as Reality itself. In the Sikh view it is throughout marked by a feminine aura. The two feminine entities – *mati* and *joti* – remain linked together.

### *Mati as the churning of butter*

*Mati* in the Sikh perspective is not solely a matter of intellect. The term central to Suhrāwardian epistemology, *al-hikmat al-dhawqiyyah* (translated by the late Henry Corbin as "tasted knowledge," *goûter*),[98] would be helpful in comprehending the eyesight–insight process, because the vision of the Transcendent does not entail speculations and abstractions, but intense experience and tasting. In Sikh speculation as well, such intense experience is essential to the epistemological procedure. A scriptural hymn articulates this through images of milk, butter-milk, and butter commodities subject to taste. Furthermore, *mati* is related to action and deeds, since without these wisdom remains merely intellectual. For this reason, the Sikh view does not espouse *jñāna mārga* (the path of knowledge) as one of the three paths towards Ultimate Reality propounded in the *Bhagavad Gītā* (the other two being *karma*, the path of action, and *bhakti*, the path of love). Wisdom, which is experienced and tasted, encompasses ethical deeds too, and the idea finds symbolic expression in the predominantly "feminine" occupation of churning butter from milk:

> bhāṇḍā dhoi baisi dhūpu devhu tao dūdhai kao jāvhu
> dūdhu karam funi surati samāiṇu hoi nirās jamāvhu
> japhu ta eko nāmā
> avari niraphal kāmā . . .
> rasnā nāmu japau tab mathīai in bidhi amritu pāvhu.[99]

First wash the vessel clean and disinfect it with incense,
Then get the milk.
Milk is the deeds, consciousness the culture,
Desirelessly ferment the milk.
Meditate but on the Name of the One,
All other actions are fruitless.
With the tongue reciting the Name, the milk is churned
and the butter (nectar) obtained.

This *śabda* pictures a typical Punjabi scene: almost every household in a Punjabi village awakens to the sound of curds being churned early in the morning. This daily morning task, an exclusively feminine occupation, here becomes the prime instance of experiential wisdom which men and women must enact. There are several steps involved in this procedure carried out diligently by the Punjabi woman.

The vessel has to be cleaned and all dirt removed, a domestic image for the cleansing of the heart. The nuances of the image become all the clearer when we consider that the word for vessel, *bhāṇḍā*, is closely related to *bhaṇḍu*, a common expression for a woman in Sikh scripture. The cleaner and the cleansed are thus intimately connected. In the cleansing, the five lower passions, *kāma* (lust), *krodha* (anger), *lobha* (greed), *moha* (attachment), and *ahankār* (egocentricity), which have been enumerated in the Gurū Granth many times, have to be cast away. Then, the vessel is to be touched with fragrance. The fragrance, according to Taran Singh, is the consequence of one's virtuous deeds.[100] The milk is then received into the pot. Thus, prior to getting the milk, a course of preparation has to be gone through. Insight, then, is not instantaneous; the way to it is paved with ethical deeds.

In the second line, an analogy has been drawn between milk and action (*dūdh karam*). Gurū Nānak attached the highest merit to moral and just action and to the service of fellow-beings. In his words, "*sacu urai sabhu ko upari sacu ācāru* – truth is higher than every thing else but higher than truth is the living of truth."[101] For his followers, practical virtue is an important ingredient of piety. Their approach to religion is in this sense "existentialist." Gurū Nānak's teaching came to be summarized in the words, "*kirat karnī vaṇḍ chhakṇā te nām japṇā* – to earn one's living by honest labor, to share the earnings with others, and always to remember the One." This forms the complete existential formula emerging from Gurū Nānak's teaching. Therewith everyone – man and woman – is expected to live fully in the world, to exist in the etymological sense of the word, *ex sistere* – to stand out of oneself, out of being. Engaged in normal activity, never forswearing one's moral obligation, one is to become an active agent in promoting the moral ends of the community. "No one ever attained spiritual merit without serving fellow-beings."[102] The obligation to serve others falls on men and women equally. According to Gurū Nānak, "unethical are those who renounce their duty and give up (*gavāini*) the occupation of their mother (*māū*) and father (*pīū*)":

māū pīū kiratu gavāini ṭabar rovani dhāhī.[103]

Implied here is the equality in the professions of mother and father. The analogy, then, of action with milk, which is an essentially female product, reflects not only the motherly and nurturing qualities of the woman but also the esteem in which she is held in the Sikh way of life.

Another subtle and illuminating analogy follows the one dealing with milk and action. Here the culture required to make yogurt from milk before it can be churned has been rendered as *surati*, which could be translated as awareness or consciousness or wisdom and is both grammatically and lexically similar to *mati*. The exact quantity of culture determined by the mental faculty of *surati* is important, for a tiny bit more or less would affect the curdling process. It is the culture which the woman, in a state of utter desirelessness (*nirāsā* = *nir* "without" and *āsā* = "desires"), puts in the milk, thus bringing about its perfect jelled state of yogurt. In a way, the yogurt is not different from the milk, but the minuscule "epistemological" ingredient of culture transforms the milk into yogurt, which is essential for the butter to be churned.

Finally, the yogurt in the pot is churned, and this churning is the tongue (*rasnā*) reciting the Name of the One (*eko nāmā*). What comes up is butter. A symbol for *amrita*, the divine elixir, butter is the ultimate food, tasted and relished above all other food. The butter has been in the milk throughout, just as the Transcendent One *is* there. But the procedure – reminiscent of the equation between eyesight and insight – from the cleansing of the vessel to the mixing of culture to the churning of yogurt has to be followed through with diligence and equanimity. Only then is the butter (always present in the milk) visibly seen and palpably relished. The metaphorical churning up of the butter – the envisioning of the Transcendent – is the most important deed, for all others are worthless, literally fruitless: *avar nirāphal; kāmā* (*nir* = "without" and *phal* = "fruit"). The fact that the most important action is illustrated through a feminine occupation (the churning of butter every morning), though her product (the butter), through her faculty (*surati*), indeed through her, herself, brings into relief the significance attached to the feminine principle in the Sikh envisioning of the Transcendent.

### *Mati as sister*

A superb exemplification of the equation between mother and wisdom can be found in a hymn in the measure Malār. Here a brother asks his sister if she has seen the Transcendent One:

> bāge kāpar bolai baiṇ
> lanmā nakk kāle tere naiṇ
> kabhūṅ sāhibu dekhiā bhaiṇ?[104]
>
> Your clothes are sparkling white, dulcet are your words,
> Aquiline is your nose, your eyes are dark,
> Have you seen ever, anywhere the One, o sister?

"Sister" (*bhaiṇ*) here could be a real sister, or a generic term for a companion. Nevertheless, it is a *she*. As portrayed in the hymn, she is a charming, adorable person – both in her physical characteristics (aquiline nose and dark eyes being symbolic of facial elegance and beauty) and in her deportment (her words are sweet). Her immaculately white dress contributes to the distinctive qualities being referred to by the brother. That she is someone who commands respect is obvious. What is remarkable is that it is the male who inquires about the Transcendent from *her*, as if she would have the answer. "Have you seen the One?" asks the brother, not in a rhetorical manner but in earnest hope. His hope signifies if not the actual, then the potential proximity of the feminine to the knowledge of the Transcendent, a knowledge acquired through the phenomenon of seeing. The sister's dark eyes aptly portray her ability to see into the Beyond. Extending the metaphor, we might say that she is in fact *bāṇī* – the expression of the Transcendent Itself.

In the Upaniṣads also we come across some instances of highly intelligent women such as Maitreyī and Gārgī who pose some very difficult and intricate questions to men. However, they are questioners in search of answers, and the possessors of wisdom are the men. In "Gārgī at the King's Court," Ellison Banks Findly makes a perceptive remark about women and philosophical "innovation" in ancient India:

> Maitreyī, from the narrative point of view, may be nothing more than a foil for Yajnavālkā's questions, a partner in dialogue only in so far as Yājnavālkā [the male]'s brilliance becomes even more obvious in comparison with her ignorance.[105]

In the Sikh scriptural instance, the role is reversed: the sister has the knowledge and wisdom which are sought by the brother. It is *her* deep, beautifully dark eyes which have penetrated the Mystery. She has got the insight.

## SOTERIOLOGICAL

The vision of the Transcendent is the soteriological goal for the Sikh: It can be obtained in life; It can be obtained after life. Paradoxically, though, to see the Transcendent – whether now or in the hereafter – the Transcendent Itself has to look upon the individual. In Sikh philosophical speculation, the latter phenomenon is indicated through the feminine noun *nadar*. Loosely translated as "grace" and interchangeable with the Persian *nazar*, meaning "sight" or "vision," *nadar* is the principle underlying the soteriological objective in Sikh philosophy. But Sikh philosophy does not dwell upon what happens *after* the vision; that is totally unknown, ineffable. The emphasis instead is on the individual who seeks and envisions the Ultimate Reality. This, as we have said, is not possible without the individual receiving *nadar*, the divine vision of the Transcendent's glance of favor. In this section, then, we shall try to discern the Sikh understanding of *nadar* and analyze the five stages of ascension towards the vision of the Transcendent One. These five stages are enumerated at the end of Gurū Nānak's *Japu*.

### *The Sikh understanding of nadar*

The most important Sikh belief about *nadar* is that it reveals the power of the Transcendent. Everything, everyone, is within the divine vision, as Gurū Amar Dās (Nānak III) points out in a hymn in the measure Sirī:

> sabh nadarī karam kamāvade nadarī bāhari na koi
> jaisī nadari kari vekhai sacā taisā hi ko hoi.[106]

> All action takes place within Its sight; nothing happens outside of it.
> As Its eye falls upon one, so does one become.

Gurū Nānak had spoken in measure Dhanāsarī in almost identical words, stressing that the *isness* of all is contingent upon the divine sight: "vinu nadarī nānak nahī koi[107] – without the Divine glance, no one comes into existence." Again, the divine sight can perform miracles: she can transform an ugly crow into a beautiful swan, as one of Gurū Nānak's poems relates:

> kiā hansu kiā bagulā
> jā kau nadari karei
> je tisu bhāvai nānakā kāghau hansu karei.[108]

> Be it a swan, be it a crane,
> All depends upon the Divine Eye,
> If it so pleases the One, a crow is transformed into a swan.

It is not only the physical universe that comes into Its orbit; the mental and psychological faculties of the individual are also under Its control. The individual recognizes the presence of the One only through Its glance upon her or his consciousness. "Najarī bhaī gharu ghar te jāniā[109] – the glance fell upon the inner self and the self recognized the Self." Through *nadar* one becomes so purified and lucid that "the mind penetrates right into the Beyond – parkhai nadari nihāl."[110] And as the true glance falls upon one, so does one get absorbed in contemplation. Human beings are constantly subject to the *nadar* of the Transcendent.

It is through *nadar* that the individual crosses over the worldly ocean which is described as vast and awesome. Where is the shore? Where is the bridge? A verse goes on to say that there is neither a boat nor a raft; neither oars nor an oarsman. This points to the utter helplessness of the individual's present situation. It is almost as if – to use the Heideggerian term – the individual had been "thrown into"[111] this life-ocean. But there is one thing, and in fact the only thing, that takes one safely ashore and that is *nadar*: "nadarī pāri utāru – through the divine glance, the other shore is reached."[112] Thereby the Transcendent One intervenes soteriologically. Its power is exercised through the feminine principle of *nadar*. The Transcendent *sees*, and Its seeing denotes creation, nurturing, sustaining, and benevolence – all feminine qualities. *Nadar*, as we have already observed, is not only feminine grammatically but also in its intrinsic value.

*Nadar* is something very special. It has been called *ratanu*, that is, a jewel. "Jis no nadari kare tisu devai nānak gurmukhi ratanu so levai – whomsoever the One favors receives the jewel," says Gurū Amar Dās (Nānak III).[113] It is a precious gift. The association of *nadar* with *ratanu* conjures up images of beauty and radiance, and artistically weaves it with the feminine dimension of wisdom (*mati*) that we just discussed. The bestowal of it is a mark of extraordinary favor. "Sabhanā vekhai nadari kari jai bhāvai tai dei[114] – the One looks upon all with a benevolent eye, but confers the gift upon those chosen for favor." Who is chosen for favor? To whom the gift is bestowed and to whom it is denied is not quite clear here. In a later *śabda*, however, we find these two categories of people represented through the images of *duhāgan* and *suhāgan*. While *duhāgan* is the unlucky woman who has been deserted by her husband or has lost him, *suhāgan* is the fortunate one who enjoys *nadar* and the love of her husband. *Suhāgan* is described by Gurū Nānak as the woman who is reaping the fruit of her past actions.[115] *Nadar* or the union with her husband is, therefore, the outcome of her good deeds (*karam kamāi*). It is obviously one's actions, one's ethical conduct, that determines the bestowal of *nadar*.

Through *nadar*, one achieves freedom from the cycle of birth and death. To quote from the *Japu*, "karmī āvai kapṛā nadarī mokhu dūāru[116] – through actions (*karmī*) one achieves the body, but, through *nadar*, liberation from the cycle of birth and death." Kartar Singh interprets *karmī* as the grace, from Arabic *karam*, of the One through which one achieves *kapṛa*, literally cloth or garment, which Kartar Singh interprets as the garment of "God's love."[117] The inside of the individual is then cleansed, and one obtains the gateway to God. I would tend to think that *karmī* here is the Sanskrit word denoting "action." The line would then mean: "By one's deeds one obtains the garment, that is, one's body or birth; by *nadar*, the gateway to liberation." Liberation depends upon *nadar*, the benevolent glance of the One. It is *nadar* that leads one to freedom – out of the migratory process from one womb to another, from one garment to another. That we shall not return back into the "womb," and that we shall be liberated from the cycle of birth and death, are reckoned to be a consequence of the vision of the Transcendent. "Satigur baṅdan tori nirāre bahuri na garabh majhāri jīo – the bonds will be shattered and there will be no return to the womb," says Gurū Nānak in a hymn in the measure Soraṭh.[118] However, the non-return into the "mother" is not an elaborated theory in Sikh philosophy, as it is, for example, in the *Bhagavad Gītā* and the Upaniṣads. In the *Bhagavad Gītā*, Lord Kṛṣṇa expounds the two paths that the *ātman* or the individual soul takes after death. They are *devayānā* and *pitṛīyānā*. Through the former, the *ātman* travels through light and reaches Brahman, with which it exists eternally thereafter; through the *pitṛīyānā*, the soul travels through darkness and returns into the bodily form again. These two paths are also central to the eschatology of the Upaniṣads and are delineated in the Bṛhadāraṇyaka (VI.2) and Chāndogya (V.10) Upaniṣads. Such speculations are absent in Sikh scripture, where the individual, *nadar*, and the vision of the Transcendent are all-important.

Finally, what the seeker longs for through *nadar* is union – something that has been latent throughout our discussion and was explicitly stated by Gurū Nānak:

> sahu merā eku dūjā nahī koī
> nadari kare melāvā hoī.[119]
>
> There is my One, none other besides It,
> Were It to look upon me with favor, union would occur.

The singularity of the One is reiterated, and the wish for the One to see the individual so that they can unite! Another instance from the Gurū Granth:

> nadari kare tā meli milāe
> guṇ saṅgrahi augaṇ sabadi jalāe.[120]
>
> If the favorable glance, then the union,
> Then virtues will be gathered, vices annihilated.

Through *nadar*, all vice is annulled; only the qualities and virtues (*guṇa*) are seen by the Transcendent, and this leads to the union. The union seems to be a two-way meeting of "vision." The individual strives to see from her or his world; the benevolent glance comes from the Transcendent. The union is the crux of the equation of eyesight with insight: the individual yearns to see the Transcendent One, and something from the Divine – Its *nadar* – reaches out to the individual.

What follows is unknown. This union, coming to the individual through the feminine principle of *nadar*, is the climax of the human quest. It is also the fifth and final state of ascension, known as *Sac Khaṇḍ*, the Realm of Truth. To the five *Khaṇḍs* or stages we shall now turn.

## *The five stages of ascension*

In his justifiably popular work *Gurū Nānak and the Sikh Religion*, McLeod remarks that "there is much that is obscure in Gurū Nānak's exposition [of the five *Khaṇḍs*]."[121] The obscurity that McLeod finds here (as he did in the Mūl Mantra) can in this case be traced to his preoccupation with a genetic approach to Sikhism. Like many other historians of religion, he is overly concerned with attempting to categorize neatly the origins of the Sikh faith into a Hindu or Islamic context. The five stages as recounted in the *Japu* have given rise to much controversy. McLeod criticizes those who see here a Sūfī parallel. According to him there is no correspondence between the *maqāmāt* of the Sūfīs and the fivefold spiritual ascent set down in the *Japu*, so he concludes that it cannot be a Sūfī suggestion or contribution. Adhering to his own point that the pattern evolved by Gurū Nānak is a reworking of the Sant synthesis,[122] he asserts: "A much closer one [parallel] is to be found in the pattern of salvation enunciated in the *yoga-vasiṣṭha*."[123] McLeod does not, however, explain why the Sant parallel is so much more acceptable than the Sūfī one, and he does not pay enough attention to the Sikhs' own understanding of the issue, which is a very pertinent factor. As we saw in Chapter 1, the *Japu* which enumerates the five stages of spiritual ascension was recited during Gurū Nānak's crucial mystical encounter. It is, like all other *bāṇī*, regarded by Sikhs as revealed Word, Word from the Beyond, and therefore beyond categorization in historical terms. To attempt to explain it by simply tracing it back to a pre-existing tradition would be to succumb to the temptations of the genetic fallacy. Rather than ascribe "obscurity" to the seer who brought it forth, we must endeavor to grasp the import of these *Japu* stanzas[124] – not by tracing their historical origins but rather by understanding them as a metahistoric phenomenon.

As we proceed to analyze the stanzas, we shall discover how the feminine principle pervades the enunciation of the path of spiritual progress – something theologians and commentators have failed to take notice of. One exception was the latter-day Sikh poet and mystic Bhāī Vīr Singh, who, in his epic *Rāṇā Sūrat Singh*, traces the five stages through the heroine Rāṇī Rāj Kaur and her ethereal female companion. We will return to Rāṇī Rāj Kaur's ascension in Chapter 8.

The five stages as envisaged in the *Japu* constitute a path leading onward and upward to higher and higher levels of experience. The first is the *Dharam Khaṇḍ*, or the Realm of Duty. This is where we human beings along with other creatures exist and can actually practice our way of life with its ethical standards.

> rātī rutī thitī vār
> pavaṇ pāṇī agnī pātāl
> tisu vici dharatī thāpi rakhī dharamsāl.[125]
>
> Amidst nights, seasons, solar and lunar days
> Amidst air, water, fire and netherworld
> The earth is placed, the place for righteous action.

It is described as a region made up of nights (*rātī*) and seasons (*rutī*) and dates (*thitī*) and days (*vār*). Time is a major factor at this level of existence. All the elements – air, water, fire, and earth – and all the compounds produced from them are a part of this region. In other words, the physical universe in time and space and in form constitutes the *Dharam Khaṇḍ*. And what is the center of the Universe? *Dhartī*! "Vic dhartī thāpi rakhī dharamsāl – the earth is set within," goes the verse. The planet Earth, the Mother Earth (*dhartī*) is the axial point of the physical universe. The Earth unites all species:

> tisu vici jīa jugati ke raṅg
> tin ke nām anek anant[126]
>
> Within this infinite matrix are myriads of species,
> Infinite are their names and forms.

Although there are innumerable varieties of species, they all remain interconnected through her. There is no implication of any disjunctions or divisions of gender, race, and class in this organic Earth. The designation of *dharamsāla* (House of Dharma) brings together her ontological and epistemological functions: she is the womb to which all beings owe their origin; she is the matrix where the infinite number of creatures can *act* ethically and purposefully. Her being the stage for righteous action is reaffirmed by Gurū Arjan in the measure Gauṛī Guāreri:

karma bhūmi mahi boahu nāmu.[127]

In the field (*bhūmi*) of actions (*karma*), sow the seed of devotion (*nām*).

The Earth, referred to as *dhartī* or *bhūmi*, provides us first with existence itself and then with the opportunity to engage in moral and ethical action. Earthly existence is not to be renounced but to be lived fully and intensely. Without the Earth, no being, and without her, no meaningful or wise action. There is no inherent nature–culture split. She is necessary. The ascent begins with her.

We discover that this primal stage has a soteriological function as well: "nadari karami pavai nīsānu – through *nadar* the actions (*karam*) are acknowledged (*pave nīsān*) by the One."[128] The Truthful One is true, and Its Earth is also true; and by means of the benevolent glance, ethical conduct in the physical universe is rewarded, and the person can then be launched onto the second stage.

The second stage is called *Gyān Khaṇḍ*, the Realm of Knowledge. Here the mind expands. The individual becomes cognizant of the vastness of creation. The vastness of creation seems to be evidenced in two ways – through physical nature and through metaphysical deities. As for the former, innumerable varieties of atmosphere, water, and fire are acknowledged (*kete pavaṇ pāṇī vaisantar*). The region is made up of millions of inhabited planets like our Mother Earth (*ketiā karam bhūmi*), countless mountains (*mer kete*), countless moons (*kete cand*), suns (*sūr*), and constellations (*maṇḍal des*), and an infinite number of species (*ketiā khāṇī*). This sphere also contains innumerable gods and goddesses.

kete kān mahesa
kete barme ghāṛati ghaṛīahi rūp raṅg ke ves . . .
kete siddha buddha nātha kete kete devī ves.[129]

Zillions of Kṛṣṇās and Śivas,
How many Brahmās were created in millions of forms!
Countless *siddhas*, *buddhas*, *nāthas*, and so many, many goddesses.

Here the goddesses take equal place with the male gods.

This knowledge of infinity – of nature and deities – paradoxically leads to the experience of the infinitesimalness of the individual. The littleness of the self is experienced in contrast with the infinitude. The Ego is shattered. The selfish manipulation of others gives way to an all-embracing sorority.

We find here yet another paradox: The countlessness of deities diminishes their significance in the Sikh view, enhancing, at the same time, the power of their maker, the Transcendent One. Gods and goddesses are part of the created world. The individual's horizons are widened through seeing the vastness of nature and her innumerable gods and goddesses; this knowledge makes her or him stand fully in awe of the Invisible One, the Mysterium Tremendum.

The feeling that the individual is infinitesimal is experienced in this realm of "knowledge." Knowledge here is not abstract; it is not an "idea." In Rudolph Otto's *Idea of the Holy*, mysticism is characterized by two distinctive notes: "We come upon the ideas, first of the annihilation of the self, and then, as its complement, of the transcendent as the sole and entire reality."[130] This is what happens in *Gyān Khaṇḍ*. Realizing the infiniteness of the cosmos with its countless gods and goddesses, one experiences self-annihilation and recognizes the Transcendent as the sole and entire reality. In Otto's mystical world, however, it is ideas that constitute the realization; in *Gyān Khaṇḍ* it is experience. This experience is described as follows:

> gyān khaṇḍ mahi gyānu parcaṇḍu
> tithai nād binod kod anandu.[131]
>
> In the sphere of knowledge, knowledge blazes forth;
> Mystic melodies, gaiety, and countless joys reign.

The "blazing of knowledge" immediately evokes the image of *joti*. The experience of knowledge in this second region is delineated through feminine imagery which captures its beauty, radiance, power (the vertical ascension of the flame), and joy (the music and dance are prevalent in this sphere). In a way, *joti* – the transcendental light, totally immaterial and insubstantial – appears at this stage, shining forth palpably and physically. The mental illumination of the individual is the core of this sensuous experience, and it is appropriately expressed in such concrete imagery. Ironically, *Gyān Khaṇḍ* or the Realm of Knowledge in the Sikh *Weltanschauung* does not parallel the concept of "Pure" Knowledge that we find, for instance, in Greek philosophy. In the writings of Plato and Aristotle, transcendent mind remains far above feelings and passions. Feminist thealogians have condemned this division, which has remained the basis of western philosophy. Speaking of Aristotle's *Politics* and Plato's *Timaeus*, Rosemary Ruether writes that Greek philosophy has subjugated matter or body to be ruled by or shunned by transcendent mind.[132] In the *Gyān Khaṇḍ* of the *Japu*, experiences – feelings and passions – are totally fused in with the mind and ideas! Mind and body are not split apart.

The third stage is the *Saram Khaṇḍ*. All expositions of this *Khaṇḍ* begin by stating how "unclear," "cryptic," or "disputed" the term *saram* is. Indeed, there are three possible origins for the word: the Sanskrit *śarma*, meaning "effort"; the Sanskrit *śarman*, meaning "joy" or "bliss"; and the Persian *sharm*, meaning "shame," with connotations of humility and surrender. We have thus three choices: this third stage could be the Realm of Effort; it could be the Realm of Joy; and it could be the Realm of Humility. I do not wish to argue for any of these. Instead, I would like to focus upon the definitions of the stage itself, which is:

saram khaṇḍ kī bāṇī rūpu.[133]

The form of *Saram Khaṇḍ* is beauty itself.

The artistic form (*bāṇī* here does not mean "word," but is derived from the term *banāvaṭ*, meaning "creation" or "formation" or "art") of this region is beauty itself (*rūp*)! It is the Realm of Art, where things are chiseled and beautified. Their exquisiteness is beyond description:

tā kīā gallā kathīā nā jāhi
je ko kahe pichhai pachhutāe.[134]

Its praise cannot be put into words,
Whosoever tries must regret [the inadequacy].

Although nothing of this region of beauty itself can be described in words, several human faculties are mentioned which get sharpened here:

tithai ghaṛīai surati mati mani buddhi.[135]
Here are sharpened consciousness, wisdom, mind, and discrimination.

Thus a lot of activity is taking place here. Wisdom (*mati*), which we discussed earlier, is at this stage refined (*ghaṛiai*, from the infinitive *ghaṛnā*, literally "to shape" or "chisel") along with consciousness (*surati*), mind (*man*), and the power of discrimination (*buddhi*). The chiseling, refining, and sharpening lead to such wondrous forms that any attempt to portray them would be futile. In this path of spiritual ascent, aesthetic refinement is important. Without this sensitivity, the goal will remain unapprehended. As Gurū Nānak says, "rasīā hovai musak kā tab phūlu pachhāṇai[136] – one who can appreciate fragrance will alone know the flower."

The feminine principle pervades this Realm of Art and Beauty also. According to Heidegger the constant strife between Earth and sky, the Earth being feminine, dark, solid, substantial, and the sky being male, light, ethereal, and flamboyant, leads to the birth of art. The two opposing forces are equally important, and they have to be at strife with each other for art to be born. Both forces are present in this realm and represented in its name: *saram* as strife or effort (from the Sanskrit root *śarma*) and *saram* as joy and bliss (from the Sanskrit *śarman* = "joy"). And the creation of art comes from the psychological state of worthlessness and shame, known as *sharm* in Persian, an ideal which is also found in the Sūfī concept of *fuqarā*ʿ (humility and poverty). We see that all the different meanings co-exist in the term *saram*. However, there is no syncretic motive at work here: the instance of *saram* simply reflects the rich and dynamic character of Gurū Nānak's vocabulary.

From this stage of art and beauty the person moves on to the *Karam Khaṇḍ*. This movement from the Realm of Art finds a remarkable parallel in the thought of twentieth-century western artist Kandinsky. In *Concerning the Spiritual in Art*, Kandinsky states that "art is not vague production, transitory and isolated, but a power which must be directed to the improvement and refinement of the human soul – to, in fact, the raising of the spiritual triangle."[137] Aesthetic refinement of the faculties opens the way to the next stage of the spiritual development.

The fourth stage, that of *Karam Khaṇḍ*, is the Realm of Grace. Macauliffe, Tejā Singh, and Khushwant Singh, taking *karam* to be the equivalent of the Sanskrit *karma*, have translated *Karam Khaṇḍ* as "the Domain of Action."[138] McLeod argues against this view, for, according to him, if *Saram Khaṇḍ* is to be regarded as the Realm of Effort and *Karam Khaṇḍ* as the Realm of Action, there is scarcely any difference between the third and the fourth stages. Instead, he translates *Karam Khaṇḍ* as "the Realm of Fulfillment," wherein *Karam* still retains the Sanskrit meaning of *karma* but with an emphasis upon fulfillment, the reaping of the rewards of previous action. I agree with McLeod in not accepting *Karam Khaṇḍ* as "the Domain of Action" (though not for the reason he provides), but I do not agree with its translation as the "Realm of Fulfillment." Fulfillment of action will not come at this later stage. The action performed and its reward belonged to the first stage, the *Dharam Khaṇḍ*, where, in the True One's Truthful Court, the good and the bad are judged. It was this fulfillment that led to the second stage of the widening of horizons, which then led to the aesthetic plane, the *Saram Khaṇḍ*.

*Karam*, it seems, retains its Persian meaning, and *Karam Khaṇḍ* is more aptly rendered as "the Realm of Grace." Bhāī Jodh Singh, Gopāl Singh, and Bhāī Vīr Singh subscribe to this interpretation.[139] McLeod very perceptively states that grace occupies a position of primary importance in the thought of Gurū Nānak and that it extends over the whole process.[140] Grace should be relevant to the first stage as well, for without divine grace one would not take to this path at all. The benevolent, female aspect of the Transcendent sustains the seeker throughout her or his spiritual quest. But it is of crucial importance at this fourth stage, for from here will begin the last stage of the journey to the omega point, the *Sac Khaṇḍ*. That *nadar* or grace lies so close to the ultimate Realm of Truth enhances its relevance. It may also be mentioned here that both *Karam Khaṇḍ* and *Sac Khaṇḍ* are described in the *Japu* in the same stanza – no. 37, which is indicative of their close interrelationship.

*Karam Khaṇḍ* is described as the abode of those who cherish none other than the Transcendent One. "Here live warriors and heroes of mighty power – tithai jodh mahā bal sūr."[141] Who are these warriors and heroes? Gurū Nānak provides the definition in a verse in the measure Sirī:

> nānak so sūrā varīām jini vichhu dusṭu ahankaraṇu māriā.[142]
> The true hero, says Nānak, is one who kills the evil of egotism within.

The real might and strength lie in one's conquering her or his own self. Herculean muscle and power is not the ideal. "Mani jītai jagu jītu[143] – by conquering oneself, one conquers the world."

What requires special notice is that in the *Karam Khaṇḍ* heroines are given equal importance with the male heroes. In fact, Sītā in all her beauty receives pride of place in this fourth sphere:

> tithai sīto sītā mahimā māhi
> tāke rūp na kathne jāhi.[144]

> Here abide many heroines like Sītā of surpassing praise,
> Their beauty beyond words.

Gurbachan Singh Talib, in his commentary, passes this by: "It would be superfluous to dilate on the symbolic character of Sītā as representative of all that is noblest and purest in human nature."[145] For us the presence in *Karam Khaṇḍ* of "heroines" along with "heroes" is very significant. Among the heroines and heroes, Sītā alone is mentioned by name. We need to ask why she receives so much importance. Sītā's power includes fertility (*sītā* literally means "furrow"), and she is related to plants and animals. Her character as portrayed in the *Rāmāyana* is very familiar: a princess and the designated future queen, she renounced all her material comforts and security to accompany her husband Rāma into exile. Rāma renounced his throne for his younger half-brother Bharata and went into exile to protect his father's honor. During the hardships of exile, Sītā was a constant source of strength and joy to Rāma. When abducted by the demon Rāvaṇa, who tried to tempt her in various ways, Sītā remained steadfast. She went through many trials and ordeals, but stuck to her love and faith.[146] Cornelia Dimmitt has also shown Sītā as the source of Rāma's political power: as *śaktī*, the female energy, Sītā inspires King Rāma to action.[147] It is for her virtues of inner power, devotion, and love that hers is the most popular, most revered, name in Indian classical tradition. It is not so much the historical Hindu wife Sītā that is evoked in the Sikh scriptural passage: here, in fact, that role is transcended by the use of the name in the plural – *Sīto-Sītā*, i.e. Sītās. She is presented here as the ideal to be emulated by men and women. That *she* and other women like her are mentioned as the denizens of *Karam Khaṇḍ* is not without meaning. Women like Sītā are the models and archetypes for heroism.

Heroines and heroes in *Karam Khaṇḍ* are exempt from the cycle of birth and death. "They do not die and they are beyond all allurement – nā uhi marahi na ṭhāge jāhī."[148] That they cannot now be beguiled or enticed indicates that they are approaching Reality, the Truth. "They are rejoicing for that True One is close to their hearts – karhi anandu sacā mani soi."[149]

Firm in their conviction and full of joy, they blithely ascend to the final stage, *Sac Khaṇḍ*, the Realm of Truth.

> sac khaṇḍ vasai nirankāru
> kari kari vekhai nadari nīhāl.[150]

> In *Sac Khaṇḍ* (the Sphere of Eternity), dwells the Transcendent
> (*nirankār*, *nir*, "without," and *kār*, "form"),

> Who having created watches over Its creation with a benevolent eye.

Again, the process of watching over is depicted through the feminine power, *nadar*, of the Transcendent. Here in the Sphere of Eternity, this fifth and highest stage, unity is achieved with the Divine. What this unity actually means is hard to describe – as hard as iron is the simile employed by Gurū Nānak. The only way the unity is expressible is through a sense of infinity:

> tithai khaṇḍ maṇḍal varbhaṇḍ
> je ko kathai ta ant na ant . . .[151]
>
> Here are continents, constellations, and universes,
> Their counting never ending, never . . .

The individual thus comes face to face with Infinity Itself. Countless in this region are the continents (*khaṇḍ*), constellations (*maṇḍal*), and universes (*varbhaṇḍ*). The focus here turns from the individual to the Transcendent. The One, says the verse, "watches over [the creation] ever in bliss, in contemplation – vekhai vigsai kari vīcāru."[152] In the *Sac Khaṇḍ*, the self and the One have become a unity, an ineffable juncture wherein the seeing by the individual becomes the seeing by the Transcendent!

The power and validation of the female that feminists such as Ruether, Christ, Downing, Bruteau, McFague, and Gross seek in the "goddess" image is present here – paradoxically – in the Transcendent. For the One watches over (*vekhai*), blissfully rejoices (*vigsai*), and contemplates (*kari vīcāru*). The terms here picture a mother watching over her child lovingly, being happy and reflecting upon her or him, being concerned about her or his future. A continuous and unconditional love pours forth from the Transcendent, and there is no sense of conflict between the individual and That One: the relation between the creatures and the Creator is a harmonious one. It is indeed the Infinite Matrix which gives birth and sees her creation flourishing; she contemplates her offspring and rejoices in it. The contemplation by the One evidences a real concern for what exists rather than taking existence to be a random play. Being and becoming are mutually validated.

## CHAPTER 3

# *The bride seeks her Groom: an epiphany of interconnections*

*merā manu locai gur darsan tāī*
My mind pines for a sight of the Gurū.

The symbol of the bride has been central in religious literature all over the world. Her image has dominated the literary imagination of the prophets of the Old Testament, Christian saints, Hindu Bhaktas, Sūfī Shaikhs, and the Sikh Gurūs. Whether we pick up the sixteenth chapter of Ezekiel, the twenty-first of Revelation, St. Teresa's *Interior Castle*, Mīrā Bāī's *Padāvalī*, Ibn al-Arabī's *Tarjumān al Ashwāq*, or Gurū Nānak's *Bārah Māh*, we find the figure of the young and beautiful bride depicted in the most vivid images. In her excellent essay "The Bride of Israel: The Ontological Status of Scripture in the Rabbinic and Kabbalistic Traditions," Barbara A. Holdrege has written about the prevalence of bridal imagery in rabbinic literature, where Israel is referred to as the bride of God and the Torah in turn as the bride of Israel.[1] The Church has also been designated as the bride of Christ in the New Testament. The presence of the bridal symbol acquires an even more interesting dimension when we think that many of these authors have been men. To express the ineffable urge for union with the Divine, humans have resorted to the relationship most intimate to them: that of the bride and the bridegroom.

From the countless brides who are endowed with such immense symbolic significance throughout world literature, it is the bride of the Gurū Granth that we shall single out. This image is one of the most important representations of the feminine in Sikh scripture in addition to the Mother. Whereas the Mother image focuses on the creative and nurturing aspects of the Transcendent, the bridal symbol develops the nuance of intimacy and passion in the human relationship with the Divine. Throughout the Gurū Granth, the individual is presented as the bride who is forever seeking union with her Groom. This is a longing for the vision of the Transcendent, for coming face to face with It: "darsan piāsī dinusu rāti[2] – day and night, I thirst for a sight of the Groom." The bride longs to see the Groom with her eyes: "kev nainī dekhīe? – when will these eyes see?" Through this symbolic search for the Divine, Sikh metaphysical speculations are rendered in the Gurū Granth most artistically, most poignantly. The bride symbol further confirms the feminine principle which pervades the Sikh vision of the Transcendent.

In this chapter, then, I wish to analyze the various ways in which the parts of a dismembered universe are recollected in the bridal symbol. I shall be drawing mainly upon the poetry of Gurū Nānak, for it is his poetic utterances that form the philosophical core and stylistic model for the Gurū Granth as a whole. The bride is often portrayed in the Gurū Granth as the center of the cosmos. Such a representation symbolically discloses varied images of how humankind can – and does – participate in varied interlinking realms of the family, society, nature, cosmos, and the Transcendent. The young bride is essentially embodied, passionate, relational, communal, and she is intimately connected with the Transcendent! In her we have a paradigmatic person who weaves a network of interconnections and enables us to do away with traditional antitheses and dualisms. These dualisms are seen by feminists as a major feature of patriarchal thought which has subjugated and oppressed women, and the effort to demolish them is of great importance to feminist philosophy. Scholars in various disciplines have underscored the alienation of the masculine from the feminine as the source of all dualism. It has generated all other forms of alienation, the emotional from the rational self, the subjective self from the objective world, the individual from the social community.[3] The Sikh bridal symbol in the scriptural hymns provides us with an approach towards resolving this problem. The duality which differentiates, opposes, separates, and excludes the Other is gently erased by the bride; the duality which trivializes and denigrates women is obliterated in her person. She exemplifies a life which is lived not in fragmentations and either–or divisions but as a dynamic and flowing continuum. Indeed, she strikes me as an epiphany of the interconnections that feminists in the West are searching for.

A secondary reason for focusing on the bride symbol lies in the history of Sikh scholarship. Is Sikhism a "reinterpretation" of Hinduism, as has many a time been asserted? Certainly, there are similarities in the bride symbol of the Gurūs and the Hindu Bhaktas, but we cannot stop there, for we also find similarities between the bride in the Gurū Granth and the bride in the Old Testament. In Psalm 45 the bride in "clothing of gold" and "raiments of needlework" who walks with her companions is remarkably similar to the one depicted in the Gurū Granth with all her jewels and crimson robes as she walks out of her parents' home with her friends! Indeed, the omnipresence of the bridal symbol points to our human shared consciousness and imagination, to our fundamental oneness. But historians of religion, instead of looking at the rich texture of parallels amongst the various religions, busy themselves in tracing thin strands of historical dependency. In the case of Sikhism this means confining the Sikh religion to the Hindu heritage. This I find to be a misinterpretation of Sikhism and of religious experience in general. Even if we were to look at the bridal symbol in these two traditions alone, we would in such a comparison find a refutation of this genetic approach to religion. This chapter will concentrate on exploring the implications of the bridal symbol in Sikhism, but at the end of the chapter we shall look into the bridal symbol in the poetry of Sant Kabīr, the most important of Hindu Nirguṇa saints. As was noted in the Introduction, modern scholarship has tended to posit Kabīr as a precursor of the Sikh religion and to describe Gurū Nānak as a follower of Kabīr.[4] But as soon as we compare the bridal symbol in the poetry of Gurū Nānak and that of Bhagat Kabīr, we encounter two totally divergent points of view. This contrast shatters any assumptions that the Sikh Gurū was a follower and reinterpreter of the Sants of Northern India.

## THE BRIDE AND HER TRANSCENDENT GROOM

The very fact that the male Gurūs identify with the female affirms a *human* situation. The ardor of their longing for the Infinite Reality is expressed in *her* voice. Male authors and poets in the Gurū Granth do not confront the female, but seek to merge themselves with feminine feelings and thoughts. The male–female duality which violates the wholeness of human nature and deprives each person of the other half is overcome, establishing, in turn, the significance of being human. Men and women are united and share their human Angst and human hope.

The bride symbolism is also extended to include females in the animal world, thereby connecting the human and animal worlds. For instance, in a passage of superb poetic beauty, Gurū Nānak seeks to identify himself with the females of several species to express his yearning for union. He wishes he were a doe (*harṇī*) living in the jungles, or a koel (*kokil*) singing in the mango grove, or a fish (*machulī*) dwelling in the waters, or a she-serpent (*nāgin*) within the earth, in each case enjoying the proximity of the Beloved.[5] Gurū Nānak's predilection for the feminine image is evidenced by the parable of the elephant and the sparrow. The male elephant, says the Gurū, devours mounds of *ghee* (butter) and *gur* (molasses), and huge quantities of corn. Satiated, he puffs and belches and raises dust. Content with his material existence, he passes away when his time comes and gains nothing in the end. On the other hand, the delicate female sparrow eats but half a grain and flies towards the skies giving vent to her longing for the Beloved. She is acceptable to the Groom, for she is always warbling, "khudāi khudāi[6] – Lord! Lord!" Gurū Nānak does not utilize animals as empty images for humanity, as they might appear in a fable. His literary imagination does not simply construct a comparison between lowly animals and high humans but rather discloses the intimacy between human and animal worlds. The two worlds are not parallel and separate; they are essentially one and the same. The identification with the sparrow and other "she" figures from the natural world reveals Gurū Nānak's unity with palpable and living nature. Linking the various species together, the Sikh view posits the female as the one who has the insight into the Transcendent One and who possesses the spiritual refinement to pursue That One *actively*.

The bride undoes the usual polarization of body and mind. In the very person of the bride converge a variety of meanings and values.[7] Her physique and beauty are described in great detail. She is a young maiden, charmingly embellished, waiting to be united with her Groom. The bride has done everything to make herself attractive for the Groom: "hār dor kaṅkan ghaṇe kari thākī sīgāru[8] – she has put on heavy necklaces and braided strings and bracelets." "She gets her hair plaited, puts vermilion in the parting – māṭhi guṅdāīṅ paṭṭīā bharīaī māṅg sandhūre."[9] The wearing of such articles of jewelry as bracelets (*kaṅkan*) and embroidered tassles (*dor*) and the sprinkling of vermilion in the parting of the hair are typical of the Indian bridal make-up. The bride's female friends (*sakhīāṅ*) joyfully make arrangements for the nuptial ceremonies, for the Groom is soon to come to wed his bride. At the center of the ceremony is the young bride who dresses up, who fondly oversees the arrangements made by her friends, who revels in the glory of the scene, and who waits ardently for the Bridegroom.

> khelu dekhi mani anadu bhaiā
> sahu viāhaṇ āiā
> gāvahu gāvahu kāmṇī bibek bicāru.[10]
>
> The heart is joyous at the marvel,
> The Bridegroom is coming to wed his bride,
> Sing, sing O friends,
> Sing songs full of the Truth of life.

But the bride's ritual embellishments embody the sanctification of the human personality. Her bodily adornment is representative of her mental purification. Her cosmetics do not only enhance her physical appearance, but also contribute to her intellectual strength. For example, the mascara (*aṅjanu*) that she uses to darken and beautify her eyelashes is to be interpreted as *jñāna* (knowledge). There are some lovely verses in the Gurū Granth which describe the very positive and powerful consequences of her make-up: as the eyeliner of knowledge is gently put on, the pitch-heavy darkness of ignorance disappears.[11] Made up with mascara and eyeliner, the bride's eyes become striking; these in turn can see through the material and glimpse into the transcendent dimension. The equation between eyesight and insight, physical eye and mental eye, seeing and knowledge has here been arrestingly brought out. Likewise, her jewelry is related to her mental state:

> karṇī kāmaṇ je thīai je manu dhāgā hoi
> māṇaku muli na pāīai lījai citi paroi.[12]
>
> If the bride were to make good deeds her ornaments
> and her mind the thread,
> She should be able to string the diamond of *nām*
> which is beyond all price.

The bride's necklace, then, consists of amulets composed of her own good deeds and the jewel of *nām* strung in the thread of contemplation. The diamond-like *nām*, symbolizing her absorption in the Divine Name, is itself her finest ornament.

The bride's garments too have a symbolic meaning. The bridal gown is dyed in the deepest hue, indicating binding love.

terā eko nāṃu manjīṭharā ratā merā colā
sad rang ḍholā . . .[13]

Your Name alone, O Beloved, is the scarlet dye fast and unchanging.
With this fast dye have I dyed my own raiment . . .

The color of the garment is bright red – *manjīṭharā* – and it is fast, at once brilliant and unfading. "It is not like that of the false garment of lust and anger – kāma krodka kī kaccī colī." The rich hue of the bride's dress is a reflection of her mind, which is richly imbued with the love of the Divine. The depth and intensity of this Punjabi bride's *manjīṭharā* dress certainly creates a resonance with the color purple that womanists aspire to today! They seek a more passionate ideal of woman than the model proposed by white middle-class feminists, a distinction expressed by Alice Walker through the difference between the colors purple and lavender. With intense love, the bride stitches the deeply dyed fabric. Dyeing fabrics and stitching them – everyday feminine occupations – become here the signs of complete devotion and single-minded attachment to the Transcendent One. Traditional feminine chores acquire a significant value.

Overall, the poetry of the Gurū Granth is replete with elaborate descriptions of the bride's physical attractions and her mental tenacity. The duality of body and mind, which not only splits one part of the self from the other but also has an in-built mechanism that degrades the one and exalts the other, is negated. For, as the bride shows, body and mind are both equally essential for the passage towards the Divine. The Sikh scripture, as we noted, does not debase the female body and does not place taboos around menstruation, childbirth, or any other female functions. There is nothing inferior or abhorrent about feminine sexuality. Female activities and accoutrements are assigned a high value, even a transcendent value. The bride's necklaces, ribbons, jewels, clothes, cosmetics, and her acts of dressing, applying make-up, and overseeing the arrangements for the wedding are all imbued with spiritual significance. At one level they serve to establish the bride's worthiness for the Groom; at the other, they are the conditions for the soul's union with Ultimate Reality. The Sikh affirmation of the feminine as a category of being with essential values and strength is expressed through the symbol of the bride.

Another polarity that is interwoven by the bride is that of matter and spirit: The bride is the symbol for the presence of the Divine Spirit intimately within each of us. Feminists in the West have objected to androcentric theology which posits that "The physical world is made as an artifact by transcendent, disembodied mind or generated through some process of devolution from spirit to matter."[14] In this bi-partite framework, the sensual and material dimension is not only subordinated to the mind and spirit, but also given a negative identity. The Gurū Granth clearly establishes an identity between spiritual light and physical body: "ekā joti joti hai sarīrā[15] – there is one light and the light is also the body." Bodiless ego or spirit is certainly not demarcated as primary. In the Sikh scripture, all Sikhs are encouraged to interpret the bride as the divine spark, the *joti* within all of us. We are thus provided with a multivalent and complex bridal imagery through which we can see who we are and what we might hope to become. The beautiful and radiant young woman carefully groomed and dressed for her wedding is *joti*, the light within every person. She is the symbol of the divine potential within each and every one of us. The Gurū Granth maintains that *joti* inheres within all humans – high and low. Similes of fire, which is within all vegetation, and of butter, which is within all kinds of milk, elaborate the point that all of us are informed by the divine light.[16] In fact, the Gurū Granth asserts, "e sarīrā meriā hari tum mahi joti rakhī tā tu jag mahi āiā[17] – everybody takes on material form only because of *joti*, the spiritual insertion by the Transcendent One."

Over the last decade feminists and womanists have been redefining God. They have rejected the ideal notion of a white male God sitting *out there* and instead revisioned a spirit *within*. This emphasis placed by contemporary writers on an inner experience of the Divine seems to emerge from the Sikh conception and perception of *joti* as well. Furthermore, the thealogical emphasis on the connection between body and spirit, body and mind – a connection denied through the splits created and maintained over the centuries by patriarchy – is accomplished in the bridal symbol. The Gurū makes an appeal: "man tūṅ joti sarūpa hai apnā mūlu pachāni – recognize the spiritual treasure with which you are endowed."[18] From such scriptural verses we can infer that *joti* in the Sikh worldview is the spiritual ingredient of the entire cosmos, and that it is the impulse behind both mind and body.

The bride forges a most sensual and palpable union with the Infinite and Transcendent Reality. In the Gurū Granth, the Groom (*sahu*) is referred to as *agam* (infinite), *agocaru* (unfathomable), and *ajonī* (unborn); it is utterly metaphysical and beyond all sense perception, and it brings to mind Rudolph Otto's characterization of the Transcendent as "the Wholly Other."[19] The bride perceives and proclaims the infiniteness of her Groom: "mere lāl jio terā aṅt na jānā – O my beloved, your limits I cannot fathom." She is perplexed and wonders how she is going to "see" her True Groom when "The True One has no color, no garb, no form – varanu bhekhu asrūpu na jāpī kiokari jāpasi sācā."[20] How is she going to know the unknowable? She seeks the help of her sisters and friends. "Tell me, my sisters and friends, how to apprehend the Ineffable One – uhu alakhu na lakhīai kahhu kāi."[21] She pines to visualize the Infinite. She imagines him to be "a deep and unfathomable ocean full of precious jewels – *gahir gaṁbhīr sāgar ratnāgar*," and "she dedicates herself entirely to him – *avar nahi an pūjā*."[22] The bride is cognizant of the Singularity of her Groom and declares that she would attach herself to none other. "Without the One, I know no other," she affirms later in the same hymn.

The bride is the one who succeeds in creating proximity to this distant Groom: she is the one to chart out the way that will make the Transcendent accessible to human experience. She addresses the "Wholly Other" in the most personal terms: "mere sundar gahir gambhīr lāl[23] – O my handsome, unfathomable Beloved"; "mere piru raliālā rām – my future Husband is the most delicious inebriation." The Wholly Other is perceived so intimately that the bride announces, "My loved Groom isn't far at all – dūri nāhī mero prabhu piārā."[24] She praises him lavishly in another verse:

> merā prabhu rangi ghaṇau ati rūṛau
> dīn daiālu prītam manmohanu
> ati rasa lāl sagūṛau.[25]
>
> My Groom is utterly glorious, brilliantly crimson,
> Compassionate, beneficent, beloved, enticer of the hearts,
> overflowing with *rasa*, like the *lāla* flower.

The backdrop to this scenario is nuptial union. The red color, the *lālā* flower, the enticing of hearts, the latent joy – all point to this consummation. The bride in this phenomenal world sees her transcendental Groom directly and physically. In her eyes, He is like the *lālā* flower. He is dyed deep in glorious beauty; He is mind-bedazzling. He is overflowing with *rasa*. The senses of sight (crimson, brilliant), smell (like the fragrance of the flower), and taste (*rasa* – the juice, the essence) all unite to convey to the reader the bride's complete, and thoroughly sensual, unity with the Transcendent Groom.

This unity between the bride and her Transcendent Groom points in the direction of a more egalitarian and open-ended social structure. In his *Systematic Theology*, Paul Tillich reflected at length upon the impact of religious symbols in the western Christian tradition; they enhance rather than diminish the reality and power of religious language. For Tillich the two symbols of the Godhead are "Lord" and "Father."[26] Theologically and psychologically they fully represent his conception of God. "Lord" betokens fascination, mystery, authority; "Father," love and sentimentality. But the Lord–Father symbol basically upholds a hierarchical, patriarchal frame of reference from which the female experience is excluded. The Christian God is a loving God, but the Freudian "father figure" is not afar.[27] The bride symbol in Sikh scripture, on the contrary, exalts feminine love. Here equality is the basis of the relationship. Underlying the bride–Groom relationship is love, which, according to Sri Aurobindo, the Hindu mystic-philosopher, is the source of fullness and joy:

> Love is the power and passion of the divine self-delight and without love we may get the rapt peace of its infinity, the absorbed silence of the Ananda, but not its absolute depth of richness and fullness.[28]

The bride, simply by loving, not by fearing, or remaining in awe, or being totally dependent, senses the proximity of her Transcendent Groom and is then able to share that feeling with her sisters and her friends. Through her intense love, she is able to establish a free and non-authoritarian relationship with the Divine. Feminist scholars have pointed out that love underscores the mutuality and bonding of both partners.[29] Love is passionate and takes lovers to those depths of richness and fullness where there is freedom from all kinds of limitations and barriers. Liberation by the bride is thus experienced not against, but in and through her relationship with her Groom. In her love for the Transcendent Groom, the bride indeed has much to offer women who are struggling to free themselves from a Father–Lord symbol that they find oppressive.[30]

Furthermore, the bride symbol denotes a very direct encounter between the individual and the Transcendent Groom, and it offers a reversal of the symbolic hierarchy: God–male–female. In many cultures, women do not stand in a direct relation to the Ultimate Reality and are connected to It secondarily, through the male. Western feminist scholars have voiced their regret over the structure of patriarchal law in the Old Testament, where only the male heads of family are addressed directly. On Indian soil also, we find patriarchy as the dominant motif: paṇḍits and priests – the mediators between Brahman and the people in the case of Hinduism – are invariably male. Ulemā – the religious lawyers and theologians – play an analogous role in the Islamic world. Gurū Nānak's bridal symbol suggests a freedom from patriarchal mediums; without anyone standing in between, the bride directly and passionately seeks to embrace the Wholly Other, her Transcendent Groom.

The bride symbol reveals "a perspective in which diverse realities can be fitted together or even integrated into a 'system.'"[31] Through a multitude of structurally united meanings in the bride symbol, the unity of the cosmos with the human beings who are integral parts of it becomes manifest. Integrating the physical and spiritual dimensions, she further integrates herself with nature and society. The bride translates the human situation into cosmological terms and vice versa; she reveals the unity between human existence and the structure of the cosmos. And she does this because of, rather than in spite of, the feminine imagery evoked.

## THE BRIDE AND HER COSMOS

The theme of cosmic unity is especially prominent in Gurū Nānak's calendar poetry, a collection of hymn-verses called *Bārah Māh* or "Twelve Months" which belongs to a genre called the *viraha* (separation).[32] The Sikh literary tradition uses the *viraha* classification to depict month by month the suffering of the bride separated from the Groom against the backdrop of the changing seasons, including the lunar and solar cycles. Simultaneously, the poem depicts the changes in space, that is, the impact of the seasons upon its inhabitants of diverse species – those born from the egg (*aṇḍaj*), those born from the fetus (*jeraj*), those born from the sweat (*setaj*), and those born from the earth (*utbhuj*). Integral to this cosmic time and space is the bride. Through her ardent search for the Bridegroom, cameos of the changing reality are captured in vivid, poignant images and fitted harmoniously into a "system."

The Indian calendar begins with the month of Chet or Chaitra (mid March to mid April). It is a month of splendor. Flowers in the woods are in bloom, the bumblebee hums rapturously, the koel sings on the mango tree, and the bee hovers around the bush fully in blossom. Chet is springtime, and the air is saturated with joy. Every creature seems to have someone to celebrate the season's glory with: the bumblebee its blossoms, the wood its flowers, the koel its mango tree . . . But there is one exception:

> piru ghari nahī āvai dhan kio sukhu pāvae?
> birahi birodh tanu chhījai.[33]
>
> The Groom hasn't come home;
> then how will the bride be comforted?
> She shrivels away in pangs of separation.

The bride, then, is the only one who stands isolated, without her Groom by her side. The beauty and lusciousness of springtime sharpen her sense of deprivation. Whereas everything in nature is blooming, she, afflicted by separation, is withering away. Paradoxical though it may sound, her complete contrast with her surroundings presents a picture of an organic structure to which she belongs and of which she indeed is the center. Unfortunately, at this stage, she is unable to participate in the reigning beauty of the season, for her Groom is not with her. Perhaps because of her separation and forlornness, she becomes all the more aware of the togetherness and rapture of everyone and everything around her, and all seems to her to fit into a perfectly integrated joyous "system."

Following Chet is the month of Vaisākh, when the tree boughs get clothed in fresh leaves. The bride "sees" (*dhan dekhai*) the newness in verdure and begs the Groom to come home. Since this is the month of harvest, the farmers negotiate business deals. Commerce enters the bride's vocabulary too: "tudhu binu aḍhu na molo kīmati kaun kare tudhu bhāvāṅ[34] – without you I am not worth a penny, but if you are with me, I become priceless." She then wishes that "Someone, somehow, would see her Beloved and help her to see Him

– dekhi dikhāve ḍholo." Nature, commerce, fellow human beings, spiritual quest become synthesized in the bride's worldview.

In the month of Jeṭh, "why should the Groom be forgotten? – prītamu kio bisarai?"[35] sighs the bride. In the heat of Jeṭh, the earth burns like a furnace. This external heat drives all beings toward inwardness. In search of the cool, all creatures are on the lookout for the deepest interior. The bride too – like St. Teresa – moves into her "Interior Castle,"[36] contemplating the Divine Groom and his virtues. The geographical locale is in harmony with her psychological state. Inherent here is an allusion to the biological heat with which life generates and in which it incubates – an acknowledgment that it is from *agni*, the heat of the womb, that the varied species derive their primal sustenance and nourishment. The procreative energy of the bride and her geographical locale are versions and inversions of each other.

In the scorching month of Āsāṛh, the sun blazes in the skies. Its fire sucks the sap of the earth. The earth roasts and suffers. Even the crickets wail. But the chariot of the sun marches on. Here the bride is portrayed as a full participant in the cosmic scene: she shares the suffering of the earth and of the cricket. "She too seeks shade – chhāiā dhan tākai."[37] The great earth, the human individual (the bride), and the tiny cricket represent the gamut of creation. All suffer. And they are all united in their search for the cool shade.

After the blazing heat of Āsāṛh comes the month of Sāvan, bringing welcome rainshowers. The earth is cooled and quenched, but not the bride, for "Her Groom is still in distant lands – pir pardesi sidhāe."[38] She lies alone on the bed. Along with the pain of solitude is the fear: the lightning amid the monsoon clouds terrifies her. What she sees around does not soothe the anguish of her heart. She addresses her mother: "maraṇu bhaiā dukhu māe[39] – O mother, it is death for me." Having lost her sleep and her appetite, the bride in the month of Sāvan lives a death-like life. The integration of polarities – life and death, lightning in the skies above and the bed on which she tosses and turns alone here on earth – is accomplished in the person of the bride.

Bhādoṅ is the month of abundance: both land and river are in flood. Throughout the dark night it rains. Birds and animals feel invigorated. They shriek as if they cannot contain the fullness within: peacocks sing, the frogs croak, the *papīhā* cries forth, "prio prio – Love, O my Love." Overflowing with life, the snakes sneak out to bite, and the mosquitoes swarm out to sting. And the pools overflow with water. The pulsating animate and inanimate worlds are coordinated into a vivid pattern. Juxtaposed to this bursting forth of nature is the bride's desolation. She yearningly contemplates the fullness, the energy, the joy surrounding her. Standing in the center of it all, she exclaims, "binu hari kio sukha pāīai[40] – where, where is comfort for one without the Groom?" The female psyche perceives the unity of nature. Absent here are all vertical hierarchies; absent here are all horizontal divisions. The snake is not cursed and the frog is not any uglier or the peacock any prettier. From her point of view, they are all – equally – enjoying the season.

In Asuni (Asūj), the seventh month, the bride sees her own reflection. Both cosmic time and space mirror her situation. On the ground, "kukah kāh si phule[41] – the country-shrubs bearing white flowers are in bloom." These white flowers represent her own white hair; the bride is greying. The coming season frightens her: "āgai ghām pichhai ruti jāḍā dekhi calat manu ḍole[42] – Gone is the summer, and cold winter is not far away; this makes my heart tremble." What the bride realizes at this seasonal juncture is the loss of her youth and the setting in of old age. She shudders at the thought. But she also sees in this autumn month some green boughs which instill optimism in her. The possibility of meeting with her Groom again strikes her. "Sahaji pakai so mīṭhā[43] – that alone is ripe-sweet which ripens slowly in its own sweet time," the bride tells herself. During this autumnal period, the bride's physical self is identified with that of the cosmos.

In the month of Katak (Kārtik), the days begin to get shorter. Lamps are lit earlier in the evenings. The lamp itself becomes a symbol rich in nuance. It represents the refined emotional and intellectual faculties of the bride which will eventually lead her to apprehend the Divine. The traditional lamp or *dīpak* is a tiny clay bowl, pointed at one end, with a cotton wick, and filled with oil. But the only lamp that shines steadily is "the lamp lighted by the match of knowledge – dīpaku sahaji balai tati jalāiā," whose oil is *rasa*, the aesthetic essence of love.[44] Love and knowledge together can bring the union of the bride's inner light with the Bridegroom's Transcendent Light. This fusion of knowledge (kindling match) and love (oil) within the lamp image helps illuminate the bride's psychological condition. The *dīpak* connects her physically with "cosmic" time, with the evenings of the month of Katak. In this state she feels she is closer to achieving her goal – union with the Groom.

In the month of Maghar, "The bride listens to the praise of her Divine Groom through song, music, and poetry, and her sorrow departs – gīta nād kavit kave suṇi rāmnāmi dukhu bhāgai."[45] We can see here the effect of aural art upon the human mind: Music and sound, which travel in the atmosphere, penetrate into the very being of the bride. Thereby, her sorrow (*dukhu*) literally vanishes away (*bhāgai*). By reciting and hearing and reading the artistic evocation of the Divine Groom, she assuages her pain of separation. The passage vividly portrays the bride sitting amidst other men and women listening to song, music, and poetry. She is part of a symphonic gathering, the congregation or *saṅgat*, as the Sikhs call it. The *saṅgat* is a community in Tolstoy's sense of the word, a community created by art.[46] In it all members are viewed as equal, irrespective of caste, gender, or race. We see in the month of Maghar the bride as a participant within a community which cherishes the recital of the Divine Name.

The description of the month of Pokh begins with these words:

> pokhi tukhāru paṛai vaṇu triṇu rasu sokhai.
> In Pokh comes the snow, sapping the *rasa* from woods and grass.

And it ends as follows:

> Nānak raṅgi ravai rasi rasīā hari sio prīti saneho.[47]
>
> Says Nānak, the bride who is in love with her Groom
> savors the *rasa* of her charming Beloved.

The contrast between the opening and the final line of the hymn is conspicuous: the cold white snow covering the earth sapping away the *rasa* of all vegetation is juxtaposed to the bride, who in her love for the Groom would be savoring his *rasa*. Perhaps it is the panorama of the starkly white snow which ignites in the bride's imagination that warm and vibrant fantasy. We notice here the transformation in the meaning of *rasa*: From its literal meaning of juice or the physical essence of vegetation, it becomes an aesthetic and philosophical sentiment to be savored by the bride. But then again, in the figure of the bride, there is no Cartesian split; the body is not pitted against the mind. In fact, as the passage states, she imagines the experience to be simultaneously totally mental (*mani*) and sensual (*tani*).

Also, in the month of Pokh, the bride realizes her intimate relationship with all other creatures:

> aṇḍaj jeraj setaj utbhuj ghaṭi ghaṭi joti samāṇī
> darsanu dehu daiāpati dāte gati pāvao mati deho[48]

> Egg-born, fetus-born, sweat-born, earth-born – all pulsate with the Light.
> Do bestow a glimpse, O compassionate Beloved . . .

The one light (*joti*) permeates (*samāṇī*) the hearts (*ghaṭi ghaṭi*) of all species, be they egg-born (*aṇḍaj*), fetus-born (*jeraj*), sweat-born (*setaj*), or earth-born (*utbhuj*). Absent again are hierarchies and divisions: humans (fetus-born, *jeraj*) are not any higher than bugs (sweat-born, *setaj*). Through the singular *élan vital* the bride perceives the unity of the universe. From within this linked circle she ardently implores her compassionate Groom (*daiāpati dāte*) to bestow upon her a vision of Himself (*darsanu deho*). In her words can be heard an alliteration of "d"s – the "d"s dance around the circle she weaves.

In Māgh, the month of pilgrimage, the bride realizes that the pilgrim seat is within herself. The sacredness of all holy places and of all time would be hers, were her Transcendent Groom pleased with her:

> prītam guṇa aṅke suṇi prabh baṅke tudhu bhāvā sari nāvā
> gaṅg jumun tah beṇī saṅgam sāt samuṅd samāvā
> puṅa dāna pūjā parmesur jugi jugi eko jātā
> nānak māghi mahārasu hari japi aṭhsaṭhi tīrath nātā.[49]

> Listen, O Beauteous Groom, if I were to acquire
> your virtues and please you,
> that would be my pilgrimage.
> This would be my bath in the Gaṅgā, the Jamunā and
> their point of confluence with the Sarasvatī,
> and in the seven oceans as well.
> All charity and worship for me is the cognizance that,
> throughout the yugas (time-cycles), there is but the
> Singular Groom.
> Says Nānak, in the month of Māgha, to taste the great
> essence of the meditation upon the Beloved
> is alone the bath in the sixty-eight holy waters.

For the bride, then, the so-called sacred rivers of India – Gaṅgā, Jamunā, and Sarasvatī – are not separate; nor are the seven oceans. In her vista, the different rivers and oceans exist as a whole. Relishing the essence of the Groom replaces for her the various traditional Indian pieties associated with visiting and bathing in particular spots. The very self becomes the center of all the variegated places of pilgrimage. This passage reinforces the Sikh view that external ritual and even outward actions are empty and unnecessary. The relationship with the Groom being sufficient devotion, "puṅa dāna pūjā – meritorious deeds, charity, and worship" are all lumped together as essentially worthless. The woman is conceived as the paragon of Sikh ethical principles.

Also, the bride is an integrator not only of space but of temporality as well. As we see above, "yugas" or time-cycles do not appear chopped up to her; rather, they are in the literal sense "yoked together" (for the Indo-European root of yuga is *yuj*, to yoke) by the knowledge that the Singular Beloved pervades time past, present, and future. The bride figure, while spinning the twelve months, also spins together all time with its three tenses.

Finally, in the month of Phalgun, "the bride would lose herself – āpu gavāiā."[50] With the ego gone, "desires are eradicated – man mohu cukāiā."[51] Paradoxically, with the "integrator" of time and space gone, what remains is the *integration* itself. Continuous bliss is anticipated. All duality vanishes. Even night and day are conjoined, and what is experienced continuously is utter ecstasy: "andinu rahasu bhaiā[52] – night and day joy prevails."

The discussion above illustrates that the twelve months are very important, for within them the intersection of the timeless with time takes place. The Timeless Groom is brought by her into her personal and historical context. The twelve months, the six seasons, the days, the hours, the minutes, the seconds are *bhale* (blessed) in the Sikh scripture. For, it is sometime now, somewhere here, that the Ontological Being pervading all time and space is instantaneously found:

> be das māh rutī thithī vār bhale
> gharī mūrat pal sāce āe sahhaji mile.
>
> Two plus ten months, seasons, lunar and solar days are all blessed;
> Hours, minutes, seconds are all true too; for they lead to the union with the True One.

The bride thus establishes a link with cosmic time and space. During the course of the year, nature with its changing hues and moods has a profound impact on her. It transports her into a mood of ecstasy; at another moment it intensifies her sense of lonesomeness; and still again, it inspires hope and optimism. The young bride clearly sees herself belonging in her own and different way to the seasons and the terrain around her. Through the intimacy established by her, we do not feel "isolated" in the cosmos; "we become open to a world which, thanks to the [bridal] symbol, becomes 'familiar.'"[53] In her recent book entitled *Staying Alive: Women, Ecology and Development*, physicist, active feminist, and ecologist Vandana Shiva argues that "development" (or as she would have it "maldevelopment") is a western, patriarchal concept that ignores the connection between women and nature.[54] The protagonist in Gurū Nānak's *Bārah Māh* clearly bridges the connection and in fact seems to share the holistic vision "of planetary harmony and coexistence among all peoples, all creatures, all elements, all plants, all stars, all of everything we are cognizant of that resides outside our individual selves."[55]

## THE BRIDE AND HER SOCIETY

The bride thus brings meaning to human existence. As we learn from Eliade, symbols have an existential value; symbols always point to a reality or situation concerning human existence; symbols preserve contact with the deep sources of life; symbols express the spiritual as life experience.[56] In her quest for the Transcendent Groom, the bride projects an existential revelation: The Transcendent does not belong to the world beyond, but is directly related to our situation, to our here and now. The Divine Groom belongs to our world in a very palpable manner. Effectively, the antithesis of flesh and spirit, here and yonder, is shattered.

The particular reality of the institution of marriage thus "explodes beneath the irruptive force of a deeper reality." In Sikh literature marriage is seen as an important event in the life of a human being. By seeking to "wed" the Transcendent, the bride is able to add something extra, something of the Divine to human life, and vice versa. A specific and human activity acquires a universal and divine importance. As Eliade puts it, the person who understands a symbol not only "opens himself" or herself to the objective world, but also succeeds in emerging from his or her personal situation and reaching a comprehension of the universal.[57] Similarly, the bride symbol both awakens and transmutes the individual experience into a spiritual act. With her moral discipline and spiritual quest, the bride is a symbol that can be "lived." By correctly deciphering her message, we too can open ourselves to the Transcendent.

Interestingly, even from our worldly point of view, the bride symbol combines an array of options, opening wider horizons for women in society. The bride is a potential mother, but motherhood with babies and feeding and diapers is not her only prerogative in life.[58] The mother archetype induces in a woman an anxious overprotectiveness and possessiveness of the "other" who has outgrown such support or never really needed it. The mother type, meaning either literally a mother with children or figuratively a maternal woman with a strong capacity for helping, nourishing, and answering needs, has been the predominant image of femininity in western culture. There has even been a tendency within the Jewish and Christian traditions to equate a feminine identity with the maternal instinct.[59] In the Hindu worldview, the woman without a son has the least social standing. Women who do not conceive in their first year of marriage are even today often sent back to their parents' home, and the husband takes another wife. Bearing children (especially sons) is the woman's highest obligation – the tendency in India to equate femininity with maternity is thus even stronger.[60] The bride symbol marks a departure from this one-sided framework. The picture that emerges of the young bride in Gurū Nānak's poetry is that of an independent person in possession of her own time and space. She is free to think and reflect upon herself and her relationship with the cosmos and the Transcendent beyond. And yet, this completely autonomous woman may choose to be a mother as well.

The bride portrays a bonding between the individual and her society, for she always maintains a closeness with her friends. We hear her address them so often in affectionate terms like these: "merī sakhī sahelī sunhu bhāī merā piru rīsālū – listen, O my sisters, O my friends, my Groom is very handsome."[61] Here she is sharing her joy with her sisters and female friends (*sakhī sahelī*). In sharing her trepidations and enthusiasm, the bride reaches out to other women; her female consorts, in turn, reach out to her. Indeed, she affirms her experience through a process that is communal in essence. Inherent in this instance is her moving away from isolation as a woman to a sense of community with other women, a condition which the Sikh tradition both idealizes and implements. According to Judith Plaskow, in "The Coming of Lilith: Toward a Feminist Theology," this same personal evolution is at the heart of the women's movement and feminist thealogies.[62] In seeing other women as real people and friends, the bride discovers a source of energy for personal and social growth and transformation; her rediscovery in turn is very valuable for raising our consciousness. Through the bride the bonds of female friendship are strengthened and extended.

Insofar as she stands on the threshold of marriage, the bride aptly combines the polar situations in a woman's life – life in her parents' home and life with her in-laws. In the life of an Indian woman, marriage marks a radical break in her lifestyle: it is almost a painful event when the carefree young girl has to start assuming responsibility for her husband and her in-laws. But in this case, a pattern of psychic integration is woven by the bride. The parents' home (*pekā ghar*) is representative of the many years that the bride spends purifying and refining herself for the day when the Bridegroom will come and escort her to her real home, that of her in-laws (*sauhrā ghar*). The intrinsic distinction between *pekā ghar* (parents' home) and *sauhrā ghar* (in-laws' home) is illustrated by Gurū Nānak from the point of view of the bride:

> sahuraṛī vathu sabhu kichhu sājhī
> pevakaṛai dhan vakhe.[63]
>
> In the in-laws' home, she experiences Unicity;
> in the parents' she lives in duality.

*Sauhrā ghar* represents total unity. It is all One Light. Everything partakes of that Wholeness without divisions – "sabhu kichhu sājhī." *Pekā ghar* marks our world, the world into which we are born, in which we grow up, and continue living in alienation (*vakhe*) from ourselves. Instead of envisioning the whole, the individual views reality in divisions and parts. It is the bride who, with her unique sensitivity, recognizes the Singular source and longs for union, thus forging a link between her *pekā ghar*, the world of dualities, and *sauhrā ghar*, the Realm of Total Unity. The transport to *sauhrā ghar* – the wedding – is dependent upon the bride, for she has to take the initiative:

> piru dhan bhāvai tā pir bhāvai nārī jīo.[64]
> If the bride loves her Husband, the Husband will love her, too.

The Bridegroom will wed the bride only if she truly loves him. She is thus the active one who searches for the Groom. She initiates the marriage which in fact forms the nexus of life here and life after.

In the wedding symbolism we further discover a fusion of the polar rites of marriage and death. The young bride bedecked in all her finery is immersed in the most critical rite of passage, the wedding ceremony. This latter facet of her life not only marks the cyclical flow of human existence but also evokes patterns of eternal destiny. In a subtle way, her being and the event itself contribute to an understanding of Sikh ontology. She says to her friends:

> saṁbati sāhā likhiā mili kari pāvhu telu
> dehu sajan āsīsaṛīā jio hovai sāhib sio melu
> ghari ghari eho pahucā sadaṛe nit pavaṅi
> sadaṇhārā simarīai nānak se deh āvaṅi.[65]

> The day of my wedding is fixed,
> In unison, O friends, pour ritual oil (in blessing),
> Bless me that I unite with my Husband.
> From home to home these summons are received daily;
> Remember the Summoner, O friends,
> For this day must come to one and all.

In this passage the bride is telling her friends that the day of the wedding is already fixed (*likhiā* meaning "written down"). While implying a festive invitational message, the term *likhiā* also denotes inevitable fate. It refers not only to the time when she makes a transition in her personal life (from her parents' home to that of the Groom's) but also to the destined day of her departure from the Earth. The dual meaning is extended further when she asks her friends to pour oil. The pouring of oil is an auspicious ritual which is performed several times in the course of the wedding ceremonies. During the period of bridal preparation, for instance, the bride is massaged with oil. Again, when she enters the Groom's house, oil is poured over the threshold as a mark of welcome. The wedding ceremonies thus begin and culminate with the pouring of oil. Yet friends will one day pour oil on the funeral pyre. Oil is an essential ingredient in both wedding and death ceremonies, and it is one's friends who have the duty of pouring it on both occasions. The request "mili kari pāvohu telu – in unison pour the oil, O friends" synthesizes the wedding and death rituals. The bride then beseeches her friends to give her their blessing so that she may be able to unite with her Groom. The phrase "joti jot samaunā – light merging with light" visualizes the union of the individual light with the Universal; this first "physical" meeting of the bride and the Groom is also a figure of speech for death. In the bride symbol we can find expressions of a holistic worldview.

We also discern here the active participation of women in rituals. In many instances during a given Indian ceremony, women are traditionally excluded. In the Hindu death rituals, for example, the son alone is permitted to light the funeral pyre. Upon his officiation depends the salvation of the father or the mother. The parent's *atman* cannot proceed on the right route, i.e. the path of light, if there is no male offspring to perform this rite. The funeral procession also consists only of men. The wedding party again consists solely of male friends and relatives who are expected to carouse their way to the bride's home and bring the newly wed bride to her in-laws' home. In stark contrast to such predominantly male participation in ritual, this Sikh text reveals the centrality of women in the process of consecrating ceremonies – be they related to marriage or to death.

Daily these invitations – to a wedding? to a death? – come to different homes. The bride asks her companions to remember their Summoner. It has often been noticed that in both eastern and western literature, the phenomenon of death is never encountered directly by human beings. To take an example from the Hindu tradition: When Yudhiṣṭhra, the oldest of the Pāṇḍava brothers, is asked about the most wonderful aspect of life, he answers that it is the living of life "as if death were never to come to me." Similarly, in Tolstoy's *Death of Ivan Ilyich*, Ivan's friends cannot even face the corpse of their friend lest it remind them of their own mortality. That "death always comes to someone else, never to me" is a universal human illusion expressed in the literatures of both the East and the West. It is of some significance, then, that the young bride in the Sikh tradition is fully aware of the inevitability of her own death and reminds her companions about their situation as well. The bride projects the linking of the worldly and the other-worldly dimensions: Since existence is transitory, each moment must be lived with the utmost intensity; in each instant, time and timelessness co-exist.

Finally, the bride fuses the distinct realms of religion and aesthetics. Some years ago, Samuel Laeuchli in his provocative book *Art and Religion in Conflict* showed that there is an antithesis between aesthetic appreciation and religious belief.[66] Philosophy in the West has created many splits and hierarchies between the dimensions of religion and aesthetics. We may recall how Kierkegaard degrades aesthetics to the bottom rung, way below the realm of ethics and religion. Bypassing all such divisions and hierarchies, the bridal symbol manifests the intimacy between heightened aesthetic joy and the perception of absolute Truth.

The bridal symbol is indeed an arresting example of the blending of the religious with the aesthetic, and this blending flows directly from the feminine element in Gurū Nānak's artistic vision. By reading or reciting *śabdas* (hymns) with the bridal motif at the core, or by listening to such *śabdas* being recited, one encounters a pervasive feminine presence, power, and mystique. The poetic devices, besides image and metaphor, include alliteration, assonance, and consonance, and they enrich the tonal quality of the verse. The multiple meanings and paradoxes, pictures and significances co-existing in the bridal symbol make it susceptible to interpretation at various levels – aesthetic, religious, and ethical; and each time we are presented with some aspect of the richness, complexity, and sacredness of female energy. But the revealed Word here is art par excellence. And it is the woman – her figure, her voice, her desire, her action, her psyche – who weaves together the carded strands of the androcentric universe. She has the power to awaken the mind to Ultimate Reality, to the love of the Transcendent, to the quest for Its vision. Religion and aesthetics are not two separate dimensions. The many meanings and nuances of the bridal symbol itself and the never-ending search of the bride launch the imagination of both male and female Sikhs individually or collectively on a religio-aesthetic journey into the Beyond. The bride symbol, to use Ismail al Faruqi's words, "creates deferred esthetic effort of intuiting the unintuitability of That which can never be the object of immediate intuition."[67]

### THE BRIDE IN THE POETRY OF GURŪ NANAK AND SANT KABĪR

The bride thus integrates and synthesizes many dualities: The varied demarcations and bifurcations and either–or distinctions have been colorfully knitted together by her. We must now turn to my secondary reason for focusing on the bride symbol: Is Sikhism a "reinterpretation" of the Sants of Northern India? Beginning with H. H. Wilson in 1828, many scholars[68] have stated and elaborated in diverse ways the thesis that Gurū Nānak was a follower of Kabīr, the forerunner of the Hindu school of Nirguṇa Bhakti. This misconception may have arisen partly from the fact that some of Kabīr's compositions have been included in the Gurū Granth. As we have seen, Gurū Arjan (Nānak V) while compiling the holy book recorded in it the poetical compositions of several Indian saints and Sūfīs besides his own and those of his four predecessors. Whatever was in consonance with the Sikh teaching was admitted, with the result that a considerable body of Kabīr's verse found its place into the Sikh scriptures. Much, however, was left out. In her penetrating article, "Kabīr in the *Gurū Granth Sāhib*: An Exploratory Essay," Karine Schomer makes a comparative textual study, and she attempts to identify those Kabīr themes which have been excluded from the Gurū Granth. While compiling the Granth, the Gurū included in it those of Kabīr's verses which, as noted by Schomer, related to the themes of Divine Omnipotence, love of God to the exclusion of all else, the importance of prayer, the worthiness of saintly people, the meaninglessness of a life empty of devotion to God, and the distinction between hypocritical outer display and genuine interior devotion. She writes, "In the remaining 628 dohas [couplets] of the KG [*Kabīr Granthāvalī*], however, we find several important themes which are largely absent from the GG dohās."[69] Though Schomer's reasons why those several themes were not included in the Gurū Granth may not be exhaustive, her exposition is very valuable in apprehending the points of divergence between Kabīr and the Sant tradition on the one side and Gurū Nānak and the Sikh tradition on the other. Without taking into account the philosophical and social implications of the teachings of Gurū Nānak and Kabīr, the bride symbol alone, as employed by them in the Gurū Granth and the *Kabīr Granthāvalī* respectively, strikingly reveals the differences between them. The fundamental contrariety between the two orientations comes out conspicuously in three important aspects.

Firstly, the bride symbol has been used by Kabīr to describe his mystical union with the Divine. The *Kabīr Granthāvalī* consists of a section of forty-one couplets entitled "Parcā kau Anga" (the Chapter of the Mystical Experience), which, according to Schomer, is considered the heart of this Sant text.[70] In this section, Kabīr describes his moments of union in radiant colors, of which the following is just one example:

> Kabīrā tela anaṅta kā, manaū ugī sūraja senā
> pati saṅga jāgi suṅdarī, kautiga diṭha teni.[71]
>
> Kabīr, the radiance of the Infinite
> was like the rising of a host of suns:
> The bride woke up next to her husband
> and marvelled at the wonder!

Kabīr uses the symbol of the bride to describe his mystical experience. The bride wakes up *with her husband*; she has *already beheld* the Infinite radiance. Such actual union is missing in Gurū Nānak's usage of the bride symbol. The bride in the Sikh conception remains but in ardent quest of the vision of her Transcendent Groom. She is invariably depicted as being alone, her bed remaining unoccupied. We may recall the image from *Bārah Māh* where in the month of Sāvan she is sitting lonesomely on one half of the vacant bed; the flashes of lightning stabbing the skies frighten her. In the Sikh poetic tradition, then, there is the constant striving on the part of the bride to *envision* her Infinite Groom, and not a reminiscence or recollection of a sensual experience of union, as we find in Kabīr's *dohās*.

A second difference between the two interpretations of bridal imagery concerns the path of devotion. Central to *Kabīr Granthāvalī* is the arduousness of the path of devotion:

bhagatī duhelī rāma kī, nahī kāyara kā kāma
sīsa utārai hātha sau, so lesī hari nāma![72]

The bhakti of Rām is hard to practice,
  it is not for cowards!
Sever your head with your own hands,
  and then invoke Rām's name!

kabīrā bhāṭhī prema kī bahutaka baiṭhe āi
sira saūpai soi piai, nātara piyā nā jāi![73]

Kabīr, in that liquor-shop of love,
  many have come together:
He who pawns his head can drink,
  none other!

Couplets such as these depict the trials the devotee has to go through. According to the bride symbol in Gurū Nānak's compositions, this is an enjoyable path – invitingly so. The young bride, handsomely bedecked with the longing for the Bridegroom in her heart, is indeed a captivating figure. Her yearning, in all its delectable painfulness, is rendered in aesthetic and romantic images. Kabīr's image of "severing your head with your own hands" is in total contrast with the bridal preparation of pouring fragrant oils onto the hair, braiding it, sprinkling vermilion in the parting, and putting on ornaments and bejeweled ribbons. This world is not to be rejected or renounced; it is the place where the Transcendent is actively pursued by the bride. She has the capacity to draw the handsome Beloved to *this* beautiful spot.

Thirdly, in Kabīr's latter couplet it is stressed that very few who set out on the path of devotion ever reach their goal. "He who pawns his head can drink, none other!" On the other hand, the bride symbol in Gurū Nānak's *Weltanschauung* opens the path towards the Transcendent to everyone: every girl can become a bride one day.

Deep down, there is a major difference between the two outlooks on women. Kabīr's opinion of women is contemptuous and derogatory. Women historians of religion, such as Karine Schomer and Wendy O'Flaherty, are familiar with Kabīr's misogynist bias.[74] Schomer has pointed out some blatant examples of Kabīr's deprecatory attitude: For Kabīr woman is "Kālī nāginī" (a black cobra), "kundā naraka kā" (the pit of hell), "juthānī jagata kī" (the refuse of the world).[75] She is an impediment to spiritual progress:

> nāri nasāvai tini guṇa, jau nara pāsai hoi
> bhagati mukutinija gyānamai paisi na sakai koi.[76]
>
> Woman ruins everything when she comes near a man:
> Devotion, liberation, and divine knowledge no longer enter his soul.

Kabīr and the Sants of Northern India generally valued an ascetic life in which women played no significant role. They were, perhaps, prisoners of the fear of the erotic. In our own time, feminists like Audre Lorde have pointed out the openness, the fearlessness, and the empowerment which comes with erotic knowledge, "a lens through which we scrutinize all aspects of our existence, forcing us to evaluate those aspects honestly in terms of their relative meaning within our lives."[77] Living in fifteenth-century India, Gurū Nānak was quite familiar with the prevailing mores of his milieu and spoke extensively against abstinence and asceticism, which denied this knowledge. Acknowledging the spirituality as well as the sensuality of human life, the Sikh existential ideal posits an integration of the two; our bridal symbol indeed values the palpability and sensuality of the bride along with the spirituality of her quest for the Transcendent. The deprecation of woman is totally alien to the Sikh worldview.[78] In Sikh scriptural texts, the bride – the quintessence of womanhood – is the prime symbol of the virtuous individual in quest of the Ideal, seeking union with the Divine. She incarnates physical beauty and grace, morality, discipline, and spiritual awakening. She is the model: "Devotion, liberation, and divine knowledge" – in contrast to what Kabīr says – enter the human soul only by following the path shown by *her*.

The viewpoints of Kabīr and Gurū Nānak are thus diametrically opposed. Gurū Nānak certainly was not Kabīr's follower in his attitude towards women! Gurū Nānak's thought as manifested through the bride symbol is radically divergent from the Sant tradition as represented by Kabīr, its most eminent exponent.[79] If Gurū Nānak differs so radically from the most prominent Sant on this crucial subject, he surely could not have been a follower or reproducer or reinterpreter of this tradition. Gurū Nānak and his Word have a *raison d'être* all their own. The celebration of the bridal imagery in Gurū Nānak's poetry is a measure of the originality and autonomy of the Sikh identity.

The great importance of this new and independent worldview is that the bridal symbol central to Gurū Nānak's poetry is a great resource for uplifting women's psyche. Throughout his verse is expressed the wish to "feel like her." The feminine remains the ideal. It may be the human bride, or the deer in the jungle, or the koel perched on the mango tree. Her experience is always cherished. *She* has the longing; *she* seeks the Transcendent; *she* launches upon the quest.

Some feminists in the West may object to the longing bride as a model. They might see an inherent dualism in the relation between the bride and her Groom, and the role of the bride seeking her Beloved may be viewed as restrictive and stifling. As far as the first objection is concerned, the dualism is but a temporary and superficial one; the individual is called upon to overcome this division by achieving union with the Ultimate One. The bride is a paradigmatic figure who opens the way towards the union. The second objection is a more serious one. How can a western woman of the 1990's identify with a bride whose *raison d'être* is union with her Beloved? The yearning woman, by longing for something or someone outside herself, indicates a lack of autonomy; by needing her Beloved she becomes the *de*pendent one. How then can a liberated, *in*dependent woman look up to her?

To understand the bridal symbol fully, we must remember that it emerged in Sikh literature at a point in time and space when the Indian woman was humiliatingly subjugated. The customs of *purdah*, *satī*, and child-marriage prevailed. Such practices were indicative of the pervasive degrading attitude towards women. As we saw in the poetry of Kabīr, who is the most respected of the Nirguṇa saints of medieval India, the woman was depicted as a black cobra, stalling the male's spiritual progress. In such a milieu, women's desires were rarely articulated. In Gurū Nānak and the Sikh literary tradition, woman's desire is expressed, presenting her in turn as the paragon of physical and spiritual refinement. *Her* experience is given precedence over that of the male, and *she* enjoys an active involvement in the social, cosmic, and transcendent spheres. For centuries, "bride" and "mother" have been the only symbols of womanhood. To deny the bridal symbol would be to deny our heritage as women. We cannot reject these generations of brides, our mothers. In the case of the Sikh bridal symbol, we should not read too much into her apparent dependency. We must remember that she is, after all, dependent only upon the Transcendent One, and that this dependence is shared by men, women, and the entire cosmos. The Sikh scriptural message is not the subjugation of the female to the male, for her Groom is beyond gender; rather, it is the rising of the individual spirit towards the Absolute.

Rather than look for a paradigm in the bride, many modern women have sought the validation of the female in the image of the goddess. Rita Gross, Carol Christ, Merlin Stone, Nelle Morton, Christine Downing, have brought back the goddess as a feminine power in the world. Now, the Sikh tradition rejects all forms of idolatry and the installation of gods and goddesses, but the bride symbol does offer many of the qualities that modern feminists might seek in the goddess. Rosemary Ruether's eloquent qualification of the goddess as the "*Shalom* of our being" can easily be transferred to the Sikh bride:

> [She] liberates us from this false and alienated world, not by an endless continuation of the same trajectory of alienation but as a constant breakthrough that points us to new possibilities that are, at the same time, the regrounding of ourselves in the primordial matrix, the original harmony. The liberating encounter with [her] is always an encounter with our authentic selves resurrected from underneath the alienated self. It is not experienced against, but in and through relationships, healing our broken relations with our bodies, with other people, with nature. We have no adequate name for the true [her], the "I am who I shall become."[80]

The central message of Sikh scripture is that the gap between the Divine Reality and the individual is bridged by following the bride's example of loving devotion. But her devotion doesn't call for renunciation and asceticism; she opens the way to the Transcendent by living fully and authentically in *this* world, maintaining her connections with her own self, her family and friends, and nature around. The walls between sacred and profane are obliterated and every aspect of daily life is imbued with spirituality. The bride leads us to our ultimately real and intrinsic self – the harmonization of self and body, the very spark or light (*joti*) that we are made up of.

CHAPTER 4

# *Durgā recalled: transition from mythos to ethos*

> kautak hetu karī kavī ne satisayi kī kathā eh pūrī bhae hai
> jahi namitt parai suni hai nar, so niscai kari tahi dae hai.
>
> For the thrill of it has the poet delineated the tale of the goddess.
> My object is that whosoever reads or hears her story may be inspired with faith and determination.

Gurū Gobind Singh, the last of the ten Gurūs or prophet-teachers of the Sikh faith, succeeded to the spiritual seat of Gurū Nānak in AD 1675. His immediate predecessor, Gurū Tegh Bahādur (1621–75), died a martyr's death protesting against the religious intolerance of the rulers of the day. In the first decade of that century, Gurū Arjan (Nānak V) had laid down his life to uphold the principles of human dignity and freedom. The event had marked the fulfillment of Gurū Nānak's religious and ethical teaching. Gurū Arjan's martyrdom generated a strong impulse of resistance and inaugurated a new era of martial *élan*. Instead of the rosary and other saintly emblems, his son Gurū Hargobind, the sixth Gurū, wore a warrior's equipment for the ceremonies of succession. He put on two swords – one he called the sword of *pīrī* and the other the sword of *mīrī*. The former was declared to be the symbol of his spiritual and the latter that of his temporal investiture, emphasizing how in the Sikh faith the worldly and the other-worldly were not disjointed.[1]

Gurū Hargobind's overt act of combining *mīrī* and *pīrī* marked an important development in the evolution of the Sikh community. This gave a military turn to its career. Since peaceful resistance to oppression had proved abortive, the Gurū recognized recourse to the sword as a lawful alternative. He raised a small armed band of Sikhs and sent out messages that disciples in the future come with gifts of horses and weapons. To defend the town of Amritsar, he built a fortress called Lohgaṛh (Iron Fort) in 1609. Another symbol of temporal authority instituted by Gurū Hargobind was the Akāl Takht (the Throne of the Timeless One) in front of the Harimandir, the Golden Temple of modern day. The Harimandir was for prayer; the Akāl Takht for the conduct of the community's secular affairs.

A martial atmosphere was introduced into Sikhism, and it came into full play after the martyrdom of Gurū Tegh Bahādur (Nanak IX). This Sikh Gurū challenged the Moghul policy of converting Hindus by force, and for this defense of religious freedom he was executed in 1675. His son and successor, Gurū Gobind Singh (Nānak X), though only nine years of age then, provided vigorous leadership to the Sikhs. His first task was to infuse a new spirit among a people long reconciled to their fallen state. His grand design to achieve this end found fulfillment in the inauguration in 1699 of the Khālsā, a casteless and self-abnegating commonwealth of Sikhs ready to take up arms to fight for justice and equality. Five of the Sikhs who had responded successively to his calls for five leaders constituted the nucleus of the new order. They were admitted into it through an initiation ceremony which marked a dramatic departure from the past. On that day Gurū Gobind Singh introduced a new form of baptism – baptism by churning water with a double-edged sword. As Gurū Gobind Singh started stirring with the steel sword the water that was poured into a steel bowl, his wife, Jītojī, came forward and dropped some sugar-puffs into the vessel. Sweetness through the feminine hand was thus mingled with the alchemy of iron. Another feminine note entered through the chanting by Gurū Gobind Singh of verses from *bāṇī* as he prepared the baptismal water.

The five to whom the rites of baptism were administered on that Baisākhī day by Gurū Gobind Singh were given the surname of Singh, meaning "lion," and were ever after to wear the five emblems of the khālsā – *keśa* or long hair and beard; *kaṅghā*, a comb tucked into the *keśa* to keep it tidy, in contrast with the recluses, who kept it matted as a token of their having renounced the world; *kaṛā*, a steel bracelet; *kachhā*, short breeches worn by the soldiers of that time; and *kirpān*, a sword. Their rebirth into the new order meant the annihilation of their previous family ties (*kula nāsa*), of the occupations which had hitherto determined their place in society (*krita nāsa*), of their earlier beliefs and creeds, and of the rituals they had so far observed. They were enjoined to succor the helpless and fight the oppressor, to have faith in the One, and to consider all human beings equal irrespective of caste and religion.[2] Gurū Gobind Singh spoke to them:

I wish you all to embrace one creed and follow one path, rising above all differences of the religion as now practised. Let the four Hindu castes, who have different dharmas laid down for them in the Sastras, containing Institutes of Varnashram dharma, abandon them altogether, and adopting the way of mutual help and co-operation, mix freely with one another. Do not follow the old scriptures. Let none pay homage to the Ganga and other places of pilgrimage which are considered to be holy in the Hindu religion, or worship the Hindu deities such as Rama, Krishna, Brahma and Durgā, etc., but all should cherish faith in the teachings of Guru Nanak and his successors. Let him of the four castes receive my Baptism of the double-edged sword, eat out of the same vessel, and feel no aloofness from, or contempt for one another.[3]

This baptism through steel was open to both men and women. Women were to wear the five emblems of the Khālsā, too. As men received the surname Singh, women received the surname Kaur, signifying princess. Thus the patriarchal structure of society was modified. Men and women no longer traced their lineage or occupation to the "father." As "Singh" and "Kaur," both were equal partners in the new family.

Before this culmination was reached, much reflection and contemlation had to be gone through. Out of Gurū Gobind Singh's moods of concentrated meditation issued poetry – poetry both spiritual and heroic. The fusion of the devotional and the martial was the most important feature of the philosophy of Gurū Gobind Singh and of his career as a spiritual leader and harbinger of a revolutionary impulse. Gurū Gobind Singh's poetry had the twofold purpose: to sing praises of the Timeless One and to infuse new vigor into a listless society. His compositions were most appropriately adapted to these objectives. Rarely has poetry in any tongue recaptured the transcendent vision in such personal terms or inspired such a spirit of courage and valor. It was the same vision of the Transcendent as had come down from Gurū Nānak; Gurū Gobind Singh rendered it in heroic diction and imagery. For him poetry was a means of revealing the divine principle and concretizing the vision of Being that had been vouchsafed to him. Through his poetry he preached love and equality and a strictly ethical and moral code of conduct. He preached the adoration of the Singular Reality, deprecating idolatry and superstitious beliefs and practices. He also employed the poetic medium to impart a new orientation to the minds of people given to passivity. For this latter purpose he picked themes from the ancient epics and mythology of India to produce verse charged with martial fervor.

Out of the myriads of gods and goddesses of the Hindu pantheon – 330 million traditionally – it is the goddess Durgā who became Gurū Gobind Singh's favorite literary subject. The protector of the cosmos from the threat of demons, Durgā is one of the most powerful and popular deities of the Hindu religion. The name Durgā is found in Vedic literature, but any resemblance with the warrior goddess of later Hinduism is missing in these early texts.[4] The image of Durgā slaying the buffalo demon begins to appear in fourth century AD, and by the sixth century, Durgā becomes a very popular deity, worshiped devoutly throughout India. By the sixth century we also have the written text *Devī Māhātmaya* in the Sanskrit language. *Devī Māhātmaya* forms chapters 81–93 of the *Mārkaṇḍeya Purāṇa* and is the most famous of all Hindu texts celebrating Durgā's mythological exploits. To this day it is used in the worship of the goddess and is greatly revered by her devotees. In this Hindu text, Durgā is the central figure in the story of the battle against the demons. She subsumes the many and various powers of the male gods who individually and collectively lacked the strength to defeat the buffalo demon.

It is this revered Hindu goddess, the subject of the *Devī Māhātmaya* text, who figures as heroine in two of Gurū Gobind Singh's compositions from the late seventeenth century in the Braj and Punjabi languages. These compositions have been included in the *Dasam Granth*, the Book of the Tenth Master (i.e. of Gurū Gobind Singh). In keeping with the Hindu tradition, the Sikh Gurū refers to Durgā (the inaccessible or unattainable one, from *dur*, "difficult," and *gam*, "reach") by her various names – Kālī, Caṇḍī, Camuṇḍā, and Bhadrakālī. The story of her titanic battle against the demons (narrated in fourteen cantos of the *Mārkaṇḍeya Purāṇa*) is retold by Gurū Gobind Singh in his ornate Braj composition *Caṇḍī Caritra* (*The Exploits of Caṇḍī*), parts I and II, and in his Punjabi work *Vār Durgā Kī* (*The Ballad of Durgā*). The latter text is commonly known as *Caṇḍī dī Vār* (*The Ballad of Caṇḍi*). Gurmukhī forms the script for these three pieces (as in all of his writings). Gurū Gobind Singh's poems are abbreviated versions of the original account, rendered in verse that employs a variety of meters and is rich in image and cadence. He describes her battles against the demons Locan, Caṇḍ, Muṇḍ, Rakatbīj, Nisumbh, and Sumbh. Even in Gurū Gobind Singh's *Akāl Ustati*, a hymn written in praise (*ustati*) of the Timeless One (*Akāl*), one part (sections 211 to 230) is a panegyric to the prowess of the invincible Durgā.

Now, the incorporation of the Durgā poems into the Sikh tradition is a controversial issue, concerning which one can clearly delineate several schools of thought. Scholars such as S. Radhakrishnan, who are given to interpreting the Sikh tradition within the Hindu framework, see in this "the profound influence which Hindu tradition and mythology has had on the development of Sikh religion."[5] On the other side of the spectrum are scholars from within Sikhism itself who totally reject Gurū Gobind Singh's authorship of the poems, claiming Hindu poets and scholars who associated with the tenth Gurū as the rightful composers.[6] There is yet another school which accepts the works as genuine, but distinguishes between two genres of Gurū Gobind Singh's poetry – secular and devotional. Here the Hindu goddess is accepted as a part of Gurū Gobind Singh's worldview, but only as a figure in his secular poetry. For example, scholars such as D. P. Ashtā[7] and Trilochan Singh[8] think that the eulogies of the goddess are appropriate to some version of the *Caṇḍī Caritra*, but they are disturbed by its presence in a purely devotional poem like the *Akāl Ustati*. Among all these scholars of Sikhism the debate over the authenticity of the works attributed to Gurū Gobind Singh continues to this day.[9] In one way or the other, these different intellectuals are unable or perhaps unwilling to recognize the relevance of this female mythological figure for the religious vision of Gurū Gobind Singh.

My own thesis is that the very popular Hindu goddess Durgā is recalled in all her Puraṇic glory by the Gurū. Such a claim completely rejects, however, Radhakrishnan's view of the Hindu influence on the Sikh tradition, for Durgā is being recalled as a figure of myth and literature; she is not invoked as a goddess by the Gurū. Nowhere does Gurū Gobind Singh profess himself to be a devotee of the Hindu goddess. The tenth Sikh Gurū but crystallizes the message of Gurū Nānak and ardently devotes himself to the One Singular Transcendent Reality. Yet, he recalls the very popular ancient goddess and artistically, almost playfully, describes her invincible deeds narrated in the *Mārkaṇḍeya Purāṇa*. At the very outset he sets forth his objective: He is going to tell the story of the goddess artistically, in "words that are beaded like jewels." The poet thus sets a rather amusing mood for his work.

The controversial Durgā compositions are Guru Gobind Singh's very own. Had they belonged to his Hindu associates, as many have alleged, they would not have been mentioned in his autobiographical composition the *Bacitra Nāṭak*. In verse 14 Gurū Gobind Singh clearly mentions his poems on Durgā: "pahile caṇḍī caritra banāyo nakh sikh te kram bhākh sunāyo – first *Caṇḍī Caritra* was composed, describing in detail deeds from beginning to end."[10] Bhāī Desā Singh in his *Rahitnāmā* also refers to Gurū Gobind Singh as the author of the *Caṇḍī Caritra* (along with the *Jāp*, *Bacitra Nāṭak*, and *Akāl Ustati*).[11] Moreover, if the *Caṇḍī* poems were not Gurū Gobind Singh's own but rather the compositions of his contemporaries, why would their opening line be incorporated in the daily supplications of the Sikhs? To this day, the first verse of *Vār Dārgā Kī* ("prathami bhagautī simar kai – having first remembered the sword") forms the beginning of the prayers recited by the Sikhs morning and evening. Nobody could deny that Gurū Gobind Singh himself was a poet of great artistic range. For something as important as their daily prayer, the Sikhs would surely have made a selection from his own creative repertoire; they would hardly have found it necessary to resort to a composition by one of his associates. The most telling argument of all, however, lies in the very content of the poems themselves: the aesthetic techniques that have been used and the religious ideal that is intimated in them belong to Gurū Gobind Singh's particular religio-aesthetic world. Only a miscomprehension of Gurū Gobind Singh's objective and perhaps a not fully conscious fear of "female power," "goddess worship," and "polytheism" would lead one to believe that he is not the rightful author of these compositions. His recalling of Durgā posits her as a literary metaphor, validating the female experience in the society, aesthetics, and religion of the Sikhs. The appropriateness of the Durgā image is not due to any particular category, sacred or secular, of Gurū Gobind Singh's poetry, but rather to his intuition as a whole. This is the thesis which I wish to explore in the present chapter.

To repeat, Gurū Gobind Singh recalls Durgā; he does not invoke her. The recalling is a deliberate utilization of the ancient myth, and, furthermore, a utilization of myth as myth. There is an utter absence of worship of the goddess in Gurū Gobind Singh's verse, a worship that is central to the *Mārkaṇḍeya Purāṇa* text and to her overall image in Hinduism. In the Purāṇic narration, Durgā is exalted by being the subject of *pūjā*, *yājnā*, *tapas*, and *bhakti*; she is placed within the context of ritual and cult.[12] For instance, chapter 12 of *Devī Māhātmaya*, named *Phala-śruti*, opens with these words:

> And whoever with a concentrated mind shall invoke me constantly with these hymns, I shall certainly put down all affliction for him.

It ends with the following verses:

> When praised and worshiped with flowers, incense, perfumes, etc, She bestows wealth and sons and a mind devoted to dharma and an auspicious life.[13]

Throughout this Hindu text, Durgā is perceived to be the source of boons – both material and spiritual. Such an invocation and homage is utterly absent in Gurū Gobind Singh's compositions. Nowhere is Durgā the subject of piety and spiritual exercise.

Gurū Gobind Singh's invocation is ever addressed to the Transcendent One. *Caṇḍī Caritra*, for instance, begins with: "ādi apār alekh anaṅt ākal abhekh alakh anāsā."[14] With the prefix alliterative "a" added to each word, the characteristics and qualities of the One are enumerated in the negative form: "Beginningless, Unfathomable, Ineffable, Infinite, Timeless, Formless, Indescribable, Undestroyable, is the Creator of all." The *Akāl Ustati* also opens with the supplication to the totally Transcendent One: "I salute the One Beginningless Being – praṇvo ādi ekaṅkārā."[15] As we may recall, Gurū Gobind Singh, in addressing the first five disciples admitted to the Khālsā baptism, had clearly rejected the worship of gods and goddesses, of "the Hindu deities such as Rāma, Kṛṣṇa, Brahmā and Durgā."[16] He was completely consistent and orthodox in his rejection of gods, goddesses, and incarnations. Among the attributes of the Supreme Being mentioned in Gurū Nānak's Mūl Mantra, which forms the preamble to the Gurū Granth, the Sikh sacred text, is *ajūnī* – the One is never born; the One does not become incarnate. The Sikh faith does not postulate any *avatār* or incarnate being co-equal or co-powerful with the Transcendent One and thereby worthy of human worship. Gurū Gobind Singh retains this view, and in his *Śabda Hazāre* he writes that whatever powers the gods and goddesses have are derived from the Primal Being. In the second passage of *Vār Durgā Kī*, Gurū Gobind Singh follows Gurū Nānak's *Japu* in stating that Brahmā, Viṣṇu, and Śiva are all creations of the

One.[17] Gurū Gobind Singh goes on to say that it is from the One that Rāma received his prowess in piercing with his arrows the ten-headed Rāvaṇa; it is from the One that Kṛṣṇa received the power to catch Kaṅsa by the hair and tear him apart. Not only the gods but also the demons are created by, and therefore subject to, the Transcendent One. As Gurū Gobind Singh says, "taiṅ hī durgā sāj kai daiṅtāṅ dā nās karāiā – You are the One who created Durgā and caused the demons to be destroyed."[18] The term *sāj kai* ("formed" or "created") denotes the creation of the goddess by the Metaphysical Reality. The doctrine that Brahmā, Viṣṇu, and Śiva are the lords of the universe – the creator, preserver, destroyer trinity of the Hindu tradition – is also refuted in *Srī Mukhibak Savayye*: "Recognize none other but the One alone," proclaims Gurū Gobind Singh.[19] A Singular, Transcendent Reality dominates his vision.

But I do maintain that Gurū Gobind Singh recalls Durgā. The "recalling" of Durgā is a retelling of the heroic deeds of the goddess as narrated in the *Mārkaṇḍeya Purāṇa*. Gurū Gobind Singh's own words make this explicit. After inscribing the invocatory "Ikk Oaṅ Kār Wahigurū jī kī Fateh – there is One Be-ing; Hail to the One to Whom belongs the Victory," he says, "ath caṇḍī caritra ukti bilās – now the tale (*bilas*) of Caṇḍī will be told."[20] Acknowledging the *Mārkaṇḍeya Purāṇa* narrative to be an extraordinary story, he wishes to retell it with due stylistic embellishment:

ratan pramud kar bacan cīni tā mai gaco . . .
adbhuti kathā apār, samajh kari citt mai.[21]

I shall bead the story with sentences full of jewel-like choicest words . . .
The story (*kathā*) which I think is marvelous (*adbhut*).

Rather than a devotee, we encounter here an artist. Gurū Gobind Singh's objective is, then, certainly not to worship or invoke the goddess, but rather to recall her, to renarrate the chivalrous deeds in words studded like luminous gems. The Purāṇic account has no historical or religious meaning for the poet; it is for him simply a wonderful (*adbhuti*) story (*kathā*) or tale (*bilās*). The poet's overall objective is the reproduction of a thrilling story – "kautak hetu karī kavī ne – for the thrill of it, the poet has delineated the tale."[22] Throughout the retelling, the tone of Gurū Gobind Singh's poetry lacks the reverence that would underlie an invocation. The *Mārkaṇḍeya Purāṇa* account of seven hundred verses is reproduced by Gurū Gobind Singh in a considerably condensed version. The martial exploits of Durgā are described by him with zest and in superb poetry, but in his compositions she is nowhere deified as she is in the original Sanskrit text. The invocations to the goddess by the gods in the Purāṇic account are absent from Gurū Gobind Singh's versions. Yet, Gurū Gobind Singh's poetic recalling brings the feminine dimension to the fore and reveals *her* power in Sikh society, aesthetics, and religion.

## SOCIAL DESIGN: TO REGENERATE AN EFFETE SOCIETY

Gurū Gobind Singh's choice of Durgā means unequivocal acknowledgment of woman's power in society. At a psychologically and politically weak moment in the history of Indian society, Gurū Gobind Singh deliberately evokes the myth of Durgā. Stories and myths are indeed essential to the make-up of the world. In Muriel Rukeyser's formula, "the universe is made up of stories, not of atoms." Mythology has been defined by James L. Jarrett as an *Urphenomenon*, i.e. something which predates our sophisticated distinctions of literature, science, philosophy, religion, and dreams, but from which these very distinguishable activities arise. He discerns five categories for myths: (1) stories, (2) pre-science, (3) primitive religion, (4) primitive philosophy, and (5) collective dreams.[23] Gurū Gobind Singh's understanding of mythology falls into the first category. He clearly regards the myth of Durgā as a marvelous story (*kathā*) or tale (*bilās*). Max Müller's simple formula declared that "mythology is history changed into fable or fable represented as history,"[24] but this is not Gurū Gobind Singh's conception of the myth. In his case, the mixing up of history and fable does not occur. Not history but sheer "fable" is the myth of Durgā for the Sikh Gurū.

Yet it is evident throughout his poetry that Gurū Gobind Singh was deeply conscious of the power of myth. Myths were for him, as for us today, what animate and direct us: they face us this way or that, open or close our horizons, orient us or disorient us, enrich us or impoverish us.[25] Myths provide "the pattern to which growth may aspire."[26] They present us with "archetypes" which can act as images and role models to build self-esteem and encourage fulfillment of individual potential. The transformation from "mythos" to "ethos" was central to Gurū Gobind Singh's perception: by reading, hearing, and reciting the myth of Durgā, the inert society could be invigorated, and the ethical principles could be upheld. The myth from the past held possibilities for the present, for the future.

From amongst all the myths of India – Hindu, Buddhist, Jaina – it is Durgā who captures the poetic mind of Gurū Gobind Singh. The strong, courageous, independent Durgā is considered to be an exception amongst Hindu goddesses by scholars of Sanskrit literature. The Gurū singled her out as a model of moral force and martial prowess for both men and women.

Almost all of the countless goddesses who figure in the Purāṇas are married, with gods as their spouses. As wives, the goddesses lack individual status and identity. Many of them, like the wives of Brahmā and Viṣṇu, appear to be flimsy, dependent creatures, having no distinctive personalities or traits of their own. According to Cornelia Dimmitt and J. A. B. van Buitenen, the marriage of gods and goddesses is probably a reflection of the synthesis that occurred between different races and cultures – Aryan and Dravidian – in the early history of the Indian people:

> Certainly the goddesses as wives are utterly dependent upon their gods, much as the indigenous race was subdued and rendered subject by the conquering Aryans. In any case, it seems that only fragments of the careers of the goddesses in Indian tradition remain in the stories found in the Purāṇas.[27]

The one exception is Durgā. She is the one goddess in the Purāṇas without husband, consort, or lover. She is independent; she is powerful. She is the central figure in the story of the battle against the demons. In her person she unites the powers of many and various gods, so that she alone is able to defeat the demons. In the *Mārkaṇḍeya Purāṇa*, her birth is described as a miraculous event, and an auspicious one for the gods:

> The Devas saw in front of them a pile of Light blazing
> like a mountain whose flames filled the whole space.
> Then that matchless light born from the bodies of all
> gods gathered into a single corpus and turned into a
> woman enveloping the three worlds by her lustre.
> Her face was produced from the light of Śiva;
> her hair from that of Yama;
> her arms from the lustre of Vishṇu;
> Her breasts from that of the Moon; her bust from that of Indra;
> her thighs and legs from that of Varuna;
> her hips from the lustre of the earth;

> Her feet from that of Brahmā;
> her fingers of the feet from the lustre of Sūryā;
> her fingers of the hand from that of the Vasus;
> her nose from that of Kubera;
> Her teeth were formed from the lustre of Prajapati,
> her triple eyes were produced from the light of Agni;
> Her eye-brows were the twin twilight and
> her ears were formed from the lustre of Vāyu.
> The light of the other gods became the goddess Śivā.
> Then the Devas oppressed by Mahishasura looking at the
> form of Devī produced by the assembled lustre of all of
> the gods became gladdened.[28]

Born thus, she charges forth mounted on her lion, paying homage to no one, acknowledging the authority of no one. She is her own mistress.

It is ironic that the significance of Durgā's autonomy would be misinterpreted by modern western scholars such as Dimmitt and van Buitenen. In their introduction to "The Goddess" in *Classical Hindu Mythology*, which they edited and translated together, they characterize the unique freedom enjoyed by Durgā as her "lack of control."

> She [the ferocious goddess, i.e. Durgā/Kālī] is raw power, energy untamed by discipline or direction. The pairing off of male and female deities in Purāṇic mythology appears to provide a check to this excess, the other side of which is found in the intense asceticism of the meditating *yogin*. Coupling these two extremes, a balance is achieved between the opposing forces of the universe that is unknown to the solitary ascetic whose self-control inhibits growth, and unknown as well to the ferocious goddess whose excesses threaten to destroy all life. Whether as wife, lover, or other half of the male deity's body, the goddess represents the energy of the universe, which unchecked wreaks havoc, but without which nothing is born, moves or lives. Controlled by its opposite force, this energy is channeled into the natural creativity of the world, and poured forth by a generative deity. As Śiva and *śakti* together demonstrate, neither one can stand entirely alone, for either pure asceticism or untamed fury by itself would annihilate the world. In balance together, they assure its fruitful continuity.[29]

Is the ferocious goddess sheer "untamed energy" and "untamed fury"? Do her excesses "threaten to destroy all life?" Would she "annihilate the world" in its entirety? On the contrary, the immense energy and fury of Durgā are thoroughly disciplined: these are directed towards annihilating and destroying only the demons, symbolic representations of evil and negative forces in the individual psyche and in society. Durgā is indeed a destroyer, but she simultaneously saves humanity from the pit of hell. In the *Akāl Ustati*, she is rightly addressed as both destroyer and savior.[30] For the male gods who come to seek her help, she is clearly their savior. This crucial point is overlooked by Dimmitt and van Buitenen. Instead, they tend to see the goddess in her common domestic role, that is, *with* a male (husband, consort, or lover), passively balancing and harmonizing the "fruitful continuity" of the world.

Moreover, they fail to appraise the magnitude of her person, for she has the power to bestow life as well as the power to withhold life. She is both the creator and the destroyer. The gods approach Durgā for succor against the demons who have dethroned them and overturned the harmonious order of the cosmos. Hearing their request, she laughs uproariously and readily consents to challenge the usurpers. She summons the lion she rides, her devourer of demons, and she comforts the gods with the words "*cintā karhu na kāi*[31] – do not worry at all." And then she goes off to battle:

> roh hoī mahāmāī rākaśi mārṇe.
>
> Infuriated, the great mother (*mahā*, "great," and *māī*, "mother") advances to kill the demons.

She can destroy, but she can also preserve and create; she even has the power to generate on her own. These powers are one and the same, for it is out of her destructive fury that Durgā creates Kālī. The goddess needs no male. Kālī, the black goddess who is addressed as both *Kāla Mātr* ("Time-Giver" – the creator, the Mother, the giver of birth and time) and *Kāla Harśiṇī* ("Time-Taker" – the destroyer, the clipper of time, and thus the one who brings death), emanates from Durgā's forehead: "From her broad forehead of curved eyebrows suddenly sprang forth Kālī of terrible countenance, armed with a sword and noose."[32] Durgā is presented here as the progenitor – the great Mother – but she is also the destroyer, and she must proceed to kill her enemies, to punish and overcome evil. She charges single-handed with full fury into the ranks of the demons. Their well-equipped and deadly armies do not frighten her, and her loud laughter echoes throughout the battlefield. She makes light of the hazards she faces, and with sovereign ease she confronts the enemy.

Her extraordinary physical strength is also the theme of a section of Gurū Gobind Singh's composition *Akāl Ustati*, wherein she is pictured as clad in armor from head to foot, with mighty white serpents coiled around her neck, hissing dreadfully at the foe. Her hand-drum makes the sound of roaring tigers.[33] She is riding a lion. The poet addresses her:

> The sovereign deity on earth,
> Enwrapped in all the regal pomp.
> To you be victory,
> O you of mighty arms.[34]

Here also the goddess's valorous deeds are described in vivid detail – how, for instance, she makes mincemeat of the demon Dhūmar, slays Mahikhāsura, and vanquishes their entire armies. Her offspring, Kālī, bursting forth from her forehead, gulps down the demons and elephants alike. Durgā herself is skilled in the use of a hundred arms and gives an astounding display of her martial prowess. The bulwark of righteousness, she moves back and forth fearlessly. Gurū Gobind Singh sees her battle as one against sin:

> dusṭ nivāraṇ dokh hare . . .
> bis-bindusan; srisṭi kare.[35]

> All sins you annihilate,
> and righteousness you countenance . . .
> Dangerous poison is destroyed
> and creative energy maintained.

The gods themselves revere Durgā as "Mother," and they look up to her for help in overcoming and destroying their enemy. They pay homage "to the Goddess who among all created beings stands firm with the form of Mother (*Mātrupen*)."[36] They perceive that she is "at once most gentle and most harsh." The one-sided analysis of Durgā developed by Dimmit and van Buitenen overlooks the "wholeness" of the woman in herself.[37]

It was the full independence of Durgā's character, her ability to challenge and quell evil, her power to embrace all of life – birth and death, creation and decay – that attracted the imagination of Gurū Gobind Singh. Gurū Gobind Singh's choice displays a singular awareness of the intrinsic importance of the female. A contemporary scholar, Miriam Starhawk, regards the goddess image as a positive model for the wholeness of the person – woman and man. According to her, the goddess inspires us to see our aggression as healthy and our anger as purifying.[38] The Sikh prophet too realizes how significant "her" existence and power are, how important she is for the maintenance of harmony, morality, and justice. Where the male gods are vanquished, she comes out triumphant. She symbolizes the moral power to challenge an oppressive system. Her aggression is indeed healthy; her anger is indeed purifying. This affirmation of female power by Gurū Gobind Singh illustrates the overall positive attitude towards women in Sikh speculation. Gurū Nānak likewise affirmed that there is nothing inferior or insidious about woman. Neither a hindrance nor a negative influence, she is necessary for the continuance of society and for the preservation of its ethical structure. She remains the paradigm for both men and women.

The role that this unique goddess played in Hindu myth fitted in well with Gurū Gobind Singh's design to renovate and regenerate an effete society. The rulers at that time were guilty of gross injustice and oppression, so Gurū Gobind Singh's own socio-political environment corresponded with the situation at the beginning of the Durgā story – the imbalance resulting from the defeat of the gods by the demons. Durgā's eventual victory over these negative forces must have appealed to the imagination of Gurū Gobind Singh. The poet in fact believed that those qualities of hers were still capable of inspiring women and men to positive action. With the literary paradigm of Durgā before them, they might overcome their weakness and cowardice, overthrow the unjust political authorities, abolish social inequalities, and ultimately forge a new structure based on more just and egalitarian values. Sikhs heard and recited his words about the goddess who embodied courage and challenged oppression. As history witnessed, men and women were charged with courage and moral fervor by the personal example of Gurū Gobind Singh and by his literary resurrection of this mythological heroine. In this period of great stress and strife, women stood side by side with men. Māī Bhāgo, from the Amritsar district of the Punjāb, was just one instance of such a woman. When she saw how some Sikhs of her area had fled Anaṅdpur, the seat of Gurū Gobind Singh, in the face of the privations brought on by a prolonged siege, she chided them with pusillanimity. She led them back to fight for the Gurū, and she herself took part in the battle that ensued at Khidrāna (now Muktsar) on December 19, 1705. She performed extraordinary feats of valor and skill, but this entire period is replete with the heroic deeds and sacrifices of Sikh men and women like her. They all fought valiantly against the mighty forces of the rulers of the day. Because of this sustained resistance, the Sikhs had become a major political force within half a century of Gurū Gobind Singh's death, and they had established a State of their own in another forty years.

### AESTHETIC: HEROIC INSPIRATION AND PHYSICAL BEAUTY

The penultimate passage in the *Caṇḍī Caritra* articulates not only Gurū Gobind Singh's object in reproducing the story of Durgā in Punjabi verse but also his aesthetic values and ideals:

> caṇḍī caritra kavittan mai barnio sabh hī rasrudra maī hai
> ek te ek rasāl bhaio, nakh te sikh lau upamā so naī hai
> kautak hetu karī kavi ne, satisayī kī kathā eh pūrī bhaī hai
> jāhi namitt parai suni hai nar, so niscai kari tāhi daī hai.[39]
>
> I have narrated the wondrous story of Caṇḍī in verse in its entirety:
> In the martial tone is it cast;
> Each verse is more captivating than the other.
> Fresh and new are the similes from the beginning to the end.
> For the thrill of it has the poet delineated the tale of the goddess, to whom seven hundred stanzas are inscribed in the Purāṇa.
> My object is that whosoever reads or hears her story may be inspired with faith and determination.

His new poem about Durgā is full of fresh and striking imagery. Gurū Gobind Singh employs all the different poetic devices to lend enchantment and vigor to his version of the Purāṇic story. In his poetry, he wants to exalt the mythical Durgā and through her all women. Modern feminist writers such as Merlin Stone and Bella Debrida point out how rare such respect is; in most cultures the image of the female has been degraded. In "Ancient Mirrors of Womanhood," Merlin Stone cites several instances from a wide variety of cultures which reveal how the patriarchal structures have attempted to "suppress," "alter," and even "erase" the luster of the female. The Sumerians, for example, replaced the ancient creator goddess Nammu with the less effective Inana. Another instance is that of Kuan Yin in China. She probably derives from the pre-Buddhist creator goddess Nu Kwa, but she is reduced to being a male Boddhisattva who decided to return to earth as Kuan Yin. A final example noted by Merlin Stone is that of the Arabian goddess Attar. She is associated with the Semitic Ishtar and the Egyptian Hathor, but she is described in later South Arabian inscriptions as a male deity.[40] Bella Debrida in "Drawing from Mythology in Women's

Quest for Selfhood" sums up this entire process: "while ancient mythology affirmed woman's power, those stories through patriarchal influence over the years have come to be "muted," "curtailed" and even "perverted."[41]

Gurū Gobind Singh's treatment of Durgā is completely exempt from any such detraction. On the contrary, through his artistic sensibility and through the breathtaking opulence of his imagery, the Purāṇic goddess and her heroic exploits have been handsomely magnified in this account. She appears here in all her legendary glory. In this recalling, she has lost nothing of her dynamism and fire.

If we examine some of the artistic devices employed by Gurū Gobind Singh in his artistic recalling of the Hindu goddess, we first notice the tone or mood of the poem. He himself concludes in the *Caṇḍī Caritra* that "all of it has been in the martial tone – sabh hī rasrudra mai hai." In *The Transformation of Nature in Art*, Ananda Coomaraswamy states that a work of art is a result of the combination of four elements: (1) determinants (*vibhāva*), the physical stimulants to aesthetic reproduction, particularly the theme and its parts and the overall setting with its time and place; (2) consequents (*anubhāva*), the specific and conventional means of "registering" emotional states, in particular gestures; (3) moods (*bhāva*), the conscious emotional states as represented in art. Here Coomaraswamy distinguishes between fugitive or transient moods such as joy, agitation, and impatience and permanent (*sthāyi*) moods such as the erotic and the heroic. "In any work, one of the Permanent Moods must constitute a master motif to which all the others are subordinate"; (4) involuntary physical reactions (*sattva bhāva*), for example, fainting.[42] It is easily discernible that the third of these elements is Gurū Gobind Singh's primary concern. The "permanent mood" of heroism is the dominant characteristic of his presentation of the story of Durgā in verse. His purpose is to evoke a heroic atmosphere, and this he does through powerful verbal images and similes and through martial rhythms and cadences, all of which delineate Durgā's person and her feats in battle.

Prior to analyzing the mood (*rasa*) pervading the poem, we need to comprehend the significance of *rasa* in Gurū Gobind Singh's artistic intuition. A critical concept in Indian art, *rasa* is indeed rich in meaning. In the *Hindu View of Art*, Coomaraswamy studies this multi dimensional term from a chronological point of view. He writes that *rasa* was used in the earliest hymns to signify water and milk. In the *Atharva Veda*, the application of the term *rasa* is extended to the sap of grain. It occurs in the *Ṛg Veda* in the sense of the juice of the *somā* plant. In the time of the later *Vedas*, it came less to signify water and milk and juice, and acquired instead a very interesting and important connotation noted by Coomaraswamy – that of savor or taste. Later, during the early Upaniṣadic period, when every Vedic concept was being transformed from a particular to a universal, *rasa* developed to mean "an abstract idea of an essential element." Finally, during the late Upaniṣadic period, we find in the *Taittiriya* and *Maitreya* Upaniṣads that *rasa* has acquired a new meaning, "the highest state of joy."[43] Gurū Gobind Singh's conception of *rasa* is more in consonance with the one prevalent in the later Vedic period. For it is neither the early Upaniṣadic ideal of an abstract "essential element" nor the later Upaniṣadic ideal of "the highest state of joy," but the concept of "tasting" and "savoring" which we find in the later Vedas and which marks his own aesthetic vision.

While the dominant *rasa* of poetry honoring Durgā is *raudra* ("martial"), the *śringār* ("erotic") flavor is not altogether missing. Durgā is depicted in her most terrifying martial aspect – her eyes rain fire, she has hissing snakes around her neck and lethal weapons in her hands, she is mounted on a roaring tiger, and she smites the enemy with stark ferocity. Yet this picture is relieved by handsome, even sensuous, elements, of which the following description is a striking instance:

> Luminous like the moon is her face,
>   and a sight of it charms away many a woe.
> Her hair hangs like Shivjī's serpents;
>   her eyes are the envy of both the lotus and the gazelle.
> Her brows are in the manner of a bow;
>   her lashes like the arrows.
> She has the waist of a lion
>   and marches with the majesty of a royal tusker.
> She abides on the mountain-top;
>   none can resist the splendor of her charms.
> She holds a sword in her hand and rides a lion;
> Flaming like gold is her presence.
> In another hand she carries a bow of war.
> The fish are shamed by her restless energy;
> The lotus and the gazelle by the softness of her eyes;

The parrots by her nose;
The pigeons by her neck;
The cuckoo by her voice;
The pomegranate by the pearly row of her teeth.
Touching the person of the goddess,
The moonbeams have become more lustrous.[44]

Here we encounter a radiant and majestic figure whose charms none can resist. Such is her loveliness that even the moonbeams – after touching her person – become more lustrous! In a verse in his *Akāl Ustati*, the poet describes her ankle bells making a silvery peal. Even when she is in the midst of the fierce battle, a passage in *Caṇḍī Caritra* describes her sword making a jingling sound and twinkling like glow-worms during a dark, stormy, monsoon night.[45] In another passage from the *Caṇḍī Caritra*, the blood oozing from her neck is compared to the spit of a Ceylonese damsel who has been chewing red betel-leaf.[46] A scholar like D. P. Ashta may consider Gurū Gobind Singh's poetic fancy "not apt due to the unseemly mixture of the heroic and erotic sentiments,"[47] but this combination of the two *rasas* in fact denotes a rich artistic sensibility. The combination is most subtle: the heroic or the martial mood dominates, and the romantic is gently woven into it. The latter sets off the former. Even though the passage cited concentrates on the physical charms of the goddess – her arched eyebrows and her long lashes and her narrow waist – the keynote of the description is martial. For Durgā's arched eyebrows are in the manner of a "bow," her long darting eyelashes are like "arrows," her narrow and shapely waist like that of a "lion" – perhaps of the roaring one she rides. Though the lotus and gazelle are put to shame by the "softness" of her eyes, Durgā's presence is flaming like gold and she marches with the majesty of a royal tusker. The "jingling" and "twinkling" may conjure up romantic images, but their subject is the goddess's sword, their surroundings, a fierce battlefield. The silvery peal of Durgā's anklets is juxtaposed to the clamor of the weapons around. And however "romantic" the analogy with the young Ceylonese woman may be, the theme is the wound sustained in the fighting. The *raudra rasa* is dominant throughout and the *śriṅgāra rasa* seeps in tenderly now and then, accentuating the former and creating a powerful aesthetic effect.

This overall heroic and martial temper is evoked by a succession of dynamic similes. In Gurū Gobind Singh's own words, "Fresh and new are the similes from the beginning to the end." *Caṇḍī Caritra* I and II both reveal the Gurū's mastery of the figures of speech, especially the simile. He has created myriads of original images and similes, and through them he has rendered eloquently and vividly the character of Durgā and the battles she engages in. The parallels drawn are at times rather homely and at others splendid – but through the genius of Gurū Gobind Singh, they come out picturesquely. All are novel and fitting.

In fact, it is the common images that are highly appealing and have the most effect for their beauty, unexpectedness, and humor. Many of the parallels come from the familiar crafts and trades of carpenters, oil extractors, dyers, and confectioners. For example, the goddess plunging into fierce action tramples down her enemies as "an oilman crushes the oil-seeds."[48] The demons are beheaded by the goddess in the manner of a carpenter chopping down trees.[49] The blood spilt by the touch of her sword runs down the field like colored water that splashes onto the ground when the dyer's basin gets broken.[50] Soldiers in chariots, elephants, and horses are hurled down by her – she flings them down like a confectioner dunking *vaṛṛās* (sweet balls).[51]

All these occupations – carpentry, oil extracting, dyeing cloth, dunking *vaṛṛās* – must have been part of the rural scenario experienced first-hand by Gurū Gobind Singh. The rendering of the heroic deeds of the legendary Durgā in images from everyday life, the intermixing of the extraordinary with the ordinary, creates an uncommon artistic effect. Latent in this aesthetic design seems to be the message from Gurū Gobind Singh: Everyone, confectioner, dyer, carpenter, or oil extractor, is endowed with Durgā-like natural energy; her story can be enacted here and now.

In order to enrich his portrayal of Durgā, Gurū Gobind Singh borrowed his decorative devices from nature as well. The phenomenal sights and sounds of nature are used to produce exquisite pregnant similes to characterize Durgā and her warlike prowess. But as is the case with most artists, nature is not introduced by Gurū Gobind Singh for its own sake. Durgā's attack on the enemy is likened to her "crashing upon them like lightning."[52] The connection with lightning conveys the speed and velocity with which Durgā falls upon the army of the demons. Intimately relating the goddess with lightning, the comparison makes for vigor and realism. It is for the purpose of presenting the goddess in a life-like, in a most "natural" manner that phenomenal objects, sounds, and scenes are drawn upon in the imaginative scheme of Gurū Gobind Singh.

Many of the other analogies are once again drawn from the agrarian landscape with which Gurū Gobind Singh and his readers or hearers must have been familiar. The customary spectacles, however, become alive and meaningful as they turn into vehicles for the delineation of the martial exploits of the invincible goddess. The heads of the demons struck down by Durgā are likened to "dates fallen off the tree as the storm blows."[53] To quote from another stanza, "the goddess's eyes blaze forth like wildfire burning her enemies to ashes, and like poison, they send bees to sleepy death."[54] The arrows of the goddess strike a great many demons and penetrate through their bodies "like the sprouts of the paddy seeds breaking forth from the soil in the month of Sāvan."[55] The lanced demons struck by the goddess hang on spears "like olives on a tree bough."[56] In another verse, soldiers hung on arrows shot by Durgā are likened to "flowers on a pomegranate tree."[57] The huge demons wounded by Durgā's sword writhe in pain and roll on the ground like unconscious drunkards.[58] In the same passage, they are pictured fallen in the battlefield as if bitten by black serpents.

The similes are thus never conventional or hackneyed, but always fresh and original. And in spite of their abundance, the poetic style does not become monotonous. Apart from the newness of the images, this may be attributed partly to the poet's avoidance of words such as *jāpani* ("as if") or *jivain* ("like") which are commonly used in similes. Instead, as we saw, the parallels are established in novel modes:

> The fish are shamed by her [Durgā's] restless energy;
> The lotus and the gazelle by the softness of her eyes;
> The parrots by her nose;
> The pigeons by her neck;
> The cuckoo by her voice;
> The pomegranate by the pearly row of her teeth.[59]

The comparisons come out strikingly; the quintessential models of energy and beauty are "put to shame" in Durgā's presence. The comparisons are not platitudinous and they do not conform to any specific technique. The innumerable parallels studding the narrative bring to the reader and hearer the marvelous image of the goddess and her equally marvelous deeds, but they never take the form of direct equations. The mind never stops calculating the magnificence of the goddess. The stairlike parallelisms continue . . .

The whole sequence of parallels from nature as well as from the human world flows out in a heightening rhythmical tempo. A dignified, echoing music of the richest timbre accompanies the visual analogies. The aural rhythm thus created intensifies the *raudra rasa.* He uses several devices to achieve this end.

One is repetition of sounds. It seems as if Gurū Gobind Singh had woven *raudra rasa* into the warp and woof of the language itself, into the very texture of the words! His frequent use of alliteration, assonance, and consonance lends a stimulating rhythm and music to the narrative. The constant repetition of sounds like *bha*, *gha*, *jha*, *ḍha*, and *ṛa* reproduces the heavy sounds of combat. In "durgā sabhe saṅghāre rākhaś khaṛag lai,"[60] for instance, the use of *bha*, *gha*, and *ṛa* makes the verse throb with excitement. The sound here itself suggests that the goddess is felling the giant-like demons. In another verse, "bhakā bhuṅk bherī ḍahā ḍūh ḍaṅkaṁ . . . ḍhakā ḍhukk ḍhalaṁ,"[61] the martial rhythm is ringingly audible. The readers become saturated with the frenzy of battle and are carried away with it, feeling it flow turbulently in their own blood and nerves. In another line, "taṇi taṇi tīr calāe durgā dhanukh lai,"[62] the sound alone – a combination of the alliteration of *t* and the consonance of *lai* – reproduces the speed of action in actual fighting. Durgā is pictured here shooting arrows (*tīr calāe*) with all her might (*taṇi taṇi*). These devices are very appropriate to the description of battle-scenes.

Another favorite device is the use of onomatopoeia. Gurū Gobind Singh subtly chooses words whose sound suggests their meaning. He reinforces *raudra rasa* by the aural effect of his diction. The different names used for Durgā like Caṇḍī, Bhavānī, and Durgshāh have a heroic ring. Furthermore, polysyllabic words or compound epithets – aurally very resonant – enrich the poetry. Durgā has been variously called *Siām-barṇī* ("dark-complexioned"), *Dait-darṇī* ("demon-slayer"), *Garab-harṇī* ("pride-vanquisher").[63] In such instances a multiplicity of characteristics are brought together, heightening both sound and sense.

In describing her battle-scenes, Gurū Gobind Singh employs vocabulary echoing the actual sounds of the action, as in this example from *Caṇḍī Caritra* II:

kah kah su kūkat kaṅkīyaṁ
bahi bahat bīr su baṅkīyaṁ
lah lahat bāṇi kripāṇyaṁ
gah gahat pret masāṇyaṁ
dah dahat davar daṁkyaṁ
lah lahat tegh traṁkyaṁ
dhramdhramat sāṅg dhaṁkyaṁ
bab kant bır su bankyaṁ
chhutkaṅt bāṇ kamāṇyaṁ
harraṅt khet khatrāṇyaṁ
dhahkaṅt dhāmar dhaṅkaṇī
kah kahak kūkat juggaṇī.[64]

Even without a translation, the above verses convey the awesomeness of the scenes of war. The crows crow ("kah kah su kūkat kaṅkīyaṁ"); the heavy weapons produce dull sounds ("bahi bahat"); the swords clash ("lah lahat"); ghosts make weird sounds ("gah gahat"); the drums are beaten ("dah dahat"); the rattling spears are brandished ("lah lahat"); the strong warriors hurl defiance ("bab kant"); the arrows are discharged ("chhutkaṅt"); the soldiers fall stunned ("harraṅt"); the war-drums are reverberating ("dhahkaṅt"); the wives of the demons are wailing ("kah kahak kūkat").[65]

In another passage, a scene from Durgā's war against the demons is depicted as resounding with the roaring of cannons ("ṭakā ṭukk topaṁ") and the clashing of swords and shields ("ḍkakā ḍhukk ḍhālaṁ"), the slashing of bodies ("tacchā muchh"), shrieks of confused warriors ("halā cāl bīraṁ"), and the rattling of spears ("dhamā dhaṁi sāngaṁ"). The reverberations of the clamor are heard even in the netherland.[66]

The crescendo of the varied sounds reenacts the battle-scene. We hear the blasting of cannons, the rumble of the drums, the crackle of arrows, the screaming of the warriors, the wailing of the wives of the fallen demons, the cawing of crows flying over corpses. As the ears hear these weird sounds, the eyes envision the gruesome images. The entire scene comes vividly alive – the goddess spitting the demons out to their wailing wives (watching from far away) and the crows greedily awaiting to pounce upon corpses. This coalition of the visual and the aural in the poem imparts to Durgā and her battles a reality belying her mythical character.

We might also note that Gurū Gobind Singh frequently coins new words. Very often he alters a word or varies its phonetic form, investing it with fresh musical, pictorial, or suggestive values. He also uses archaic words and words from other languages, particularly Persian and Arabic. In the following verse, the Persian *bolaṅd* has been altered to *bilaṅd* for the sake of meter:

> pharī bilaṅd maṅgāiosu,
> farmāiś kari multāṇ kao.[67]

> He [Nisuṁbha] took his mighty (*bilaṅd*) bow,
> especially ordered from Multān.

The criterion for Gurū Gobind Singh's choice of words may seem simply to match the sound and fury of the battle. But as we reflect a bit further we find that his choice is governed by a deeper philosophical purpose. For, in the above instance, the adjective for Nisuṁbha's sword ordered all the way from Multān is the Persian *bolaṅd*. A foreign term is aptly used for an object from an almost foreign region. Moreover, Multān in the Gurū's days was an important Sūfī center, and it seems rather natural that in connection with this region the poet adopt Persian terms like *bolaṅd* and *farmāiś*.

Likewise, the poet uses to great aesthetic and meaningful effect a term from the Arabic, *rahimah*. When Durgā emerges victorious over the demons, he applauds her triumph:

> jiṇi ikko rahī kaṅdār kao
> sad rahimati tere vār kao.[68]

> Upon her who single-handed conquered the army of demons
> May a hundred blessings be!

In invoking blessings upon her prowess, the word *rahimati* has been employed by the poet. Coming in between *sad* and *tere vār*, *rahimati* has an immense artistic value. Through it, the whole verse becomes rhythmic, but it also has an intrinsic import. In Ibn 'Arabi's speculation, the basic meaning of the term is "womb," the meaning of "mercy" (or "blessing," as in my translation above) being derivative.[69] *Rahimati* contains intimations of the feminine principle of creation. Gurū Gobind Singh must have been conscious of it for, while the legendary heroine is applauded for the destruction of evil, the Transcendent, the very Principle of creation, is invoked for blessing. Death and life are brought together through the Female. Whether through myth or through Ultimate Reality, the feminine principle is dominant in Gurū Gobind Singh's intuition.

A final artistic device, very distinctive in the Durgā compositions, is the meter chosen by the poet. The meter is a short one called Sirkhaṇḍī Chhaṅd, and it was used for the first time in Punjabi poetry by Gurū Gobind Singh in *Vār Durgā Kī*. A peculiar feature of this meter is the rhyme in the middle of the verse which produces a stairlike momentum. Within the symmetry of the short and rapid meter there is a varied and flexible sound movement. With consummate artistry Gurū Gobind Singh uses this meter, and the words most apt to it and to the theme, to recreate the tempo and excitement of the action. Just as Durgā gallops triumphantly, so do the verses, as in this example:

karaki uṭhī raṇī caṇḍī faujāṅ daikhi kai
dhūhi miānoṅ khaṇḍā, dhāi sāmhaṇe
sabhe bīr saṅghāre, dhūmar naiṇ de
jaṇu lai kaṭṭe āre, darkhat bādīā.[70]

Beholding the host, Caṇḍī in the battlefield thundered.
Pulling out the sword from the sheath,
she dashed towards the demons.
All the warriors of Dhumar Naiṇ were slain,
Like wood sawn by the carpenter
And the tree hewn.

Durgā's passion for challenge, the fierceness of the contest, and the alacrity with which she vanquishes the demons are projected through word images and metrical rhythms of great beauty and power. The pauses in the narrative etch out well-marked climactic patterns. The rhythm and style of the poetry are appropriate to the atmosphere, to the mood the poet wishes to evoke. Each verse, each word, each rhythmic tone is instinct with martial fervor – the *raudra rasa*.

Gurū Gobind Singh adopted such a dynamic art form with the object of inspiring bravery, dispelling cowardice, and infusing the hearts of his people with confidence and courage. The philosophy of art for art's sake is certainly not applicable to Gurū Gobind Singh's recalling of Durgā. In his work we find, rather, the Tolstoyan view that the "infected" artist should transmit his feelings to the reader or spectator or hearer and therewith create a community of people united together with the same feelings.[71] This view seems to be the objective of Gurū Gobind Singh's artistic transmission of the Durgā story. It is significant, however, that from the vast and rich ancient mythology of India it is the feminine figure of Durgā who infects the

Sikh Gurū's imagination! The action of the Female is picked up, and without being curtailed or muted her story is retold. The phenomenon of "remythologizing," which entails the retelling of stories and myths from the past from the female point of view, is put at the heart of the contemporary feminist movement by spokeswomen like Ellen Umansky[72] and Bella Debrida. In Debrida's words, "By discovering our true mythological roots we can demystify, inspirit, remythicize them; we can reclaim the power usurped by patriarchal control; we can begin to fill the overwhelming need for female models of strength and wisdom so lacking in contemporary culture."[73] Such remythologizing seems to govern Gurū Gobind Singh's recalling of Durgā. The tale of the invincible Hindu goddess was retold artistically and powerfully in vivid image and in speedy meter and cadence by the Gurū. The cumulative effect of the visual and the aural poetry was the creation of an inspired and invigorated community of Sikh men and women.

## RELIGIOUS: THE METAPHOR OF THE SWORD IN SIKH RITUALS

Thirdly, Gurū Gobind Singh's recalling of Durgā manifests the feminine dimension in Sikh rituals and ceremonies. In envisioning the Transcendent One, Gurū Gobind Singh introduced a new metaphor, the metaphor of the sword. Being Itself began to be intuited in terms of *kirpān*, *sarabloh*, *kharag*, *bhagautī*, *khaṇḍā*, and *tegh* – all these terms signify the sword. And the sword is the metaphor for Goddess Durgā! Thus in Gurū Gobind Singh's recalling of Durgā is present a metaphor within a metaphor. The metaphor of the sword, specifically, was intended to give a new orientation to the common people, demoralized and debilitated by prolonged subjugation. Passivity had seeped into their blood. They needed a new vocabulary and a new principle of faith. This Gurū Gobind Singh provided by coining the new figure and making it a part of Sikh identity and religious ceremony.

From the time of Gurū Gobind Singh's initiation of the Khālsa (March 30, 1699), both Sikh men and women carry the sword, as one of the five Ks, as one of the five emblems of the Sikh faith each beginning with the letter "k." The *kirpān* or sword may be worn in the form of a tiny symbol studded in a comb and tucked in the hair, or a charm-like image worn on a chain around the neck, or it may be a real sword varying in length and size and slipped into a waist sheath. Sikhs of both genders continue to be baptized with the water churned by a double-edged sword. The Sikh supplicatory prayer called the *ardās* is recited daily by the Sikhs, whether individually or as a congregation, at the end of their morning and evening prayers, and at the beginning and conclusion of any significant undertaking. The *ardās* opens with the words "prathami bhagautī simarkai – having first remembered the sword." "Bhagautī," in the invocatory line in *Bhagautī dī Vār* (*The Ballad of the Sword*) is a variation on the title "Vār Durgā Kī" (*The Ballad of Durgā*) and is followed by the remembrance successively of the ten Gurūs of the Sikh faith – from Gurū Nānak to Gurū Gobind Singh. This portion of Gurū Gobind Singh's composition, with his own name added later, now forms part of the Sikh *ardās*. The words "prathami bhagautī simarkai" are thus part of the living Sikh tradition. Durgā – though in her metaphorical aspect – continues to be recalled to this day and forms a link between the image of the sword and the Transcendent One.

In his act of metaphor-making, Gurū Gobind Singh approaches the Transcendent with a new freedom, a new power that articulates his vision of the Metaphysical One. The function of the metaphor lies in its transformation. As stated by Philip Wheelwright in *Metaphor and Reality*, the test for essential metaphor is not only a rule of grammatical form (i.e. the addition of "as" or "like") but rather the quality of semantic transformation.[74] Metaphor in the Punjabi–Hindi lexicon is *rūpak* – the beautifier, "-fier" indicating that it makes some kind of transmutation. In both eastern and western thought, its undercurrent is motion (*phora*). Marcia Falk describes the metaphor most appropriately: "it bridges and it leaps; it points out likeness even as it affirms difference; it connects without assimilation, without blurring distinction." She cautions us that the empowering quality of metaphor exists only as long as we remember that it is metaphor we are speaking, not literal truth and not fiction: "When a metaphor is treated as though it were literal truth, then it becomes a lie."[75] For her, any dead metaphor makes a strong idol. When the Sikh Gurū addresses the One by any of the several synonyms for the "sword," the One totally beyond is "metamorphosed" into a concrete and invigorating clue towards envisioning the Metaphysical Reality.

In Gurū Gobind Singh's *Akāl Ustati*, the Timeless One is addressed as All-Steel:

akāl purakh kī rachhā ham nai
sarab loh kī rachhiā ham nai.[76]

My only refuge is the Timeless Being (*Akāl*),
My only refuge is the All-Steel (*sarab loh*).

At the opening of his *Bacitra Nāṭak* the sword is addressed as a synonym for the Timeless Being:

namaskār sri kharag ko
karoṅ su hitu citu lāi![77]

Honor to the holy Sword:
I bow to it with love and devotion!

In the invocatory line to *Caṇḍī dī Vār*, Gurū Gobind Singh remembers the Transcendent One by the term *bhagautī* – "prathami bhagautī simarkai." Here the word for the One is *bhagautī*, which could mean both "sword" and "the goddess." We shall soon be exploring the implications of the use of this term.

While being a synonym for the One, the sword in *Vār Durgā Kī* is also conceived as Its generative function:

khaṇḍā prathami manāikai
jin sabh saisār upāiā.[78]

After the primal manifestation of the sword,
the universe was created.

The creation of the universe is thus dependent upon the primal manifestation, that is, of the *khaṇḍā* or the sword. As Eliade would say, the sword is the *axis mundi* which holds the skies vaulted over the earth. Only after the manifestation of the double-edged sword (*khaṇḍā*) did the cosmos come into being. In a couplet in the *Jāpu* Gurū Gobind Singh envisions the Formless One simultaneously as "the wielder of the sword" and the "mother of the cosmos." In his words, "namo sastrapāṇe, namo astramāṇe, namo param giātā, namo lok mātā[79] – I bow to the wielder of the sword, I bow to the owner of arms, I bow to the possessor of ultimate knowledge, I bow to the mother of the cosmos." The creative powers are fused in with the omniscience and omnipotence of the Transcendent One. Whether it be used for the Transcendent Itself (as evidenced in the verses from the *Akāl Ustati*, *Bacitra Nāṭak*, and *Vār Durgā Kī*) or for Its power of generation and sustenance (as in instances from *Vār Durgā Kī* and the *Jāpu*), the sword is a crucial metaphor in the poetic intuition of Gurū Gobind Singh.

In this metaphor-making process, verbal idols from the past – especially male gods and their weapons – are shattered. Weapons are usually associated with male gods – we have the famous images of Lord Śiva with his trident, Lord Viṣṇu with his conch, and so on. Through Gurū Gobind Singh's recalling of Durgā, the sword achieves a feminine identity. In the Sikh tradition, then, the metaphor of the sword maintains a feminine impulse. Marcia Falk suggests that it is not hatchets and concepts and abstract ideas about God's being neither male nor female which break verbal idols, "but new, living metaphors, verbal images possessing powers of transformation."[80] This is the type of vital metaphor and transforming image that Gurū Gobind Singh projects in the sword. It must be observed, however, that the metamorphosis brought about by Gurū Gobind Singh through the sword is in no way a substantial representation of the Reality; it is only a starting point from which the imagination can launch into intuiting the Yonder. A recognition of Gurū Gobind Singh's metaphor of the sword leads us towards a recognition of the female principle.

What is interesting to observe is the particular way in which the sword is identified with Durgā. Several functions, religious in nature, embodied in the goddess, are represented in the sword. It is not by chance, then, that the sword is personified: she is bathed in blood, which is compared to "her descending gracefully like a princess dressed in a crimson sārī – jāṇu rajādī uttarī, painhi sūhī sārhī."[81] It is the poetic genius of Gurū Gobind Singh which can render metaphorically, indeed so richly, the wielder and the instrument as one and the same. In the recalling of Durgā through the term *bhagautī* what was essentially sought by the poet was the remolding of the religious spirit of the people.

In either sense – as goddess or sword – *bhagautī* is the annihilation of negative forces. The geographical battlefield could also be the psyche of the human being wherein contrary forces are at war with each other. The infirmities of the psyche like ego, deceit, and desire are obstacles which hamper knowledge; mental darkness eclipses the knowledge of the Singular Being. The chief demon's massive head and club also stand for opaqueness, violence, and resentment; the demons as a whole are like dark and thunderous, rather ominous clouds – "jaṇu ghaṇīaru kāle"[82] – or like proud roaring clouds – "māno ghor-ghamaṇḍ."[83] But on the other side, Durgā's eyes blaze forth as she sees the army of the demons; the sharp sword dazzles like lightning. "So luminous is the sword that even the sun is overshadowed – laśkani tegāṅ barchhīāṅ sūraj nadari na pāi."[84] Both the goddess and the sword are thus metaphors for the piercing light of intelligence which destroys nescience and the dark brute forces. In the *Markaṇḍeya Purāṇa*, the goddess is directly addressed as the concrete form of knowledge (*buddhīrūpeṇa*), consciousness (*cetnetybhidhīyate*), memory (*smritīrūpeṇa*), and contentment (*tuśṭirūpeṇa*), and Gurū Gobind Singh symbolically reiterates her intellectual and psychological qualities.[85]

In recounting the exploits of Durgā, Gurū Gobind Singh is in fact reminding his Sikhs of the triumph of knowledge over nescience. In minute detail he depicts Durgā's feats – interchangeable with those of her sword. A very vivid instance from the account in *Vār Durgā Kī* is of the sword's attack on the demon Mahikhāsura. "Gulping down kidneys and intestines, she moves on to rip out his lungs and liver – gurde āṅdāṅ khāī nāle rukkaṛe laindī aghāṅ sidhāī phiphar kāljā."[86] Another instance, equally fearsome, is the sword's action against the demon bull: "shattering the skull of the demon and cleaving through his horse's saddle into the earth, she penetrates into the very horns of the bull – kopar cūri cuvāṇī latthī karag lai pākhar turā palāṇī, raṛkī dharti jāi laiṅdī aghāṇ sidhāṇī, siṅgāṅ dhaul diāṅ."[87] One by one, the dreadful armies of the demons headed by Mahikhāsura, Locana, Dhūma, Caṇḍa, Muṇḍa, Nisuṁbha, and Suṁbha are extinguished by Durgā. The Story of the Invincible Sword (*Kahāṇī Tegh Dī*) will be remembered for many, many yugas or time-cycles, says the poet.[88]

Besides being the sharp and penetrating power of intelligence, *bhagautī* is also a symbol for crusade against evil. The *dānava* (devils) have been victorious over the *deva* (gods). The principal god Indra has been exiled from his kingdom, along with the other gods; Mahikhāsura, the chief of the demons, has taken over the realm of the gods with the title "vaḍḍā bīr" ("the Great Warrior"). He sits regally under a canopy, with the rest of the demons prancing around over their victory.[89] In utter dejection Indra comes to Durgā, beseeching her for help. Mahikhāsura, who successively assumes various menacing forms, would uproot righteousness if not checked. The goddess accedes to the request of Indra and the other gods. She is ready to fight against the demons with a view to maintaining the moral balance – upholding good against evil.

The means for the restoration of the gods, as achieved by the goddess, or for the restoration of an ethical order, as envisioned by Gurū Gobind Singh, is the sword. Like the goddess, the sword performs the dual role of preserving the good and demolishing the evil, the negative elements. In his *Bacitra Nāṭak*, Gurū Gobind Singh salutes the sword as the savior of creation: "You who bring fortune to the good, you who terrify the evil . . . I salute you, creator of the world, savior of creation!"[90]

The sword is meant to uphold righteousness, to resist tyranny. The glorification by Gurū Gobind Singh of the sword was to secure the fulfillment of divine justice. For him, "the sword was never a symbol of aggression and it was never used for self-aggrandizement. It stood for righteous and brave action for the preservation of truth and virtue."[91] The sword, like Durgā for the gods, was to be invoked only in self-defense and as a last resort. This point is stressed by Gurū Gobind Singh in his Persian poem *Ẓafar-nāmah*:

> cu kār az hamah hīlate dar guzasht
> halālast burdan ba śamśīr dast.[92]
>
> When the matter is past all other remedy,
> It is but lawful to take up the sword.

Unlike a dagger, which is associated with secret attack or sudden defense, the sword is associated with open combat, governed by certain ethical principles. Thus, *bhagautī* – whether as Durgā riding her lion or as the sword carried by a Sikh citizen, male or female – is the assertion of this right to freedom. To quote a modern Sikh intellectual:

> [the sword] is, by ancient tradition and association, a typical weapon of offense and defense and hence a fundamental right to wear, of the free man [and woman], a sovereign individual. All governments and rulers, whether ancient or modern, have insisted and do insist on their right to control and curtail the right of a citizen to wear arms. Indeed, in final analysis, a government or the State is sustained and supported by the organized might and exclusive right of possession of arms, a citizen's right to wear arms being conceded as only of a permissive and licensed character. It follows from this that, the measure of freedom to possess and wear arms by an individual is the precise measure of his freedom and sovereignty. Since a member of the Khālsa Brotherhood [and Sisterhood] is pledged not to accept any alien restrictions on his [or her] civic freedom, he [or she] is enjoined to insist on, and struggle for, his [or her] unrestricted right to wear and possess arms of offense and defense. This is the third meaning of the symbol [sword].[93]

While on the one hand Gurū Gobind Singh reminds his people of the heroic deeds of *Bhagautī* (Durgā), on the other hand, he enjoins them to carry the *bhagautī* (sword) in their hands – thereby to proclaim their self-esteem and freedom.

After depicting the fearless character of Durgā and recounting her marvelous deeds of valor, Gurū Gobind Singh ends his *Caṇḍī Caritra* with this supplication:

> deh sivā baru mohi ehai subhu karman te kabhūṅ na taroṅ
> na daro ari so jab jāi laro, niscai kari apunī jīt karoṅ
> aru sikhoṅ āpne hī man ko, eh lālac hau gun tau ucaroṅ
> jab āv kī audh nidān banai, ati hī ran mai tab jūjh maroṅ.[94]

> Grant me, O Gracious one, this boon that I may never turn away from doing good deeds.
> I should have no fear of the enemy when I enter the battlefield, and when I return, may I be triumphant.
> Grant me, O Gracious one, this wish that my mind be always greedy to sing Your glory and praise.
> When the moment reaches its finale, may I die fighting in the thick of battle.

Through this supplication, through the protagonist Durgā, Gurū Gobind Singh presents his ideal religious person. Such people should, in the first instance, be moral, making their choices in life strictly by the ethical criterion. They should be prepared to act in behalf of the moral choices they make. They should be ready to act not only for themselves but also for others where injustice and oppression are involved. They should be fearless and launch upon action unfalteringly. They should be convinced of the righteousness of their choice and be optimistic of their success. Moral fervor, moral commitment: these are essential values which enrich the human state. Spiritual quest and action are not disparate or antithetical; they are in fact complementary states. Men and women of action must be men and women of spiritual will. While engaged in action, they should not be oblivious of the Just One. The Name of the One should in fact be ever upon their lips. They should be above the fear of death. Death in a philanthropic cause is posited as the acme of existence – a consummation devoutly to be wished for.

Unfortunately, Gurū Gobind Singh's recalling of Durgā could be misinterpreted as a polytheistic trend and his encouragement of the martial spirit as deviating from Gurū Nānak's vision of universal harmony and the oneness of humanity. It is my contention that

Gurū Gobind Singh does conform to Gurū Nānak's vision. By no means does Gurū Gobind Singh invoke the goddess – on the contrary, *Akāl*, the Timeless One, the Formless One, remains the sole object of his devotion. As we noted, he categorically rejects the worship of deities. Gurū Gobind Singh's could not be a polytheistic view of Reality, for he does not visualize Durgā as an idol from the Hindu pantheon. Even if we look at her name, Durgā etymologically signifies the unfathomable one (*dur*, "difficult," and *gam*, "reach"), which is typical of Gurū Nānak's understanding of Ultimate Reality as totally Transcendent. Her being the single power against the hosts of contrary forces underscores the Sikh belief in the utter singularity of the Transcendent. Like Gurū Nānak, the tenth Sikh Gurū acknowledges the power of the female, for she forges a link between the ideals and rituals of the community. Clearly, she is the subject of his poem and not just its object, a role that women too often play in other stories. Like Gurū Nānak, Gurū Gobind Singh believed in universal harmony and equality. It is, after all, the words of Gurū Gobind Singh that Sikhs recite when they proclaim in the Punjab and abroad that "the singular caste of humanity be recognized – mānas kī jāti sabai ekai pahicānbau."[95] Gurū Gobind Singh perceived the Oneness from Gurū Nānak's thealogical worldview, and his very tone and imagery are reminiscent of those of the first Sikh Gurū. Indeed, we hear Nānak X soliciting humanity "to know the one light – *joti* – pervading all – ek . . . ek hī joti jānabo."[96] Again, like Gurū Nānak, Gurū Gobind Singh worships the Transcendent One as "Mother of the cosmos – namo lok mātā."[97] But when Gurū Gobind Singh found oppression standing in the way of Gurū Nānak's message of equality and harmony, he tried to inspire his people by renarrating and embellishing the valorous stories of the invincible Durgā. Through this *female* figure he urged them to resist oppression and injustice and to be ready to take up the sword in the cause of righteousness and freedom.

Gurū Gobind Singh's message is best summed up in his verse: "jin prem kīo tin hī prabhū pāio – it is those who love who attain the Ultimate."[98] In keeping with Sikh scripture, both love (*prem*) for the cosmos and love for the Transcendent were important to him. Gurū Gobind Singh did not veer away from the ideal of universal peace and love; rather, he crystallized in a definitively feminine metaphor the vision of the Transcendent One that he had inherited from Gurū Nānak.

CHAPTER 5

# *The maiden weaves: garlands of songs and waves*

mere geet,
mere sāiāṅ!
tusāṅ laī gāe gae geet . . .
uṭṭhan taraṅgāṅ sāgaroṅ āē pauṅ vāṅgūṅ.

My songs,
My Beloved!
Songs sung for you . . .
The waves rise like wind from the ocean

I shall now focus on the works of a modern writer – Bhāī Vīr Singh (1872–1957). His writings clearly do not belong in the category of sacred scriptures. Nonetheless, they illumine a later age with insights derived from the holy writ. This is a big leap in time, but the intervening period proffers little creative or philosophical writing of any significance. The turmoil which overtook the Sikhs after the passing away of Gurū Gobind Singh in 1708 at once brought the dominance of heroism and restrained the profusion of learning. Gurū Gobind Singh's own epoch was anything but quiet; yet he had striven to preserve and enrich the literary tradition bequeathed to him by his spiritual predecessors. The elements of disturbance were to rule the day when he was no longer on the scene. It is for this reason that we encounter very little philosophical or scriptural exposition for most of the eighteenth century.

One new genre of Sikh writing which developed during this period was the *rahitnāmā* series. The *rahitnāmās* (from *rahit*, "conduct," and *nāmā*, "manual") were codes regulating Sikh practice and custom. They came to be composed in the name of Sikhs who had been close to Gurū Gobind Singh and were meant to carry the authority of the Gurū himself. They were terse, apophthegmatic, and hortatory in style. Here, the necessity and immediacy of the announcement took precedence over the spiritual and metaphysical nuances of early Sikh writings. Austerity overrode imagination. The moral stipulations for a community under siege could not but be mundane and direct.

Some historical works also emerged during this period. The first among them was *Gurbilās Chhevīṅ Pātshāhī* (AD 1718), which is an account of the life of the sixth Gurū, Gurū Hargobind. That was followed by Koer Singh's *Gurbilās Pātshāhī 10* (AD 1751), the life story of the tenth Gurū; Kesar Singh Chhibaṛ's *Bañsāvalīnāmā* (AD 1769), a genealogical account of the Gurūs and their families; Sarūp Dās Bhallā's *Mahimā Prakāsh* (AD 1776), lives of the ten Gurūs; and Sukkhā Singh's *Gurbilās Dasvīṅ Pātshāhī* (AD 1797), a biography of Gurū Gobind Singh. All these books are in verse, with flashes of poetic imagination and embellishment, but metaphysical or philosophical speculation seldom belong to this class or writing. There is hardly any other work worthy of mention falling within this period.

The more settled period of Sikh rule followed in the Punjab from 1799 to 1849, but these years also failed to produce any important speculative writing. History continued to dominate the world of Sikh writing. Two important works of this period were Ratan Singh Bhaṅgū's *Prācīn Paṅth Prakāsh* (AD 1841), a versified account of the history of the Sikhs from the time of Gurū Nānak to the third quarter of the eighteenth century, and Bhāī Santokh Singh's *magnum opus, Srī Gur Pratāp Sūraj Granth* (AD 1843). This work consisted of the lives of the ten Gurūs and of Gurū Gobind Singh's disciple, Baṅdā Singh Bahādur. It was in verse and abounded in a wealth of detail and poetic imagery. Another important work of this period was again historical, *'Umdat-ut-Tawārīkh*, written in Persian by Sohan Lāl Sūrī. He was the court diarist of the Sikh sovereign, Ranjīt Singh, and his book was a comprehensive story of the Sikhs in five volumes. It included the lives of the ten Gurūs, the early struggles of the Sikhs during the eighteenth century, and biographies of the Sikh rulers, Mahārājā Ranjīt Singh, Mahārājā Kharak Singh, Nau Nihāl Singh, Mahārājā Sher Singh, and Mahārājā Duleep Singh. It ended with the annexation of the Punjab to the British Indian dominions.

Some theological writing appeared during this period in the form of commentaries on the scriptural texts. These works displayed an intellectual disposition that was predominantly Hindu. Rather than accepting the straightforward meaning of the text, they proffered an esoteric interpretation. Two such schools of Sikh scriptural interpretation then were Udāsī and Nirmalā schools, and scholars within these traditions were essentially reared in classical Indian exegesis. They amplified Sikh thought through classical Hindu texts. The works of Anaṅdghana and Bhāī Santokh Singh – representatives of the Udāsī and Nirmalā schools respectively have been carefully researched by Nripinder Singh. His study shows that the Udāsī and Nirmalā exegesis of Sikh scripture was saturated with Upaniṣadic and Purāṇic learning. The style and content of their speculations brought about a reincubation of Hindu ideology in Sikh thinking.[1] For instance, an eminent scholar of that period, Anaṅdghana, commenting upon a line from Gurū Nānak's *Japu* – "Guru īsaru Guru gorakhu barmā Guru pārbatī māī" – construes him to be a follower of the six Hindu deities. Anaṅdghana explains that Gurū Nānak in this verse acknowledges Īśar (Śiva), Gorakh (Viṣṇu), Barmā (Brahmā), Pārbatī (Pārvatī), Mā (Lakśmī), and Ī (Sarasvatī) as his Gurūs.[2] It is ironic that Anaṅdghana would provide such an explanation for the fifth stanza of the *Japu* which opens with a ringing statement of the unicity of the Infinite. The Sikh vision of the Transcendent began to get eclipsed by the Hindu *Zeitgeist*.

The Punjab was the last of the Indian provinces to succumb to British rule. It was also the last to be exposed to western ideas and western education, but when it experienced this modern influence, the Punjab was quick to respond and interact. The first Christian center was established in 1834 at Ludhiānā across the Sikh border. This was under the auspices of the Western Foreign Missionary Society of Philadelphia. After the occupation of the Punjab by the British, missionary activity was extended to cover the newly acquired territory, and it received government patronage. The Christian enterprise also penetrated into spheres of social welfare such as education and medical care. After the famous Wood's Despatch of 1854, the government's policy was directed towards opening schools and colleges and encouraging private initiative by the grant-in-aid system. The effect was twofold. The mutual contact of the two cultural streams encouraged some western scholars to devote themselves to the study of Indian thought and to discover its richness; on the other hand, it initiated among the Indians a new process of literary, social, and cultural resurgence. Christian missionary activity led to a fresh appraisal by the people of their own religious traditions. Three powerful movements of reform and renewal arose in the three major traditions of India – Brahmo Samāj in Hinduism, Aligaṛh in Islam, and Singh Sabhā in Sikhism. The

Brahmo Samāj founded by Rāmmohun Roy in Bengāl in 1828 comprised western-educated intellectuals who wished to create a synthesis of enlightened Hinduism and European liberalism. Founded by Sir Sayyid Ahmad Khān, Aligaṛh initially began as a secondary school patterned after European models in 1875 in India and soon established itself as an influential modernizing movement in Islam.[3]

In Sikhism, the religious doctrines and practices had suffered considerable retrogression during the century preceding the rise of the Singh Sabhā movement. With the establishment of Mahārājā Ranjīt Singh's rule in the Punjab and the elaboration of pomp and ceremony at the royal court, formal ritual and ceremonial were also ushered into the Sikh faith. Brahmanic rites discarded by the Gurūs entered into the Sikh way of life. The loss of political power following the annexation of the Sikh kingdom to British India encouraged conversion to the faith of the new rulers and, oftentimes as a response to that phenomenon, reversion to ceremonial Hinduism. Conversions by Christian missionaries particularly added to the gravity of the identity crisis. The Sikhs, roughly estimated to be about 10 million in Mahārājā Ranjit Singh's Punjab, dwindled to a mere 1,141,848 in the census made in the Punjab in 1868.[4] The Sikhs articulated their apprehensions with a sense of helplessness:

> An English newspaper writes that the Christian faith is making rapid progress and makes the prophecy that within the next twenty-five years, one-third of the Majha area will be Christian. The Malwa area will follow suit. Just as we do not see any Buddhists in the country except in images, in the same fashion the Sikhs, who are now, here and there, visible in turbans and their religious forms like wrist-bangles and swords, will be seen only in pictures and museums. Their own sons and grandsons turning Christians and clad in coats and trousers and sporting toadstool-like caps will go to see them in the museums and say in their pidgin Punjabi: "Look, that is the picture of a Sikh – the tribe that inhabited this country once upon a time."[5]

It was in the face of such a tragic situation that the Singh Sabhā arose. It issued from the deliberations of leading Sikhs of the time such as Thākur Singh Sandhānwāliā, Bābā Sir Khem Singh Bedī, and Kanwar Bikrama Singh of Kapūrthalā, who met in Amritsar in 1873. Less than a year old at that time, Bhāī Vīr Singh eventually became its most ardent exponent and eloquent spokesman. According to Harbans Singh, Bhāī Vīr Singh's central aim was the furtherance of the Singh Sabhā enlightenment: "He was able to comprehend the significance of the Sikh traditions so accurately and interpreted them to his generation so powerfully that Sikhism experienced a much-needed revival."[6]

The Singh Sabhā aimed at recapturing the original message of the Gurūs and recovering and reestablishing Sikh identity. While it looked to the past to revive the original purity of belief, it also looked to the future with a view to leading the community into the modern age.[7] Bhāī Vīr Singh possessed this dual vision of a past and a future and concretized it through his writings. The source of his inspiration was the Sikh faith, and the resurrection of the message of Gurū Nānak was the singular principle of his literary creation. He made simple Punjabi the medium of his writing. Since the time of Gurū Gobind Singh, two hundred years before this, Punjabi had been neglected as a literary language by the Sikhs. Through his study of Sikh scripture, Bhāī Vīr Singh had acquired a deep respect for the Punjabi language. His versatile genius modernized the language and gave a new life to it as a literary medium. He marks the beginning of a renaissance in Sikh culture. His revival of the popular tongue found literary expression in a wide variety of genres, some of which had never before been attempted in Punjabi. His literary production is voluminous, and includes eight collections of poetry, four novels, a play, five biographies, and nine texts that he meticulously annotated and commented upon. Throughout his literary career, he kept up with his journalism and his tractarian writing. Late in his career, he devoted several years unsparingly to the monumental project of writing a formal commentary on the Gurū Granth, which was published posthumously in seven large volumes. Bhāī Vīr Singh's exegesis of the *Japu* in 178 pages is a telling illustration of his erudite scholarship. The verses are analyzed in great depth; allusions and symbols are explained; a glossary of terms is provided; individual words are traced etymologically; extensive references to preceding commentators are included. He also revised the *Gurū Granth Kosh*, a dictionary of the Gurū Granth which explains important terms and allusions in great detail. It provides valuable information on the musical notation adopted for the Gurū Granth as well.[8] In Bhāī Vīr Singh's works we have an authentic renaissance of the spiritual legacy of the Sikh faith. As an interpreter of the Sikh metaphysical and philosophical thought, he served as an outstanding model for his own and later generations. It is with his writings, especially his poetry and the novel, that we shall continue the exploration of our theme.

The female principle dominates Bhāī Vīr Singh's creative vision. When he felt that Gurū Nānak's vision of the Transcendent was becoming blurred amongst the Sikhs as a result of the challenge from Hindu and Christian ideals and values, he created female role-models for his people like Suṅdarī, Rāṇī Rāj Kaur, Satvaṅt Kaur, Subhāgjī, and Sushīl Kaur. These women were paradigms of moral strength, spirituality, boldness, and keen insight for the Sikh psyche, which was now at a low ebb. Through them Bhāī Vīr Singh wanted to remind his people of the revelation of the One mediated through Gurū Nānak and of its implication for society, that is, the oneness of humanity. All of his major novels – *Suṅdarī*, *Bijay Singh*, *Satvaṅt Kaur*, and *Bābā Naudh Singh* – have a female character at the core, be it Suṅdarī or Sushīl Kaur, Satvaṅt Kaur or Subhāgjī. He handles these characters with the utmost delicacy and esteem, and projects through them his cherished worldview.

In his poetry also, Bhāī Vīr Singh identifies himself with the woman character: it may be the widow Rāṇī Rāj Kaur, who is imbued with an intense spiritual longing, or it may be the beautiful maiden in the prime of her youth who asks the fundamental existential question – "Jīvan kī Hai? – What is life?" The identification of the poet with the female and the creation of female protagonists as the paradigms of morality, courage, spirituality, and philosophical quest manifest not only the tenderness of Bhāī Vīr Singh's poetic perception but also his, that is to say, the Sikh, worldview in which women enjoy great esteem. These characters are not abstractions of an "eternal feminine." Each is a living and breathing individual. They are not fairyland characters, but human beings of flesh and blood. Each in her own and separate way is a model worthy of emulation by women as well as by men. The young maiden who weaves painful and lyrical songs in the anthology entitled *Mere Sāiāṅ Jīo* (*O, My Beloved*), the maiden who seeks to comprehend the meaning of life in the composition "Jīvan kī Hai? (What is Life?)" from the anthology *Lahirāṅ de Hār* (*Garlands of Waves*), Suṅdarī, whose name provides the title for the first novel in the Punjabi language, and Rāṇī Rāj Kaur, who ascends from tribulation to beatitude in the epic *Rāṇā Sūrat Singh* – will be the focus of my study. The individual roles of these four women elucidate the

Sikh vision of the Transcendent from the romantic, existential, ethical, and mystical perspectives.

*Mere Sāiāṅ Jīo* (*O, My Beloved*) is an anthology of short poems that Bhāī Vīr Singh brought out at the end of his poetic career. This form of the short poem was an innovation in Punjabi literature and became popular instantly. While ushering new and quicker lyric tunes and measures into Punjabi prosody, the short poem introduced new words and images as well. *Trel Tupke* was Bhāī Vīr Singh's first collection of poems, to be followed at quick intervals by *Lehrāṅ de Hār*, *Bijlīāṅ de Hār*, *Preet Veenā*, and *Kaṅt Mahelī*. An anthology of songs in praise of the Sikh Gurūs was published in 1933 under the title *Kambdī Kalāī* (*The Trembling Wrist*), and *Mere Sāiāṅ Jīo* itself was his last collection of verse. The dominant strand underlying this prodigious output was his use of poetic strategy to evoke, elucidate, and expand the Sikh scriptural message. Poetically Bhāī Vīr Singh grasped the Gurū Granth, making it diaphanous and alive for his readers. He is, to use Emerson's analogy from "The Poet," a glass through which later generations can see the Gurū Granth in all its richness.

### *MERE SĀIĀṄ JĪO*

*Mere Sāiāṅ Jīo* was published in 1957, when Bhāī Vīr Singh was eighty-one years old. But this last specimen of his poetry, in Harbans Singh's words, "had the same morning-dew's distilled beauty, the same deeply-felt longing of the heart and the same sensitive energy of expression as his precious Rubāiyāts or haunting Kashmir poems written in the beginning of the century."[9]

The basic Sikh philosophical concept is elaborated by the heroine of *Mere Sāiāṅ Jīo*. In ardently addressing her Beloved, she is but substantiating the opening statement of the Gurū Granth: *Ikk Oaṅ Kār*. The existence, the Being of the Beloved, is affirmed in her very salutation:

mere geet
mere sāiāṅ!
tusāṅ laī gāe gae geet . . .
uṭṭhan taraṅgāṅ sāgaroṅ āē paun vāṅgūṅ,
chhiṛ paea merā cup galā, boldī bulbul vāṅgūṅ,
hāṅ bāl-gale dīāṅ thibakdīaṅ thibakdīaṅ
tusāṅ – mere sāiāṅ jīo – dī
hazūrī vic![10]

My songs,
My Beloved!
Songs sung for you . . .
The waves rise like wind from the ocean;
My silent voice has now burst forth like the nightingale singing;
Like from a child's throat
May the tremors reach forth.
To your presence,
O, my Beloved!

These are the opening lines of the poem and provide a personal witness to the is-ness (*Kār*) of the Beloved. The expression is imaginative. The woman's silent voice (*cup galā*) now rings like the nightingale's song. The vibrations gushing forth from her heart have been compared to the gusty wind from the ocean on the one hand, and to the tiny tremors in a baby's throat on the other. But where are these sound waves heading towards? "Tusāṅ – mere sāiāṅ jīo – dī hazūrī vic! – To your presence, O, my Beloved!" is the answer. The presence of the Beloved is thus acknowledged and celebrated. The destination may be far – the gusty wind indicates that – but it certainly exists. The woman needs no ontological, cosmological, moral, or teleological proofs: she knows, she feels, and therefore yearns for the presence (*hazūrī*) of her Beloved. She lyrically asserts the scriptural view that the One is present everywhere, a view we find stated by Gurū Nānak, "jah jah dekhā tah tah soi – in whichever direction I turn my eyes, I see You,"[11] and by Gurū Arjan, "Nānak kā pātisāhu disai jāharā – Visibly present everywhere is the lord of Nānak."[12]

The origin of her longing for the Beloved she traces to the Beloved himself: "You are the One who implanted this sapling – tuhoṅ būṭī e lāī sī." In this short poem, the woman states that his single glance of benevolence – *ikk nadar* – breathes new life into her; his single beautiful gesture – *ikk nāz de gamze* – fills her with fragrance:

muśk ikk phir macī
magan surati hu aī sī . . .

An aroma struck the mind again;
Intoxication overtook consciousness . . .[13]

The Beloved is thus the one who created her, sustained her, and awakened her. The aroma, a hint from him – the yonder, formless, intangible, yet powerful and aesthetically pleasing – touches her, and she becomes inebriated with longing for him. Interestingly, the sense of fragrance intoxicates her mentally, dissolving the usual dichotomy of body and mind. Clearly, her desire is not only material in nature but also spiritual. It comes from the depths of her very being. This combination of materiality and spirituality underscores the message of the Gurū Granth: it is the physically attractive woman dressed up in all her finery – with perfumes and jewels – who has the longing for the Divine Groom.

With the vista of the garden as a backdrop, she also makes the philosophical point that the entire universe is dependent upon its singular gardener, her Beloved. In the Gurū Granth, the totally abstract and metaphysical One is also addressed metaphorically as the gardener: "ihu jagu vāṛī merā prabh mālī sadā samāle ko nāhī khālī – the world is the garden; my lord is its gardener; ever he guards it, leaving none without protection."[14] Through his twentieth-century protagonist, Bhāī Vīr Singh is paraphrasing the creating and nurturing functions belonging to the Gardener. Through the course of the brief poem, we hear her repeat several times that he is the one who has implanted the sapling (*būṭī*). For their origin and sustenance, the individual shrub and the garden as a whole depend upon him: "If you forget us even for a moment, how will we remain in bloom or be fragrant?" she asks. The fragrance which the gardener bestows upon the *būṭī* is both her elemental energy and the desire for him; the identity between her *élan vital* and the longing for the Gardener, the Beloved, constitutes the core of the thematic burden of the poem.

Bhāī Vīr Singh is simultaneously highlighting another element from the Sikh worldview: the feminine dimension of the Transcendent One. The One beyond (*Ikk*) is a Gardener – ever caring and nurturing the world. A harmonious and loving relationship between the Creator and creation is postulated.[15] The Beloved (*Oaṅ*) is transcendent – beyond reach and beyond all categorizations. Nowhere are any contours drawn sketching his form or personality. The metaphor of the Beloved is quickly and skillfully moved into the second person, *tūṅ*. Although in our references (and in translation as well) the specification of gender occurs, in Bhāī Vīr Singh's composition itself there is scarcely any. *Sāiāṅ Jīo* is constantly beckoned, grammatically, in the gender-neutral form of the second person – as *tūṅ*, the neuter "you." The Beloved is thus encountered informally, intimately, but without any emphasis upon "Its" form. Therewith, the utter unicity and singularity – the *ikk*-ness of the Sikh ultimate reality – is also projected. In one passage she rhythmically repeats "you, you, you – tūhīṅ, tūhīṅ, tūhīṅ," which but echoes the scriptural style of saluting the *Ikk Oaṅ*. Gurū Arjan's words "tūṅ merā pitā tūṅ hai merā mātā tūṅ merā bandhapu tūṅ merā bhrātā – you are my father, you my mother, you my friend, you my brother,"[16] shatter the monopoly of male symbols in depicting the unicity of the Ultimate Being, and they also express the intimate relationship between one and the One. Again, we find that the "I–Thou" encounter put forth by Buber echoes the Sikh communion between the individual and the Divine.

Instead of creating or employing male images, we hear and see the singer of *Mere Sāiāṅ Jīo* trying to visualize the One – the totally abstract and metaphysical Being – in aesthetic terms. A prominent "form" for the Infinite Beloved comes from the aural sphere. It is rendered through the term *rasa* and its variations. These terms form the very title of the poem "Rasa, Rasīā Rasāl," which ends with the following lines:

> vāh vāh coj tere, mere sāiāṅ
> tere geetāṅ dīāṅ taiṅu vadhāiāṅ
> tūhon geet, saṅgeet, te suād
> ras, rasīā te āp rasāl.[17]
>
> Wondrous, wondrous are your sports, my beloved;
> Congratulations to you on the beauty of your songs;
> The song, the music, and the essential taste are you;
> You yourself are the joy, the enjoyer, and the bringer of joy.

These lines are truly untranslatable, and there can be no adequate version. First the maiden expresses her amazement at the marvelous aspect of the Beloved. She then celebrates the richness and beauty of his songs (*geetāṅ*). In line 3 she goes on to identify her Beloved with the song (*geet*), the music (*saṅgeet*), and the essential taste (*suād*). Finally, she addresses him in a play on the word *rasa*: he is the aesthetic delight (*rasa*), the relisher of aesthetic delight (*rasīā*), and the provider of aesthetic delight (*rasāl*). The Beloved is therefore all-encompassing: he is not only the aesthetic joy but its savorer and bestower as well. He is the primal cause and ultimate end of joy. His Oneness is repeated over and over again. Again, Bhāī Vīr Singh is expanding upon scriptural ideas and vocabulary. Song, music, and tasting were, as we saw, very important factors in the creation of the Gurū Granth itself. The songs that Nānak sang, the songs of which the holy book is composed, had their genesis in the Divine Beloved. The image of the Transcendent as possessor of *rasa* also has its archetype in the Gurū Granth. For, we may recall, our bride addresses her Beloved as "dīn daiālu prītam manmohanu ati rasa lāl saguṛau – compassionate, beneficent, beloved, enticer of the hearts, overflowing with *rasa*, like the *lālā* flower."[18] In fact, the passage quoted above from *Mere Sāiāṅ Jīo* echoes much of Gurū Nanak's terminology and is evocative of his verse in the Gurū Granth: "āpe rasīā āpu rasu āpe rāvanhār – It itself is the relisher of *rasa*, it itself is the essence, it itself is the bestower."[19]

In her perception of the Beloved, Bhāī Vīr Singh's heroine also avails herself of the symbol of light. For instance, she exclaims that one ray of the Beloved, from his luminous form (*nūrī rūp*), enchanted her. The Arabic and Persian term for light (*nūr*) is also used in two other instances to qualify the Transcendent: "Your light pervades the earth and skies"; "I am desirous of the vision of your luminous form." In another verse she implores her transcendent Beloved:

> Bestow your vision upon me,
> Oh radiance of radiance(s).

Here she alludes to him as light of lights or radiance of radiance(s) – *ujjalāṅ de ujjal* – which recalls the perception of Ultimate Reality as *Jyotiśam jyoti* and *Nūr al-anwar* from the Hindu and Islamic traditions, respectively. In the Gurū Granth, as well, "light" in its Sanskrit and Arabic equivalents has been extensively used as a symbol for the Absolute. The following instance in the Gurū Granth comes from Gurū Nānak himself:

> jahi jahi dekhāṅ tahu joti tumhārī
> terā rūp kanehā!
>
> Wheresoever I turn, I see your light;
> What a wondrous form you have![20]

The concept of light and wonderment at the brilliance of this form is reiterated in *Mere Sāiāṅ Jīo*.

The distance from him – underscoring his transcendence – constitutes the core of the intense experience for Bhāī Vīr Singh's heroine. He remains an enchanting paradox: he is infinite; he is infinitesimal! In either fashion, he is totally beyond her grasp. In the poem entitled

"Nikkī God Vic" ("In the Tiny Lap"), she marvels at the all-pervasive Beloved playing in the tiny lap of a rose:

aj nūr de taṛke
jadoṅ lai rahī sīsaver aṅgṛāiāṅ . . .
ikk khiṛé gulāb dī kūlī god vic
tusīṅ kheḍ rahe sāo mere sāiāṅ
kiṅjh, hāṅ kiṅjh! ā gae sao
os nikkī god vic?
mere aiḍhe vaḍhe viśāl sāiāṅ![21]

At the touch of light (*nūr*) today
When the morning was beginning to stir . . .
In the silky lap of a blossomed rose,
You were playing my Beloved.
How, yes, how
Did you enter that tiny lap?
My great and vast Beloved!

The reader is not to infer that her Beloved was literally playing *in* the silky rose! It would be a gross misunderstanding of the poet's intent and message to believe that the Beloved was encapsulated in the rose. The maiden is struck with the sight of the rose in full bloom during the glory of the morning. So overpowering is the scene that she imagines the infinite Beloved playing in the little rose. The Transcendent is never enclosed; It is never *in* the rose as such. That Its infinity and formlessness can never be confined in a finite frame is categorically affirmed in the Gurū Granth: "thāpiā na jāe – It cannot be molded; It cannot be shaped," says Gurū Nānak in the *Japu*.[22]

Similarly, in "Sadke Terī Jādūgarī De" ("Homage to Your Magic Feats"), she states that he is within her:

mere aṅdar, dhur aṅdar, dhur aṅdar de
kise ohle luke mere prītam!
hāṅ,
tuṁbaṅe o apṅiāṅ saṅgeetak tuṁbāṅ nāl
jagā dene o tarbāṅ tārāṅ
aṅdarle dīāṅ
gāoṅdīāṅ han uh geet
– tusāṅ jī de birhe, tusāṅ jī de milan de tarāne –
jo karde han jādūgarī mere hī utte
merī main bir bir takkadī
rahi jāṅī e kaṁbdī te tharrāṅdī

āh prītam
dissan de ohle luke prītam

kol kol par dūr dūr,
dūr dūr par kol kol
sadke terī jādūgarī de[23]

In me, deep inside, deep inside somewhere
is hidden my Beloved!
Yes,
You strike me with your melodious tunes,
Touching
My inner strings.
They sing songs –
Songs of separation from you, songs of the anticipation,
of union with you.
These do cast magic upon me.
I gaze all around.
Trembling, quivering.

Oh Beloved!
Behind sight hidden Beloved!
Very near (*kol kol*), but far far (*dūr dūr*)
Far, far (*dūr dūr*), but near, very near (*kol kol*)
Homage to your miracle!

Paradoxically, closeness to and distance from the Beloved, as well as his infinitesimalness and infinity, are felt deeply by the woman. He is "ure ure par agamo agam – close close, but farther than the farthest." He is so close and so small that he abides in her innermost being. But he is hidden (*ohle*) somewhere. Thus even though he may be very close, very near, he remains inaccessible, totally transcendent. Again, it is clear that he is not enclosed in her; his form is not present within her. Formless, he remains hidden somewhere in her being. Simultaneously, he is infinite and far, far away, and the categories of time and space do not delimit him. In "Dil Saddhar," she proclaims his infinite nature:

agamo agam agam he mere tūṅ pyārnā.

Unfathomable amongst the most unfathomable are you, my Love.

Finally, she accepts the utter ineffability: "Tongue, be silent! Trembling and quivering tongue, be silent! Friends! Nothing can here be uttered." The paradox therefore cannot be verbalized. Silence alone can be the only indicator. Having him so close and yet so far, experiencing his infinitesimalness and infinity together is totally overwhelming and defies articulation in human speech.

What we have here is a poetic exposition of the scriptural dialectic of the transcendence and the proximity of the One (*Ikk*). While maintaining the utter unfathomability and infinity of the Ultimate Reality, the Gurū Granth posits Its presence within everyone:

> tūṅ ādi purakhu aparaṅparu kartā
> terā pāru na pāiā jāi jīu
> tūṅ ghaṭ ghaṭ aṅtari sarab niraṅtari
> sabh mahi rahıa samai jīu.
>
> You the Primal Being, you are the Infinite Creator;
> None can fathom you.
> But within each and every being you are
> Equally, constantly ever.[24]

These words of Gurū Rām Dās (Nānak IV) are reiterated by his successor Gurū Arjan (Nānak V): "tu sabh mahi vartahi āpi – you are present within all."[25] In the *Āratī*, Gurū Nānak exclaims: "sabh mahi joti, joti hai soi – within all is the light and the light is That One."[26] The symbol of the insubstantial and non-material light is used extensively in the Gurū Granth to portray the Transcendent One in all of Its manifestations. In another passage, the Gurū Granth declares Its infinite nature directly: "agam agocaru sacu sāhibu merā – unfathomable, ineffable, truth is my lord."[27] The holy book also contains passages expressing the marvel of the dialectic: "nirgunu āpi sargunu bhī ohi kalā dhāri jini sagalī mohī – formless and yet archetypal, it takes on substances that enchant all."[28] This enchantment felt by the fifth Gurū finds a precedent in the thought of Gurū Nānak: "sahas tav nain nan nain hahi tohi kau sahas tav mūrati nanā ek tohī . . . sahas tav gaṅdh iv calat mohī – you have a thousand eyes, but without eyes you are; you have a thousand forms, but without form you are . . . you have a thousand noses, but without a nose you are; I am left thoroughly enchanted."[29] Through the word "thousand" Gurū Nānak is describing the One in terms of the entire gamut of comprehension. Additionally, he juxtaposes Its immensity and infinity, and thus delineates It as beyond all expression and thought. In line with the concept of the *Ikk Oaṅ Kār* as expounded in the Gurū Granth, the woman's vision renders a very positive and joyous image of the Transcendent. Yet, it is no image, for the aesthetic delight is devoid of all materiality and substantiality; its intangibility and transcendence can never be formalized into a figure. Pure form is the Beloved – but form realized only in experience. Thus, the marvel of the paradoxical nature of the Metaphysical One, which was expressed in the Gurū Granth and in Gurū Nānak's encounter with the Divine (as recorded in the *Purātan Janamsākhī*), is recreated with a sense of wonder and joy in Bhāī Vīr Singh's poetry.

In spite of her expansive imagination and varied idealizations of the Beloved, the heroine of *Mere Sāiāṅ Jīo* retains a remarkable consistency. Whether as light, knowledge, beauty, *rasa* or artist, as innermost or farthest-off, her Beloved is envisioned as formless, transcendent, totally beyond her grasp. Throughout he remains the absolute Source and the acme of beauty, love, and art. In her we thus have a true exponent of *Ikk Oaṅ Kār*, the fundamental Sikh ideal. As noted earlier, even in her most intimate poetry she uses the vocabulary, symbols, and metaphors of the Sikh scriptures. Her very yearning for the Beloved also has its prototype in Gurū Nānak's hymn *Bārah Māh* (discussed in Chapter 3). Bhāī Vīr Singh's work is, in a sense, an exposition of the scriptures, but instead of being aridly intellectualized, it uses the medium of romantic poetry. The concept of the Existence of the One Being is not expounded; it is experienced by our heroine at its very deepest.

In presenting through his poetry the central Sikh concepts enshrined in the Gurū Granth, Bhāī Vīr Singh has succeeded remarkably in emulating the mood and idiom of the Sikh scripture. The anthology of poems *Mere Sāiāṅ Jīo* is saturated with the personal pronoun *tūṅ* – encountered in the Gurū Granth. The vocabulary, metaphors, and symbols of that text – *agam, mālī, rasa, nūr* – occur frequently in his own poems. The very title, *Mere Sāiāṅ Jīo*, seems to be both based upon and in turn unfolding the scriptural verse: "kar kirpā mere sāiṅ – be gracious, my Beloved."

Besides interpreting the fundamental theological concept, Bhāī Vīr Singh's *Mere Sāiāṅ Jīo* also unfolds the essential epistemological ideal enshrined in the Sikh holy text. The basis of Sikh epistemology is that the *Ikk Oaṅ Kār* is not intellectually apprehended or made the object of reasoning, but felt. The One cannot be objectively proved – it cannot be tested out in mathematical equations; rather, it is subjectively recognized. The *Ikk Oaṅ Kār* is not posited as an impossible goal; rather, it becomes an object of ardent quest, of ardent longing to be undertaken by the self to attain supreme knowledge.

In "Sāiāṅ Jīo dī Siān" ("Recognition of the Beloved"), Bhāī Vīr

Singh's protagonist actually refutes those who think that the Metaphysical One is impossible to know. The poem opens with this question:

> e kaun han jo ākhde han:
> "tere sāiāṅ jī siān nahīṅ huṅde?"
>
> Who are they who say:
> "Your Beloved cannot be known?"[30]

After posing this question, she directly addresses her Beloved, saying that those who see, hear, smell, touch, and taste discern him. Again, it is a short poem, but of great artistic and philosophical import. The maiden asserts that "those who have eyes discern him from his overflowing beauty (*dhulh dhulh pai rahī suṅdartā toṅ*), which is reflected from the scenes around (*nazāriāṅ toṅ*) and upon the eyesight (*nazāriāṅ te*)." She continues in the same lyric style: "Those who have ears know him from his melodious word, which reverberates everywhere . . . those who drop their fears know him from his sensation-creating touch." His brimming ambrosial drops fall into the mouths of those who, like the *papīhā* (a mythical love-bird), longingly sing for him. At some auspicious moment these ambrosial drops provide the taste of his existence (*hoṅd*). It is thus a clear announcement about the certain possibility of the apprehension of the Beloved – of the *Ikk Oaṅ Kār*, the Ultimate Reality.

Her emphasis is upon *siān* or recognition, an immediate and exhaustive recovery, a reseeing. The Beloved is here, there, everywhere. The vast and magnificent panoramas, the dulcet symphony echoing throughout the universe – these are hints of Its ontological presence. But it is the human being who has to apprehend that through her or his five senses. The physical senses are thus a crucial channel. The process is not an arduous one; it does not call for asceticism; it does not call for the stifling of the senses. Knowledge too is not of any new theme, nor a garnering of new abstract or scientific facts. On the contrary, the physical senses have to be sharpened and heightened in order for them to recognize the spaceless and timeless Beloved. It is as if Bhāī Vīr Singh were illuminating for the reader and hearer the third stage of the *Japu*, the *Saram Khaṇḍ*: "tithai gharīai surati mati mani budhi – here are sharpened consciousness, wisdom, mind, and discrimination."[31] The heightening of the senses means sharpening the perception so that instead of dull and ordinary sensations one experiences deeply the extraordinary. As Bhāī Vīr Singh's heroine says: "paṅjāṅ de rasiāṅ toṅ rasa uciāṅ nūṅ, hāṅ, lakhā deno ho tusīṅ āp – those who transcend the ordinary seeing, hearing, smelling, touching, and tasting, yes, you yourself reveal yourself unto them."

The process of recognition (*siān*) which underlies the Sikh envisioning of the Transcendent is further elaborated in the poem entitled "Andarle Nain" ("Inner Eyes"). In this poem the maiden throws light upon the phenomenon of insight, which combines physical seeing with knowledge and intelligence; *siān* (recognition) by the individual with *lakhānā* (revelation or showing) from the Beloved. The poem in its entirety may be translated as follows:

Eye – the human eye
Could not see you,
My Beloved!
Darkness has overtaken
Knowledge (*ilmu*) and intelligence (*'aql*).
Yes, the strong light of intellect.
It still cannot see you:
The brilliance is too dazzling.
Do cast a favorable glance (*nazar*),
Do please open the inner eyes,
Which would see you –
Whether it be light, dark or bedazzling,
You, my Beloved! Beloved!
In every place (*har jā*) in every color (*har raṅg*)
  in every direction (*har sū*)
Playing (*kardā khelāṅ*), yet remaining apart (*rahindā asaṅg*).
Handsome, you are the acme of splendor.[32]

It is reiterated that the Beloved is all-pervading. The One is in all space, in every color,[33] and in all directions. That he is not only in light but also in darkness is an interesting perception by the maiden. And he pervades everything. Yet, paradoxically, he always remains apart (*rahindā asaṅg*) from everything. Again, he is not in anything – he plays within each and every thing, but constantly maintains his distance. The Transcendent always remains transcendent.

In the poem "Bithun Pathar" ("Amorphous Stone") it appears that the maiden even gives up her attempt to envision her Beloved. She seems to accept the sheer impossibility of imaging the Formless and Transcendent One. The Beloved cannot be seen! The maiden emerges as a deeply thoughtful character, constantly making smooth and liquid transitions between art and metaphysics. At the opening of the poem, she describes a stone lying on the wayside, amorphous and shapeless. A sculptor chances upon it and perceives in it the form smothered by the unwanted mass of rock. He takes a chisel in one hand, a hammer in the other. Carving and cutting, he takes off the unwanted mass. "Behold, it turned into handsome form – *suhaṇī tasvīr* – that formless piece of stone."

She then compares her own mental state to that of the amorphous stone – in its former shapeless and lifeless condition. Perceiving her Beloved as the artist whose art is full of grace, she wishes that he would chisel away all the unnecessary and extraneous matter, leaving but the imprint of his own picture upon her. She thus asks of her Beloved himself to carve his image upon herself. The chiseling away of the superfluous matter is a symbolic expression of her wish to get rid of material desires and, maybe, of her own ego also, so that the intrinsic, essential image, the beautiful picture of the Beloved, alone would remain. The Transcendent's portrait would breathe life into her present condition. The short poem leaves us with two empowering facts: that our very constitution, our *élan vital*, is the Transcendent Reality; and that the female body, the female form, is fully capable of mirroring the Infinite One. *She* is the one made in the image of the Transcendent Creator.

While maintaining her inability to conceive an image of the Beloved and therefore imploring him to imprint his image on her mind, she simultaneously sees him as the supreme artist. "Bithun Pathar" ends with these words:

> My Beloved, you are an artist;
> Your art is full of grace.
> Give me the power to understand this;
> Do rip off the surrounding veil of ignorance.

The Beloved, then, is an artist, but one whose art is full of grace – *mehar bharpūr*. Loving and nurturing aspects of the singular formless Artist are clearly identified.

The image of God as artist is well known. But in our maiden's articulation, the emphasis is on his grace. Human knowledge and intelligence are deficient; the physical eye is precluded from discerning It. But a favorable glance (*nazar*) from the Other would open the inner eye and thus provide insight into the Divine Reality. It is, then, the inner eye which perceives the omnipresent Being. This is the fourth stage of spiritual ascension as delineated by Gurū Nānak in the *Japu – Karam Khaṇḍ*, the Realm of Grace. Grace (*nadari*), i.e. his glance (*nazar*) of favor, is what the maiden seeks. Touched by his grace, her inner eye would encounter the bedazzling brilliance. The merging of eyesight with insight brings about this juncture where human effort is touched by divine grace. It is also the moment of revelation.

Central to Sikh epistemology is the vision of the *Ikk Oaṅ* as a perennial movement. As originally experienced by Gurū Nānak and as illustrated by the heroine of *Mere Sāiāṅ Jīo*, it remains the objective, the goal for every man and woman. The longing for the vision of the Beloved, a mystic consummation between one and the One, is the dominant motif of this anthology of poems; yet the longing remains sheer longing. The finale of *Mere Sāiāṅ Jīo* is the poem called "Nām Piālā" ("The Cup of Nam or Word"):

> The cup of the beautiful Word
> Is overflowing, O friends.
> Who will have a sip of it?
> Keep watching, O friends.
> She whose own cup of longing is brimming,
> She alone will receive the cup of nectar . . .[34]

The poem recalls the historical moment portrayed in the *Purātan Janamsākhī* – the moment of Gurū Nanak's mystic experience some five hundred years earlier.[35] That is when he received the ambrosial cup of the Divine Name and was launched on his mission. Bhāī Vīr Singh's interpretation of that event through the medium of twentieth-century Punjabi poetry acknowledges that primal moment in Sikh history and projects its application towards the present and future. In "Nām Piālā," the heroine is addressing her female friends. The future of society depends upon them and their male counterparts. Interestingly, the female (*sakhī*) is the generic term, inclusive of men. Their mission will get launched with the drinking of the ambrosial Word. But who gets to have a sip of it? Who savors it? Paradoxically, it is the individual whose cup brims (*dhulh dhulh pai rihā hovai*) with longing (*saddhar*) who stands to gain! For the emptier the inside, the stronger the urge; and, hence, the greater the chance of receiving the divine nectar. Bachelard's prayer for "hunger" is implicit here.

Thus we see the solitary maiden and we hear her. She weaves garlands of songs and waves. Naomi Goldenberg, modern feminist writer, observes that the image of a woman weaving is a positive one:

A woman who weaves is concentrating on changing natural materials into something useful for civilized life. She is skilled at a craft, which she has studied to the point of its becoming second nature. When she weaves, she uses this skill to bring something she alone can visualize psychically – like the shape of a basket or the design in a tapestry – into a material form which everyone else can see and use in their world.[36]

The image of weaving portrays, we could add, the woman's meditative and reflective proclivities. Bhāī Vīr Singh's maiden weaving garlands of songs and waves is certainly highly skilled in her art, for her words are so natural and intrinsically so powerful. The garlands – "like the shape of a basket or the design in a tapestry" – are visualized psychically by her and presented to the reader.

What is finally woven by the maiden are polarities, polarities such as proximity and distance, infinitesimal and infinite, human and divine, male and female, past and future, empty and full. The heroine of *Mere Sāiāṅ Jīo* weaves garlands of songs for her Beloved, who, though close by, remains constantly far away. The *Ikk Oaṅ* is felt intimately by her – within her very self. Yet That One, transcendent, remains ever transcendent. Through the maiden's songs one realizes that distance and proximity in the Sikh tradition do not violate each other; instead of being mutually exclusive they enhance each other. The Unfathomable Infinite Beloved is "seen" by her in the dew-drop shimmering on the silky lap of a rose at the break of dawn. The shimmering minuscule droplet presents the indescribable vastness. Human language explodes and participates in the communication with the Divine, for how else would there be garlands of waves? Fearlessly, the maiden expresses the emotion of love delineated in the Gurū Granth and in spite of the chasm that lies between them she weaves together the human and divine realms.

Bhāī Vīr Singh's heroine has the power, the skill, and the sensitivity to work on this cosmic loom. Like the bride figure in the Gurū Granth, she restates the primacy of the feminine consciousness in the search for the Transcendent One. Through her, the crucial moment in Sikh history – the experience of the "Primal Paradox" by Gurū Nānak – is thrust into the future. And the emptier the cup of longing for a vision of the *Ikk Oaṅ*, the fuller will be the experience of union.

CHAPTER 6

# *The woman asks: "What is life?"*

kī hai, te e kioṅ hai sārā
peṭa tānā taniā?

What is it? And why is it all?
For what purpose is all this warp and woof woven?

Written in 1922, "Jīvan kī Hai" ("What is Life?") is one of Bhāī Vīr Singh's earlier poems. The young woman with this existential inquiry is the sole human figure in the composition. Magnificent scenes of nature form the backdrop. In fact, her question is put to the transparent waters of the lake. So vivid are the descriptions – both of the nature around and of the woman's psychological state – that the reader seems to be present with her during her five visits to the lakeside. Her first visit is during a bright moonlit night, the second at the break of dawn, the third as the sun is setting on the horizon, the fourth at crisp midday, and the fifth on a dark and rainy day. Through this sequence, a journey is made from intense anguish to supreme joy. Basically this journey revolves around her perception of the Transcendent One, and it could be interpreted as a statement of Sikh existentialism.

Now we do not often come across the terms "Sikh" and "existentialism" together. How could they relate to each other? Are they not in fact apart from each other, as if they belonged to two different realms? The difficulty is compounded by the fact that "existentialism" is not easy to define: "Like the unicorn, whom legend endows with wondrous attributes, but whom the empirical eye has never calibrated, existentialism is a kind of poetry of the philosophical imagination, defying rational systematization."[1] Furthermore, the term has been coined by the western mind: would the reflections of Kierkegaard, Heidegger, and Sartre have meaning for an Indian religious faith such as Sikhism?

The fact is that religion in its intrinsic core is existential. Some years ago the illustrious historian of religions Wilfred Cantwell Smith, in his book *The Meaning and End of Religion*, rejected the term "religion." He said that it is "notoriously difficult to define. It is a distorted concept not really corresponding to anything definite or distinctive in the objective world . . . religion is confusing, unnecessary and distorting."[2] Smith's point is that a systematization and reification of religion (as in Christian-ity, Hindu-ism, Sikh-ism . . .) takes it away from the locus of religious truth which lies in persons – Christians, Hindus, Sikhs. For example, Christianity is not true absolutely, impersonally, statically; "it becomes true as we take it off from the shelf and personalize it, in dynamic and actual existence."[3] As in existentialism, systematization is to be denounced; the human being becomes the central protagonist. It is from this point of view that we discern an existential perspective in the Sikh religion.

In fact, among the various religious traditions, Sikhism provides a striking instance of urgently addressing the human condition. The Sikh religion originated with Gurū Nānak in a region which, as we have seen, was religiously a very rich area, with Hindus and Muslims particularly engaging in mutual commerce. But Gurū Nānak did not accept any of the existing worldviews: "Neither the Veda nor the Qateb know the mystery."[4] Not conforming to any of the prevailing opinions, he set out to investigate for himself the reality and meaning of existence. Because of the simplicity of both the content and style of his teachings, people started to follow him, seeking enlightenment for themselves. The individual search and inner wrestling thus lie at the very root of the Sikh religion. The Sikh maxim "Truth is higher than everything else, but higher than Truth is true living" stresses the priority of human existence over metaphysical abstraction. That existential truth is more important than propositional or absolute Truth forms the core of the Gurū Granth teaching. Like all of Bhāī Vīr Singh's vast literary productions, *Jīvan kī Hai* fully and authentically reiterates Sikh ideals and values. The young heroine of this poem ardently wrestles with the whole issue of existence, and her transformation from one human condition to another forms its central theme.

It is interesting to observe that the Sikh author does not assign to her any social or religious category, or indeed any other category for that matter. He perceives her as a human individual, which is the essential category for existential philosophy. The existentialist nature of the Sikh religion is embodied in the first words pronounced by Gurū Nānak after his mystical encounter with the Divine: "There is no Hindu; there is no Musalmān." The human being exists essentially, authentically as a human being, not as a Hindu or a Muslim, a Christian or a Buddhist. This message forms the basis of Sikh philosophy. In a society structured on a four-tier hierarchy with caste as the final determinant of one's role and destiny, this was a radical message. It was Gurū Nānak's way of proclaiming the validity of human existence as such. The woman in Bhāī Vīr Singh's poem stands in her own right as a woman, a unique and vital being. Thus does the poet come face to face with her fundamental identity.

We can discern yet another link between existentialism and the Sikh religion. Gurū Nānak and his successors all used the poetic technique to convey their philosophical reflections. The Gurū Granth contains no dogma; no societal code is prescribed. Without any resolutions, with only intimations, Sikh thought has felt itself at home in poetry. The poetic text then is the *Gurū* – the enlightener. What Edith Kern says about existentialism applies to Sikh writings as well: "Because of its intense 'inwardness' and the 'commitment' of its proponents, it has expressed itself more strikingly in imaginative writing than in theoretical issues."[5] As in much of existential literature, the Gurū Granth and later Bhāī Vīr Singh, who imaginatively interprets the Sikh sacred text, make the human being the central protagonist, his or her individuality the focus of the drama, the journey inward – a probing of the layers of the self – the main action, and reaching into the innermost core of the self its finale. Indeed, the Sikh scripture overall and Bhāī Vīr Singh's *Jīvan kī Hai* in particular are "a kind of poetry of the philosophical imagination, defying rational systematization." Both in content and in style, the poem constitutes a significant articulation of the existential affirmation in the Sikh religion.

In the context of the present work, this poem elaborates both the intrinsic meaning of the vision of the Transcendent in the Sikh worldview and the importance of the feminine in the envisioning of the Transcendent. The poem basically records the woman's journey from ignorance of the Being of the Transcendent to an intimation of Its Being, and finally, to the absolute certainty of Its Being. She exemplifies for us that the vision of the Transcendent is not simply a concept or an ideal in the abstract; rather, it is an experience that is experienced here and now – very much in our human situation.

What is most illuminating is the fact that in this Sikh depiction, it is not a male sage or a prophet or even a male voice, but a young fully embodied female who both *quest*-ions and envisions the Transcendent. The usual preeminence of the male is reversed here. The Absolute Reality is sought through *her* struggle and anguish; Its disclosure is celebrated through *her* joy and bliss.

The poem opens with the woman walking softly one evening to a lake. She is young and beautiful and tall like a reed. Her eyes are dark and deep and melancholic. The specific spot visited by the lady is a lake "as white and luminous as a ball of mercury."[6] At the lake, she beholds a "wondrous sight – *ajab dikhāvā*." The fullness and luxuriance of the scene are portrayed exquisitely by the poet. The lake is full to the brim; little waves play upon it as the gentle breeze fondles them. The moon, "browsing in the skies," peeps into the water, which in turn rises up to embrace it. While one moon radiates its beauty in the skies, the other shines resplendently in the lake, swinging back and forth tenderly. The stars hang like lamps in the blue celestial expanse, but they reappear – as though swimming – in the blue waters. This double luminosity with the celestial reflected in the terrestrial, this overpowering sight, projects the cosmological expansiveness of the lake. It leaps towards the skies; it extends into the unknown depths below. The reader is thus introduced to the woman in this very harmonious and picturesque setting. But she is not a part of it. She is standing out (*ex sistens*) from the surroundings, existentially alienated from everything around her. There is something unique about her. She is, as we know, alone – away from her family and friends and society – but juxtaposed to the myriad forms of nature around her. In this situation, her solitariness becomes even more conspicuous. Whereas nature is at peace with itself, the young woman is in the throes of a deep emotion: she is in Angst. She is fully aware of the difference between her mode of being and that of her environment. Of the lake she inquires, "kioṅ santuśt, rajiā, rāzī bin hasrat dis āveṅ? – Why serene, content, and at harmony and without any apprehensions do you appear?" She pleads with it, "Give me first the answer to the meaning of existence, then laugh." Her tears drip against the gleefully rippling waters. In these perfect surroundings she seems to feel uneasy, not at all at home. Unable to tranquilize herself and escape the radicalness of her human condition, she painfully questions:

"I exist" I know, "I exist,"
Yes I know that.
But this "existence" (*jīvan*) – what is its objective?
What is its meaning (*mainā*)?
Millions like me have seen it and departed,
None comprehending *why* they came to be.
None grasped the source,
Without understanding, they passed away . . .

Here she is restating the question of being, and we may recall that at the outset of *Being and Time*, Heidegger underscores the necessity for looking the question in the face.[7] She knows she exists spatially and temporally, but wants to know what lies beyond that. The contradiction of human life is presented here poignantly: the human being is of *this* world, in *this* time and space and yet aspires for the other, the Transcendent! Limited, the human seeks freedom. The contrast between her and Bhāī Vīr Singh's heroine of *Mere Sāiāṅ Jīo* is obvious. Whereas the heroine of *Mere Sāiāṅ Jīo* knows the Metaphysical One, her Beloved, and yearns in agony for a vision of him, the woman here is in anguish because she does not know THAT. She lives without the knowledge of the Transcendent. *Ikk Oaṅ Kār* has not yet been recognized by her. As a consequence, she feels split from her environment, even from her own self. The meaning, the fundamental *isness* of it all – whether of the world around or of her own self – eludes her. Somehow, the wondrous lake incites something in her, for she begins to inquire the source and purpose of "existence" itself.

In her ardent inquiries, our protagonist even addresses her life as *aṛīe* or *sakhī* (denoting a close female friend) to get an answer. Such terms are indicative of her split and division from her own being. Over and over again, she asks of the "other" "*what* are you," "*who* are you?"

Tell life, what are you, my dear friend (*aṛīe*)?
A bundle of emotions? . . .
Tell me, who are you? What are you, my friend (*sakhīe*)?
Now don't run away without giving the answer . . .
You sit behind veils (*purdeh vic*).
Do reveal a bit of yourself . . .

She has a keen desire to know the being of her existence. In a way she "knows"; she lives, but what the significance of it all is, what its real meaning is, is beyond her grasp. Her life is a contradiction. Self-evident, it is still 'veiled in darkness – purdeh vic," as she says.

Later in the poem, we hear her alluding to Hindu and Buddhist views of the self:

> What is this life? Tell me . . .
> Is life this round circle?
> Should I know it simply as one flash? . . .
> Where did you all come from? Why?
> What did you come for?

The image of roundness is reminiscent of the Hindu theory of life and death; the "one flash" of Buddha's first noble truth which states that all life is in motion and flux. Our woman seems to encounter an array of philosophical choices, but continues to wrestle without accepting any.

The fact that she comes out alone and comes face to face with herself on the lakeside reveals her Angst and therewith her "authentic existence." Angst is put at the center of things by Heidegger because the meaning of the human being – its whole structure – is grasped through anguish. "Real anxiety is rare," says Heidegger,[8] but Bhāī Vīr Singh's heroine is engulfed by it. The philosophic exposition of Angst in *Being and Time* is applicable to her. She actually lives it. In real anxiety, the individual is threatened but does not see any definite "here" or "yonder" from where it comes.

> That in the face of which one has anxiety is characterized by the fact that what threatens is *nowhere*. Anxiety "does not know" what that in the face of which it is anxious is . . . that which threatens . . . it is already "there," and yet nowhere; it is so close that it is oppressive and stifles one's breath, and yet it is nowhere.[9]

This is precisely the situation in which the woman finds herself: she is anxious without being threatened by anything in particular, from any particular direction, or at any definite time. She just does not know what that is in face of which she feels so filled with anxiety. It is not this or that particular thing but rather the world, or being-in-the world. And indeed the threat is so close that she feels extremely oppressed and stifled; her "heavy breathing – garam garam sāh" is indicative of her state of suffocation.

Heidegger goes on to say that "only because Dasein is anxious in the very depth of its Being, does it become possible for anxiety to be elicited physiologically."[10] So intense is the woman's Angst that it is visibly reflected in her person. It is physiologically elicited not only in her heavy breathing, but also through her complexion and through her movements and gestures. Her face is pale, "deep yellow like the egg yolk – cehere chhāī zardī."

> She falters at every step,
> She glances up and down,
> Forward and backward she rolls her eyes,
> And suddenly stands still, shutting them.
> One moment her whole self is lost in thought,
> The next she abruptly opens her eyes;
> From her dark and deep eyes,
> *Chhamān̄ chham*! water gushes forth . . .

The sound of anklets – *chhamān̄ chham* – has been used poetically to denote the trickling of tears from her eyes. The emphasis on eyes – their beauty, their depth, their darkness, their shutting and sudden opening – illustrates that she is looking for something desperately in all directions; her abrupt actions and fainting are reflexes of it.

In this state of utter dejection and forlornness, she hears a melodious voice coming from across the waves:

> phir ānā, phir ānā ānā
> ānā ānā ānā
> phirjī phirjī phir phir phir
> phir ānā phir ānā.

The repetition of just two words – *phir* ("again") and *ānā* ("come") – flowing in the above rhythm has a mesmerizing effect upon her. She is for the moment somewhat assuaged, and she returns home. The source of these enchanting words is described by the poet "as if it were an *apsarā's*." *Apsarās* are in the Indian world feminine angelic beings. Our agonized heroine is thus presented not only against the backdrop of joyous nature but also against the rapturous divine beauty. Neither nature nor the Divine appears to suffer from any anxiety. It is then her peculiar constitution as "human" that makes our heroine subject to Angst.

Thus through the young woman Bhāī Vīr Singh artistically states the positive role assigned to anxiety in the Sikh worldview. According to Gurū Nānak, a life lived inauthentically is a life lived in utter oblivion. Tension and dynamism as qualities of human existence are a theme running throughout Sikh scripture: "dukh dārū sukh rogu bhaiyā – suffering is medicine; contentment is disease." In another verse Gurū Nānak says:

> raini gavāī soi kai divasu gavāiā khāi
> hīre jaisā janamu hai kauḍī badale jāi.[11]
>
> Night is lost to sleep, day to eating;
> This life (*janamu*) worth a diamond for a farthing goes.

Life is not merely biological or quantitative. What is cherished in the Sikh tradition is the intensity of life. Living in apathy, simply sleeping and eating, would be an inauthentic mode of existence, and our heroine in that instance would have stayed at home, fully immersed in everyday being-in-the-world and being-with-others, and we certainly would not have been introduced to her in this pain-ridden solitary situation of hers. The young woman finds little satisfaction in the pleasures of the world; she is allured by none of them:

> The usual eating and drinking she enjoys not;
> No flavour (*suād*) is attractive;
> Nothing visible (*disdā*) is enchanting . . .

With her unique psychological make-up, she experiences anxiety in solitude, and through her emerges the Sikh view that anxiety is propaedeutic to realization. To endure anxiety is to have one's eye opened to the reality of the human condition, as Gurū Nānak says:

> They have called the physician to try his physic
> And he grips the wrist and searches it for ailment.
> Little does the naive physician know
> That the ache is in the heart.[12]

The mood of Angst leads the woman to a very significant disclosure.

At this point, however, Heidegger and our young woman, I would say, move apart. For, in *Being and Time*, Heidegger states, "Being anxious discloses, primordially and directly, the world as world."[13] For Heidegger, then, the world is finite, with death as its utmost possibility. The maiden by the lakeside, on the contrary, comes to realize in this second phase that the world holds infinite possibilities. The world is pregnant with richness and mystery – just like the brimming and shimmering lake. Nowhere is nature denigrated. We observe, throughout the psychological passage, the intimate relationship of the protagonist with her environment. At the outset, the young woman feels estranged, at times, even jealous of the calm surroundings, but never superior to them. This is the secret unveiled to her. In a way, "the world as world" becomes in her experience "the world more than world." That the disclosure has an impact on her psychological state can be inferred from her outburst: "ṭhanḍ paī taiṅ dekh rūp nūṅ! – seeing you I feel cooled!" This happens during her second visit to the lake early one morning. The disk of the sun has not yet emerged on the horizon and the redness has not broken out in the skies. There is no sign of the birds. This is the moment before dawn, called *amrit velā* in Sikh terminology. This is the time of day most conducive to reflection. It is also the time when the *Japu*, the composition with which the Gurū Granth opens, is recited by the Sikhs. At this ambrosial hour our heroine walks over to the lakeside. What she perceives are circular and rather dark leaves caressing the waters of the lake. On many of these, pearl-like droplets glisten. These drops of water tremble and then delicately sliding settle upon the olive-colored leaves. "They sparkled like longing eyes – nain jiveṅ koī sikde." As the dawn breaks, whiteness embraces the entire lake, and she beholds the inebriating freshness of this scene.

A series of questions is directed at these lotus leaves fondling the shimmering drops. Last time there was no sign of them; now they are luxuriantly spread out. As they come to light suddenly at daybreak, they stir the mind of the woman with the fundamental issue of existence. *Where* did they come from? *Why? What for?* Their round form makes her reflect upon the circularity of life. Is life a circle? Does "life" keep coming and going and returning forever? Or, like the bright droplets resting on the leaves, is it transitory and ephemeral? "Is it merely a flash, a single flash – nirī ḍhalak ikk jānā?" During her next two visits, she sees the lotus leaves grow. On her third visit, the leaves come up higher, and by the fourth, they are laden with buds. Each time she repeats her question seriously and passionately.

Prior to her fifth and final visit to the lake, the woman makes a stopover under an old and huge *boṛh* tree. It is dark and cloudy. The weather is hot and humid. The air is stuffy. She sits down to rest. Immediately a sweet drowsiness overtakes her and she falls sound asleep in the very position in which she had sat down. Soon, there is a thunderstorm. Stuffiness gives way to a buoyant breeze, darkness to light. The breeze becomes very cool, auspicious; it seemed as if it had on its way down from the Himalayan peaks sensuously touched a glacier. The woman's eye suddenly opens up – "khulī acānak akkh nārī dī," and she begins to wonder at the miracle that happened during that short spell:

> is akkh-mīṭe de hai aṅdar
> kī kautak vartāe?
>
> Within this blink of an eye,
> What wonders have taken place?

The coolness of the atmosphere seeps into her inner being. She finds the heaviness in her chest also lightening. Her feet at this moment begin to move towards the lake. Most delicate, suspenseful, is Bhāī Vīr Singh's evocation of the scene.

Reaching the lake, she witnesses a wondrous spectacle – the buds have bloomed. The lake is totally concealed: innumerable lotuses in a variety of hues blanket it from one end to the other. Such is the intricacy of their designs and the radiance of their colors that it seems "as if nature had herself set up an enamelware bazaar – mīnā laggā bazaar kudaratī." Each is in the pattern of a sliced bowl; like beautiful eyes they appear. According to the woman, these "beautiful eyes" (*nain jiveṅ koī suhaṇe*) are fixed on the luminous sun:

> karan dīdāre, caran sarūrā
> jhūm jhūm rasa laiṅde.
>
> Seeing, getting crimson,
> Rhythmically and joyously they swing.

The lotuses thus gaze at the sun sucking in its joy. Not only do they become bright red seeing the sun (their getting red suggests their healthy nourishment), but they also get inebriated. This description could be read as an artistic extension of Gurū Nānak's verse: "sarvari kamalu kirani ākāsī bigsai sahaji subhāī – in the lake is lotus, sun-ray in the skies, [yet] it blossoms forth instantly, so naturally."[14] The major elements from Gurū Nānak's verse have been recaptured by the modern poet – the non-material distance between the lotuses and the sun, the vision of brilliancy, the ensuing blossoming forth and therewith the intimate relation between seeing and existing or blooming.

Savoring the vision, "the lotuses swing to and fro ecstatically – jhūm jhūm rasa laiṅde." The repetition of *jhūm jhūm*, referring to their rapturous movement, provides a handsome rhythm for the poem. But even more importantly, it highlights their symbolic significance: swinging lotuses are carefree, non-attached, happy. Their freedom is further expressed:

> āshak te māshūk āp ho
> khūdi hȧndole jhūlan.
>
> Lover and beloved they themselves are:
> By themselves they joyfully sway.

The lotuses are themselves the beloved and the lover. They thus exist as the quintessence of non-attachment and self-contentment. The sight is too overwhelming for the visitor. While her gaze is still fixed on the lotuses, as theirs is on the sun, she faints. For a while she loses all consciousness. Her eyes, however, remain wide open:

> kheṛā arshī raṅgāṅ vālā
> vic kāljē aṛiā
>
> The joy of celestial colors
> Gets imprinted on the heart.

In this state of unconsciousness, the eyesight itself imprints splendid motifs upon her mind. This imprinting is a momentous transformation: "her doubting intellect melts away – aqal saṅsiāṅ vālī ruṛ gaī"; "the questioning fever which plagued her vanishes – puchhan tāb nasāī." No trace is left of doubt or hesitancy. From the sight of the blossomed lotuses, the maiden gets an insight into certitude:

> jioṅ khiṛiā sī sarvar sārā
> dil-nārī khiṛ āiā.
>
> Just as the whole lake blossomed,
> The heart of the woman (*dil-nārī*) blossomed forth, too.

The former Angst has disappeared; hope and expectancy have finally bloomed. This ultimate state that our heroine experiences is summed up in the following stanza:

> kheṛā te āpā ikk hoe
> lūṅ lūṅ gaī paroī.
> kheṛā dil dā, kheṛā tan dā,
> kheṛā sarvar vālā,
> sabh kheṛā ikk rūp ho gae,
> kheṛā bhanīāṅ pālān.
> heṭhāṅ uppar cār cuphere,
> kī aṅdar kī bāhar,
> kheṛā kheṛā hoī sārī
> kī bātan kī zāhir . . .

The blossom and herself became one;
Each and every pore was beaded together.
Blossom of the heart, blossom of the body,
Blossom of the lake,
All the blossoms became One form,
The blossom broke all barriers.
Below, above, all four directions,
All inside, all outside,
All became a blossom.
Who could say what is hidden?
Who could say what is revealed?

This crucial passage marks the high point of the maiden's enlightenment. She has awoken from her "slumber"; she has regained her consciousness, a consciousness that is a sequel to a spell of unconsciousness. And, finally, she has the answer to her question. "What is life?" – it is a blossom, a joy! But this recognition requires further amplification.

As the first line states, in this blossom (*kheṛā*), there is a loss of individuality. *Kheṛā* and *āpā* (selfhood) become *ikk* (one). The ground of her individuality is *haumai* (ego). *Haumai* in Sikh scripture is conceived as a veil (*purdah*) which obstructs insight into Reality, as Gurū Arjan (Nānak V) explains in the following lines:

aṅtari alakhu na jaī lakhiā
vic puṛdā haumai pāī.[15]

The Unfathomable within is not fathomed,
The veil of ego separates the two.

During all her former visits, there has been a "veil" hindering her from seeing into the transparent lake. In Sikh existentialism, *haumai* is also regarded as a disease (*rogu*), a point made by Gurū Rām Dās (Nānak IV):

haumai rogu gaiā
  dukkhu lāthā[16]

When the disease (*rogu*) of *haumai* goes,
  suffering ends.

We may recall that during her second visit to the lake, the maiden envies the lake for appearing without disease (*rogu*). Bhāī Vīr Singh's usage of the term may have been a coincidence; nonetheless, there is in his composition the reiteration of the Sikh existential tenet that "ego" or "*me*-ness" is the root of all suffering. When the maiden loses her sense of duality and becomes one with the abundant lotuses, her doubting, her suffering ends. Her high running "fever" – i.e. her barrage of questions – ceases. No longer does she stand by the lakeside wondering about or questioning the other*s* – the lake, the skies, the myriad stars, the sun, the moon, or their reflections. Those dualities and polarities have now disappeared. Those separate "existences" are not seen anymore. There is no other half of her left. The friend whom she addressed as *aṛīe* and *sakhīe* has vanished. "Each and every pore was beaded together!" Bhāī Vīr Singh's poetic genius is here at its zenith. The spiritual wholeness has its manifestation in the material body: the boundaries of millions of pores are erased. The woman's body becomes a unity, and this unity is a blossom – the blossom of the heart, the blossom of the body, and the blossom of the lake become "One form – Ikk rūp." Plurality (the different blossoms – that of the heart, body, and the lotuses) becomes singularity. This experience of the woman's loss of individuality and the gain of "oneness" is a superb exemplification of Gurū Nānak's principle:

> sarab jīā mahi eko jāṇai
> tā haumai kahai na koī.[17]
>
> Recognizing oneness in all beings,
> "me" is no longer uttered.

Gone is the "me" who doubted and suspected:

> kithe hai uh puchhan vālī?
> kī? eh jīvan kī hai?
> kheṛe kheṛ laī hai sārī . . .
>
> Where is she who questioned?
> She who questioned about *what*, about what is life?
> The blossom has blossomed her in entirety . . .

Only *a* blossom – *a* joy – pervades. In this "oneness" there are no circumferences. As we know, the woman used to see the myriads of round leaves and wonder about the circularity of life. But the "blossom broke all barriers." The breaking (*bhanīān*) of barriers (*pālān*) is the process of transformation whereby she obtains an insight into transcendence. A variety of concrete images come in a speedy meter and cadence to render this phenomenon. For example, there is an allusion to the torrent of joy which accompanies the drinking of *soma*, the divine intoxicant. "It springs up like *soma* – aṅdar phuṭṭ piā jioṅ somāṅ." Her blossoming forth is "like the breaking of a dam – kaṛ khusīan dā phuṭiā," it is "like the sudden burst of a water-spring – caśmen jioṅ phuṭ chhuṭiā" and "the spurting of fountains – chhuṭe phuāre." Freedom, velocity, suddenness, expansion, and rapture mark her transformation.

The breaking of barriers and the depiction of it through water imagery bring to mind a scene from Kate Chopin's *The Awakening*. In this feminist classic, the main character, Edna, is a charming mother of two children married to a moderately wealthy Creole businessman. But she finds no satisfaction in life. Needlework, conversation, and entertainment fill up her empty days. Under the impetus of a newborn love for a young bachelor and as a direct challenge to her husband, Edna learns to swim. She is out in the waters, by herself; this signifies her awakening:

> She turned her face seaward to gather in an impression of space and solitude, which the vast expansion of water, meeting and melting with the moonlit sky, conveyed to her exciting fancy. As she swam she seemed to be reaching out for the unlimited in which to lose herself.[18]

Here too the woman has the vision of the sea and the sky becoming a unity – "meeting and melting . . ." Losing her finite self, she reaches out for the Infinite. The breaking of barriers – a transcendence of their limited selves – is experienced by the women of the Punjab and of New Orleans. It is noteworthy that a male author writing in India in the early part of the twentieth century would anticipate this modern feminist *Weltanschauung*. Our Punjabi heroine perceives all space – above and below, in every direction, within and without – as one. For her the material world does not exist in parts and particles: rather, the world is *an* atom; it is *a* cell. In the singular circumference, nothing obstructs anything. It is a statement of her experience of ultimate freedom.

That the Oneness is not intellectually apprehended or made the object of reasoning, but rather felt to the very depths of the being, derives from the existential basis of Sikh epistemology. The young woman's ecstatic disclosure is but a vivid and poignant illustration of the quintessential statement of Sikh scripture: *Ikk Oaṅ Kār*. The numeral One, which stands at the outset of the Sikh text and is the very foundation of the Sikh religion, underscores the total unicity and singularity of the Ultimate Reality. After her intense anguish, our protagonist gets an insight into That Oneness. But the starting point of That Oneness is her being one with herself, both psychologically and physically. This experiential dimension is marked by the numeral 1 (One), with which the Sikh Holy Writ begins and which is so crucial to Sikh philosophy.

The numeral 1 is followed by the sound of *Oaṅ* or *Aum*, the mystic syllable of the Hindus. Out of all the varied and rich Sanskritic and Arabic terminology available to him, Gurū Nānak chose *Oaṅ* or *Aum* to designate the Singular Reality. *Aum* is the most significant word in the Sanskrit language. Mystics and philosophers have meditated upon it and have grappled with its meaning for centuries. Our heroine's inward realization is an existentialist embodiment of this term.

*Aum* is expounded with much intellectual sophistication in the Māṇḍūkya Upaniṣad as a four-tier psychological journey.[19] The fourfold Māṇḍūkya analysis begins with the first stage, "A," which is the Realm of Consciousness in which the world exists out there. It is basically a stage in which the subject is contrasted with the objects, I versus It or them. This was the stage where we first encountered the tall, beautiful woman wistfully questioning herself, the scenery, and the objects around. Later, when she perceives the two moons, the stars swimming in the lake, the lamps hanging from the celestial ceiling, the waters embracing the skies above . . . , we have entered the second stage. This is the psychological state of the semi-conscious where absolute categories start breaking down. The logical one-moon world begins to dissolve. In the Māṇḍūkya Upaniṣad it is referred to as the "U" stage. The third stage, that of "M," is the deep-sleep state, the state of utter unconsciousness. We may recall that prior to her fifth visit to the lake, the woman fell asleep under a big old *boṛh* tree. She fell asleep in the position she sat in, slipping into total unconsciousness. The final stage, the fourth one in which the A and the U and the M are fused together, is the experience of totality. It is referred to as *turīya* in the Upaniṣads. This is the ultimate unity, the transcendence that Bhāī Vīr Singh's protagonist is deeply aware of. This is what she has attained to; this is what brings her joy unbounded.

Her disclosure has epistemological value. For, as the woman says, there is nothing that is hidden or revealed any more. The focus here seems to be the oneness of knowledge. Absolute certainty has been reached. The Arabic terms *zāhir* ("exoteric") and *bātin* ("esoteric") are employed by her to restate that the exterior and the interior, the outer and inner dimensions, coalesce harmoniously in her experience of Oneness. But rather than entail an objective truth, her disclosure is subjective. One could not, for instance, test it out like the proposition 2+2=4; the only kind of testing would be for other human beings to participate in that experience. The concern here is not with ordinary matters of fact, and Bhāī Vīr Singh's heroine does not leave us with any system to follow. This is keeping in line with Gurū Nānak and his successors, who did not categorize the Transcendent One in any form. According to Gurū Nānak, the One cannot be reduced into any form or shape or installed as an idol; the *Sac Khaṇḍ* or the Realm of Truth cannot be described in any way.[20] The only way to know the Transcendent is by experiencing It oneself.

In this stage of certitude, all questions and answers become one. No longer does she inquire "What is life?" or wonder "Is it a circle? Is it a droplet? . . ." Some years ago Elie Wiesel provided an aphoristic definition of eternity. Towards the beginning of *Night*, when Elie as a little boy would avidly read the Cabbalistic texts late into the night with Moché the Beadle, he anticipated eternity as "that time when question and answer would become one."[21] That highly ambiguous statement is rendered intelligible through Bhāī Vīr Singh's protagonist. Indeed, in her vision of the blossom, question and answer become one. Wiesel helps us discern that her "oneness" is inclusive of the realization of eternity or timelessness.

A distinctive point that emerges from the Sikh existential perspective is that life is a joyous mode of being. Intense Angst leads to ultimate bliss. Life authentically is a blossom. Most likely, our heroine after her experience will return to her normal routine, but then she will live more fully, more meaningfully. Unlike Edna (in Kate Chopin's novel), who is unable to integrate spiritual liberation with participation in society and therefore commits suicide, our heroine is bound to retain the smile which she had finally attained. A cheerful attitude (*kheṛā*) is prized in the Sikh way. Life, then, is not to be shunned. One should not retreat and become a recluse. Instead, one should, as Gurū Nānak says, "battle in open field, with one's mind perfectly in control and with one's heart poised in love, all the time."[22] Liberation is attained in the world itself. Another verse in the Gurū Granth reads: "hasaṅdiā khelaṅdiā paiṅandiā khāvaṅdiā vice hovai mukti – amidst joyous fun, play, wearing fineries, and eating delicacies does one achieve liberation."[23] Liberation or *mukti* is being like the lotuses which swing back and forth ecstatically. Although in the lake, the lotuses do not get caught up in its murkiness. This image from the Gītā which pervades the Gurū Granth[24] is also used by Bhāī Vīr Singh in our own century to exemplify the life of freedom and liberation. The lotuses literally exist: they stand out – *ex sistunt*. For how long? That is not the point. The woman does not seek to know or inform us about the duration of life, and she does not reflect upon the after-life. The moment here – the now, the Heideggerian *Augenblick* – is what she experiences, through and with the blossomed lotuses.

What we recover from this analysis of a twentieth-century Punjabi poem is that existentialism is not just a western experience. Anxiety and disclosure are human experiences, shared by Punjabis and Europeans alike, and shared across the centuries. In fact, the phenomenon of anxiety is revelatory of the human condition. In the Sikh religion, however, existentialism takes on a transcendental dimension, for it is the Transcendent One that is to be realized by the individual here and now.

Thus Bhāī Vīr Singh's "What is Life?" underscores and explains the importance of "vision" in the Sikh tradition. The unity with the overwhelming "blossom" is an insight into the beauty and the *élan vital* of the lotuses. The maiden's anguish arose from her inability to fathom the mystery of the lake, and her hope is prompted by the sight of the buds growing into leaves on its surface. But the certainty is her blossoming with the blossom, her becoming "one" – through the phenomenon of vision – with the luxurious and buoyant abundance. The paradox of the proximity and distance of the Transcendent One is vividly illustrated through the symbol of the singular sun: although it is far away in the skies, the sun is the ontological foundation for the existence of the myriad lotuses. Experientially, it is the *Ikk rūp* – the One Form, in reality, the formless form, that the woman realizes. The "vision" of the *Ikk rūp* is bliss: in the merging of the microscopic spark with the Macrocosmic Light, ego and individuality are lost; instead, transcendence, ultimate freedom, and eternity are gained. Absolute joy pervades. And this unity? Nothing of material substance, it is sheer "vision."

Most of all, the twentieth-century poet promotes the importance of women in Sikhism. That life is a blossom – the Sikh existential ideal – is apprehended and communicated by the "female" herself. She is the one in quest of the meaning of life. We discover that the questions posed by the heroine of the poem "Jīvan kī Hai?" bear a striking resemblance to the ones contained in the new literature created by women. In "Images of Spiritual Power in Women's Fiction," Carol Christ calls upon women to awake and question our world:

> Women's *spiritual quest* concerns a woman's awakening to the depth of her soul and her position in the universe. A woman's spiritual quest includes moments of solitary contemplation, but it is strengthened by being shared. It involves asking basic questions: Who am I? Why am I here? What is my place in the universe? In answering these questions, a woman must listen to her own voice and come to terms with her own experience. Because she can no longer accept conventional answers to her questions, she opens herself to the radically new – possibly to the revelation of powers or forces of being larger than herself that can ground her in a new understanding of herself and her position in the world.[25]

Bhāī Vīr Singh's protagonist embodies the concerns of this contemporary feminist thealogian. We notice that each of the five times the woman visits the lake, she is by herself. We do not see her as daughter, wife, or mother. Free, with her freedom further pronounced by the fact that she walks alone, she experiences "moments of solitary contemplation." She raises questions – questions about existence, her own existence, the existence around, the relationship between her and the cosmos, and the relationship amongst all the parts and particles of the universe. She is the one in quest of knowledge about Being. Without any "male" interventions, without any male protagonist like Yājnavālkya or any other seer or prophet, the woman herself, from within herself, while hearing the beautiful female voice and seeing the lake giving birth to the lotuses, becomes cognizant of Being Itself. Most complex spiritual and philosophical issues are grasped by *her*. Thereafter, *her* life is a "blossom." That existence – for men and women – is bliss is portrayed in *her* journey from deep Angst to utmost joy. *She* raises questions; *She* provides answers. She personifies the Sikh scriptural statement: "mātā mati – mother is wisdom."

CHAPTER 7

# *Suṅdarī: the paradigm of Sikh ethics*

tūṅ jihā amrit safal kītā hai tihā harek istrī purukh kare.

As you [Suṅdarī] have succeeded in living your pledge with the Divine, may each and every man and woman likewise succeed.

What does she do after the re-cognition? Where does she go? What happens when the young woman returns home after having viewed that vista of the singular blossom of lotuses? How does a Sikh person lead her or his life after a vision of the Transcendent? Although chronologically, the poem "What is Life?" came twenty-four years after the publication of the novel *Suṅdarī*, it seems to me that ideologically the novel begins where the poem ends. For Suṅdarī in flesh and blood *lives* the Sikh ideal of insight into the Singular One.

*Suṅdarī* is one of Bhāī Vīr Singh's earliest literary creations. The story was conceived when he was still at high school, and a part of it was written then as well. As a young boy, Bhāī Vīr Singh had fed on stories of Sikh heroism and sacrifice from the eighteenth century. The encounter with Moghul governors like Mīr Mannū (1748–53) and Afghan emperors like Ahmad Shāh Durrānī invigorated the Sikh spirit, leading to the creation of a sovereign Sikh kingdom. With the kingdom now under British rule, there was again a testing of faith. It was with a view to resurrecting Sikh moral values that Bhāī Vīr Singh chose to recreate that stirring period. He chose a woman to be his principal character, personifying the Sikh virtues of faith and courage. We find that a reestablishment of Sikh identity was indeed the leitmotif of *Suṅdarī*, as the author himself states explicitly in the following passage:

In writing this book our purpose is that by reading these accounts of bygone days the Sikhs should recover their faith. They should be prepared actively to pursue their worldly duty as well as their spiritual ideal . . . They should learn to own their high principles . . . and adhere to the Gurū's teaching: "Recognize all humankind as one."[1]

The renaissance writer wanted to bring back for his readers the message of the Sikh Gurūs: "mānas kī jāt sabhe ekai pahacānbo – recognize all humankind as one." Like Gurū Gobind Singh, who coined this motto, Bhāī Vīr Singh wanted to reawaken his society. *Suṅdarī* was published in 1898, and the novel gained immediate popularity:

It caught the imagination of the Sikhs as no other book has. Perhaps no other Punjabi book has been read more . . . For vast numbers of people Suṅdarī has been a real person, an embodiment of faith, chastity and courage. They have loved and admired her. They have shed tears over her trials, and they have heaved sighs of relief at her providential escapes. Her name has become a byword in Punjabi homes. Many were inspired by her deeds of chivalry to initiation into the Khālsā.[2]

The legend of Suṅdarī has since lived on in the Sikh consciousness as an exemplar of the moral ideals bequeathed by the Gurūs. For generations Punjabi readers have been touched by her qualities of dedication, daring, and charity.

His choice of a woman as the central character in recreating that stirring period of faith and chivalry is atypical. It establishes Bhāī Vīr Singh as a radical artist for his times. With the Afghan invasions into India, Hindu and Sikh men became overly protective of "their" women, which led to an overall degradation of the position of women. The harem scene from the novel itself is a perceptive illustration of their situation:

The *zanān khānah* (women's quarters) too is bustling. On a carpet, five or six begums are seated and several maids are attending on them. Each begum surpasses the other in beauty. They are wearing silks and their jewels are sparkling . . .[3]

Soon the begums are served sumptuous meals. We hear them chatting, and some of them are even joking. When the drunken Nawāb enters at night, each receives a blow or two for having misbehaved towards the "newly encaged bird." After all, the *zanān khānah* is no better than a golden cage, breeding frivolous chatter, jealousy, and enmity. Many of these begums may have been forced into marriage, as indeed were many, many women of Bhāī Vīr Singh's century. With the luxurious palace as the backdrop, we come face to face with the painful imprisonment and victimization of women. The consciousness of our male author comes through as he tries to portray their tragic situation and their contrast with Sundarī. Against the bevy of victims in the harem, Sundarī gallops freely in the jungles, sometimes by herself, sometimes with brave Sikh men – the picture of self-assurance, courage, and defiance. The novel is not merely a passive lament about the position of women. It is a call to action, and it provides a role model for defiance. It involves an active commitment demanding a shift in consciousness and a transformation of society. It is indeed remarkable how the young Sikh author in the late nineteenth century establishes the importance and sovereignty of woman.

The book opens with the jubilant anticipation of the marriage of the young and beautiful Surastī. Her father Shāmā's house is defined as belonging to one "whose daughter was to get married."[4] Even in modern India, this for many may sound an anomaly for the daughter traditionally belongs to the father's house (as is clearly specified in the *Laws of Manu*[5]). Bhāī Vīr Singh thus reverses the order: it is the daughter who in this instance gives identity to Shāmā (the father)'s house. Her name, "Surastī," can be traced to the Vedic goddess Sarasvatī, who has been worshiped by millions of male and female Hindus as the bestower of knowledge and learning. We first encounter Surastī in the courtyard outside where she is singing, dancing, and laughing amidst her friends. In beauty Surastī outshines all the maidens. She is like the "moon amidst the stars." Soon thereafter, she is abducted from the jocund crowd by the Moghul chief who was out hunting with his entourage; laughter in the house immediately turns into mourning and tears.

Surastī's father, her brother, the would-be bridegroom, and two members of her village Pancāyat go to the chief to plead for her return. The father joins his hands and respectfully begs the Moghul to return his daughter. The son follows him, requesting that the Nawāb return his sister as "charity." The fiancé falls at the chief's feet, offering all his wealth in exchange for Surastī. The Pancāyat members also humbly make the request. "But why would the Nawāb give back a dazzling jewel?"[6] Surastī's father begins to cry. Her brother falls unconscious. Her fiancé, in fear lest the chief ask him to surrender his property, runs away. Over against this fragility and weakness, Surastī boldly unveils her face and authoritatively asks the members of her family and village to return. To her still unconscious brother she undauntedly says, "The Moghul's water I will not drink. Die I will in the fire."[7] Surastī then decides to immolate herself.

As she gathers wood and prepares the pyre, Surastī reveals her resolve and her faith. The self-immolation on her part is understood as an effort to escape the clutches of her captors, but a contemporary Sikh scholar notes its true significance:

> The act is contemplated not in despair, but as a means of demonstrating fortitude. She combines patience with strength of mind and courage to suffer adversity. As she gathers wood and prepares the pyre she reveals resolve and faith: there is no remorse and, instead of frenzy, there is trust in the eventual goodness that shall prevail.[8]

For that reason, Surastī is heard reciting passages from Gurū Nānak's *Japu* when her brother arrives. The holy text does not contain any specific injunctions regarding the moral obligation of a woman faced with such a situation.[9] However, she receives fresh succor from reciting it, specifically the opening lines, which are a sterling affirmation of the existence of the Transcendent One.

Another brother of Surastī, Balvant Singh, who had become a Sikh and was initiated into the Khālsā, lived in the jungle along with his companions and carried on a desperate, though unequal, battle with their persecutors. On the evening of Surastī's wedding, he chances to visit his home. Hearing of the tragedy that has befallen his sister, he immediately turns his horse in pursuit of her. As he draws near the Nawāb's camp, he sees a pile of logs, a corner of it alight. Into his ears comes a familiar voice reciting the *Japu*. He rushes to the spot and pulls away Surastī from the top of the pyre. His words are "piārī bhain, ātmān dā ghāt karnā vaddā pāp hai[10] – dear sister, to commit suicide is a grave sin." (We hear the very same words repeated by the sister later in the novel.) Once rescued, Surastī faces the choice of returning to her family and leading the usual lifestyle, or going to the in-laws and living with her husband, or accompanying her brother to the Sikh camp and living a hazardous life in the jungles. The decision for the bold, fearless woman is not difficult to make. Life in the jungle is what naturally attracts her, and she asks herself why she should not choose it:

> Why should I not serve those brave people who fight for righteousness? Why don't women ever join action to uphold righteousness? If they haven't so far, why should I not be the first woman to fight courageously like my brother?[11]

Now, for a woman, the ability to make decisions over her own life and thereby experience the power of self-determination is in itself a winning of freedom.[12] The Sikh author portrays his heroine as autonomous from this point on. After making her decision we see Surastī very confidently mounting a horse and hear her demanding a sword from her brother. Resolutely, she starts riding with her brother towards the camp.

Surastī is the first woman to join the camp. Coming face to face with innumerable strong Sikh men, she proclaims the power of woman. Her address to the gathering is bold and eloquent:

> You might be thinking that just as a woman appears delicate from the outside, she must be fragile inwardly too. Do not entertain such a thought even for a second. A woman's mind is soft like the wax and strong like a rock; once she is confirmed in her faith, nothing can deter her.[13]

There is applause from the members. Clearly, through Surastī's statement and the positive response that it elicits, Bhāī Vīr Singh affirms the strength and tenacity of women. A synthesis of the commonly polarized virtues of tenderness and strength is affirmed.

Early next morning all join to pray together to the Transcendent One. *Āsā kī Vār* by Gurū Nānak is recited. Surastī receives the initiatory *amrita* and enters into the Khālsāhood launched by Gurū Gobind Singh (Nānak X). She becomes one with the brothers and receives the name Suṅdar Kaur, affectionately shortened to Suṅdarī.

Suṅdarī is now part of the people driven into jungle asylums under the pressure of State persecution. She takes a leading part in the bitter struggle they have launched to regain freedom and justice for themselves. Dauntlessly she gallops out with her warrior-comrades on their desperate sallies. As the story unfolds, we see her involved in many a hair-raising adventure. We see her tending the sick and the wounded, cooking food in the camp kitchen, and leading worship and prayer. We hear her expound high-minded principles of the faith espoused by Gurū Nānak three centuries earlier, and we see her live up to these principles under the most trying conditions. Bhāī Vīr Singh's portrayal of the Sikh ethical ideal in a fictional setting is a most comprehensive statement on this theme at the beginning of the modern period of Sikh history.

The Sikh moral imperative is best summed up in the maxim: "kirat karnī, vaṇḍ chhakṇā, te nāmu japṇā, – to labor for one's keep, to share with others, and to practice the repetition of the Divine Name." At the head of the triple formula is the phrase *kirat karnī*. *Kirat*, from Sanskrit *krit*, in Punjabi means the labor of one's two hands. It means manual work – honest, upright work in pursuit of one's living. The term has extended implications in the Sikh worldview. It stresses the values of honesty and activity. It underscores the dignity of labor and deprecates parasitism. More significantly, it prescribes a positive attitude towards life. Withdrawal is rejected; home and family are made the rule. The Janamsākhī accounts and the ballads of Bhāī Gurdās allude to the first Gurū's visit to the mountains where he met Siddha ascetics sitting in a conclave. The Siddhas ask Gurū Nānak how it went with the mortals below. "To the mountains," says the Gurū, "have the Siddhas escaped." "Who," he asks, "will save the world?"[14] According to Gurū Nānak, "Living amid wife and children would one attain release."[15] A truly religious person did not retire from the world but "battle[d] in open field, with one's mind perfectly in control and with one's heart poised in love, all the time."[16]

This is exactly what Suṅdarī does. She does momentarily contemplate self-immolation, but soon proclaims the importance of living, and she lives positively and authentically. She becomes part of the campaign resisting invasions from across the border of the country and against religious fanaticism and intolerance. Bhāī Vīr Singh portrays Suṅdarī as being both mentally and physically strong – "rock-like," as she pronounces all women to be. She is a warrior among her warrior brethren and is not shy of wielding the sword. Bhāī Vīr Singh presents her fighting in the historical battle of Kāhnūvān (AD 1746) against the troops of the governor of Lahore. According to the novelist, in a fierce action she wounds a Moghul general by the name of Nawāb Faizullāh Khān, well known in history. We also read about Suṅdarī's heroic acts in battles against Ahmad Shāh Durrāni, who led many incursions into India.

*Kirat* also implies *sevā*, which is an important concept in the Sikh system. *Sevā* means a deed of love and selfless service. It means contributing the labor of one's hands to serving fellow human beings and the community. *Sevā* is presented as the highest ideal in Sikh ethics. By *sevā* one cultivates humility. By *sevā* one overcomes one's ego and purifies one's body and mind. *Sevā* is an essential condition of spiritual discipline. As the canon runs, by *sevā*, i.e. by practicing deeds of humble and devoted service, alone does one earn a seat in the next world (*vici dunīā sev kamāīai tā dargah basiaṇu pāiai*).[17] To quote Gurū Arjan (Nānak V):

> āo sakhī saṅt pāsi sevā lāgīai . . .
> taji āpu mītai saṅtāpu āpu nah jāṇāīai
> saraṇi gahījai māni līјai kare so sukhu pāīai.[18]
>
> Come friends, come to the saint,
> let us devote ourselves to deeds of service . . .
> Conquering the self, suffering ends and the ego vanishes,
> We receive refuge, obtain honor, and whatever we do
> brings comfort.[19]

Gurū Arjan is here referring to the comfort that is achieved through *sevā*. Dedicated to service, one conquers one's self. With the curbing of egotism, all suffering ends. Absorption in action – whatever it be – brings calmness and happiness. Gurū Amar Dās (Nānak III) said that a person engaged in *sevā* becomes pure, *nirmal* (*nir*, "without," and *mal*, "dirt" or "impurity"). *Sevā* is the way of a truly religious person. Engaged in *sevā* one becomes purified and soothed personally, and simultaneously one becomes an active agent in promoting the welfare of society.

Sundarī's spirit of *sevā* is the dominant key of her character. Her *sevā* takes many forms. Early in the story as she joins the Jathā (the camp of Sikh warriors), she implores its members:

> It is my wish that I fulfill my life serving the community. I should, if you would allow, live here amid my brothers. In peacetime, I shall serve in the *laṅgar*. When you launch out into combat, I should be in the ranks too.[20]

In the novel we see her cooking in the community kitchen. Her love of service manifests itself in yet another way as she gently and devotedly nurses the wounded and the sick. Her *sevā* is not limited to the Sikhs alone; she nurses the wounded irrespective of their religious or political affiliations. She draws no distinction between factions. With great concern and tenderness she bandages the injured – Sikhs and Hindus, Paṭhāns and Moghuls. Many a time, fragments shredded from her own garments form the bandage. This reminds one of an incident from Gurū Gobind Singh's life. One of his followers, Bhāī Kanahiyā, used to tend the wounded on the battlefield without making distinctions between friend and foe. When complaints were made to Gurū Gobind Singh, Bhāī Kanahiyā explained that when rendering service to those who needed it, he saw no friend or foe but only the Gurū's face all around.[21]

Engaged in her tasks of *sevā*, Sundarī is often heard reciting the *bāṇī*, passages from the Gurū Granth. Her words are gentle and sweet and they bring a breath of peace and comfort to the Jathā during its arduous moments. Hearing Sundarī speak, the injured person says, "Your sweet words are like a balm on my wound."[22] Sundarī thus renders *sevā* through both deed and word.

*Vaṇḍ chhakṇā* (from *vaṇḍ*, "distribution" or "sharing," and *chhakṇā*, "to eat") is the sharing of monies and goods before the individual partakes of them. It is another important aspect of Sikh ethics and is based on the principle of mutuality. It does not imply charity, but sharing among equals. Just as members of the family share their earnings and goods with the other members of the family, so should the Sikhs, according to the Gurū's injunction, conduct themselves in the larger family of the community. This principle of sharing underlies the institutions of *saṅgat* and *laṅgar*, which have been primary factors in shaping the Sikh moral ethos. As we saw in Chapter 1, *saṅgat* in the Sikh tradition consists of the fellowship of seekers. Such groups and communities came into being in places visited by Gurū Nānak during his extensive journeys. They consisted of groups of Sikhs who got together to recite the Gurū's word. All members were equal in it, equal partners in religious and social activity. The same ideal of equality and togetherness is symbolized by the institution of *laṅgar*. Gurū Nānak established the *laṅgar*, or community refectory, where all sat together to share a meal irrespective of caste, creed, or gender. The *laṅgar* as an instrument of social transformation continued to gain in importance during the time of the successive Gurūs. In Gurū Aṅgad's day, his wife Mātā Khīvī, providing shade "like a thickly leafed tree," i.e. comfort to everyone, used to serve rich food in the *laṅgar*.[23] During the time of Gurū Amar Dās the writ prevailed: "pahile paṅgat pācche saṅgat – first *paṅgat* (the row in which all sit together to partake of the *laṅgar* meal) and then meeting with the Gurū." Eating and serving in the *laṅgar* have always been considered meritorious.

This element of *sevā* is tellingly illustrated in Sundarī's person. When she joins the Jathā, she takes charge of the *laṅgar* and lovingly prepares meals to feed the members morning and evening. Assisted by several men, she goes about her task cheerfully. The *laṅgar* in the camp is not limited to the "indoor kitchen." For when the supplies run low, which often happens, Sundarī goes into the jungle to gather fruit and sweet roots. She thus keeps an eye on the outdoors to see what is growing and when something is about to ripen. One day she goes up a hill and surveys the entire area. She then discovers a little bazaar located amidst green fields. She begins to go there to buy vegetables, grain, and spices. With great devotion and humility Suṅdarī carries out the many duties involved in the running of the community kitchen. When she finds out that the kitchen supplies have run out and that there is hardly any money to buy anything, she decides (without telling anyone) to go into the village to sell her engagement ring. The meal for the members overrides her personal sentiment and any sense of possession. As she has taken charge of the *laṅgar*, she undertakes responsibility for the *saṅgat* as well. She is the moving figure behind the morning and evening congregations and takes a leading part in the religious service.

*Nāmu Japṇā* (*nāmu*, "name" – referring to the Divine Name – and *japṇā*, "to repeat," "to meditate upon"), absorption in the remembrance of the Divine by constantly repeating Its Name, is the prime spiritual value in the Sikh tradition. It is, at the same time, the spontaneous source of ethical conduct. According to Gurū Amar Dās, "jatu satu saṅjamu nāmu hai vinu nāvai nirmalu na hoe – chastity, truth, continence are all contained in *nāmu*; without contemplation on *nāmu*, one does not become pure."[24] Another line in the Sikh scripture describes *nāmu* as action par excellence – "Superior to all acts of piety, charity, and austerity, is *nāmu* (pun dān jap tap jete sabh ūpari nāmu)."[25]

Bhāī Vīr Singh presents Suṅdarī as a living example of this Sikh religious precept. The action of the novel begins with her rescue from the pyre by her brother – as she is reciting Gurū Nānak's *Japu*. The story ends with her death – as she is meditating on the Divine Word, her head bent in reverence. Gurū Nānak's words are recalled as the novelist describes her last moments, death staring her in the face:

> antari nāmu kamalu pargāsā
> tinh kau nāhī jam kī trāsā.[26]
>
> They within whom the lotus of *nāmu* blossoms
> Totally free from the fear of death they become.

That Reality is felt by her to be with her constantly. She is never in doubt; never alone. As a result she always remains cheerful, even after being severely wounded:

> All the time she appeared happy (*khiṛī*). She would be in pain, but she would not utter a sigh; her temperature would rise, but she would not be

perturbed. On her face radiated the love for the feet of the Absolute Gurū. Because of that love she knew, no, she had total faith that she belonged to That Supreme Being and That Being was always with her, never, never for a moment apart.[27]

Love and knowledge are superseded by Sundarī's total faith in the Supreme Being. "Her love for the feet of the Absolute Gurū" does not mean that she bows before any physical or living person or Gurū; rather, it is a symbol of her complete submission to the Transcendent One – Who is always with her. Not for a moment does she feel separated from that Reality, so that she always is *khiṛī hoī*, "in blossom." The melodious *nāmu* rings constantly in Sundarī's being. Consequently, her existence is like a lotus in bloom. She dies totally without fear. We notice that the vocabulary from the poem "What is Life?" has been used to describe the joy, power, and strength that Sundarī derives from her belief in the presence of the Transcendent with her all the time.

With the love for the Truth Beyond, she continuously exists in *kheṛā*. This term was used for the blossom of the lotuses. This blossom is always the expression on her face – whether she is contentedly working in the kitchen or is lying in bed suffering from a high temperature. *Kheṛā* is a symbolic depiction of her true living. Severely wounded and running a high temperature, she lies in bed, her strength visibly ebbing. She realizes that her end is near, but this does not affect her:

even in such great suffering she was happy. She always appeared to be like a blossomed lotus . . . She knew . . . that life and death are two conditions, not two objects. If there is a love for the Divine in one's heart, one need fear nothing in either condition.[28]

This was because of her deeply realized consciousness of the Divine Reality. She cherishes the body which, "when it remembers the One, is *harimandir* – Supreme Reality's temple itself."[29] On her death-bed Sundarī requests her brothers for a *darśana* (vision) of *bāṇī*. With the utmost respect and jubilation, the Gurū Granth is brought into the camp. Recitation begins. When she hears the Divine Word, each and every pore of Sundarī's body gets saturated with *ānanda* or bliss. She reverently bows in front of the *bāṇī* and, thus paying homage to the Holy Word, she breathes her last. The verse brought forth, "tujh binu dūjā nahī koi – there is none other besides You," continues to reverberate; Suṅdarī's forehead continues to kiss the ground in front of the Gurū Granth. Throughout the novel we never see her have recourse to any superstitious practice or ritual; morning and evening she recites only the Word and remains absorbed in it. In all the critical episodes in her life the Divine Word is her sole standby.

Through her recognition of the One Divine Being, Suṅdarī transcends contemporary socio-political reality. Her society was divided into different religious and racial factions which were continually at war with one another. Abductions, robberies, and killings abounded. It was a period of strife and conflict. But rather than blame the opponent, Suṅdarī accepts a mutual blindness. She states this at one point:

> All this suffering is owing to the deviation from the path of the One (*Ikk*). Devoted to the One all actions become fruitful. Following the One, all human beings become beaded together ... Through love we become one (*ikk*) force.[30]

Thus the political and social ills of the eighteenth-century Punjab are traced by Suṅdarī to the non-recognition of the One. The Oneness of the Reality implies the oneness of human beings – be they Hindu, Muslim, or Sikh. Contemporary problems are, according to her perception, the consequence of the refusal of men and women to perceive the One Transcendent, their inability to perceive the oneness of all Its creation. In the plurality of realities, the one Reality is missed, and ironically such plurality threatens real pluralism. A tragic consequence is the attempt to convert or coerce others into seeing one's own reality. But by realizing the One, all human beings, according to her, become "beaded together" in love. She possesses a collective understanding of the transforming possibilities for her society, and thus shares in the ethical perspective recovered by modern feminists. It rejects a strictly individualistic view and embraces a pluralistic attitude to moral issues.[31]

The chief of the Sikh Jathā, Shām Singh, seems to echo Suṅdarī when he explains the oneness of creation: "sārī sriśtī sānūṅ ikk samān hai – all of nature is one and equal to us." The group are described as though they were the "offspring of One mother and father – ikk mātā pitā dī aulād."[32] We notice that Bhāī Vīr Singh maintains Gurū Nānak's style: the mother (*mātā*) clearly precedes the father (*pitā*) in his conception. Since the children come from the *One* which is both mother and father, there cannot be differences amongst them. All are equal. Shām Singh claims that he and his band oppose injustice and inequality, *not* the religious conviction of anyone. At that point in time, they must fight the rulers who perpetrate atrocities against the subjects, against those whom they should be protecting. By defeating such rulers, irrespective of their religious persuasion, they were chastising tyranny and injustice. "We have enmity towards no caste or faith – kise zāt jān mat nāl sānū koī vair nahīṅ,"[33] declares Sardār Shām Singh.

Under his leadership Suṅdarī fights in the ranks of the Jathā against the Moghul forces. Once on her way back from the day's action, she hears the faint voice of one wounded trooper crying "āb āb barāe khudā āb – water, water, for the sake of God, water!"[34] From his Persian vocabulary Suṅdarī can make out that the soldier belongs to the enemy forces. However, she immediately dismounts from her horse. Not only does she pour water into his mouth from her own flask, but she also tears strips from his turban to make a bandage for the wounds on his thigh and chest. Gurū Nānak's message "There is no Hindu; there is no Musalmān" is a living moral for Suṅdarī.

Through Suṅdarī's character and actions, Bhāī Vīr Singh underscores the Sikh faith in the transcendence of the One. As we saw in Chapter 5, much of the eighteenth century interpretation of Sikh scriptures had been filtered through Vedic and Purāṇic lenses and the Sikhs had begun to lose sight of the Transcendent Reality. That the Transcendent is to be regarded as *the* Gurū in place of polytheistic deities is the very basis of Gurū Nānak's teaching. The Infinite is never incarnated. Nevertheless, such commentaries were current and led to an incubation of Hindu ideology in Sikh thinking. By the late nineteenth century Brahmanical ritual and orientation had come to sway the Sikh way of life. An editorial in the *Khālsā Advocate* summed up the situation:

> false Gurūs grew up in great abundance whose only business was to fleece their flock and pamper their own self-aggrandizement. Properly speaking, there was no Sikhism. Belief in the Gurūs was gone. The idea of brotherhood in the Panth was discarded. The title of "Bhāī" [brother], so much honored by Sikhs of old, fell into disuse and contempt. Sikhs grovelled in superstition and idolatry . . . It [the Sikh faith] had thus lost all that was good and life-giving in the faith . . .[35]

With a view to ending the "grovelling of Sikhs in superstition and idolatry," Suṅdarī is presented as the paradigm for a staunch belief in the Transcendent. Throughout the novel the author shows that Suṅdarī's only ritual, her only ceremony, and her only worship are the recitation of the *bāṇī*, the Word from Beyond. He singles her out as the archetype of faith in the One Transcendent and calls upon the women of his own time, "gharīb te amīr sikkhāṅ dīo dhīo, bhāīno te māvo – daughters, sisters, and mothers of poor and rich Sikhs alike." He urges them to reflect on the suffering and faith of Suṅdarī, who under all circumstances remains firm in her love of the One Absolute. He condemns their falling away from the faith:

Having denounced the Transcendent and Its message couched in the teachings of the Gurūs, you worship stones, trees, spirits, and cemeteries . . .[36]

Bhāī Vīr Singh's message is loud and clear, and his criticism of the decadence of contemporary society unsparing. He straightforwardly remarks that the women of his century have become forgetful (*gāphal*) of the Sikh vision of the Transcendent and have veered instead towards superstition and idolatry:

Forgetting the ever-living One you have fed cakes (*pūṛé*) to the serpents; becoming oblivious of the One beyond life and death, you have taken to the path of ignorance towards which you draw your husbands and sons as well. For a second, remember Suṅdarī . . . Like Suṅdarī become courageous, like Suṅdarī, adopt the path of Truth . . .[37]

In contrast to these women worshiping images, snakes, cemeteries, trees, and ghosts is Suṅdarī, who worships the Transcendent One alone. The power of the woman in the Sikh household is latent in this critique of women who worship idols and in the vivification of faith in the Infinite through Suṅdarī. *She* "draws the husbands and sons" towards the ideals she holds. The woman is the nucleus of the home, and she gives direction to society as a whole; she is the central agent in both the microcosmic and macrocosmic spheres. The renaissance writer clearly attaches great importance to the role of Woman: the rise and downfall of a civilization depend upon her. This view comes across through the words of Shām Singh, the leader of the Jathā:

The core of the Paṅth (Sikh community) is righteous women like yourself (Suṅdarī).[38]

The novel is about a woman, and it is addressed to women; implicitly through the model of Suṅdarī and explicitly through his direct exhortations to his readers, the author urges Sikh women to regenerate their culture. Bhāī Vīr Singh deliberately subverts the androcentric dichotomy between nature and culture, which regulates woman to an uncultivated world, excluding her from the world of patriarchal civilization. For Bhāī Vīr Singh it is natural that a woman, Sundarī, would renew Sikh culture.

Through Sundarī, Bhāī Vīr Singh also voices the handicaps and subjugation that were particularly suffered by women in his society. While she finds herself treated fairly by the men in her group, Sundarī is deeply conscious of the inferior position assigned to woman in traditional scriptures. Her moral consciousness is typically feminist in its anguished awareness of victimization, violence, and pain. She does not concentrate on her own individual situation, which is relatively good; she remains constantly aware of the inferior status of her sisters, and wants to advance them too. She realizes that the freedom and equality she experiences is juxtaposed against the bondage and inequality of her sisters. Just before passing away, she makes this plea to her Sikh brothers:

> It is my prayer that you know your women as your equals (*sāthī*) and not subordinates . . . In the *śāstras*, woman is written down as *śūdra*, but our ten Gurūs have praised her . . . Do not forget my request, respect women . . .[39]

In her last moments, Sundarī reminds her comrades of the esteem enjoyed by women in the Sikh scripture; how from Nānak through Gobind Singh the Gurūs were champions of women's position and rights. The status of women must clearly have been a very crucial issue for her. Close to her last breath, she also reminds the Jathā of the role of women in Sikh history like Mātā Sahibā, who put sugar-puffs in the alchemical nectar prepared by Gurū Gobind Singh to invigorate his Sikhs. Men and women alike drank it. Although she does not mention any specific *śāstras*, Sundarī alerts her companions to the prejudices based on sex and caste which are written into the traditional texts, and she illuminates for them the special message of sexual and creedal equality brought forth by the Sikh Gurūs. Sundarī's final wish is that disparity between men and women end: woman ought to be a *sāthī* – an equal partner of and companion to man, no more and no less.

Of course for Sundarī the root of a sexist and divided world lies in the failure to see the Transcendent One. Her very being resonates with a complete faith in the message of the Gurūs that there is a Singular Reality:

nānak soī jīviā jini ikku pachhātā.[40]

Only that individual lives who recognizes the One.

Existence is deemed authentic only when the Oneness of the Ultimate Reality is seen. The metaphysical insight into That One transforms the social fabric: it weaves a pattern with a multiplicity of colors, each one equally maintaining and celebrating its intensity and richness.

Bhāī Vīr Singh's Suṅdarī is a living embodiment of the ethical ideals espoused by Gurū Nānak. There is no doubt that Suṅdarī is a highly idealized character, but this was in keeping with the declared object of the novelist. He wished to create a character marking the acme of Sikh virtue to serve as a model for others. His own time was a period of decline for the Sikhs. They had lost their grasp of the teachings of the Gurūs, and after losing their political power to the British, their morale was at a low ebb. But even in these dark days, there were already intimations that a process of renewal was coming into effect. This renaissance had a dual purpose, for it urgently demanded that the Sikhs recapture the purity of earlier customs and precepts, but it required with equal urgency that they look to the future and change with the times. Bhāī Vīr Singh, a literary genius of uncommon sensitivity, felt in his heart the power of these nascent stirrings and articulated them through book and tract. The first book he wrote was *Suṅdarī* itself, followed by two others in the same style – *Bijay Singh* and *Satvaṅt Kaur*. His fourth novel was *Bābā Naudh Singh*. The inspiration behind all these works was the same: the same intent of portraying the Sikh character at its very best. Women are the protagonists in most of them. This was the author's way of recalling his contemporaries to the ideal of Sikh faith and tradition.

*Suṅdarī* was then Bhāī Vīr Singh's first such creation. Technically, the novel is rather tentative. From a literary point of view, the tone tends to be somewhat didactic. Instead of tantalizing the reader's imagination, the author imposes his moral principles. The artistic play is thus subordinated to Bhāī Vīr Singh's ethical ideals. The plot of the novel itself is weakened by the abundant presence of coincidences. For example, Suṅdarī is captured by her enemy four times, and each time she is rescued in some unrealistic and miraculous way. Furthermore, the novel too often combines historical and imaginary characters and events, reducing the authenticity of its character as a work of fiction or history. The co-existence of the two dimensions needed to be worked out on a larger framework, and the two strands might have been developed more rigorously and artistically. As it stands, the fictitious character of Suṅdarī is juxtaposed to figures from Indian history such as Kauṛā Mall and Ahmad Shāh Durrānī; the story of Suṅdarī, to actual events such as the Little Massacre of 1746. The result is that the reader at times is unable to decipher fact from fiction. Even Harbans Singh, Bhāī Vīr Singh's most devoted admirer, criticizes him for his historical substantiation of an imaginative piece: "The footnotes added to later editions of the book to document some of the statements and events further weaken the illusion of the story."[41] For me, however, Bhāī Vīr Singh's most serious mistake is the death of Suṅdarī at the end. The emotional appeal of this scene is so overwhelming that the readers lose sight of the author's message, which was really embodied in Suṅdarī's *life.*

But in his own way, the novelist has tried his best to bestow care and affection on his principal character. Suṅdarī is cast as the model of Sikh morality. In his undisguised homiletic manner, Bhāī Vīr Singh during the course of his narrative invites contemporary womenfolk "to reflect upon the suffering and faith of Suṅdarī who under all circumstances remains firm in her love of the One Absolute."[42] We heard the leader of the Jathā in exile, Shām Singh, acknowledge that "the core of our people are righteous women like yourself."[43] The impelling instinct in Suṅdarī's nature is her total submission to the Reality of God – the fundamental principle of Sikh belief. She is presented by the novelist as a typical example of faith in the One Transcendent. She is seen at several points in the narrative and in several different situations as completely rapt in *nāmu*, the devotional remembrance of the One. Her only ritual, her only worship is devoted to *bāṇī*, the Word from Beyond. From her awareness of the Divine Reality spring many natural qualities of love, humility, and tolerance; this is the source of her spirit of *sevā*, which leads to action-oriented, selfless, and courageous living. When the situation so requires, she is ready to resist tyranny and fight against injustice. In this sense she belongs to the line of archetypal women heroines of Sikh history such as Māī Bhāgo, who, in the time of Gurū Gobind Singh, fought valiantly in the battle of Muktsar (AD 1705). Bhāī Vīr Singh thus invests Suṅdarī with the noblest of Sikh merits derived from Sikh teaching and history.

Suṅdarī is the incarnation of all that is best in Sikh life and tradition, yet she does not remain a remote paragon of excellence or a distant goddess to be worshiped on a pedestal. Physically and psychologically she embodies the power that is being articulated by the modern feminists. In her valor and physique, the author compares her with the Hindu goddess Durgā, who, as we know, was selected by Gurū Gobind Singh (Nānak X) as an ideal character from the corpus of Indian mythology. Durgā-like Suṅdarī performs feats worthy of the goddess. She reacts with the alacrity of a "lioness" and the quickness of "lightning."[44] She possesses the strength of the goddess, of a lioness, of lightning: in Bhāī Vīr Singh's artistic realm, there is no hierarchy amongst the Divine, the terrestrial, and the celestial. Images come together from these different worlds to depict *her* vitality and strength.

In many works of fictional literature, the heroine is supposedly exalted as a "desired object."[45] Or in religious life and literature she is often imaged as a distant and ideal goddess. Suṅdarī, on the contrary, is a living person, living in actual life truths and morals enjoined by the Sikh faith. She is a person in flesh and blood who gallops freely with men, cooks with them, and, with them, worships the Transcendent One. She is not a sleeping beauty awaiting her prince charming; nor is she a Sītā devotedly following her beloved Rāma. We find Suṅdarī putting Madonna Kolbenschlag's maxim "Kiss Sleeping Beauty Good-bye"[46] into practice: she abandons all traditional texts and mores that proclaim the passivity and subjugation of women; instead, she provides a holistic model for men and women, opening up new avenues for self-empowerment and transcendence.

CHAPTER 8

# Rāṇī Rāj Kaur: the mystical journey

dhīāṅ māvāṅ bhet ikko hoṅvadā
amīn! tūṅ main ikk doveṅ ikk hāṅ.

Daughters and mothers share but one single mystery,
Mother! You and I are one; we are both one indeed.

The portrayal of Rāṇī Rāj Kaur in *Rāṇā Sūrat Singh* represents the zenith of Bhāī Vīr Singh's creative art and consciousness. To enter the imaginative and mystical world of *Rāṇā Sūrat Singh* is itself, in Harbans Singh's words, "to encounter the poet's mind and soul at their subtlest and most intimate."[1] The poem is more than twelve thousand lines long, and it is unique in Punjabi literature for its form and size as well as its artistic qualities. It was published in 1905 and instantly became a major inspiration for the other writers of the Sikh renaissance.

The epic is a vitally important statement of Sikh mysticism, for it recounts the experience entirely from a Sikh perspective. Mystical experience does, of course, have a universal core, as Evelyn Underhill brought out in her classic work on mysticism from an ecumenical perspective.[2] For her, the intimate and passionate love for Ultimate Reality is the distinctive mark of all mystics irrespective of their racial and religious backgrounds: "There is little difference in this between the extremes of Eastern and Western thought: between A Kempis the Christian and Jalalu'd Din the Moslem saint."[3] If the notion of mysticism is to have any meaning, there must be some truth to this view, but it is somewhat overstated. Even if we can refer to people from very different traditions as mystics and recognize a common element in their experience, they are still mystics within a particular tradition, and this tradition shapes their experience in a very important way. Every mystical experience is, as Steven Katz has argued, mediated through the distinctive tradition of the mystic:

"the experience itself, as well as the form in which it is reported, is shaped by concepts which the mystic brings to, and which shape, his experience."[4] It is within the Sikh context, therefore, that Bhāī Vīr Singh's text expresses the mystic ascent towards the Absolute and with a return, in the fullest and deepest sense, to the particular here and now. Once again, the renaissance writer has chosen a female character to be the central protagonist. A woman's person and psyche thus form the expression for his ultimate ideals and values. A woman, Rāṇī Rāj Kaur, accomplishes the metaphysical journey through the five *Khaṇḍs*, a mystical path that forms the finale to the *Japu*.

Gurū Nānak's *Japu* is the opening text in the Gurū Granth. It has become the morning prayer for the Sikhs and is regarded as the quintessence of Sikh philosophy. The finale to the *Japu* recounts the five stages that lead the individual towards a direct experience of the Transcendent. These five stages are the Realm of Duty (*Dharam Khaṇḍ*), the Realm of Knowledge (*Gyān Khaṇḍ*), the Realm of Beauty (*Saram Khaṇḍ*), the Realm of Grace (*Karam Khaṇḍ*), and the Realm of Truth (*Sac Khaṇḍ*). These five *Khaṇḍs* or stages constitute a path leading onward and upward to higher levels of experience, and they remain the aspiration of every devout Sikh. These five stages of ascension enumerated in the Sikh scripture provide the framework within which Bhāī Vīr Singh artistically depicts the heroine's quest.

One wonders about the title *Rāṇā Sūrat Singh* (*King Sūrat Singh*), for the epic is in fact the story of his queen, Rāṇī Rāj Kaur. It is the story of her heartache and its resolution. Another intriguing aspect of the title is the very name of the king, for *Sūrat* literally means "form." In the story, however, Rāṇā Sūrat Singh is dead, incorporeal, form*less*. The "Sūrat" or form that we are introduced to is one in white marble. It is a statue of a Sikh warrior in the prime of his youth. His body is exquisitely proportioned and his face drawn in chivalrous action. He is firmly seated upon his fiery steed and appears to be galloping swiftly away. The "form" in stone is just a surrogate for the real form, which is in fact a formless form. This formless form resides in the *Sac Khaṇḍ* (the highest stage), which Rāṇī Rāj Kaur ultimately envisions. The epic takes its title from the name of the erstwhile ruler, whom we never encounter directly; but the story is really about the wife, Rāṇī Rāj Kaur. The title *Rāṇā Sūrat Singh* is in the hands of Bhāī Vīr Singh a subtle artistic device: it is what the epic is *not* about. Advancing beyond the normal expectations of the reader, the epic leaves the formal title far behind and instead raises the reader's consciousness towards the Formless.

The book opens with Rāṇī Rāj Kaur's utter dejection. We first meet with her as a tragic widow, forlornly offering flowers at the shrine of her dead husband. The book closes with her attaining perfection and we find her actively engaged in her queenly duties, her hands firmly holding the reins of the kingdom. Rāṇī Rāj Kaur's transformation is the critical juncture of the epic. But the transformation is not merely a change of heart, a dramatic device used by the author to set the plot in motion; it is the transfiguration brought about by her mystical enlightenment. Rāṇī Rāj Kaur enters into this mystical state as she tragically contemplates the loss of her beloved husband. The course of Rāṇī Rāj Kaur's onward and upward journey brings her from a state of utter inaction to a full participation in worldly affairs. She herself narrates the journey to her mother, and this narration constitutes three chapters of Bhāī Vīr Singh's text: "Uḍārī" ("The Flight"), "Darśan" ("The Vision"), and "Utarāī" ("The Descent"). "Uḍārī" represents the protagonist's gradual movement through the *Khaṇḍs* of *Gyān* (knowledge), *Saram* (beauty), and *Karam* (grace) as these realms are understood in Gurū Nānak's *Japu*; "Darśan" is Rāṇī Rāj Kaur's apprehension of the *Sac Khaṇḍ* (Realm of Truth); and "Utarāī" is her return to her earthly existence, charted through the very same stages. These three chapters constitute the core of Rāṇī Rāj Kaur's mystical experience, and will be the focus of this chapter. Through them, the reader is provided with an empirical rendering of the metaphysical structure of the *Khaṇḍs* as enunciated in the *Japu* and as refracted through the prism of Bhāī Vīr Singh's artistic consciousness.

*Dharam Khaṇḍ* (the Realm of Duty) is stated in the *Japu* to be the point at which one's spiritual odyssey originates. As we discussed in Chapter 2, this is the realm in which the "earth" is the infinite matrix. Human beings are nurtured in this sphere; morality and ethics can be fostered here; here lies the opportunity to develop one's personal qualities and engage with the world; here one prepares for the path of ascension. However, of the five realms that are specified in the *Japu* and are central to Sikhism, the *Dharam Khaṇḍ* is the only one that is not mentioned by Bhāī Vīr Singh. Its elimination from the scheme of the epic cannot be construed as indicating the author's disregard of it; Bhāī Vīr Singh in fact suggests that Rāṇī Rāj Kaur has already fulfilled this stage. This is in keeping with Sikh ethics:

stanza 21 of the *Japu* declares that hardly anything is gained from visiting places of pilgrimage or performing austerities or acts of charity. Instead love is appropriated as the highest form of action:

> suṇiā maniā mani kītā bhāo
> antargati tīrathi mali nāo.[5]
>
> Those who hear, appropriate and nurture
> [the disposition of] love in their hearts,
> They cleanse themselves by bathing at the
> sacred fount (*tīrath*) which is within.

We meet with Rāṇī Rāj Kaur when she is consumed in her love for Rāṇā Sūrat Singh. As the story unfolds, we learn that she is the only child of Rājpūt hill monarch ruling in one of the Himalayan principalities. Her father had embraced the Sikh faith under the influence of Sādhū Singh, a Sikh of saintly character who had been driven by State persecution to the safety of the Himalayas. Rāj Kaur was married to Sādhū Singh's son Sūrat Singh, and upon her father's death, her husband succeeded to the title "Rāṇā" ("king"). Like his own father, Sūrat Singh was a saintly person. However, to his intense spirituality he joined the characteristics of a warrior. Even as the ruler of the hill principality, he never failed to answer the call of his fellow-Sikhs who were engaged in a bitter struggle against tyranny and injustice. In one such campaign Rāṇā Sūrat Singh was killed, a tragic event which completely shattered the world of his young bride, Rāṇī Rāj Kaur.

Purgation through love and devotion is the starting point of Sikh mysticism, and Bhāī Vīr Singh elaborates this point throughout his detailed descriptions of the agony of the young love-sick widow. Often he resorts to hyperbole: she weeps tears of blood for him; her life is one long-drawn sigh; nothing assuages the ache in her heart; her youth, beauty, and entire being – "willowy like a virgin sprout freshly sprung" – are wilted by the bereavement of her heart; the glow, native to her years, has evaporated; her face, lovelier than the moon, has from pain of separation become pale like an autumn leaf; her yearning is so intense that she seems to have lost all substantiality; she has become a sheer "love fairy" (*prem dī putalī*); she walks towards the center of the garden as if fragrance itself were wafting; her eyes of wondrous charm are begirt with sadness; by constant weeping they are washed clean and have sunk low; her continuous flow of tears is compared with the unceasing downpour of rain and also with the overflowing river during the month of Sāvan; she sits by the river, and her tears merge in with its waters and flow towards the infinite sea . . .[6] The varied references to water imagery represent the process of purification. Rāṇī Rāj Kaur purges herself by her constant weeping. Through her intense love, she discards the veil of illusion.

Throughout Sikh scripture, love is applauded as the supreme virtue:

> bhagati prem āräditaṁ sacu piāsa paraṁ hitaṁ
> billāp bilal binantīā sukh bhāe cit hitaṁ.[7]
>
> They who worship the One with adoring love and
> thirst for Its True Love,
> They who beseechingly cry out – discover peace,
> for in their heart lies love.

The values idealized in this scriptural verse – worship, adoring love, thirsting for love, crying out beseechingly – are all concretized in the person of Rāṇī Rāj Kaur.

The duties of state which fall to Rāṇī Rāj Kaur on her ascending the throne do not engage her attention. She has the ashes from the cremated body of her husband enshrined in a tomb of white marble along the banks of a cool river, and all her actions revolve around its worship and adoration. Her mother, a powerful figure, dissuades her from all this and asks her instead to consider her social and political position:

> tūṅ rāṇī, sirtāj, mālak desh dī
> duniā tere pair, tarse pūjane.[8]
>
> You are the Rāṇī, the crown and ruler of this country.
> The world but waits to pay homage at your feet.

The sovereign enslaved in her love is an irony the mother cannot unlock. What adds to her confusion is that she knows her daughter to be a highly efficient administrator. In her dialogue with the minister we hear her specify Rāṇī Rāj Kaur's characteristics:

> Rāj Kaur is endowed with many virtues – intelligence, firmness, and wit; she is far-seeing, wise and accomplished in statecraft. If only she would take to her work . . .[9]

But the capricious play of destiny keeps Rāṇī Rāj Kaur engrossed in her love for her departed husband and away from her queenly duties. What also gets verbalized here is that Rāj Kaur's training did not pertain, or at least was not limited, to the palace: the princess was educated and trained in matters of statecraft. The qualities of intelligence (*buddhi*), firmness and strength (*bal*), and wit (*hoś*)[10] attributed to her are certainly cherished by women in the modern world. But for a male writer to spell them out in a place and time where the jewel of woman was (and has still continued to be) her silence or docility, and her arena, the home was daringly innovative.

Of course Rāṇī Rāj Kaur listens to no one. She occupies herself quite differently. She has sent for sculptors from Āgrā and has a life-size white statue of the Rāṇā made. It is a stately figure of a horseman in chaste marble set upon a white pedestal. The statue is placed in a temple specially designed for the purpose. Row upon row of perennial rose encircles the monument. Its boundary wall is made of white stone delicately latticed – the artistic device converting the stone into lace. Minarets adorn the monument. The whole edifice appears to be incorporeal, and the lotus dome itself wafts gently on the horizon.[11]

Totally disengaged from the affairs of state, Rāṇī Rāj Kaur immerses herself in "worshiping" her love. Every day, before the sun rises, she pays her homage at the shrine of Rāṇā Sūrat Singh. Prior to reaching the shrine, she picks up roses and jasmines from the garden which she then delicately rinses in the river. She beads the fresh flowers together with the assiduity of a devotee and makes assorted wreaths and garlands – some single-stringed, others multi-stringed. Their very designs evoke a meditative calm and serenity. The circularity of the wreaths and garlands could also be interpreted as a symbolic extension of the contemplative mood behind the feelings and thoughts of the protagonist.

The meditation through the beading is followed by Rāṇī Rāj Kaur's reverent circumambulation of Rāṇā Sūrat Singh's shrine. At the foot of the statue she lovingly replaces the withered wreaths from the day before with fresh ones from her lap. She "kisses the marble slab – cumdī sil nūṅ" and implores the river to "run by noiselessly – rumke rumke jāhu" lest the murmur disturb him who is enjoying his felicitous sleep.[12]

Face to face with the statue of the Rāṇā, Rāṇī Rāj Kaur joins her palms in obeisance and beseechingly cries out:

ṭhahirīṅ ṭukdam, mīt! sadke jāniāṅ
sarpaṭ assav nā saṭ . . .[13]

Stay, stay a moment dear friend!
Spur not your horse to such hasty speed . . .

She begs the rider in white marble to stop, to stop for a single second. The play between the real and the imagined comes out superbly in these soulful lines. She continues:

vāgān thalh lai
cummān pair rakeb vārā kar lavāṅ
sihare mālā hār jad main pā cukkān
aḍḍī lā ke pher agge jāvanā.[14]

Hold the reins (and stay a while)
So that I may kiss the stirrup upon which your foot rests.
When I have garlanded you with flowers and wreaths,
Then may you gallop away.

On the one hand the figure is as motionless and static as it possibly can be. The reins are tightened to the degree that the stoppage can be forever! But on the other hand, all that the Rāṇī sees is movement: the rider is galloping away too swiftly, so swiftly that "he appears to be conversing with the winds – gallāṅ nāl havāo kardā jāvaṅdā . . ."[15] In the static statue she perceives fierce motion; the distance from her is ever increasing. And, therefore, she keeps on imploring sorrowfully:

kūnj vāṅg kurlāṭ ro ro pāṅvadī.[16]
Like the *kūnj* bird she plaintively cries.

Crying she loses consciousness many times. At one time, while overwhelmed by her yearning, "her temperature drops and she becomes cold and white like ice – thaṅḍī ciṭ, ciṭṭāk, surtoṅ sakhanī, baraf śilā de vāṅg,"[17] and for several hours remains in a swoon. Her maid searching for her mistress eventually reaches the spot where the Rāṇī lies, and she is baffled at the sight. The ever-faithful maid, Rādhā, cannot decipher what has happened to her mistress: "Is she asleep, dead, or unconscious? O my lovely Rāj – suttī, moī kī hoś nassī es ton? Hāi piārī Rāj!"[18] Upon realizing that the Rāṇī is unconscious, Rādhā runs to the river, soaks her handkerchief in the running waters, and applies it gently to her mistress's forehead and brings her back to life.

The intensity and fervor of Rāj Kaur's love is similarly depicted in the scene where she is circumambulating the image of the Rāṇā. Something inside her snaps, and she falls to the ground cold like a stone:

mūrat vargī hoi mūrat sāhmane
sathar paī cufāl, pathar jāpdī
butt de pairīṅ butt māno pai rihā.[19]

A lifeless image she became
In front of a lifeless image.
A statue prostrate in homage before a statue.

Once again the maid Rādhā rescues her and exclaims:

eh jīvegī nahīṅ kuṭhī prem dī
khāṇā pīṇa tyāg hoī bāulī
thaṇḍe laindī svās rondī, kūkdī.[20]

She is not going to live for long
her heart is pierced by love.
She touches neither food nor drink;
Sighs and tears are what she lives on.

The Mūl Mantra is, quite appropriately, inscribed on the shrine of the Rāṇā, highlighting the centrality of the Singular Reality – *Ikk Oaṅ Kār* – in the Sikh faith. However, it is not clear whether the inscription was put there under explicit instructions from the Rāṇī. Indeed, so much in Sikh life (art and letters) is marked by the Mūl Mantra that the author probably did not think it necessary to mention any overt statement from the Rāṇī requesting its placement. What is relevant is that she has other verses from *bāṇī* inscribed below the Mūl Mantra. An explication of these verses can provide us with an understanding of the author's intention. He wishes to relate the Rāṇī's love for the Rāṇā to the Sikh moral virtue of adoring love for the Transcendent Being, the Singular Reality of the Mūl Mantra. Engraved in stone, the following verse intimates the Yonder:

muā jīvandā pekhu jīvande mari jānī
jinā muhabbati ikk sio te mānas pardhān[21]

They alone live who to their own selves die,
Not they who live for their selfish selves.
They who love the One, they form the acme of humankind.

The choice of these lines relfects Rāṇī Rāj Kaur's essential disposition: the love (*muhabbati*) she bears the One (*Ikk*). They also reveal Rāṇī Rāj Kaur's condition: she is "dead to herself." Devoid of any egotistical or selfish motives, the Rāṇī's being is saturated with elemental love and longing.

Furthermore, love is perceived by Rāṇī Rāj Kaur as a concretization of the Formless. In her own words, "prem prabhū dā rūp – love is the image (*rup*) of the Divine (*prabhū*)."[22] Love is the Reality Itself, and for her it also constitutes the *path* to union with that Reality.

> jāṇan hovai gyān, keval jāṇanā
> bhaktī vālā prem hovai prāpatī.[23]
>
> Through knowledge one obtains but knowledge;
> Through love one obtains union.

Here she is giving precedence to devotional love over gnosis. The quest for knowledge is laudable and can bring about an enlightenment of the spirit which draws one towards the Supreme Reality. Yet, it does not establish unity with the Transcendent One. For that, adoration and love are required.

In her discourse with the Queen Mother, Rāj Kaur voices the immutability and eternity of her "transcendental love." The mother asks her not to waste herself away in mourning and longing, but to engage instead in the affairs of state, for work would cure her sickness. Time, she adds, is the greatest of remedies for the affliction of separation. The daughter gently controverts her mother's logic:

> prem guṇāṅ dā hor – ātam – prem jo
> eh jo lāve tīr dūṅghā vinnadā
> is vijhaṇ dā phaṭṭ samāṅ nā meldā
> ātam amar sadīv – ātam nā mare
> prem jo ātam saṅg uh bī jīvaṅdā.[24]
>
> Love of the form is different from the love of the essence,
> When this strikes, the arrows pierce deep,
> Its wounds no time can heal,
> The essence is eternal – it is constant
> And so, too, the love of it.

Rāj Kaur in the opening line distinguishes between "love for the form" (*prem guṇāṅ dā*) and transcendental love or "love for the essence" (*ātam-prem*). The former is subject to time. Just as qualities and forms (*guṇa*) are themselves modalities subject to change, so the love (*prem*) for them cannot of necessity be permanent. However, what attaches to the Eternal Reality cannot but be immutable. Indeed, because the object of *ātam prem* is Pure Essence and the Formless, that love itself transcends all time, space, and causality. For the Rāṇī, love's ultimate goal is union with the Transcendent.

Despite her apparent yearning for this heroic Sikh, her love for Rāṇā Sūrat Singh is in fact for the immaterial, substanceless, *non*-Sūrat Singh. For her the Rāṇā is light, formless, and immortal.

Very early in the story we begin to feel that Rāṇī Rāj Kaur's pining for her husband is unusual. As a young wife who suddenly loses her much-loved husband, why does she not reminisce in the traditional way: recount past joys, power, and privileges? Regret not having children with him? Express an inability to cope with her new situation? Instead, we hear her full of remorse for not having discerned him as the "light" he was. In her own words:

tūṅ ātam prakāś miṭṭī aṅdh maiṅ
tūṅ saiṅ ṭukṛā nūr dehī jāṇiān
tūṅ saiṅ preṁ prakāś, suhṇā jāṇkai
– patī jāṇke – nitt tainūṇ seviā
tūṅ saiṅ cāṇan sāf, aṇīn maiṅ rahī
merī buddhi malīn aṭkī deh te.[25]

You were the intangible light, I a lump of darkness;
You were a particle of light itself; I knew you, but as substance only;
You were the brilliance of love itself; I knew you only as handsome –
As my husband – constantly I adored you.
You were the transparent lustre, but I remained opaque and blind –
My understanding stuck on tangible form alone.

As we saw in Chapter 2, the Transcendent in Sikh scriptures is expressed through light (*joti* or *nūr*). Here again Bhāī Vīr Singh depicts Rāj Kaur availing herself of this symbol from the Gurū Granth in apprehending the spirituality and immateriality of the Rāṇā. Several nuances of the term "light" are implicit: *prakāś*, *nūr*, and *cāṇan*. Furthermore, light as a symbol is approached from different angles – as spiritual light (ātam prakāś), as light itself (*nūr*), as light or effulgence of love (*prem prakāś*), and as transparent light or luster (*cāṇan sāf*). These terms, with varying shades and emphases, portray Rāṇā Sūrat Singh as the immaterial "light." And the Rāṇī's great regret is that she did not recognize him as such when he was alive. Opaque and blind, she saw him only as a husband and failed to see in him the radiance through which she could recognize the light. In her ignorance she thinks that she is "like the intoxicated bee fed on the honey of flowers and the drunk deer inebriated with its own musky fragrance – ḍiggī mastī khāe bhaure vāṅg maiṅ kastūre mrig vāṅg mattī hoe ke."[26] She is guilty of having been oblivious to the light itself. She grieves for having continually fed herself, like the intoxicated bee and the deer, upon the materiality, the *sūrat* (form) of Rāṇā Sūrat Singh.

Through the image of light emerged the second important idea associated with the Rāṇā, that of insubstantiality and formlessness. Rāṇī Rāj Kaur clearly states that the object of her love is formless. To her mother she says:

samajh nā bholī māoṅ! bacārī bāolī,
miṭṭī nāl sneh karke mar rahī.
miṭṭī vic samādh mere kol hai,
sūrat bhī hai pas butt dikhāṅvadā.
miṭṭi, sūrat prem jekar honvadā
kī sī maithoṅ dūr? doveṅ kol se.[27]

Think not, O innocent mother, that your daughter is insane,
Or that she is destroying herself pining for dust which is to dust returned.
I possess the dust – in the shrine it remains embodied,
The form too – it is there in solid sculpture.
Both the dust and the form I possess.
If I loved the dust or the form,
What would I want? Both these I have closely within my reach.

Rāṇī Rāj Kaur tells her mother that she has the dust, the matter, the body (ashes) of her husband. So, too, she has the form, for Rāṇā Sūrat Singh's form or *sūrat* definitely stands tangible and triumphant in the marble statue. If she loved these, she still has them. But it is the formlessness, the essence, the being of Rāṇā Sūrat Singh which is not there, and that is what she yearns for. To seek the one beyond the form is the true object of Rāṇī Rāj Kaur's love.

It is ironic that even the "form" in stone somehow remains beyond her grasp. This is indicated at least twice in the narrative. As we saw earlier, its inaccessibility is seen when she encounters the perpetual movement of the sculptured figure. Riding his horse, the Sikh warrior seems to be speeding along, and the Rāṇī implores him over and over again to tighten the reins and stop for a moment. It is seen again when she is ready to put garlands around the neck of the marble Rāṇā Sūrat Singh and realizes she cannot reach up to him! Again we hear her beseech him:

sīs nivāo sujān! seharā pā lavā
uccī hai dastār hath na apaṛe
mālā lao puvā piāre kant jī
maiṅ nirbal hāṅ nār ucce āp ho.[28]

Pray bend your head, good husband!
so that I may put these garlands around you.
Your turban is high, my hands don't reach you.
Do accept my garlands, dear husband.
I am a feeble woman and you stand up high.

Thus even in the static stone, directly across from her, he is inaccessible. Whether by galloping away with the velocity of wind or by being too tall, Rāṇā Sūrat Singh remains beyond reach. He inhabits the distant world of the Formless.

This world is that of immortality, the third major characteristic of Rāṇā Sūrat Singh. He is portrayed as one who was the very personification of morality. Rāṇī Rāj Kaur sees in him a rarefied individual who had achieved immortality in this world through his highly ethical conduct:

āp sadā ikk raṅg turgaye jīvaṅde
āp na moe mūl sad hī jīvaṅde.[29]

Always of single color were you,
and alive passed away from here.
You did not die: you dwell in the here and now.

The singleness of color (*ikk raṅg*) marks Rāṇā Sūrat Singh's constancy and his equipoise. He remained in one stable mental state, above all the fluctuations that time, space, and causality can create. He thus obtained immortality within life. His death, then, does not mark a transition from one condition to another; he *is* as he *was*: permanent, immutable. His "light" and "formlessness" are but pointers to his having attained intrinsic knowledge of the Transcendent, to his existing without the proclivities normally associated with mortality, its heaviness, laziness, ignorance.

Thus the Rāṇā Sūrat Singh whom Rāṇī Rāj Kaur yearns for day and night is neither the gallant Sikh warrior and chieftain of the hill kingdom nor the handsome husband whom she knew him to be. For her, he is sheer light, without form, totally impalpable, and the embodiment of morality. The vocabulary, symbols, and concepts used in *bāṇī* to point to the One Beyond are applied by Rāṇī Rāj Kaur to Rāṇā Sūrat Singh. In this manner she is able to forge a link between the Transcendent One and Rāṇā Sūrat Singh. It is as though the universal Transcendent had been particularized in "Sūrat" Singh. This particularization renders depth and concreteness to the Rāṇī's love and adoration. It is also in keeping with the theme of the bride seeking for her Absolute Bridegroom, which is central to the metaphysics of the Gurū Granth. The Rāṇā exists, but as a symbol, a surrogate,[30] for the Rāṇī's Transcendent Ideal.

The union with the ideal that Rāṇī Rāj Kaur seeks is a metaphysical seeing. She says:

locāṅ din te rāt piāre mel nūn
dehu daras ıkk var dildevāliā.[31]

Night and day I crave for the union:
Grant unto me the favor of a single glimpse, my beloved!

Here she identifies the *mel* ("union") with *daras* ("glimpse," "vision"). Her overwhelming desire is not to reside with him in the afterworld, not to embrace him physically; rather, it is to snatch a glimpse of him. The same wish is couched in the following words:

labhdī hārī hāi! niklo tāṅ kadī
devo daras dikhāi darśan locdī.[32]

I am exhausted searching for you! Do appear sometime.
Let me once see you with my eyes; I so hunger for a glimpse of you.

Whereas in the former passage she seems to be seeking a vision, in the latter she seems to be soliciting a revelation. In both instances, however, her objective is to obtain an insight into the Beyond. Her eyes long to see the meta-physical.

Her craving and hunger are a palpable manifestation of Nānak's injunction cited in Chapter 1:

jhūthu alāvai kāmi na āvai
nā piru dekhai naiṇī.[33]

One utters untruth and accomplishes but little,
If one does not see the Infinite with one's own eyes.

At the core, then, is the quest for the vision of the Transcendent. On the one hand, Rāṇī Rāj Kaur's ardent devotion to Rāṇā Sūrat Singh shows her availing herself of the great potentiality of love in the *Dharam Khaṇḍ*; on the other, it prepares her and spurs her onward and upward on the path of spiritual ascension. Her deep love qualifies her to go beyond the *Dharam Khaṇḍ*.

Having established love as the point of departure, Bhāī Vīr Singh artistically renders the mystical voyage through the next four stages of Sikh mysticism. When analyzed closely, Rāṇī Rāj Kaur's case reveals some remarkable parallels with the characteristics of mysticism described by William James. During the early part of the twentieth century, James made his great investigation of religion. His study included both western and eastern subjects and culminated in his famous text *The Varieties of Religious Experience*. Here James describes the four characteristics of the mystical experience shared by all mystics: (1) ineffability, (2) noetic quality, (3) transiency, and (4) passivity. The Jamesian outline illuminates the nature of Rāṇī Rāj Kaur's experience, though I would like to modify the order in which he enumerates these categories. At the moment of the mystical experience itself, one cannot be actively seeking the divine object; one is grasped by the Other only in a state of utter passivity. The mystical journey begins therefore with passivity, and this is what I have chosen as the starting point of my analysis. The other characteristics can be recognized only later, for in this stage of passivity we are clearly unable to discern its ineffability and noetic quality. And finally, it is only when we look back upon a mystical experience that we can reflect upon its transiency. In examining this experience, I would like to follow the order of the process itself, rather than to explore its characteristics in the abstract.

### *Passivity*

James lists passivity as the fourth characteristic of mysticism, and yet he acknowledges that it is the true beginning of the mystical state:

> Although the oncoming of mystical states may be facilitated by preliminary voluntary operations, as by fixing the attention, or going through certain bodily performances, or in other ways which manuals of mysticism prescribe; yet when the characteristic sort of consciousness once has set in, the mystic feels as if his own will were in abeyance, and indeed sometimes as if he were grasped and held by a superior power.[34]

We find that in the case of Rāṇī Rāj Kaur, the setting-in of the mystical state is not facilitated by any preliminary voluntary operation. One day she is sitting in the loft and looking out of the window at nature's miraculous scene. On the distant horizon, the sun is lowering, and the day, along with the sun, seems to be vanishing. Innumerable thoughts assail her grieving heart. She imagines the Rāṇā as the sun and herself as the day. Why, alas, did she not follow him as dutifully as the day did the sun!

sūraj āthan nāl din nahīṅ āthiā
rāṇe jī de nāl main nā kyoṅ gaī?[35]

Did not the day set with the setting sun?
Why then did I not accompany Rāṇāji?

Tears overwhelm her, and she falls into a swoon. In that state she witnesses something very strange happening. Her volition is suspended and her weight holds her down no more. Her "self" has escaped from the body and starts to soar upward:

main jātā chhaḍ deh nikalī bār hāṅ
nikal callī hāṅ uḍḍ uppar vār nūn . . .[36]

I felt as if I had stolen out of my body,
And was flying upwards . . .

She describes this state to her mother in vivid detail: "she felt as if she were a kite or a bird flying high on the horizon – jikkur uḍadī jāi guḍḍī aṁbarī." The title of the chapter – "Uḍārī" – signifies flight. From above, Rāṇī Rāj Kaur can see her earthly surroundings. She sees the palace, the forest, the pastures, the trees, the river, the mausoleum, gardens, orchards, servants, maids, and her mother. She also sees her own body lying on the earth below:

atī acaraj main hoī dekhāṅ āp nūn; –
ch kī vartayā khel? kitheh ā gaī
dehī paī bihoś! main hāṅ jāgadī![37]

In utter amazement I looked upon myself;
What strange phenomenon was this? Where had I come?
Below my body lies unconscious; yet here I soar fully awake!

This marks Rāṇī Rāj Kaur's crossing of the *Dharam Khaṇḍ*, the Realm of Duty. Having transcended it, she can now observe the physical universe whose center is the earth, a center she has broken away from and from which she feels no gravitational pull.

In James' language, "the characteristic sort of consciousness" has indeed set in. But it was not induced by any bodily performances or behavior prescribed in traditional manuals on mysticism. Rāṇī Rāj Kaur, we must remember, was looking out of the window at the sun setting on the distant horizon when the mystical experience seized her; she was not self-consciously fixing her attention on anything particular in an effort to induce that state. Her love-sick plight provokes the ascension, and not some conditioned mandatory action. By medieval times, yoga, with its varied schools, practices, myths, theologies, and elaborate manuals had proliferated throughout northern India. Haṭha Yoga along with Rāja Yoga, Śaktism, and Kuṇḍalīnī, emphasizing *āsana* (bodily postures) and *prāṇāyāma* (breath control) and other bodily exertions to induce levitation and exalted states of consciousness were prevalent.[38] Rāṇī Rāj Kaur's "non-activity" is in congruence with Sikh religious practice, wherein prescribed texts, bodily exercises, and ritualistic techniques to induce higher states of consciousness find no place. In the scriptures (for example, in the *Japu*, *Siddh Goṣṭi*, and *Rāg Mārū*) their significance is even denied. Gurū Nānak made this point in *Rāg Mārū*.

ikki nāge bhūkhe bhavehi bhavāe
ikki haṭhu kari marehi na kīmate pāe . . .
ikki tīrathi nāvehi ann̐u na khāvehi
ikki agani jalāvehi deh khapāvehi
rāmnām binu mukti na hoī
kitu bidhi pāri lan̐ghāī he?[39]

Some wander about naked and hungry;
Others force themselves to death by undergoing austerities (*haṭha*) . . .
Some go on pilgrimages, fast, and starve themselves;
Others burn away their bodies before blazing fires;
But without the Divine Name, there is no liberation.
Without the Divine Name, how to cross this ocean?

He repeated his disapproval of yoga techniques in *Vār Rāmkalī*:

haṭhu nigrahu kari kāiā chhījai
varatu tapanu kari manu nahī bhījai.[40]

Through practice of *haṭha* (yoga) the body is emaciated;
Through fasting and penances the mind is not absorbed in the love of the One.

Gurū Angad (Nānak II) does the same in *Rāg Mārū*:

niolī karam bhuian̐gam bhāṭhī
recak kumbhak pūrak man hāṭhī
pākhaṇḍ dharamu prīti nahi hari sao . . .[41]

Ritual cleansing of the intestines and igniting the furnace of *bhuiangam*,
The inhaling, exhaling, and controlling of breath,
All these are but outward shows of religion and do not lead to true love for the One . . .

In all these verses the Sikh Gurūs reject enfeebling the body, fasting and starving (*bhūkeh bhavae* or *annu nā khāvehi*), and practicing austerities (*haṭhu kari*); they reject kindling the power of the hidden serpent in one's body known as *bhuiangam* or *kuṇḍalīnī*; they reject the technique of breath control (*recak*, "exhaling," *pūrak*, "inhaling," and *kuṁbhak*, "keeping the breath in"); and they reject physical pain such as withstanding the heat of burning flames (*agani jalāvehi*). Instead, the Gurū Granth proclaims an inward, natural, and thorough phenomenon – drenching (*bhījai*) in love (*prīti*).

We find Rāṇī Rāj Kaur simply sitting in the loft and looking out of the window. Her eyes are not focussed on anything specific; she is not waiting to be induced into any higher mental state. Nor is she involved in any external physical exercise. She is only drenched in love, body and soul. Through the instance of Rāṇī Rāj Kaur, Bhāī Vīr Singh rejects any possibility of reaching the mystical stage and transcending *Dharam Khaṇḍ* except through a devout love of the Divine. Towards the close of the epic, he explicitly restates the scriptural disapproval of all conscious and outwardly ritualistic and bodily exercises as a means to liberation:

joga na ākhān uh muṁdarāṅ kan pā . . .
nāṅ main hāṅ haṭh joga etheh dassadā –
kaśṭ sādhanāṅ nāl dehi sādhaṇī . . .
rāj yoga, nāṅ yoga ākhāṅ sāṅkha dā
par juṛ sāīṅ nāl nāl prem de.[47]

I am not asking you to observe Yoga, which requires
the wearing of big earrings and having split lobes . . .
Nor am I here expounding Haṭha yoga –
And the arduous techniques it prescribes for the control of body
and mind . . .
Nor am I asking you to take up Rāja yoga or Sāṁkhya,
But I do say to you: unite with the Husband and with love alone
do so.

Through these words (spoken by an elderly and wise Sikh to Rāṇī Rāj Kaur) the practices and philosophies of Haṭha, Kanphat, Rāja, and Sāṁkhya are further discountenanced.

As Rāṇī Rāj Kaur floats upward, unaided, she sees one vast luminosity spread all around which for her is more dazzling than the dazzle of lightning itself. In this brilliance there appear millions and millions of blithesome spirits, swimming across the skies. One of them comes forward swiftly:

naṭhi dūroṅ āī maiṅ val dhāuṅdī
āke lityus pāī ghuṭ galvakkaṛī
kardī aidāṅ pyār bhaināṅ kardīāṅ
bhainoṅ bi uh vaddh, āpaṇe āp dā
dūjā addhā bhāg maiṅūn jāpdā
usde miliāṅ ṭhanḍ maiṅūṅ pai gaī.[43]

From far away she came rushing towards me,
And embraced me tightly.
She caressed me lovingly as only a sister would
Yet more than a sister she seemed to me –
The other half of my own self,
So soothed was I at meeting with her.

Passivity as characteristic of mysticism contains, according to James, the element of being "grasped"; and Rāṇī Rāj Kaur has certainly been "grasped." The beautiful and joyous figure comes rushing towards her and "embraces her tightly (pāī ghuṭ galvakkaṛī)." Although she may in fact be "superior," for she is a permanent resident of this lustrous realm and also has the answer to the Rāṇī's queries, the divine figure is perceived as an equal by Rāṇī Rāj Kaur. This we infer from the Rāṇī's acknowledgment of her as more than a sister – "the other half of my own self – āpane āp dā dūjā addhā bhāg." The grasping or seizing, moreover, is not an awesome or overwhelming phenomenon; rather it is characterized by gentleness. In the Rāṇī's words, "so soothed was I at meeting with her." The Punjabi word *ṭhanḍ* ("coolness") appropriately captures the effect. This fairy-like companion bringing solace to Rāṇī Rāj Kaur's heart is reminiscent of the beautiful feminine voice resounding over the waters of the lake in Bhāī Vīr Singh's poem entitled *Jīvan kī Hai?* It is this sisterly figure which then guides the Rāṇī onward:

uh hor uḍḍī upare
maiṅūn laike nāl āpane āsare[44]

She soared further aloft
Bearing me alongside.

In an embrace, the two females glide higher and higher. Rāṇī Rāj Kaur's own self and will are effaced; she soars under the care and with the momentum of the celestial figure. At the opening as well as at the close of the narration of her extraordinary experience, the Rāṇī tells her mother that she has no control over herself. Towards the beginning of the chapter entitled "Uḍārī," she says:

amī, nahīoṅ vass mere kujj bī.[45]

Mother, I have no power over myself.

And towards the end of the same chapter, she again says:

par mere nā vass dekho āp hī
– soc samajh ke hāl – merī be-vassī.[46]

But I have no power over myself – see for yourself.
Do think of my condition – my utter helplessness.

In both these instances, Rāṇī Rāj Kaur expresses her state: she has no control or power (*vass*) over herself. In order for her experience to be understood correctly, she pleads with the listener, her mother in this case, to recognize her condition of utter "passivity" (*be-vassī*).

*Ineffability*

William James maintains that ineffability is the foremost characteristic of mysticism:

The handiest of the marks by which I classify a state of mind as mystical is negative. The subject of it immediately says that it defies expression, that no adequate report of its contents can be given in words. It follows from this that its quality must be directly experienced; it cannot be imparted or transferred to others. In this peculiarity mystical states are more like states of feeling than like states of intellect. No one can make clear to another who has never had a certain feeling, in what the quality of worth of it consists.[47]

In the category of "ineffability," James refers actually to two qualities of mysticism: it defies expression, and it is experienced directly. Both are prominent in the depiction of Rāṇī Rāj Kaur's ascension.

As to the first, there are several occasions during the course of her narration when Rāṇī Rāj Kaur is reduced to saying, "I cannot put it into words . . .," especially when she is asked to recount a particular experience and when she is asked for a straightforward description of something she has apprehended. At the outset of the flight, prior to her being lovingly seized by the divine sister, she sees myriads of blithesome figures, and she exclaims: "kīku karāṅ biān rūp ināh dā?[48] – How can I describe their splendor?" It was from amongst these that her "other half" came rushing forward to her. Rāṇī Rāj Kaur had never seen anything so beautiful before:

dunīān dī suhannap enhāṅ sāhmane
sīgī kāī mail jikkur hoṅvadī[49]

The beauty of the world was
as if dark soot compared to theirs.

She indeed has no words to describe the loveliness of those creatures. All she can do is to make a negative comparison, to negate all the beauty of our world in comparison to theirs.

Rāṇī Rāj Kaur asks her celestial guide about her departed husband and is told that he resides in the *Sac Khaṇḍ*, the fifth and final realm, the Realm of Truth. The Rāṇī further questions: "kithe hai uh deś kinhī dūr? ais thāoṅ toṅ, hor? kihṛī lāmbh hai?[50] – Where is that region? How far? Somewhere away from here? In which direction?" The companion laughs loudly and asks the Rāṇī in return why she does not remember the *bāṇī*. She then recites canto 37 of the *Japu* for Rāṇī Rāj Kaur. This canto is Gurū Nānak's evocation of the *Sac Khaṇḍ*, the Realm of the Transcendent One. After the recitation, she says:

dekh gurūjī de vāk kī han ākhde:
karaṛā jikur sār kathnā osdā
ākh na sakdā koī, samajh nā āvandī . . .
dekhan hī parvān us dā piāriē!
suniāṅ samajh nā āi kahinā saukh nā[51]

See what the Gurū's words say?
To describe it is as difficult as to break iron,
None can truly describe, none can truly comprehend . . .
Seeing it alone is knowing it!
For hearing of it, we do not comprehend, and speaking of it is
far from easy.

The emphasis is upon the "ineffability" of the Realm of Truth, for any effort to describe it is "as difficult as to break iron." In this passage we also discern the connection between the impossibility of expression and the directness of experience that was made by William James. For when the guiding spirit asks Rāṇī Rāj Kaur to reflect upon the canto from the *Japu* (interestingly, the imperative used for reflection is *dekh*, "see"), the guide states: "dekhan hī paravān – seeing is the only valid testimony." There can be no other one. True recognition of the *Sac Khaṇḍ* comes, therefore, only with the direct experience of seeing.

As she continues to describe the path upward through the realms of *Gyān*, *Saram*, and *Karam* to the ultimate vision of the *Sac Khaṇḍ*, the Rāṇī at each stage reiterates the impossibility of verbally expressing what she has seen. Each time there is an added, more eloquent nuance when she declares the ineffability of her experience. For instance, as they approach the Realm of Knowledge (*Gyān Khaṇḍ*), the second stage, she describes it as follows:

> sunder te ramnīk, sobhā kī kahāṅ!
> camake vāṅg balaur dhartī esdī . . .
> śristī horo raṅg, racanā hor sī
> mūhoṅ sakāṅ na ākh, dekhī sī nahīṅ
> suṇī nā aisī sīg pahile maiṅ kadī[52]

> It was beautiful and enchanting; how can I describe it?
> Its ground shone like crystal.
> This was a world of another color altogether, a creation of a
> different order totally.
> I cannot describe it; nothing like this had I seen before,
> Nor had I heard of anything like it.

The Rāṇī is amazed to see the crystal-like ground of this realm, upon which plants and trees with infinite flowers and fruits grow – each more delicate and tender than the other. She also meets with myriads of beings who appear without a frown upon their brow, all blissfully immersed in singing the glory of the Eternal One. Everything is of a different hue, of a different order. Since she had never seen (*dekhī sī nahīṅ*) or heard of anything like it before (*suṇī na aisī*), Rāṇī Raj Kaur cannot say in words how wonderstruck she felt (*mūhoṅ sakāṅ na ākh*). Faltering, she tries to convey the inappropriateness of even attempting to do so:

> ākhāṅ kī maiṅ hor vall na āvandā
> jo ākhāṅ maiṅ uhu aslī hāl toṅ
> horo laike bhāv bandā hor hai[53]

> What more can I say? I am unaware of any method.
> Whatever I say taking a hue different from the reality
> Transforms into something utterly different.

Here Rāṇī Rāj Kaur accepts her helplessness. However hard she tries to portray the splendor of the *Gyān Khaṇḍ*, she cannot succeed, for her words ever fall short of the reality and render only an unfair version of it. The finitude of human language, its inadequacy in conveying the meaning of essence, indeed its final inapplicability to the spiritual condition are all marked by Bhāī Vīr Singh.

Regarding the third sphere, the *Saram Khaṇḍ*, with its beauty and joy surpassing that of the *Gyān Khaṇḍ*, Rāṇī Rāj Kaur says:

lokī kahin bikunṭh – par uh cīz kī
ikk ikk ethe jīv race bikunṭh hai.[54]

We worldly creatures speak of heaven –
but what heaven could compare with this condition?
Here each and every being created his/her own heaven.

In her description of the third stage of the *Japu*, our protagonist resorts to the apex of human imagination, to the term "heaven" (*baikunṭh*). But what heaven could compare with the state she has observed? The highest idea or image does not suffice to describe it. After all her endeavors, she helplessly owns: "ākh na maiṅ sakāṅ[55] – I simply cannot say."

The two then enter the fourth region, the Realm of *Karam* or Grace. This for the Rāṇī is beauty itself: "this is the pinnacle of beauty that one can reach – sundartā ati tī pahuṅcī es thāṅ." Its loveliness, once again, is both inexpressible (*akath*) and immeasurable (*apār*). Hereafter, she tends to give up even her explicit pronouncements of its ineffability. Her narration becomes paradoxical and abstruse:

jo kujh sī is thāoṅ usdā rūp nā
phir par nahīṅ arūp – rūp arūp sī.[56]

Whatever was in this region, it had no form,
But again not formless – only form was formless here.

Here she is trying to make a distinction between Pure Formlessness (*arūp*) and the most subtle and "formless form" (*rūp arūp*). Still a step below the *Sac Khaṇḍ*, the Realm of Pure Formlessness, the Rāṇī in the *Karam Khaṇḍ* sees "forms" of great heroes and heroines who are formless, without attributes, completely lacking in gross materiality. The nexus between the two regions – *Saram* and *Karam* – is also rendered paradoxically:

ṭikkī sūraj dvāl jikur tej dī
manḍal bhāse vakh juṛiā nāl hī.[57]

Like the halo of light around the sun,
Which appears to be different yet is united with it.

Is the halo of light the same as the sun? Or is it something different from that? It is through the constant use of such rhetorical questioning that Rāṇī Rāj Kaur intimates the ineffability of the Realm of Grace.

Finally, when they approach the *Sac Khaṇḍ*, Rāṇī Rāj Kaur sees her husband sitting at the feet of the ten Gurūs, who are seated amidst powerful and infinite light:

> je ākhāṅ se vakkh tā bhī ṭhīk nāṅ
> je ākhāṅ se ikk tāṅ bhī bhulladī.[58]
>
> If I say they were distant from each other, I should err;
> If I say they were one, mistaken I would still be.

Rāṇī Rāj Kaur admits that no adequate description of the *Sac Khaṇḍ* can ever be attempted. Whatever words she may use, whatever distinctions or non-distinctions she may make, her vision (*darśan*) cannot be accurately expressed. The Rāṇī eventually gives up attempting to formulate in words and concepts what she has seen:

> patā na ḍithe bājh sakdā lagg hai
> ḍithe bājh suād, āve hai nahīṅ.[59]
>
> Without seeing, it cannot be comprehended;
> Without seeing, the ecstasy cannot be savored.

During her ascent, Rāṇī Rāj Kaur experiences higher and higher states of feeling. These, however, go hand in hand with the heightening of her awareness. The Jamesian priority of "feeling" over "intellect" does not apply to her case. For the more she experiences emotionally and sensuously, the more she comprehends intellectually. Bhāī Vīr Singh portrays Rāṇī Rāj Kaur in accordance with the Sikh metaphysical tradition wherein the individual exists as a unity of body, senses, perceptions, intellect, and consciousness. Rāṇī Rāj Kaur has an immediate and full experience of lightness and radiance; a sensory intensification accompanies her intellectual experience.

We may recall that the ascent begins with her undergoing a feeling of "lightness": leaving her body on the ground below, Rāṇī Rāj Kaur begins to soar like a bird in the skies.[60] Although her corporeal form remains in the loft of her mansion, her senses and perceptions are very much with her. As she herself says:

> dehī paī behoś! main hāṅ jāgdī!
> haulī phulloṅ vaddh, halkī pauṇ toṅ . . .
> uḍḍī jāvāṅ āp āpne āp hī.[61]
>
> The body is lying unconscious; here I am soaring fully awake!
> Lighter than a flower, lighter than a breeze . . .
> Flying ever higher involuntarily.

The Rāṇī is bewildered at her own condition: she is at once unconscious and conscious! To the previous analogies of flight (that of the paper kite and the bird) are now added those of the lightness of the flower and the breeze. Throughout she feels herself being caressed by the most subtle and soothing breeze: "phir aithe ikk pauṇ halkī att dī sūkham vāṅg akāś, pāve japhīāṅ[62] – then a delicate breeze, subtle like ether, was embracing me."

The lightness thus depicted keeps becoming subtler at every stage. For instance, as they leave the *Gyān Khaṇḍ* for the *Saram Khaṇḍ*:

> mār uḍārī pher ethoṅ uḍḍīāṅ
> sūkham taral ju deh merī, māo! sī
> hun palṭī u hor sūkham ho gaī.[63]
>
> Flying off again from here we flew onwards;
> My body light as it was, O mother,
> Now transformed – becomes lighter still.

Rāṇī Rāj Kaur is thus aware of her "body" (*deh*). Her body is transformed at every stage, becoming lighter and lighter. The lightness is essentially an expression of Rāṇī Rāj Kaur's weightlessness, of the ease of her upward movement, of her feeling free and liberated.

Bhāī Vīr Singh endows her with a second characteristic, that of purity. Rāṇī Rāj Kaur expresses how this happens to her:

> camkāṅ hīre vāṅg nirmal ho rahī.[64]
> Glittering like a gem, I was becoming purer.

More than indicating the outward cleansing of the person, the term *nirmal* (*nir*, "without," and *mal*, "impurity") refers to the cleansing of the heart and the descending of peace upon the mind. It recurs frequently in the Sikh scriptures, each time with a moralistic import. According to Gurū Arjan (Nānak V) "so tanu nirmalu jitu upajai na pāpu[65] – that body alone is pure (*nirmalu*) which harbors no sin." Hence in her feeling "light," the aesthetic state (*camkāṅ* – "glittering like a gem") is related to the ethical state (*nirmal* – "pure"). This is markedly different from, for example, the Kierkegaardian pattern of ascension, where the aesthetic ("Stage One") precedes the ethical ("Stage Two"). In Rāṇī Rāj Kaur's spiritual journey, the aesthetic and the moral are intertwined, and together they contribute to her ethereal voyage. Already in the *Gyān Khaṇḍ* she realizes this connection:

– sāḍī sūkham deh palṭī sī gaī
ho ati sūkham hor bahut prakāśdī
samajh, buddhi, bal, zor hoiā vadh sī.[66]

Our corporeal form altered
We became lighter and brightly luminous
Heightening manifold our understanding, intellect, energy, and power.

These lines enable us to apprehend that as Rāṇī Rāj Kaur and her celestial guide glide higher, they not only become lighter (*sūkham*) and more lustrous (*prakāśdī*), but their understanding (*samajh*), intellect (*buddhi*), energy (*bal*), and power (*zor*) also increase. As they approach the light and as they themselves grow lighter, they are endowed with greater physical and mental powers. Rāṇī Rāj Kaur's ascent is thus intimately related to a stage in which her physical, aesthetic, moral, and intellectual faculties keep getting more and more energized.

The culmination of Rāṇī Rāj Kaur's multi-dimensional states of consciousness is her vision of the *Sac Khaṇḍ*, where she sees, amidst piercing brilliance, her beloved husband sitting enthralled at the feet of the ten Gurūs of the Sikh faith:

takht ikk tej sarūp uste rājde
das pātśāhīāṅ āp satgur sohine
tejon tej vaddhīk sabh toṅ vaddh ke
gyān tej toṅ vaddh unhāṅ sarūp sī
dissan ikko rūp par dass bhāsde
carnāṅ kamalāṅ vicch mattā prem dā
rāj rihā sī āp sāīṅ meraṛā.[67]

Upon a magnificent platform of incomparable light,
The ten Gurūs themselves were seated;
The radiance of their forms excelled radiance itself.
It was far more radiant than the Sphere of Knowledge.
Though they shone in one form, ten they glowed,
And at their lotus feet, inebriated with love,
Sat my very own beloved husband.

In this visionary experience all of Rāṇī Rāj Kaur's sensory perceptions are heightened to their utmost:

sir mastiā uss gaṅdh darśan nain se.
kan mast se rāg sun jo sī liā,
jībh śukar vickār mastī sī liā,
hath mast iss swād juṛe ju kaṅt pai
merī mastī deh – sūkhaṁ deh jo –

piare jī de des jihaṛī sī gaī
ridā mast pā mel piāre kaṅt dā
mastul mast su jān – deh man ātmā
mastī sī ikk raṅg caṛhiā sohiṇā
jis vic hoś na guṁ aslī sī huī.[68]

Inebriated was my head with the fragrance, my eyes with the vision,
My ears with the celestial music,
My tongue with gratitude,
My hands with the joyous sensation of having joined together in homage,
My body – its subtle aspect – which had traversed to the realm of my beloved,
My heart with the joy of union with him.
Inebriated – body, mind, and spirit were all;
It was a singular inebriation bringing forth an effulgence
In which consciousness was not lost but had become real.

We can glean from this passage the author's intention to present the senses as a unified whole. The Rāṇī's seeing is combined with a smelling of the fragrance wafting from an unknown world whose delicacy cannot be captured in word and phrase. This in turn is enhanced by a hearing of the harmony radiated by the Realm itself, by the recitation of thankfulness, and by the sensation of the hands coming together in peaceful and profound homage. Both the material body (*deh*) composed of the five senses and the subtle self composed of consciousness (*man*) and spirit (*ātman*) are exhilarated. This exhilaration does not, however, lead to the loss (*guṁ*) of awareness (*hoś*); rather, it lends to her awareness and consciousness the element of reality (*aslī*).

## *Noetic quality*

Of this element in the mystical experience, William James writes the following words:

Although so similar to states of feeling, mystical states seem to those who experience them to be also states of knowledge. They are states of insight into depths of truth unplumbed by the discursive intellect. They are illuminations, revelations, full of significance and importance, all inarticulate though they remain; and as a rule they carry with them a curious sense of authority for aftertime.[69]

This is how James describes the noetic quality of mysticism, and it is clearly reflected in what we have termed Rāṇī Rāj Kaur's ascent.

We must note here that even in the category of ineffability (discussed above) it was difficult for us to distinguish between Rāṇī Rāj Kaur's states of feeling and her states of knowledge. Indeed, the entire journey with the celestial guide is narrated as leading to an experiential illumination in which Rāṇī Rāj Kaur is provided a glimpse of the *Sac Khaṇḍ*, the highest of all the realms mentioned in Gurū Nānak's *Japu*. Rāṇī Rāj Kaur thus obtains an insight into the Truth revealed in the sacred writ not only by knowing or reciting it, but more importantly by also seeing it, by experiencing it.

But despite this, she cannot be part of that Truth. Time and again it is mentioned that the *Sac Khaṇḍ* is beyond Rāṇī Rāj Kaur's reach: "in the Realm of Truth dwells the Formless One – sac khaṇḍ vassai nriṅkār." Although Rāṇī Rāj Kaur with the assistance of her heavenly escort glides across the *Gyān*, *Saram*, and *Karam Khaṇḍ* and stands in close proximity to this fifth and final Realm, she does not quite reach it. The guide herself expresses the impossibility of being admitted to that region:

ithoṅ tāīṅ pauṅch merī ho sakī
is toṅ agge jāi sakdī maiṅ nahīṅ
nāhīṅ sakāṅ lijāi agge tudh nūṅ
aithoṅ akkhāṅ kholh, nījh lagāike
dekh piārā deś āpaṇe kaṅt dā
dekh tej de vall . . .[70]

Thus far was my reach and no more;
Further than this I cannot go,
Nor can I escort you beyond here.
Open your eyes and behold
The lovely region, that of your beloved's.
Witness that luminosity . . .

What is stressed here is the inability to fathom or to enter the *Sac Khaṇḍ*. The celestial guide points in that direction, towards that luminosity – a sign which in itself indicates the separation between the point at which the two stand in their ascent and the omega point which they marked as their destination. It is the radiance emanating from the latter which Rāṇī Rāj Kaur beholds and the sight, in turn, so heightens her senses that she goes into a mystical trance. Bhāī Vīr Singh thus communicates through his literary imagination the Sikh philosophical belief that the Transcendent One always remains transcendent. Rāṇī Rāj Kaur's mystical experience illustrates that even in the most intense of moments, the one here and the One Yonder do not unite. The Creator inheres within the natural phenomena including the human form and condition, which share some of Its own qualities. Nevertheless, earthly existence itself is not destined to be an innate part of the Transcendent Creator, Who dwells in a region which mortals can behold only from a distance.

This region is one of such splendid effulgence that mortals beholding it can only apprehend it as a vision of "light." As Rāṇī Rāj Kaur says:

> sī ikk tej prakāś – puṅj prakāś dā –
> behad agam athāh pār urār nā,
> jhalak ḍhalak camkār jāe na jhalliā;
> lahirāṅ khāve aioṅ kroṛā bijalīāṅ
> pujj na haṅghan mūl – hon nikārīāṅ;
> camke disse sāf mainūṅ sāmhane
> cānaneh nā sīg jihaṛā dissadā
> sānūn ethe roz; uh vann hor dā.[71]

> It was an overwhelming brilliance – the very source of light, in fact,
> Limitless, impenetrable, infinite; it had no boundaries whatsoever.
> Radiating, shining it was too dazzling to behold.
> It flashed in waves.
> A billion lightnings could not match its brilliant glory – all would remain useless dim shadows.
> This lustrous panorama stretched in front of me;
> It was no ordinary light that one usually beholds;
> It was an entirely different substance altogether.

As we saw in Chapter 2, Gurū Nānak uses light (*joti* or *nūr*) as an analogical representation of the Transcendent Reality. This light, he stresses, is radically different from the light of the stars and the moon, of the sun's rays, of lightning in the skies; it subsists by itself and is the ontological basis of the universe. The *Rāṇā Sūrat Singh* allegory must be read as an illustration of this statement. The powerful image of a billion wavering lightning-flashes is an all-too-human (and therefore inadequate) verbalization of the aesthetic splendor pervading the *Sac Khaṇḍ*. In the eyes of Rāṇī Rāj Kaur light is, in a characteristically Sikh manner, the ontological core, "*puṅj prakāś dā* – the very source of light." It is both transparent and crystal clear (*sāf*), and this clarity makes the equation of eyesight and insight possible. Whether seen in its aesthetic, ontological, or epistemological aspects, the transcendent light is a holistic reality which defies conceptualization and can only be experienced. This is what the Gurū Granth declares; this is what the heroine of *Rāṇā Sūrat Singh* perceives.

In the revelation of *Sac Khaṇḍ* the effulgent harmonious picture conveys to Rāṇī Rāj Kaur the impression of a unified whole in which all the elements are totally integrated. More significantly, the Sikh Gurūs in whose august company she sees her husband seated are both One and many: "They are seen in one form, though they are ten illuminations – dissan ikko rūp par das bhāsade." In the Sikh tradition, the ten Gurūs are considered to be the personification of a single light emanating from the Transcendent Reality. This is made abundantly clear in the writings of the first Sikh theologian, Bhāī Gurdās, and in the Gurū Granth itself. Both sources refer to the succession of Gurūship in terms of the transference of light from a single source – the one flame. This Sikh conception of one light in ten different bodies is vividly perceived by Rāṇī Rāj Kaur during her mystical voyage.

Along with the ten Gurūs, the protagonist also perceives the infinite luster surrounding the Gurūs and the Rāṇā sitting at the feet of the ten. The scene which may appear to have three elements – the infinite luster, the Sikh prophets, and the beloved – is seen as a composite whole by Rāṇī Rāj Kaur:

> ikk piya, ikk dīdār, ikk anaṁd sī
> tine ikk sarūp baṇke ikk hī
> jhalkaṇ ḍhalkaṇ att pārāvār nā.[72]
>
> The beloved spouse, the vision, the bliss,
> These three merged into one form
> And shone as one single light of infinite brilliance.

After getting a glimpse of the *Sac Khaṇḍ*, the Realm of Truth, Rāṇī Rāj Kaur loses all sense of duality and obtains a view of the essential oneness which, in Sikh metaphysics, is the hallmark of salvific knowledge. Illuminated in the *Karam Khaṇḍ* or the Realm of Grace, she sees the One Light which is yet Yonder (*sāhmane*). This vision, of a most piercing brilliance, brings her bliss (*ānaṁda*).

Her consciousness of the oneness of, and her oneness with, the Transcendent Reality is important in the Jamesian context, for it carries within it what the psychologist himself calls "a curious sense of authority for aftertime." For, even during her narration of the account to her mother, she feels a tremendous charge of energy. From the Rāṇī's gestures made during the narration and the interjections made by the Queen Mother, one can make some inferences in this regard. When Rāṇī Rāj Kaur is about to narrate the final episode, she tightly grasps her mother:

rāj kaur eh ākh pāsā partiā
baiṭhī sī huṇ tīk kucchaṛ – māon jo:
phir galvakaṛī pāi . . .[73]

So saying, Rāj Kaur, who lay in her mother's lap,
Turned on her side
And clasped her tenderly . . .

She asks her to seat herself reverently:

sāvdhān huṇ hoi pallā pā gale.[74]

Be mindful now and pull the scarf around.

She explains to the Queen Mother her excited behavior and authoritarian demands:

ḍāḍhā hai oh hāl tejāṅ vālaṛā
ati bhai adab su nāl kahiṇā cāhīe:
suṇan baṇe bhai nāl adbāṅ nāl o.[75]

The dazzling light was so overwhelming
That it must be described with great awe and respect,
And only with awe and respect must it be heard.

Hearing these words, the Queen Mother sits cross-legged, pulls the scarf around her neck, joins her hands in a pious gesture, and tries to fill her being with humble thoughts.[76] Meek and serene, she slides closer to Rāj Kaur, indicating the trepidation, the *mysterium tremendum* she too feels, for its noetic energy is communicated with its verbalization.

The narration of the ineffable experience is itself an arduous task that drains the speaker:

huṇ mathe hath pher "uf" mūnh ākhke
rāṇī kahindī, "māon! śukar akāl dā."[77]

Now wiping her brow and exclaiming "uf!"
The Rāṇī says, "Mother! thanks be to the Timeless One!"

The recounting has been a physical strain on the Rāṇī; she perspires. The depiction of that moment has been demanding; she tries to release her tension by an exclamatory sound. But in spite of being completely consumed she is ever grateful to the Eternal One (*Akāl*) for bestowing on her a glimpse of that wondrous moment. In her attempt to express her gratitude, the magnitude of her journey and its abiding power are highlighted.

lūṅ lūṅ jībh baṇāi karīe je kadī
lakh lakh geṛā dei ikko vār hī
karīe sadā ucār – sad hī jīvaṅde –
ākh na sakīe kiṇkā mātr bī.[78]

If each and every pore of the body had power to speak like a tongue,
If each uttered gratefulness, a million times over and over,
If I recited every moment of life,
I would still not be able to render even a fraction of the debt I bear.

As she further states, "the entire endeavor will value no more than a particle of sand in a vast, boundless desert."[79]

The mystical experience thus has an energy of its own which it transmits to the subject experiencing it. A sense of overwhelming power pervades his or her being; once so charged, this person can deploy its potentialities advantageously at a later stage. Rāṇī Rāj Kaur, we learn, renounces her melancholy and becomes an active participant in life. This overwhelming experience grounds her in a new sense of self and a new orientation in the world. Her domestic, social, and political life is completely changed thereafter. The administrative duties that she had refrained from she now begins to carry out vigorously, intelligently, and justly. Her performance in the political realm, the story goes on, is superb. She falters nowhere. After the mystical journey, Rāṇī Rāj Kaur takes over as sovereign queen, and her queendom is most content, peaceful, and creative.[80]

### *Transiency*

The final characteristic of the mystical experience which we have borrowed from James, its "transiency," is explained by him in these words:

Mystical states cannot be sustained for long. Except in rare instances, half an hour, or at most an hour or two, seems to be the limit beyond which they fade into the light of common day. Often, when faded, their quality can but imperfectly be reproduced in memory; but when they recur it is recognized; and from one recurrence to another it is susceptible of continuous development in what is felt as inner richness and importance.[81]

The duration of Rāṇī Rāj Kaur's overall ascent is nowhere specified. However, we are time and again told that her vision of the *Sac Khaṇḍ* has been only a fleeting one. She expresses its transiency in poetic language, which is so characteristic of the rest of the narration:

bijlī lāve ḍer jad hai kheoṅdī
is darśan ne ḍhill karī na utanī
ḍāḍhī kāhlī nāl ohle ho giā
jāṅ ho bhāsyā oh maiṅūṅ kāhlā:
jāpyā maiṅūṅ tej akh palkāṛṛā.[82]

Even lightning waits, however fractionally, before it disappears;
This vision, alas, tarried not even so much.
It vanished out of sight with exceeding speed;
Rapid it was;
A burst of brilliance which lasted less than an eyewink.

The simile is with lightning, but even that does not work for Rāṇī Rāj Kaur. For evanescent though it is, lightning still stays longer in the skies; her own vision did not even linger that much. The burst of infinite luster was but for an eyewink.

After the visionary flash, Rāṇī Rāj Kaur and her celestial escort begin their downward journey. They descend together the regions they had soared through earlier – *Karam Khaṇḍ*, *Saram Khaṇḍ*, and *Gyān Khaṇḍ*. At every stage their forms become grosser and their bodies weightier. Then comes the moment of parting. The divine companion asks for Rāṇī Rāj Kaur's leave to depart to her native world and suggests that she return to her own body. The Rāṇī is tormented to hear these words, but the companion in all her gentleness and love explains to Rāṇī Rāj Kaur that they two are indeed one. Embracing her affectionately, she says, "main nā taithoṅ dūr, neṛe jān lai[83] – know that between you and me no distance exists."

Having said these words, she disappears into space like a drop of milk in a pool of water. Immediately thereafter, a soft darkness envelops Rāṇī Rāj Kaur. The darkness keeps opening; she feels stifled and becomes totally confused. In her bewilderment, she tries to grope her way around and faints. When she opens her eyes, she finds herself calm and serene. She has the sensation of being lighter than a flower, her heart cool, her being soothed. This feeling is followed by one of amazement. She begins to wonder what indeed had come to pass, what had she been through, and what awaits her:

supnā sī, bhakhlāi jāṅ e sac sī?
kion hoī eh kār? kikur ho gaī?
kisne kītā eh? kis de vāste?[84]

Was it a dream? An illusion? Or was it something real?
Why did it happen? How did it come about?
Who brought it about? And for what purpose?

The moment Rāṇī Rāj Kaur recovers her strength, she rises and walks out of her room and reaches the garden. Here she sits and attempts to recapitulate all that had happened prior to the "opening of her eyes." It is not that the past has faded from her mind; she is simply perplexed. Sitting in the garden she tries to put together, piece by piece, the snapshots registered on the inward eye as she sailed on her mystical journey:

joṛ joṛ ke nāl parovān sangli
aṅt ban gaī sāf laṛī khiāl dī
ho bītiā hāl partakh ho giā.[85]

One by one I stringed the images together
Finally creating a coherent chain of thoughts;
Whatsoever had happened became lucid and clear.

This recreation of the voyage itself suffuses her with gratitude. She folds her hands in reverence, goes down on her knees, and bows her forehead to the ground. Fully absorbed in expressing her thankfulness, she becomes oblivious of time and space. So strong is the vision of the past in her mind that the present is lost:

samāṅ kī mahal kī māoṅ! sāre vissare
ikk raṅg ikk parvāh, dhārā tel jioṅ
man hoiā livlīn, samā na jāpiā
laṅghdā kihṛe dāo hai oh jāṅvdā.[86]

Time, the palace, my mother herself! – all disappeared.
Suffused with a single color, my mind flowed
like oil flowing uninterruptedly.
Thus absorbed, time eluded me;
Where it was sprinting off to, I did not know.

Rāṇī Rāj Kaur herself seems to be aware of the fact that she had lost the sense of time. When she recovers from this state (however partially), she breaks out into song; and what she sang, that too she does not remember. It is the Queen Mother who locates Rāṇī Rāj Kaur in the garden and awakens her to her surroundings. This marks the end of Rāj Kaur's mystical experience, and we hear her wondering at what has happened:

kinā laṅgiā kāl? huṇ kī hai samāṅ?
dittā tusāṅ jagāi tāṅ maiṅ jāgīāṅ.[87]

How much time had elapsed? What time is it now? I do not know!
You awakened me and so I am revived.

Totally perplexed, the protagonist is unaware of the duration of her momentous passage. The implication is that it was fleeting; how fleeting, neither Rāṇī Rāj Kaur nor the reader knows.

Rāṇī Rāj Kaur's journey through the five *Khaṇḍs* mentioned in the Sikh prayer, the *Japu*, constitutes an experience in which she intuitively comprehends the Singular Reality as understood in Sikh terms. The foregoing analysis indicates how the four characteristics of mysticism identified by a western thinker mark her own experience, too. The similarity that one discovers between a Sikh poet from India and a psychologist from America is striking, and it cannot be a coincidence. It reveals that the mystical experience of Rāṇī Rāj Kaur is not just an artistic creation of a poet; it reveals that the mystical analysis of William James is not just a theory formulated by a psychologist. They both bear witness to a universal mystical voyage which has been experienced by people from the most diverse backgrounds at all stages of history.

Paradoxical though it may seem, our analysis of Rāṇī Rāj Kaur's mystical journey along the universal Jamesian outline actually affirms the uniqueness of Sikh mysticism. Rāṇī Rāj Kaur's experience reveals some distinctive elements that are found only in the Sikh mystical tradition. Intrinsic to the Sikh perspective is the importance of love in bringing on the mystical state. Whereas for James, intense physical techniques and drugs are equally valid approaches to the mystical state, Rāṇī Rāj Kaur throughout reiterates love as the only path for the heightening of consciousness. For James all states of heightened consciousness, from St. Teresa's ardent devotion to the hallucinations of a drug user, are but "varieties of religious experience." Indirectly and poetically through his depiction of Rāṇī Rāj Kaur and often directly in a style that sometimes even succumbs to didacticism, the author Bhāī Vīr Singh categorically denounces all physical and chemical methods and practices in entering the mystical state.

Another unique dimension of Sikh mysticism is the co-presence and equality of feeling and thought. As concretized in Rāṇī Rāj Kaur's vision of the *Sac Khaṇḍ*, her senses and feelings were not subordinated to the mental conceptions. The Cartesian duality and hierarchy of the mind over the body which continues to be nurtured and substantiated by James is totally refuted in the portrayal of Rāṇī Rāj Kaur's ultimate experience.

Rāṇī Rāj Kaur also articulates the Sikh belief that a knowledge of the mystical ascension is not enough: it has to be put into practice. Throughout *Rānā Sūrat Singh* the stanzas depicting the mystical voyage from Gurū Nānak's *Japu* are recited and heard, the very stanzas that a devout Sikh would hear and recite daily; through Rāṇī Rāj Kaur the necessity of their being put into action is palpably reinforced. We find once again the contextual and, to use Katz's phrase, "mediated" nature of mysticism: Sikh concepts, Sikh images, Sikh symbols inform her experience.

However, the most striking characteristic of Sikh mysticism underscored by Bhāī Vīr Singh is that woman is the paradigmatic figure; as in the Gurū Granth, *she* is chosen to depict the intense and heightened states of consciousness. In contrast with the situation described by Judith Baskin – that "in Rabbinic Judaism no woman is deemed capable of any direct experience with the divine"[88] – the closest and deepest and "most direct" experience with the Divine in the Sikh tradition is, as we just saw, rendered through a female. As the fairy-like companion states, she cannot show her the *Sac Khaṇḍ*; Rāṇī Rāj Kaur has to experience it herself. There cannot be any mediations between the individual and the Ultimate. Bhāī Vīr Singh's message is that it is not sufficient simply to know about mysticism and reflect upon its various characteristics; rather, one must experience it as an individual. The patriarchal messages which women across ages, across cultures have fed on, that they are limited and cannot comprehend the deeply spiritual or intellectual aspects of life,[89] have been reversed in Bhāī Vīr Singh's epic. Here not only is the character undergoing the mystical ascension a woman, but the one helping to bring it about and the one to whom it is being narrated are also women.

Further, Bhāī Vīr Singh very delicately weaves the interrelationships amongst the personae in human and familial terms. Rāṇī Rāj Kaur narrates the experiences to her mother, eliciting the latter's love and empathy; the Rāṇī and the guide are portrayed as sisters, the latter the former's other half:

> so he piārī rāj! maiṅ tūṅ do nahīṅ,
> jiveṅ brichh de ḍāl hoṇ na vakkhare.[90]

So, dear Rāj! you and I are not two,
Just as the boughs of the tree are not different from each other!

The close connection between the angelic figure and the Rāṇī is presented through the simile of the boughs of a tree. Also implicit is the singular source from which the different branches receive equal sustenance.

Rāṇī Rāj Kaur's own words to her mother which form the finale to the chapter entitled "Utarāī" ("The Descent") – the sequel to "Uḍārī" ("The Flight") and "Darśan" ("The Vision") – declare her closeness to her mother:

tūṅ amīṅ, maiṅ dhīā, jāī teriāṅ
māvāṅ dhīāṅ vic vith na hoṅvadī
dhīāṅ māvāṅ bhet ikko hoṅvadā
amīṅ! tūṅ maiṅ ikk doveṅ ikk hāṅ.[91]

You are my mother, I your daughter, of you am I born,
Between mothers and daughters no distance lies,
Daughters and mothers share but one single mystery,
Mother! you and I are one; we are both one indeed.

These words echo the sentiment expressed by the celestial guide: "we two are one." Rāṇī Rāj Kaur's acknowledgment of her mother as the procreator, "tūṅ amīṅ, maiṅ dhīā jāī teriāṅ – you are my mother, I your daughter, of you am I born," is a reassertion of the importance of the Mother in the Sikh worldview. Without the mother, there would have been neither the mystic herself nor her celestial journey! At the same time, the most august moment of her life is shared with the mother. She is, as we saw in Chapter 2, "Mother: the Infinite Matrix," the ontological basis of all creation. Hence between the mother and her children there is a unity which admits of no differentiation. The analogical significance of the Mother in the Sikh sacred text receives a literal reiteration in the story of Rāṇī Rāj Kaur. This is also a rather ingenious manner of representing the truth enshrined in Sikh metaphysics: the vision of Oneness in the *Sac Khaṇḍ* – out there – permeates life here and now. The intimate relationships here and now, such as mother-and-daughter, sister-and-sister, wife-and-husband, are the *raison d'être* of the human condition, and they only exist because we are ultimately related to the Ultimate One. The vision of the Transcendent One has practical results in that it empowers us to recognize and bring into effect the fundamental unity and equality of our society and cosmos. Rāṇī Rāj Kaur's mystical voyage, which began with her solitary self sitting in agony in the loft of the palace, mourning the loss of her husband, ends with her sitting close to her mother, celebrating their oneness.

Rāṇī Rāj Kaur finds her authentic self not in isolation but in relationships. She informs us that the Sikh mystical experience – the love for Ultimate Reality, an ascent into the sacred or into the Yonder, a vision into the Transcendent – is grounded in the very love for fellow-beings, an immersion in our particular and material and secular world, and an insight into beauty and intimate relationships here and now. This is quite remarkable, for, as Underhill has remarked, mystical experience generally ignores the visible world:

> Its aims are wholly transcendental and spiritual. It is no way concerned with adding to, exploring, re-arranging, or improving anything in the visible world. The mystic brushes aside that universe . . .[92]

What Underhill says here does not apply in the instance of Sikh mysticism, where the emphasis is on the worldly relationships. In fact, after an insight into the Invisible Reality, the individual becomes fully concerned with "adding to, exploring, re-arranging, or improving" every connection with the visible world! The so-called division between the sacred and the secular, between transcendent and immanent, between spiritual and visible is shattered. The various stages and roles of the feminine – "wifehood," "sistership," "daughtership" and "queenship" – are fully acknowledged and affirmed through her personality. An analysis of Rāṇī Rāj Kaur's character leads us to rephrase the final definition of mysticism reached by Evelyn Underhill in her outstanding work: "It is to share, as a free and conscious agent – not a servant, but a son – in the joyous travail of the Universe."[93] We must hand over "this gift of 'sonship'" to Woman and transform it into a fundamental realization of *Daughtership*.

# Conclusion

Our journey through the three different phases of Sikh literary history – scriptural, transitional, and secular – illustrates the primacy of the feminine principle. To begin with the scriptural phase, we find that it illustrates this paramountcy in the very phenomenon of envisioning the Transcendent, in the subject of the vision itself, as well as in the individual process of *re*visioning the Formless Reality. What I wish to reiterate is, first of all, that the Sikh vision of the Transcendent One has its genesis in Gurū Nānak's experience – a most physical and sensual seeing into the Being and Nature of Reality. The method of the first Sikh prophet bypasses the androcentric approach, for it dissolves all kinds of patriarchal oppositions and hierarchies between the mind and the senses, man and nature. The holding of the cup of ambrosia and drinking it were in Gurū Nānak's vision synthesized with hearing the divine call and with seeing the oneness and unity of the cosmos, nature, and humanity; the heightened aesthetic experience led him to an exhaustive knowledge of the ontological reality. Indeed his epiphanic encounter with the Divine was in terms of process and movement, which feminists have long recognized as being central to women's experience. Furthermore, Gurū Nānak made spontaneous poetry rather than abstract theorizing the medium of celebrating what he saw, as he saw it. A joyous and holistic experience, it was Gurū Nānak's and Gurū Nānak's alone. As Gadamer has said, "Everything that is experienced is experienced by oneself." Gurū Nānak's vision is a particular, individual, immediate, and unique experience; we cannot go tracing it back to Kabīr or any of the other devotional Sant patriarchs, many of whom found the body and the senses in general and love for women in particular a hindrance to spiritual progress and enlightenment.

Secondly, the process of seeing, that is, the vision itself, has an important feminine component. Here, however, we encounter the problem of religious language. While including all time, all space, and all genders, the vision still extends beyond all! How can the Transcendent, which is beyond all human categories, be described in human language? Theologians and philosophers have reflected upon this issue from time immemorial. The medieval thinker Thomas Aquinas offers three ways of describing the Divine in his work *On Speaking of God*: univocal (wherein the cause is predicated exactly from the effect, but from the finite effect the Infinite Cause cannot be exactly predicated), equivocal (wherein the cause and effect may resemble each other; nevertheless, the cause is unlike the effect and therefore nothing at all of the Infinite can be predicated from the finite world), and analogical which is midway between univocal and equivocal (although cause and effect are different in relationship, there is a likeness between the two, for the "likeness of the cause is intrinsic to the effect" and thus – analogically – from the finite world, the Infinite can be predicated).[1] Of these possibilities it is the third which underlies the Sikh envisioning of the Transcendent.

By means of this analogical process, male and female principles should participate equally, and Gurū Nānak's vision is in fact significantly female. Yet, the fact is that the male principle has dominated Sikh studies. Clearly, a more holistic comprehension of the Singular Reality is required in order to do justice to the Sikh vision of the Transcendent, and it is precisely this that is provided by the term *mātā*, "Mother," and other images and concepts born of her.

The significance of the platitude "Mother Earth" is missed until it is realized that for Sikhs she – *mātā dharati mahat*, the great Mother Earth – is the analogical link between the Transcendent Cause, which has a vital feminine dimension, and its empirical effect Mother Earth, which is intrinsically and entirely feminine. Mother Earth is therefore not a platitude or a metaphor or a simile but a genuine analogy. It is thus an ontological term, for as Aquinas said, it is "rooted in the act of being (*actus essendi*)."[2] The analogical relationship between the Transcendent and the Female states that she is intrinsically in some degree or proportion what Reality uniquely is. Mother, the Infinite Matrix, and the Transcendent One are linked together by shared attributes.

Breaking all patriarchal idols and icons, the Sikh sacred literature celebrates the feminine aspect of the Transcendent and poetically affirms the various associations and images that are born from her. Beginning with the poetic utterances of Gurū Nānak, her presence and importance are affirmed throughout the Sikh scripture: she is *mātā*, the creator, the preserver, and the nurturer; she is *mati*, the epistemological ingredient; and she is *nadar*, the benevolent glance necessary for our salvation. The birth of all life begins with her *raktu* (menstrual blood), and her *agni* (heat) sustains the fetus for nine months in her *garbha* (womb). The child derives initial psychological and physical strength from her *thaṇ dudhi* (breast milk). She is revered neither as a virgin or distant goddess to be worshiped in some hidden sanctuary nor as a voluptuous erotic figure making the mind wonder whether to be attracted to her or whether to resist her. The structure of her body is honored because she goes through the natural processes of conception, gestation, giving birth, and lactation. Moreover, as *joti*, the spiritual spark within all – in humans and in the cosmos – she brings the Transcendent closely into space and time here and now. Through *joti* the Transcendent is recovered not as a power above and over but gently and harmoniously moving within and around the universe. The Sikh vision of the Transcendent therefore does not entail a reified object out there, but becomes a subjective experience of which all are a part, and through which everything and everyone is energized and empowered. The Sikh Transcendent does not remain out there; rather it is the ultimate sense – both sensually and spiritually – of Reality present in and experienced throughout our cosmos. The feminine dimension pervading the Sikh vision possesses the dynamism to interconnect all humans: it breaks all social, creedal, racial, and gender hierarchies, and it connects society with the rest of the cosmos. The monopoly of humans over nature is shattered through her force.

A third point which emerges from my work is that Gurū Nānak's vision of the Transcendent, which I termed the Primal Paradox, demands of necessity a revisioning on an individual basis, and that the revisioning generates a new context with a liberating divine–human relationship. It was not a process that happened once and for all; rather, it is to be experienced again and again. In the Sikh context no one is chosen. The historical moment of Gurū Nānak's revelation is not an event of the past, but rather it is intimately connected with the present. Gurū Nānak's experience in the river Beiṅ becomes the paradigmatic moment, and his direct encounter with the Transcendent an act to be emulated by Sikhs today and by their future generations. Everyone is equally equipped with the power to envision the Absolute. In Sikh ritual all forms of elaborate worship are discarded, which gives primacy to the inner and personal experience. All idols and images are understood as simply blocking the route to the Transcendent One. According to Gurū Nanak, "Gods and goddesses are worshiped, but what can one ask them, and what can they give? The stones [idols] are washed with water, but they sink in water; they are useless to carry us across the ocean of existence."[3] The dominance of male deities like Viṣṇu and Śiva and the authority of male members of the Brahmin caste have been discarded. Rejecting all reifications and fixtures, the Sikh religion makes *bāṇī*, the beautiful poetry, the Sikh's sole ritual. *Bāṇī* can be read, it can be recited, it can be heard. Revitalizing the sphere of the senses, the psyche, the body, the imagination, *bāṇī* remains the only approach open equally to Sikh men and women, towards intuiting the Unintuitable Transcendent.

When we turn from the scriptural to the transitional period of Sikh literature, we find that the symbols of this period's major figure, Gurū Gobind Singh (and later those of the most significant contemporary writer, Bhāī Vīr Singh), reflect the preeminence of the feminine principle. They incorporate the feminine and women's experience into the vision of the Transcendent. Indeed, just as the *bāṇī* leads to the ontology, so the literary symbols flow from it.

The primary symbol of Gurū Gobind Singh is the invincible Durgā, and by evoking her, he sought to invigorate an effete society. It is the autonomous Durgā, not a consort, who captures the imagination of the Sikh prophet. The opening verse from the *Ballad of Caṇḍī*, in which Durgā is identified with the sword, forms part of the Sikh supplicatory prayer to this day. When he created the Khālsāhood, all men received the last name "Singh" and women the name "Kaur." In this egalitarian structure, which the tenth Sikh prophet established, women were liberated from tracing their lineage to their father or adopting a husband's name after marriage.

By magnifying artistically the grandeur of the mythological figure, Gurū Gobind Singh sought to heighten the aesthetic sense of the individual as citizen and believer. Thus Durgā continues to be recalled by the Sikhs. A remembrance of her physical power, a remembrance of her destruction of the dark, gross, and brute forces, a remembrance of her heroically wielding the shining sword, strengthens the individual – man or woman. The example of the mythological goddess helps the individual triumph over egocentricity, lust, desire, attachment, and ignorance. With the dark and evil forces conquered, the path to envisioning the Transcendent is cleared. Nothing thereafter blocks the passage from eyesight to insight. Significantly, the main transitional figure in Sikh history uses the feminine principle to convey the "masculine" virtue of strength and courage. A remembrance of Durgā is a channel towards envisioning the Transcendent One.

Certainly, Gurū Gobind Singh composes poetry recalling the invincible Durgā and aesthetically embellishes her valorous deeds,[4] but she nowhere usurps the role of the Transcendent One. The incarnation of the Ultimate Reality into a particular feminine form is totally absent in Sikhism, for such a depiction would only create a chasm between the feminine in image and the feminine in flesh. There is, for example, an astounding contrast between the image of the Divine and the status of women in the very popular Sanskrit scripture *Devī-Bhāgavat Purāṇa*, a contrast perceptively studied by David Kinsley.[5] Drawing upon the *Devī Māhātmya*, this text dating from the ninth or tenth century celebrates the goddess as the Ultimate Reality in the cosmos. The scripture praises the goddess's mythological importance – all the male gods are subordinate to her; it celebrates her philosophical import – she is identified with absolute principles; it honors her ritualistic significance – its prayers and practices exalt her. However, the very same composer who venerates the goddess insults living women intolerably. A clear antithesis between the superhuman goddess and the subhuman woman is established. Women are stigmatized as base: "Falsehood, vain boldness, craftiness, stupidity, impatience, over-greediness, impurity, and harshness are the natural qualities of women."[6] Later in the text, they are compared to leeches who suck the life from men by stealing away their virile semen and "their minds and wealth and everything by their crooked love conversations . . ."[7] The final chapter outrightly forbids women (along with *śudras*) from reading or reciting the *Devī-Bhāgavata Purāṇa* itself![8] The text that lovingly lauds the goddess deplorably debases women. Although Gurū Gobind Singh may recall the goddess Durgā as a metaphor and Bhāī Vīr Singh may use her as a simile, they are completely opposed to the spirit of these ancient texts. In her last moments, Bhāī Vīr

Singh's heroine, Sundarī, warns her society against the misogynist attitude of such scriptures, and it is quite possible that *Devī-Bhāgavata Purāṇa* was what she had in mind. She reminds them that such an attitude has been denounced by Gurū Gobind Singh and the other Sikh Gurūs, so there can be no confusion between a literary technique and a religious idolization.

Contemporary thealogians should not be discouraged by the absence of the goddess in the Sikh tradition, by her appearance in this tradition as no more than a literary device. The goddess often represents a dehumanization of women rather than their genuine exaltation. Simone de Beauvoir had serious misgivings about the goddess, and she speculated upon the urge to metamorphose women into such idols, which she felt was largely a male urge: "Man wishes her to be carnal, but he would also have her smooth, hard, changeless as a pebble."[9] In India itself, the chasm between goddess and woman and its tragic consequences have been artistically brought out by Satyajit Ray. In his film *Devī* (meaning "Goddess") he traces the metamorphosis of a young Bengali woman into an oppressed and lifeless statue when she is worshiped by men as the incarnation of the goddess Durgā.[10] In the Sikh tradition, the transcendent *joti* is the formless spirit which cannot be embodied into any form; yet she is liberating. By being formless *joti* does not enforce or prescribe any role of any particular deity onto the human; nor does the transcendent spark reduce or limit her physical, palpable body into that of any incarnation. Rather, the transcendent within radiates to the external, energizing the senses that link the individual with the Absolute.

Sikh sacred art and architecture do not "incarnate" Truth in any way either, for the savoring of the poetry of the Gurū Granth is the only way towards the Absolute. They are simply mediums for inducing in the worshipers a state of mind that will launch them towards envisioning the Transcendent. The Sikh sacred space is called a *Gurudwārā*, from *Gurū* ("enlightener") and *dwāra* ("doorway") – it is not an embodiment of the Truth, but simply a doorway through which each person may pass to experience the Transcendent for himself or herself. Rhythm, repetition, momentum, symmetry, infinity are some of the artistic elements that can be discerned in the architecture of a building like the Golden Temple, the central shrine of the Sikhs at Amritsar. There are geometric patterns in stone, marble, and brick on the walls and grounds of the *Gurudwārās* which, in their repetition and momentum, prevent the eye from focusing on anything particular and instead draw it away towards the Absolute One. Sikh sacred space is without a formal focus, or idols, or any patriarchal reminders; at the center of all is the Gurū Granth, for it is the language of poetry which is conducive to evoking the urge to search within every individual. *Bāṇī*, feminine in its imagery, feminine in its tone, set in musical patterns that remain in harmony with the rhythm of nature in its daily and seasonal motions, permeates through the senses into the very depths of a person and leads to ecstatic disclosures.

The literary works of the major modern writer Bhāī Vīr Singh also abound with themes illustrating the feminine principle. His writings are not simply beautiful stories and poems. They depict with great power the varying "stages on life's way." By the end of the nineteenth century, when a period of decadence had threatened the Sikh way of life, the Sikh renaissance writer tried to purge the society with his literary creations. In his artistic *Weltanschauung*, women were the protagonists who alone could bring about the much-desired change and transformation in their society. Physically very beautiful, spiritually highly refined, existentially deeply intense, ethically most noble, and mystically so exalted, the women in his vast array of literary creations (including poems, novels, plays, and epics) live palpably and energetically. They search for their own identities, and discover their selves through their own individual journeys without any male instructors. Each of them has an intrinsic value in herself. Without a male to validate her, she exists harmoniously in a constellation of relationships. As daughter, sister, wife, beloved, queen, mother, and even as a young woman with a broken-off engagement – *she* in all her roles is equally important in her connection with the Divine. The religious and secular dimensions are never pitted against each other. Like the bride symbol in the Gurū Granth, Bhāī Vīr Singh's protagonists provide a multiplicity of options to women: whatever mode they choose, they have direct access to the Transcendent One.

A contemporary feminist may feel uneasy about the relationship of these women with the Beloved Groom (like that of the bride in the Gurū Granth) and fear that this may be confining, dualistic, and subjugating for women. But then, we need to realize that what the young woman loves is the Transcendent, and through her love she is able to connect with the Transcendent Lover most intimately. Through this very process, all dualities dissolve. The intimacy and closeness with the Divine established by the bride in the Granth and by the female characters of Bhāī Vīr Singh was a radical expression, especially when we take the religious and cultural milieu into account. Over the centuries, women in India have been viewed as much farther separated and distant from the Divine than their male counterparts. The Sikh tradition declares that woman enjoys an intimacy with the Divine that is even closer if anything. Her relationship with the Beloved Transcendent is not one of subjugation but of an apparent dependence leading to real independence. This temporary dependence is equally shared by men, women, and by the cosmos around. It is through love for the Ultimate Reality that this initial dependence is transformed into an empowering and dynamic passion. The love relationship is not one of subjugation, but one of valuing, and it fulfills the ideal that Sallie McFague put foward in her discussion of "God as Lover":

> The crux of being in love is not lust, sex, or desire (though these are expressions of a human love relationship); the crux is value. It is finding someone else valuable and being found valuable. And this perceiving of valuableness is, in the final analysis, unfounded.[11]

As Judith Plaskow has also stated, this symbol of God as lover is important, for unlike the images of king, judge, or father, the notion of God as lover is far more conducive to human empowerment and accountability. But there is a crucial corollary made by our western thealogian: "The feminist use of the image of God as lover would need to break through this patriarchal model of love relations, envisioning the lover as both female and male."[12] This ideal permeates Sikh scripture, for the Transcendent is sometimes referred to as *meerā* – a female friend or lover. So far this exciting symbol remains unexplored by the exegetes, but Plaskow has made its analysis urgent. The dependence of Bhāī Vīr Singh's protagonists or of humans in general on the Divine Lover is not a subjugation of women, which feminists in the West correctly deplore: it is a relationship of mutual valuing.

Sikh literature intentionally abolishes the traditional patriarchal polarization which contrasts women and nature on the one side against men and culture on the other. The identification of Bhāī Vīr Singh with the female and the creation of female protagonists as the archetypes of morality, courage, spirituality, and philosophical search manifest not only the tenderness of his poetic perception, but also the Sikh worldview, in which Woman is a profoundly valued human being. The analogical ontology of the Female and Mother in the Sikh scripture, the literary symbolism in the works of Gurū Gobind Singh and Bhāī Vīr Singh, indeed all periods of Sikh thought project the feminine aspects of the Sikh vision of the Transcendent. And yet this feminine principle can be fully understood only by means of the recent secular western ideology of the feminist movement. It enables one to overcome the tension between the classical Sikh vision and current Punjabi culture which has obscured *her* vitality in Sikh thought. This is ironic, because the western feminist movement arose in opposition to and in spite of its traditional religious base, whereas it is the sexist element current in Punjabi culture that survives in opposition to and in spite of its traditional religious base. But irony does not lessen truth. This movement has forced scholars to become aware of the relation between religious language and gender. Scholars have long been aware of the problem of describing the Transcendent in language derived from the finite world. Only the feminist movement has made them aware that the finite symbols applied to the Transcendent were always masculine.

In a sexist world, symbol systems and conceptual apparatuses have been from male creations. These do not reflect the experience of women, but rather function to falsify our own self-images and experiences . . .[13]

Obvious and innocuous as male God-language has come to seem, metaphors matter – on both an individual and social level. Though long usage may inure us to the implications of our imagery, religious symbols are neither arbitrary nor inert. They are significant and powerful communications through which a religious community expresses a sense of itself and its universe. Religious symbols give resonance and authority to a community's self-understanding and serve to support and sustain its conception of the world.[14]

The importance of words, the ethical significance of words, the sexist nature of language: this is what feminist ethical theory has made us aware of. To acquire a moral sensitivity to the nature of language is the first step in the complete alteration of consciousness required by this ethics. After such moral sensitivity the next stages are the ontological shock and the praxis to which this new awareness will inevitably lead. The ontological shock is necessary because once we have eschewed our sexist vocabulary and replaced it by a feminist language, we must supply our new feminist discourse with a radically new ontological foundation. Our empirical language of gender must be grounded in ontology. Otherwise we would be left merely with the struggle between a feminine ideology and a masculine ideology, rather than a masculine illusion and a feminine reality. Sikh literature clearly contains these two components of the feminist ethical theory: the Sikh Gurūs and the later poets were deeply conscious of women's victimization and pain within their milieux. As we shall see in the Epilogue, this questioning of their language and ontology led them towards a new praxis, a formulation of new possibilities for action: the institutions of *saṅgat* and *laṅgar*, coupled with action against *purdah*, *satī*, and pollution. These were the positive results of their moral sensitivity and ontological shock.

Sikh literature – sacred and secular – has at its center the feminine. Feminine phenomena, feminine tone, feminine terminology, feminine imagery, and feminine consciousness form the heart and muscle of it. Whether it is the beautiful Word of the Transcendent Itself, whether it is the analogous terminology intimating the Transcendent One, whether it is the preparation and the ardent quest for a vision of the Transcendent Groom, whether it is a mythological channel to strengthen the seeker for Its vision, whether it is a romantic perception of the Infinite Transcendent deep within, whether it is the existential inquiry about the Transcendent Being, whether it is day-to-day ethical living with the Transcendent in sight, or whether it is the consciousness of the highest mystical state and of the closest proximal point to the Transcendent Light –

She is the *subject*.

# *Epilogue*

*You must know who is the object and who is the subject of a sentence in order to know if you are the object or subject of history.*

We have spoken of the subject, but now we must turn to the object. We have been dealing with the world of ideas and words, so our Epilogue must then quite literally be that which comes after the word, after the *logos*. But the Sikh Word is not a masculine *logos*; it is the beautiful and formless *bāṇī*. The Word proclaimed by the scriptures and secular writers of Sikhism is Woman. We cannot underestimate the importance of this achievement in itself, but does anyone listen to the Word? Does anyone truly read it?

By the word of the Sikh Gurūs and poets we are invited to praxis, the third component of feminist ethics. But their word which empowers woman endangers man. The response has been either to shout it down or simply fail to hear it. In the writings of Gurū Gobind Singh and Bhāī Vīr Singh, the feminine presences of Durgā and Rāṇī Rāj Kaur are too central, too striking to be ignored, so instead they have been denounced. The patriarchal exegetes have declared that it would have been unworthy of Gurū Gobind Singh to write of Durgā, and so they have attempted to excise her from his works. They still argue that the compositions praising Durgā under his name were written not by the Gurū himself but by his contemporaries. Likewise, in the case of Bhāī Vīr Singh, the patriarchal literary critics have declared that the feminine nature and sentiment of his works is unworthy of the great writer. So they have decried it as an unfortunate weakness in his work, a lapse from their masculine standards.

That is where the twentieth-century Sikh writer is misunderstood, or rather too well understood and condemned for that very reason.

The following words by a renowned Sikh scholar represent a point of view that is, unfortunately, all too common:

> It is in his diction bearing the perfume of Punjab's sacred literature and the expression of sensibility that Bhāī Vīr Singh achieves the poetic quality. Very often his sensibility declines to sentimentality and the feminine small-change of feeling – but rises with recurring spurts to the true emotional level.[1]

In a metaphor that falls to the true sexual level, we hear that women experience the mere small-change of passive feeling and sentimentality, whereas men have sensitivity and true emotions that rise and gush out in recurrent spurts. The assessment that Bhāī Vīr Singh's "sensibility declines to sentimentality and the feminine small-change" only indicates the critic's glossing over the delicacy, the refinement, the multivalency attributed to the female person and psyche in the work of Bhāī Vīr Singh.

In the poetry of the Gurū Granth itself, the importance of the feminine in a relation so vital as the one with the Transcendent has been neglected by the patriarchal exegetes. This neglect can be ascribed to a basic prejudice on the part of commentators, translators, and teachers of Sikh literature. Over the years, these scholars have been excising female symbolism and imagery and replacing it with a male one. Because the sacred text has not been meaningfully read, Sikh women do not enjoy the status that Gurū Nānak wanted them to have. Its extraordinary potential for empowering women has been ignored.

The Sikh Gurūs and the great modern writer who was so close to their spirit have been remarkably radical in supporting and undergirding social equality. Unfortunately, the subject of their sentences has been the object of history. She has not even been properly recognized by Sikh culture. Why she has such significance in Sikh literature but so low a position in Punjabi culture is extremely perplexing. Once again, the image of my grandmother comes back to me. I can see and hear her asking a male member to read her the opening of the *Bārah Māh* on the first day of the new month, even though the bride is the central figure in this text!

Gurū Nānak did not want the feminine principle to be just a figure of speech or a literary device; the feminine principle was to pervade the life of the Sikhs. From the very beginning of the tradition, he took special care to give women a position of equality with men in matters religious and secular. In Gurū Nānak's new community that grew on the banks of the river Rāvī, men and women enjoyed complete equality. There was no priesthood, and men were not designated to play any more important role as liaisons between humanity and Divinity than were women. When Gurū Amar Das, the third Sikh Gurū, organized districts of religious administration, women too were selected to head them.[2] In the first Sikh society taking shape at Kartārpur, worship consisted of men and women sitting together and reciting and savoring the Divine Word in unison. Both men and women took equal part in day-to-day tasks as well: both drew water from the well, both reaped and ground corn, both cooked food in the kitchen, and both cleaned the utensils. The food was eaten in common by all, sitting in rows together as equals, irrespective of sex, caste, or rank. In the words of a Sikh woman scholar, "The transformation the Sikh Gurus brought in woman's status was truly revolutionary. The concept of equality of woman with man not only gave woman an identity of her own, but freed her from all kinds of fetters to which she was bound in the Hindu society."[3]

It is sad to see today that many Sikh women have their space confined to the kitchen and are bound within the home to carry out essential tasks. Women stay in the places ascribed to them in society and family by the male members – be they fathers, grandfathers, older brothers, brothers-in-law, or patriarchal bosses. The role of women is narrowly circumscribed. It is tragic to observe how the literature of this culture includes them so fully and the society excludes them so despairingly. The practice of *satī* was forbidden by the Gurūs, and it is of course outlawed, but widows are still ostracized; they may not be forced to die like the Satī, but they lead a life that is almost dead. The Gurūs rejected the notion of pollution. The Gurū Granth celebrates womanhood and constantly reminds its readers of their origin from menstrual blood; in practice, however, menstruating women are discouraged from touching the Book that esteems them. The Gurūs opposed the custom of *purdah*, but although women are not literally veiled, they are still marginal and almost invisible today, their voices are not heard, their desires are not discerned. It is indeed tragic to see that the birth of a daughter, who would have been honored by Gurū Nānak as a would-be bride, a would-be mother, a would-be queen, is to contemporary society a source of sorrow. Parents in the Punjab even weep at the birth of a daughter! The very female who would be opening up the way for liberation is imprisoned by her culture in the confines of her in-laws' home! Modern technology is abused to promote the abortion of fetuses that are determined to be female!

The societal and geographical context of Sikhism is another reason why the Sikh message has not been fully heeded and put into practice. The developing Sikh religion was surrounded and confined by an androcentric society. Gurū Nānak tried to break the existing mold. But the overwhelming Hindu and Islamic presence has over the centuries reinforced and even today continues to reinforce patriarchal values which are difficult to break. The relatively young Sikh religion is unable to sustain the radical changes intimated in its sacred literature. The Sikhs after all constitute less than 2 percent of the Indian population. The unique thealogical message of the Gurū Granth remains buried under the weight of past tradition and the continued pressures from its environment. In the past many Sikh commentators have displayed a predominantly Hindu intellectual disposition. Udāsī and Nirmalā were two early schools of Sikh scriptural interpretation, and scholars within both these traditions were essentially reared on classical Indian exegesis. Saturated with Upaniṣadic and Purāṇic learning, the style and content of their analyses and speculations brought about a reincubation of Hindu ideology within Sikh exegesis itself.[4] The Sikh vision of the Transcendent has been eclipsed by the Hindu *Zeitgeist.* My contention is that until the symbolic value of Sikh literature is truly understood and its difference from the neighboring traditions is acknowledged, Guru Nānak's and his successor Gurūs' aim of uplifting the role and status of women cannot be fulfilled. The new and separate message of Gurū Nānak has to be re-cognized as new and separate. By continuing to categorize it under the rubric of Hinduism (or Islam or a syncretism of Hinduism and Islam), readers, hearers, and scholars unconsciously transfer the role and image of women in those societies over into the Sikh world. The issues and concerns raised by western feminists equip one with a sensitivity to avoid such a pitfall, to discover the centrality of the feminine in Sikh literature, and to re-cover the significance that is *hers.*

In addition to the context, the texts themselves present difficulties even for Sikhs. The poly-structured vocabulary of the Gurū Granth, which includes Sanskritic, Arabic, and Persian terms, poses problems for an average Punjabi. Decoding the poetry of Gurū Gobind

Singh, laced as it is with highly subtle and ornate metaphors and imagery, and replete with mythological allusions and linguistic innovations, is an even harder task. Furthermore, the British legacy spurs young Punjabi Sikhs to study English and western philosophies and literatures, drawing them away from their own mother-tongue and their own literary heritage. Indoctrinated in English-speaking schools which were founded by Victorian colonialists, many Sikhs thus do not even possess the basic linguistic tools to recognize the subtleties of their sacred text. Many youngsters are more familiar with Cinderella and Snow White than with Sundarī or Rāṇī Rāj Kaur. The Gurū Granth may continually be seen, read, and heard at all important occasions, during all rites of passage; some of Gurū Gobind Singh's poetry may remain part of the daily regimen of Sikh prayers; Bhāī Vīr Singh's poetry may be read and memorized by young Punjabi students in schools and colleges – without the import of these texts being really questioned. Thus the thealogy and feminist spirituality and power of Sikh literature remains closed.

Its disclosure can come about only through a feminist praxis. The moral sensitivity is there, and the ontological grounding is there; the words are there; the ideals are there; they have only to be read. Sikh literature is prescriptive, not merely descriptive; it is an empowering language, not "the feminine small-change of feeling." To unleash its power, every reader needs to be equipped with a poetic sensitivity and a real awareness of the primal context. Each word has to be chewed so that full nourishment and sustenance can be derived from it. Such knowledge is empowering, but it is also enjoyment; in it we find the climactic *jouissance* of Gurū Arjan, Gaston Bachelard, Roland Barthes. To understand the choice of female models as representatives of the romantic and existential consciousness, to realize the overall importance of the varied feminine symbols and images, we need to make the translation from literary symbols to social and political realities. The words should enable us to find the spark within ourselves, legitimate ourselves, fully validate ourselves. Gurū Nānak's deep crimson *manjīṭhaṛā* – which corresponds with Alice Walker's Color Purple – radiates an energy that heightens and intensifies every experience in our social and political being. Women can articulate and construct their experience through the Sikh literary heritage and transform their lives in society. We can aspire to that ideal, aspire to that message, aspire to understanding that text. Surely, as Bachelard says, the "poetic image can be the seed of a world."[5] It can deliver us a new world where women can enter the zone that we have been excluded from and that rightly belongs to us. "May she get out of the booby-trapped silence! And not have the margin or the harem foisted on her as her domain!"[6] Sikh literature breaks this silence and provides a voice for women, though we speak in a booby-trapped world. It gives visibility and relevance to women, and it provides us with an opening towards real change, a bridge between the ideal and the real, mythos and ethos, being and becoming, moral sensitivity and social praxis.

The literature of the Sikhs raises feminist consciousness, and it gives a new meaning, a new direction, and a new authenticity to feminists in the West. Theirs is not simply a discourse developed in one particular place at one particular period in history; it is rather a voicing of an eternally and universally valid ontological perspective which has often been noticed but rarely acknowledged. The voice of western feminists is in perfect harmony with the literature of Sikhism, and it only remains to turn our mutually validating experiences into an envigorating dialogue. This dialogue calls for a vigorous interaction amongst Sikh women and other Asian women and feminists in the West. Together, we need to come close and understand one another and bring about change. I ardently await the day when the Punjabi culture which sustains the paramountcy of Woman in its literature will prove a model for her full equality in the social, political, and economic spheres, not just in India but throughout our common Matrix, the Earth.

# *Notes*

## INTRODUCTION

1 Judith Plaskow and Carol Christ (eds.), *Weaving the Visions: New Patterns in Feminist Spirituality* (New York: Harper & Row, 1989).
2 Carol Christ, "Spiritual Quest and Women's Experience," in *Womanspirit Rising: A Feminist Reader in Religion* (New York: Harper & Row, 1979), 230.
3 Ibid., 229–230.
4 Christine Downing, *The Goddess: Mythological Images of the Feminine* (New York: Crossroad, 1981), 4–5.
5 Carol Christ, "Why Women Need the Goddess," in *Womanspirit Rising*, points out that "the denigration of the female body is expressed in cultural and religious taboos surrounding menstruation, childbirth, and menopause in women. While menstruation taboos may have originated in a perception of the awesome powers of the female body, they degenerated into a simple perception that there is something 'wrong' with female bodily functions. Menstruating women were forbidden to enter the sanctuary in ancient Hebrew and premodern Christian communities. Although only Orthodox Jews still enforce religious taboos against menstruant women, few women in our culture grow up affirming their menstruation as a connection to sacred power. Most women learn that menstruation is a curse and grow up believing that the bloody facts of menstruation are best hidden away. Feminists challenge this attitude to the female body" (p. 280).
6 Gurū Granth, 473.
7 Ibid., 140.
8 Plaskow and Christ (eds.), *Weaving the Visions*, 10.
9 Marion Ronan, "The Liturgy of Women's Lives: A Call to Celebration," *Cross Currents* 28 (spring 1988), 20.
10 Rosemary Radford Ruether, "Sexism and God-Language," in *Weaving the Visions*, 161.
11 Alice Walker, *The Color Purple* (Pocket Books, 1982), 202. Also the emphasis of many other feminist writers has been on the experience of the transcendent within their individual selves. Ntozake Shange, *for*

*colored girls who have considered suicide when the rainbow is enuf* (New York: Macmillan, 1975).

12 Gurū Granth, 663.

13 See, especially, W. H. McLeod, *Gurū Nānak and the Sikh Religion* (Oxford: Clarendon Press, 1968), 151–158.

14 S. M. Ikram, *Muslim Civilization in India* (New York: Columbia University Press, 1964). Ikram writes: "He [Gurū Nānak] acknowledges Kabīr as his spiritual teacher," p. 127.

15 Karine Schomer, "Kabīr in the *Gurū Granth Sāhib*: An Exploratory Essay," in *Sikh Studies: Comparative Perspectives on a Changing Tradition*, ed. Mark Juergensmeyer and N. Gerald Barrier, Berkeley Religious Studies Series (Berkeley, Graduate Theological Union, 1979), 75–86.

16 Even in the latest edition of *A History of the World's Religions* (New York: Macmillan, 1990), J. B. Noss continues to entitle his chapter on Sikhism: "A Study in Syncretism" (pp. 234–245). It is good to see that at least the title of the book in this new edition has been changed from *Man's Religions*.

17 Gaston Bachelard, *The Poetics of Reverie: Childhood, Language, and the Cosmos* (Boston: Beacon Press, 1960), 18.

18 Ibid., 18.

19 Ibid., 25–26.

20 W. C. Smith, "Methodology and the Study of Religion: Some Misgivings," Lecture delivered at Iowa University, April 15, 1974, 3.

21 Gurū Granth, 1429.

22 Juergensmeyer and Barrier (eds.), *Sikh Studies*, 13–23. There is still a neglect of Sikhism in western writings on religion. Even in such a monumental work as Mircea Eliade's *Encyclopaedia of Religion* (New York: Macmillan, 1987), the entries on Sikhism are regrettably few, and even those few are disappointingly brief.

23 Juergensmeyer and Barrier (eds.), *Sikh Studies*, 16.

24 Ibid., 17–18.

25 Stephen Dunning, "The Sikh Religion: An Examination of Some of the Western Studies," *The Journal of Religious Studies* (Patiala: Punjabi University, Autumn 1970), 1–27.

26 Theodora Foster Carroll, *Women, Religion, and Development in the Third World* (New York: Praeger, 1983), 33.

27 Taran Singh (ed.), *Gurū Nānak Bāṇī Prākaś*, vol. II (Patiala: Punjabi University Press, 1969), 1346.

## 1 THE PRIMAL PARADOX: SEEING THE TRANSCENDENT

1 For biographies of Gurū Nānak, see W. H. McLeod, *Gurū Nānak and the Sikh Religion* (Oxford: Clarendon Press, 1968); Harbans Singh, *Guru Nanak and Origins of the Sikh Faith* (Bombay: Asia Publishing House,

1969); G. S. Talib, *Guru Nanak: His Personality and Vision* (New Delhi: Gurdas Kapur & Sons, 1969).

2 W. H. McLeod, *Early Sikh Tradition: A Study of the Janam-sakhis* (Oxford: Clarendon Press, 1980). McLeod, *The B40 Janam-Sakhi* (Amritsar: Guru Nanak Dev University, 1981). In *Gurū Nānak and the Sikh Religion*, McLeod made a minute study of the Janamsākhīs. See also Harbans Singh, *Guru Nanak and Origins of the Sikh Faith*, 15–35.

3 Otto Rank, *The Myth of the Birth of the Hero* (New York: Vintage, 1959), 14–64.

4 Bhāī Bālā, *Janamsākhī* (Lahore: Rāī Sāhib Munshī, Gulāb Singh), 6. See Harbans Singh, *Guru Nanak and Origins of the Sikh Faith*, 67.

5 Harbans Singh, *Guru Nanak and Origins of the Sikh Faith*, 70–71.

6 Published in Amritsar by Khālsā Samāchār in 1948 under the title *Purātan Janamsākhī Gurū Nānak Dev Jī*.

7 Harbans Singh, *Guru Nanak and Origins of the Sikh Faith*, 25–27.

8 This hymn is also found in the Gurū Granth, 14. All quotations from the *Purātan Janamsākhī* have been taken from the edition prepared by Bhāī Vīr Singh under the title *Purātan Janamsākhī Gurū Nānak Dev Jī*, published in Amritsar in 1948. For these translations I have relied on my father's rendering: Harbans Singh, *Guru Nanak and Origins of the Sikh Faith*, 95–96.

9 Gurū Granth, 663.

10 George Santayana, *The Sense of Beauty: Being the Outline of Aesthetic Theory* (New York: Dover, 1955), 47.

11 In *Pure Lust: Elemental Feminist Philosophy* (Boston: Beacon Press, 1984), Mary Daly gives a variety of multi-dimensional metaphors inherent in "witches." See her chapter on "Be-Witching: The Lust for Metamorphosis," 386–411.

12 Gurū Granth, 1343.

13 Ibid., 944.

14 Ibid., 227.

15 Ibid., 55.

16 Ibid., 414.

17 Rudolph Arnheim in his introduction to *Art and Visual Perception* (Berkeley: University of California Press, 1966), v–xi.

18 Kaṭha Upaniṣad in S. Radhakrishnan, *The Principal Upaniṣads* (London: George Allen & Unwin, 1953), especially 623–625. Chapter III. 3 begins with.

> Know thou the self (*ātman*) as riding in a chariot
> The body as the chariot . . .

19 *Bhagavad Gītā*, trans. Franklin Edgerton (Cambridge, MA: Harvard University Press, 1972).

20 Ibid., 57.

21 Gurū Granth, 2.

22 Ibid., 283.
23 Rosemary Radford Ruether, "Sexism and God Talk," in Judith Plaskow and Carol Christ, (eds.), *Weaving the Visions: New Patterns in Feminist Spirituality* (New York: Harper & Row, 1989), 161.
24 Rosemary Radford Ruether, *Sexism and God Talk: Toward a Feminist Theology* (Boston: Beacon Press, 1983), 54.
25 See Joseph Kockelmans, *Heidegger on Art and Art Works* (The Hague: Martinus Nijhoff, 1985).
26 Bhāī Vīr Singh, *Japujī Sāhib Santhyā* (Amritsar: Khālsā Samācār, 1981), 10.
27 Gurū Granth, 464.
28 Ibid., 1156.
29 Mary Daly, *Gyn-Ecology: The Metaethics of Radical Feminism* (Boston: Beacon Press, 1978), 1–42.
30 Gurū Granth, 350.
31 Ibid., 838.
32 Ibid., 391.
33 Ibid., 966.
34 Ibid., 1291.
35 Charlotte Vaudeville, "*Sant Mat*: Santism as the Universal Path to Sanctity," in *The Sants: Studies in a Devotional Tradition of India*, ed. Karine Schomer and W. H. McLeod (New Delhi: Berkeley Religious Studies Series and Motilal Banarsidass, 1987), 28.
36 Ibid., 38.
37 Paul Tillich, "Meaning and Justification of Symbols," in *Studies in Religious Philosophy*, ed. Robert W. Hall (New York: American Book Company, 1969), 305–309.
38 Mircea Eliade, *The Two and the One* (New York: Harper Torchbooks, 1965), 189–211.
39 In preface to Carol Christ, *Diving Deep and Surfacing: Women Writers on Spiritual Quest* (Boston: Beacon Press, 1980), xxvii. Incidentally, Buber was also Carol Christ's favorite theologian. During graduate school at Yale, she was told that he was a poet, not a theologian. She writes, "Buber's notion that a person could have an I–Thou relationship with a tree, an idea I used to interpret my experiences in the ocean, was singled out as an example of what was disparagingly called the 'confusion' in his thought."
40 Gurū Granth, 285.
41 Mary E. Hunt, "On Feminist Theology," *Journal of Feminist Studies in Religion* (autumn 1985), 85–86.
42 Ibid., 85.
43 Harbans Singh, *Berkeley Lectures on Sikhism* (New Delhi: Gurū Nānak Foundation, 1983), 9.
44 Owen Cole, in his book *The Gurū in Sikhism*, lucidly describes the *Gurū* as follows: "thus a guru is one who delivers those who accept his

teaching and discipline from darkness to enlightenment, from samsara, the road of rebirths, to moksha, spiritual realization and release." Owen Cole, *The Gurū in Sikhism* (London: Darton, Longman & Todd, 1982), 2.

45 Our *Purātan Janamsākhī* account as well as Gurū Granth, 663.
46 See Harbans Singh, *Guru Nanak and Origins of the Sikh Faith.*
47 Nirmal Kumar Jain, *Sikh Religion and Philosophy* (New Delhi: Sterling, 1979), 93.
48 Ibid., 105.
49 Mildreth Pinkham, *Woman in the Sacred Scriptures of Hinduism* (New York: AMS, 1967), viii.
50 Gurū Granth, 473.
51 G. S. Randhawa, "Gurū Nānak's Vision of Human Society," *Kheṛā: Journal of Religious Understanding* (October–December 1990) (New Delhi: Bhai Vir Singh Sahitya Sadan), 4.
52 Upinder Jit Kaur, *Sikh Religion and Economic Development* (New Delhi: National Book Organization, 1990), 308.
53 Harbans Singh, *The Heritage of the Sikhs* (New Delhi: Manohar, 1983), 23.
54 Ruether, *Sexism and God-Talk: Toward a Feminist Theology.*
55 Jean Grimshaw, *Philosophy and Feminist Thinking* (Minneapolis: University of Minnesota Press, 1986), 20.
56 Daly, *Gyn-Ecology*, 39.
57 Gurū Granth, 472.
58 In *Kojiki* 1: 10, Izanagi, the male Shinto deity, says to Izanami, "O my beloved wife, if you do thus, I will each day build one thousand five hundred parturition huts."
59 In Patricia Buckley Ebrey (ed.), *Chinese Civilization and Society: A Sourcebook* (New York: Free Press, 1981), we find a list of nine taboos that a pregnant woman must respect. Among them, no. 2 reads: "She must not go to temples or houses of witchcraft. It is believed that gods and spirits are most high, pure, and powerful beings who protect all people with impartiality and must be respected. A pregnant woman, however, is an offensive sight to them, so it would be most irreverent for her to visit a temple" (p. 302).
60 Elisabeth Moltmann-Wendel, *A Land Flowing with Milk and Honey: Perspectives on Feminist Theology* (New York: Crossroad, 1986), 74–75.
61 Rudolph Otto, *The Idea of the Holy* (New York: Galaxy, 1958), 1–40.
62 Harbans Singh, *Guru Nanak and Origins of the Sikh Faith*, 215–216.
63 Gurū Granth, 660.
64 Vaudeville, "*Sant Mat*: Santism as the Universal Path to Sanctity," in *The Sants: Studies in a Devotional Tradition of India*, 25.
65 Bhāī Vīr Singh (ed.), *Vārāṅ Bhāī Gurdas* 1. 32.
66 *Purātan Janamsākhī Srī Gurū Nānak Dev Jī*, 128.
67 Nripinder Singh, *The Sikh Moral Tradition: Ethical Perceptions of the Sikhs*

*in the Late Nineteenth/Early Twentieth Century* (New Delhi: Manohar, 1990), 214–215.

68 Gunindar Kaur, *Physics and Metaphysics of the Guru Granth Sahib* (New Delhi: Sterling Publishers, 1981), 11–22.

69 *Gurbilās Chhevīn Pātshāhī* (Patiala: Languages Department, 1979), 42.

70 S. S. Kohli, *A Critical Study of the Adi Granth* (New Delhi: The Punjabi Writers' Cooperative Industrial Society Ltd., 1961), 66 114.

71 *Gurbilās Chhevīn Pātshāhī*, 43.

72 According to Giani Garja Singh, the author of this entry is Narbud Singh Bhaṭṭ, who was with Gurū Gobind Singh at Nanded at that time. For a detailed account see Harbans Singh, *Sri Guru Granth Sahib: The Guru Eternal for the Sikhs* (Patiala: Dhillon Marg, 1988).

73 Ibid., 19–25.

74 Linda Hess, "Kabir's Rough Rhetoric," *The Sants: Studies in a Devotional Tradition of India*, 148.

75 Ibid., 147.

76 Ibid., 153.

77 Gurū Granth, 1036.

78 Ibid., 153.

79 Jacques Maritain, *Creative Intuition in Art and Poetry* (New York: Meridian Books), 4.

80 In Plaskow and Christ (eds.), *Weaving the Visions*, 321–322. See also "Maintenance: Mankind at the Helm," in Wallace S. Broecker, *How to Build a Habitable Planet* (New York: Eldigion Press, 1985), 259–282: "Thus, for better or worse, mankind is now at the helm. We have the power to modify climate, to determine the habitats of other species, to control the chemical purity of air and water. Unfortunately, our activities are intervening at such an alarming pace that we are not in control of developments. How much damage will be done before we are able to take the reins in a responsible manner?"

81 Mary Daly, *Beyond God the Father: Toward a Philosophy of Women's Liberation* (Boston: Beacon Press, 1973).

82 Beverly Wildung Harrison, "The Power of Anger in the Work of Love," in Plaskow and Christ, *Weaving the Visions*, 216.

83 Hans-George Gadamer, *Truth and Method* (New York: Crossroad, 1986), 60.

84 Rosemary Radford Ruether, "The Future of Feminist Theology," *Journal of the American Academy of Religion* 53 (December 1985), 703.

85 Martin Heidegger, *Poetry, Language, Thought*, trans. Albert Hofstadter (New York: Harper & Row, 1971), 74. In Shelley's "Defence of Poetry" an identical statement is found: "language itself is poetry."

86 Heidegger, *Poetry, Language, Thought*, 72.

87 Rita Nakashima Brock, "On Mirrors, Mists, and Murmurs," in Plaskow and Christ, *Weaving the Visions*, 236.

88 See A. C. Bouquet, *Sacred Books of the World* (Baltimore: Pelican, 1967), 315; J. B. Noss, *A History of the World's Religions* (New York: Macmillan, 1990), 234–245.
89 Gurū Granth, 885.
90 Ibid., 982.
91 Ibid., 722.
92 Ibid., 566.
93 Ibid., 763.
94 Ibid., 308.
95 Ibid., 743.
96 Ibid., 515.
97 In the words of Gurū Gobind Singh: "*gurū granthjī mānio pargaṭ gurāṇ kī deh.*"
98 Gurū Granth, 1226.
99 Victor Zuckerkandl, *Sound and Symbol: Music and the External World* (Princeton: Bollingen, 1956), 2.
100 Harbans Singh, *Sri Gurū Granth Sahib: The Guru Eternal for the Sikhs*, 19.
101 Gurū Granth, 628.
102 In Plaskow and Christ, *Weaving the Visions*, 151.
103 S. Radhakrishnan, "Gurū Nānak: An Introduction," in Gurmukh Nihal Singh, ed., *Guru Nanak: His Life, Time and Teachings* (New Delhi: Guru Nanak Foundation, 1969), 2.
104 Gurū Granth, 749.
105 Ibid., 289:

*gun gāvat terī utrạsi mailu*
*binasi jāe haumai bikhu phailu.*

## 2 MOTHER: THE INFINITE MATRIX

1 W. H. McLeod, *Gurū Nānak and the Sikh Religion* (Oxford: Clarendon Press, 1968), 164.
2 Gurū Granth, 131.
3 Ibid., 139.
4 Ibid., 144.
5 Ibid., 351.
6 Ibid., 355.
7 Ibid., 1021.
8 Ibid., 1020.
9 Ibid., 930.
10 Gurbachan Singh Talib, *Japuji: The Immortal Prayer-Chant* (Delhi: Munshiram Manoharlal, 1977), 141.
11 Gurū Granth, 1020, "*ape purakhu ape hī nārī.*" (In my translation, I have italicized "woman.")
12 Leonard Swidler, "Is Sexism a Sign of Decadence in Religion?,"

*Women and Religion*, ed. Judith Plaskow and Joan Arnold (Missoula, MT: Scholars Press, 1974), 171. He writes "An effective and deliberate eradication of sexism, i.e. by a return to their original insights, if not also an extension beyond them, would also in a major way promote a general renewal of those religions and societies."

13 Sallie McFague, *Models of God: Theology for an Ecological, Nuclear Age* (Philadelphia: Fortress Press, 1987), 99.

14 Rosemary Radford Ruether, *Sexism and God-Talk: Toward a Feminist Theology* (Boston: Beacon Press, 1983).

15 Noted by Elizabeth A. Johnson, "The Incomprehensibility of God and the Image of God Male and Female," *Theological Studies* 45 (1984).

16 Sallie McFague, "God as Mother," in *Weaving the Visions: New Patterns in Feminist Spirituality*, ed. Judith Plaskow and Carol Christ (New York: Harper & Row, 1989), 140.

17 Beatrice Bruteau, "The Image of the Virgin-Mother," in *Women and Religion*, ed. Judith Plaskow and Joan Arnold (Missoula, MT: Scholars Press, 1974), 92.

18 Samuel Laeuchli, *Religion and Art in Conflict* (Philadephia: Fortress Press, 1980). In the chapter, "Icon and Idea: Aquileia and Nicaea" (pp. 111–133), Laeuchli compares the two separate and distinct research processes involved in the verbal and visual materials of Aquileia and Nicaea. According to Laeuchli, the Creed of Nicaea is evidenced through words which we read and compare and ask questions and make deductions and try to understand, analyze, reinterpret whereas, the mosaics on the floor of Aquileia's Cathedral are firsthand and the initial and primary step of this research process begins with a visual-physical impact. The materials, colors, symbols in the mosaics are *seen*; the impact of the mosaics on the person who enters this space is experienced. The overall result of these two processes is that while the idea/word (theology, philosophy) creates bifurcation amongst people, the icon/image creates a unity.

19 Gurū Granth, 152.

20 Ibid., 156.

21 Ibid., 4.

22 Ibid., 3.

23 Ibid., 580.

24 Simone de Beauvoir, *The Second Sex*, trans. H. M. Parshley (New York: Vintage, 1974), xix.

25 Gurū Granth, 1022.

26 Ibid., 706.

27 Penelope Washbourn, "Becoming Woman: Menstruation as Spiritual Challenge," in *Becoming Woman: The Quest for Wholeness in Female Experience* (New York: Harper & Row, 1977), 1–19.

28 Judy Grahn, "From Sacred Blood to the Curse Beyond," *The Politics of*

*Women's Spirituality*, ed. Charlene Spretnak (New York: Anchor/Doubleday, 1982), 265–279.

29 Judith Bardwick, *Psychology of Women: A Study of Bio-Cultural Conflicts* (New York: Harper & Row, 1971).

30 Judy Grahn, "From Sacred Blood to the Curse Beyond," in Spretnak (ed.), *The Politics of Women's Spirituality*, 275.

31 Gurū Granth, 140.

32 Ibid., 989.

33 Ibid., 74.

34 Ibid., 156.

35 Ibid., 473.

36 McFague, *Models of God*, 109.

37 Gurū Granth, 137.

38 Ibid., 75.

39 "A literal translation of *Shad* (breast) and the possessive plural for 'my,'" noted by Ellen Umansky, "Creating a Jewish Feminist Theology," in Plaskow and Christ, *Weaving the Visions*, 192–193.

40 Arthur Waley, *The Way and its Power: A Study of the Tao Tê Ching and its Place in Chinese Thought* (New York: Grove Press, 1958), 202.

41 Holmes Welch, *Taoism: The Parting of the Way* (Boston: Beacon Press, 1965), 63.

42 Rita Gross, "Hindu Female Deities as a Resource for the Contemporary Rediscovery of the Goddess" in Carl Olson (ed.), *The Book of the Goddess Past and Present: An Introduction to Her Religion* (New York: Crossroad, 1985), 225.

43 McFague, *Models of God*, 106.

44 Brihadaranyaka Upaniṣad 1.3.28.

45 Psalms 4:6.

46 Mahāparinibbāna Sutta.

47 John 1:5.

48 Qur'ān xxiv. 35.

49 Cited by David Kinsley, *The Goddesses' Mirror: Visions of the Divine from East and West* (New York: State University of New York Press, 1989), 71.

50 Gurū Granth, 663.

51 S. H. Nasr, Discussion of Suhrāwardī's *Hikmat al-Ishrāq*, bk. II, ch. 9, Class lecture, Temple University, February 24, 1982.

52 Gurū Granth, 1033.

53 S. H. Nasr, *Three Muslim Sages* (Cambridge, MA: Harvard University Press, 1964), 69. The following passage by Suhrāwardī has been cited:

> The essence of the First Absolute Light, God, gives constant illumination, whereby it is manifested and it brings all things into existence, giving life to them by its rays. Everything in the world is derived from the Light of His Essence and all beauty and perfection are the gift of His bounty, and to attain fully to this illumination is salvation.

The ontological status of the various planes of reality is dependent upon their proximity to the *Nūr al-anwār* and upon the extent to which they are themselves illuminated. The *tashkīk al-dhātī* theory of Suhrāwardī's finds a parallel in the Hindu ontological speculation. For it is maintained in the Hindu religious texts that the universe is constituted of the various gradations of light. Passage XVIII. 36 from the *Bhagavad Gītā*.

> There is no thing, whether on earth,
> Or yet in heaven, among the gods,
> No being which free from the material-nature-born
> Strands, these three, might be.

These three *guṇas* or strands which regulate the entire make-up of the universe from the highest to the lowest are *sattva*, *rajas*, and *tamas*. Immaterial and substanceless themselves, they are sheerly different intensities of light. *Sattva* is the stainless, transparent, luminous white light; it is pure light. *Rajas* is the concentration of violet. *Tamas* is the total obstruction of light; it is black.

54 Gurū Granth, 921.
55 Ibid., 140.
56 Ibid., 19.
57 Ibid., 972.
58 Muhammad Iqbal, *The Development of Metaphysics in Persia* (Lahore: Bazmi-i-Iqbal), 106.
59 Gurū Granth, 20.
60 Ibid., 1349.
61 Ruether, *Sexism and God-Talk: Toward a Feminist Theology*, 87.
62 Gurū Granth, 83.
63 Ibid., 469.
64 Ibid., 1330.
65 Ibid., 473.
66 Ibid., 1015.
67 Ntozake Shange, *for colored girls who have considered suicide when the rainbow is enuf* (New York: Macmillan, 1975).
68 Gurū Granth, 464.
69 Ibid., 1095.
70 Ibid., 287.
71 Ibid., 2.
72 Ibid., 469.
73 Ibid., 13.
74 Heinrich Zimmer, *Myths and Symbols in Indian Art and Civilization* (Princeton: Bollingen, 1974), no. 67.
75 Beatrice Bruteau, "The Image of the Virgin-Mother," in *Women and Religion*, ed. Plaskow and Arnold, 99–100.
76 Gurū Granth, 580.

77 Ruether, *Sexism and God-Talk: Toward a Feminist Theology*, and McFague, *Models of God.*
78 McFague, "God as Mother," in Plaskow and Christ, *Weaving the Visions*, 145.
79 Ruether, *Sexism and God-Talk: Toward a Feminist Theology*, 92.
80 Carol Christ, "Rethinking Theology and Nature," in Plaskow and Christ, *Weaving the Visions*, 321.
81 McFague, *Models of God*, 122.
82 Ibid., 304.
83 *The Bible Today* 22:5 (September 1984), 300–305; and *National Catholic Reporter* (January 31, 1975).
84 "God, Father and Mother," *The Bible Today* 22:5 (September 1984), 304.
85 S. H. Nasr, *Knowledge and the Sacred* (New York: Crossroad, 1981), 208.
86 Gurū Granth, 242.
87 Ibid., 2.
88 Kena Upaniṣad III.12.
89 S. Radhakrishnan, *The Principal Upaniṣads* (London: George Allen & Unwin, 1953), 589.
90 Nasr, *Knowledge and the Sacred*, 321; 331.
91 A. K. Coomaraswamy, *Christian and Oriental Philosophy of Art* (New York: Dover, 1956), 102.
92 Nasr, *Knowledge and the Sacred*, 274.
93 Gurū Granth, 767.
94 Ibid., 189.
95 Ibid., 350.
96 Qur'ān XXXIII. 44.
97 Ṛg Veda 2.23.15.
98 Henry Corbin, *Œuvres philosophiques et mystiques de Shihabaddin Yahya Sorawardi, Opera Metaphysica et Mystica* II (Tehran, 1952).
99 Gurū Granth,728.
100 *Gurū Nānak Bāṇī Prakāś* (Patiala: Punjabi University Press, 1969), vol. II, 772.
101 Ibid., 62.
102 "binu sevā kiṅe na pāiā," in Gurū Granth, 1011.
103 Ibid., 149.
104 Ibid., 1257.
105 Ellison Banks Findly, "Gārgī at the King's Court," in *Women, Religion, and Social Change*, ed. Yvonne Yazbeck Haddad and Ellison Banks Findly (New York: State University of New York Press, 1985), 46.
106 Gurū Granth, 66.
107 Ibid., 661.
108 Ibid., 91.
109 Ibid., 153.
110 Ibid., 414.

111 Martin Heidegger, *Being and Time*, trans. John Macquarrie and Edward Robinson (New York: Harper & Row, 1962). ("Geworfenheit" is the Heideggerian term.)
112 Gurū Granth, 59.
113 Ibid., 145.
114 Ibid., 53.
115 Ibid., 72.
116 Ibid., 2.
117 Kartar Singh, *Nitnem Stīk* (Amritsar, 1977), 10.
118 Gurū Granth, 598.
119 Ibid., 357.
120 Ibid., 222.
121 McLeod, *Gurū Nānak and the Sikh Religion*, 221.
122 Ibid., 161.
123 Ibid., 221.
124 McLeod, however, is correct to note that "Sikh commentators understandably attach considerable importance to the figure of the five *khaṇḍs*, for it is clearly intended to represent the ascent of the *man* to its ultimate goal" (*Gurū Nānak and the Sikh Religion*, 221).
125 Gurū Granth, 7.
126 Ibid., 7.
127 Ibid., 176.
128 Ibid., 7.
129 Ibid., 7.
130 Rudolph Otto, *The Idea of the Holy* (New York: Galaxy, 1958), 21.
131 Gurū Granth, 7.
132 Ruether, *Sexism and God-Talk: Toward a Feminist Theology*, 79.
133 Gurū Granth, 7.
134 Ibid., 8.
135 Ibid., 8.
136 Ibid., 725.
137 Wassily Kandinsky, *Concerning the Spiritual in Art* (New York: Dover, 1977), 54.
138 Their views are meticulously analysed by McLeod, *Gurū Nānak and the Sikh Religion*, 222–223. See also, Max Arthur Macauliffe, *The Sikh Religion, its Gurus, Sacred Writings and Authors*, vol. 1 (Oxford: Clarendon Press, 1909), 216. Teja Singh, *The Japjī* (Lahore, 1930), 14, 40. Khushwant Singh, *Jupjī: The Sikh Prayer* (London), 22.
139 Bhai Jodh Singh, *The Japjī* (Amritsar, 1956), 55. Gopal Singh, *The Song of Gurū Nānak, English Translation of the Japji* (London, 1955), 11. Bhāī Vīr Singh, *Santhya Srī Gurū Granth Sāhib*, vol. 1 (Amritsar, 1958), 167.
140 McLeod, *Gurū Nānak and the Sikh Religion*, 223.
141 Gurū Granth, 8.
142 Ibid., 86.

143 Ibid., 6.
144 Ibid., 8.
145 G. S. Talib, *Japuji: The Immortal Prayer-Chant*, 135.
146 Kana Mitra, "Women in Hinduism," *Journal of Ecumenical Studies* 20:4 (Fall 1983) (Philadelphia), 588.
147 Cornelia Dimmitt, "Sītā: Fertility Goddess and *Śaktī*," in Jack Hawley and Donna Marie Wulff (eds.), *The Divine Consort: Rādhā and the Goddesses of India* (Boston: Beacon Press, 1986), 210–223.
148 Gurū Granth, 8.
149 Ibid., 8.
150 Ibid., 8.
151 Ibid., 8.
152 Ibid., 8.

## 3 THE BRIDE SEEKS HER GROOM: AN EPIPHANY OF INTERCONNECTIONS

1 Barbara A. Holdrege, "The Bride of Israel: The Ontological Status of Scripture in the Rabbinic and Kabbalistic Traditions," in *Rethinking Scripture: Essays from a Comparative Perspective*, ed. Miriam Levering (New York: State University of New York Press, 1989), 180–261. Holdrege writes, "The revelation of the Torah at Mount Sinai is sometimes depicted in rabbinic literature as a wedding ceremony. In one tradition the wedding celebrates the betrothal of the Lord to his bride Israel. The Lord presents the Torah to Israel as the marriage contract (k'tubāh) binding them in an everlasting covenant. A second tradition portrays the Torah not as a mere legal document but as the bride herself, who is presented in marriage by God, her father, to the bridegroom, Israel. Year after year these different versions of the marriage ceremony are enacted in the two annual festivals dedicated to the Torah. The marriage symbolism is thus not simply a textual phenomenon. It is a part of the living Jewish tradition" (p. 184).
2 Gurū Granth, 703.
3 Rosemary Radford Ruether, *Sexism and God-Talk: Toward a Feminist Theology* (Boston: Beacon Press, 1983), 75–82. See also Betty Roszak, "The Human Continuum," in *Masculine/Feminine*, ed. Betty Roszak and Theodore Roszak (New York: Harper & Row, 1969), 304. In "Misogynism and Virginal Feminism in the Fathers of the Church," in *Religion and Sexism*, ed. Rosemary Ruether (New York: Simon & Schuster, 1974), Ruether states that patristic theology defines woman "in terms of her subordination to the male in the order of nature and her 'carnality' in the disorder of sin" (p. 156). Lynda M. Glennon, *Women and Dualism* (Longman, 1979), shows that dualism always goes on to make females "feel inferior and treated in a subservient way"

(p. 106). The medical experts in the Roman Empire explained male superiority in biological terms and buttressed their beliefs with "scientific" arguments: males were those fetuses who had realized their full potential by acquiring the appropriate amount of heat and vital spirit; the females, in contrast, were the lower, i.e. the "failed males." Aretaeus, the Greek doctor, is cited by Peter Brown, in *The Body and Society: Men, Women, and Sexual Renunciation in Early Christianity* (New York: Columbia University Press, 1988): "For it is the semen, when possessed of vitality, which makes us men, hot, well-braced in limbs, heavy, well-voiced, spirited, strong to think and act" (p. 10).

4 See S. M. Ikram, *Muslim Civilization in India* (New York: Columbia University Press, 1964,), 127; R. C. Zaehner (ed.), *The Concise Encyclopaedia of Living Faiths* (Boston: Beacon Press, 1959). See also Gurdev Singh (ed.), *Perspectives on the Sikh Tradition* (Patiala: Siddharth Press, 1986), 18.

5 Gurū Granth, 157.

6 Ibid., 1286.

7 According to Mircea Eliade, multivalence is an essential quality of religious symbolism. See *The Two and the One* (New York: Harper Torchbooks, 1965), 189–211.

8 Gurū Granth, 937.

9 Ibid., 558.

10 Ibid., 351.

11 "giānu aṅjanu guri dīā agiānu aṅdher bināsu" (Gurū Granth, 293). "timar agiānu gavāiā gurgiān anjanu gur pāiā rām" (Gurū Granth, 573).

12 Gurū Granth, 557.

13 Ibid., 729.

14 Rosemary Radford Ruether, *Sexism and God-Talk: Toward a Feminist Theology*, 54.

15 Gurū Granth, 125.

16 "sagal banaspati mahi baisaṅtaru sagal dūdhu mahi ghīā
ūch nīch mahi joti samāṇī ghaṭi ghaṭi mādho jīā" (Gurū Granth, 617).

17 Ibid., 921.

18 Gurū Nānak's term "man" itself brings together the range of thought, emotion, and spiritual being which are ordinarily distinguished as "mind," "heart," and "soul". See W. H. McLeod, *Who is a Sikh? The Problem of Sikh Identity* (Oxford: Clarendon Press, 1989), 9.

19 Rudolph Otto, *The Idea of the Holy* (New York: Galaxy, 1958), 29.

20 Gurū Granth, 945.

21 Ibid., 1170.

22 Ibid., 1233.

23 Ibid., 1169.

24 Ibid., 1197.

25 Ibid., 1331.

26 Paul Tillich, *Systematic Theology*, vol. 1 (Chicago: University of Chicago Press, 1951), 241.
27 Sigmund Freud, *The Future of an Illusion* (New York: Anchor Press, 1961), 33.
28 Sri Aurobindo, *The Synthesis of Yoga*, vol. 1 (Pondicherry: Sri Aurobindo Ashram, 1965), 286.
29 See, for instance, Carter Heyward, "Sexuality, Love, and Justice," in Judith Plaskow and Carol Christ (eds.), *Weaving the Visions: New Patterns in Feminist Spirituality* (New York: Harper & Row, 1989), 296.
30 Christ, "Why Women Need the Goddess," in *Womanspirit Rising: A Feminist Reader*, ed. Carol Christ and Judith Plaskow (New York: Harper & Row, 1979), 286. See also Carol Christ, "Symbols of Goddess and God in Feminist Theology," in *The Book of the Goddess, Past and Present: An Introduction to Her Religion*, ed. Carl Olson (New York: Crossroad, 1985), 250.
31 Eliade, *The Two and the One*, 203.
32 Charlotte Vaudeville, *Bārahmāsā in Indian Literature* (Delhi: Motilal Banarsidass, 1986), 7.
33 Gurū Granth, 1108.
34 Ibid., 1108.
35 Ibid., 1108.
36 The translation from the autograph of St. Teresa is entitled *The Interior Castle* translated by the Benedictines of Stanbrook Abbey, (London, 1912).
37 Gurū Granth, 1108.
38 Ibid., 1108.
39 Ibid., 1108.
40 Ibid., 1108.
41 Ibid., 1109.
42 Ibid., 1109.
43 Ibid., 1109.
44 Ibid., 1109.
45 Ibid., 1109.
46 Leo Tolstoy, *What Is Art?* (Scribners' Sons, 1911), 63–67.
47 Gurū Granth, 1109.
48 Ibid., 1109.
49 Ibid., 1109.
50 Ibid., 1109.
51 Ibid., 1109.
52 Ibid., 1109.
53 Eliade, *The Two and the One*, 207.
54 Vandana Shiva, *Staying Alive: Women, Ecology and Development* (Zed Books, 1989).
55 Carol Lee Sanchez, "New World Tribal Communities," in Plaskow and Christ (eds.), *Weaving the Visions*, 352.

56 Eliade, *The Two and the One*, 207.
57 Ibid., 207.
58 Rita Gross, "Hindu Female Deities as a Resource for the Contemporary Rediscovery of the Goddess," in Olson, *The Book of the Goddess, Past and Present*, 225.
59 Ann Belford Ulanov, *The Feminine in Jungian Psychology and in Christian Theology* (Evanston: Northwestern University Press, 1971), 199–200.
60 See Elizabeth Bumiller, *May You Be the Mother of a Hundred Sons (A Journey Among the Women of India)* (New York: Random House, 1990).
61 Gurū Granth, 1170.
62 In Carol Christ, *Diving Deep and Surfacing* (Boston: Beacon Press, 1980), 199.
63 Gurū Granth, 1171.
64 Ibid., 689.
65 Ibid., 157.
66 See Samuel Laeuchli, *Religion and Art in Conflict* (Philadelphia: Fortress Press, 1980).
67 Ismail al Faruqi, "Figurative Representation and Drama: Their Prohibition and Transformation in Islamic Art," unpublished paper, 21.
68 Such as E. Trumpp (1877), J. N. Farquhar (1912), R. C. Zaehner (1959), S. M. Ikram (1964), and A. Embree (1966).
69 Karine Schomer, "Kabīr in the Gurū Granth Sāhib: An Exploratory Essay," in *Sikh Studies: Comparative Perspectives on a Changing Tradition*, ed. Mark Juergensmeyer and N. G. Barrier, Berkeley Religious Studies Series (Berkeley: Graduate Theological Union, 1979), 80.
70 Ibid., 80.
71 *Kabīr Granthāvalī*, 9.15. Throughout this section, I have relied on Schomer's fine translations of Kabīr.
72 *Kabīr Granthāvalī*, 14.18.
73 Ibid., 14.34.
74 Schomer, "Kabīr in the Gurū Granth Sāhib: An Exploratory Essay," and Wendy O'Flaherty, "*Comments*: Mediation in the Sant Tradition," in Juergensmeyer and Barrier (eds.), *Sikh Studies*, 75–89.
75 Schomer, in "Kabīr in the Gurū Granth Sāhib: An Exploratory Essay," 83.
76 *Kabīr Granthāvalī*, 30.7.
77 Audre Lorde, "Uses of the Erotic," in Plaskow and Christ (eds.), *Weaving the Visions*, 211.
78 C. H. Loehlin, *The Sikhs and their Scriptures* (Lucknow: Lucknow Publishing House, 1964). Loehlin writes, "It is said that the Guru [Guru Arjan, Nanak V, while compiling the Granth] rejected the hymns of self-deification, those derogatory to women . . ." (p. 32).
79 Daljeet Singh has also noted the radical difference in the attitude towards women between the Sikh Gurūs and Hindu sects. See chapters

3–7 in *Perspectives on the Sikh Tradition*, ed. Gurdev Singh, 55–146. He writes, "In Nathism celibacy is essential. Woman, as in the other Hindu systems, is deemed to be a temptress. The Naths would not sit and eat with even Nath women. But in the Guru's system, downgrading the woman has been denounced and she is deemed to be an equal partner in man's spiritual venture . . . In all ascetic and monastic systems woman has been dubbed as evil. That is so even in systems that renounce the world either on account of Bhakti or devotion or for other reasons. But in the Guru's system her role is significant and equal to that of man" (p. 133).

80 Rosemary Radford Ruether, "Sexism and God-Talk," in Plaskow and Christ (eds.), *Weaving the Visions*, 161.

## 4 DURGĀ RECALLED: TRANSITION FROM MYTHOS TO ETHOS

1 Harbans Singh, *Guru Tegh Bahadur* (New Delhi: Sterling, 1982), 17.

2 Harbans Singh, *Guru Gobind Singh* (New Delhi: Sterling, 1979), 46.

3 Sujān Rāi Bhaṇḍārī Batāliā, *Khulāsat-ut-Tawārīkh*. Quoted in Kapur Singh, *The Baisakhi of Gurū Gobind Singh* (Jullundur: Hind Publishers, 1959), 4–5.

4 David Kinsley, "Durgā, Warrior Goddess and Cosmic Queen," in *The Goddesses' Mirror: Visions of the Divine from East and West* (New York: State University of New York Press, 1989), 3–24.

5 S. Radhakrishnan, foreword to *The Poetry of the Dasam Granth*, by D. P. Ashta (New Delhi: Arun Prakashan, 1959).

6 The most heated moment during a conference on Sikh theology at Columbia University revolved around Gurū Gobind Singh's poetic utilization of the Hindu goddess. Many other participants, all male, vehemently disagreed with a female participant for suggesting that the Sikh Gurū could refer to a Hindu goddess (conference on "Sikh Theology," Columbia University, March 31, 1990).

7 Ashta, *The Poetry of the Dasam Granth*, 38.

8 Trilochan Singh, *Sikh Review* (Calcutta, May 1955), 34.

9 For a detailed discussion of the continuing debate see Piara Singh Padam, *Dasam Granth Darśan* (Patiala: Kala Mandir, Lower Mall, 1990), 39–53; 96–109. Earlier Sikhs belonging to the Bhasauṛia school (flourishing in the 1920s) and recently Rattan Singh Jaggi and many other scholars have rejected Gurū Gobind Singh's authorship of poems with Hindu themes. On the other hand, for many scholars such an issue does not even arise. They are fully convinced about Gurū Gobind Singh's authorship. See, for example, Jodh Singh, "Bachitra Natak: Some Further Exploration," *Journal of Sikh Studies* (August 1987) (Amritsar: Guru Nanak Dev University), 34.

10 *Bacitra Nāṭak*, in *Śabdārath: Dasam Granth Sāhib*, vol. 1 (Patiala: Punjabi University Press, 1973), 91.

11 Piara Singh Padam in his *Dasam Granth Darśan* cites a passage from Bhāī Desā Singh's *Rahitnāmā*. Bhāī Desā Singh writes that he has had a dream of the Gurū in which he hears him state:

> sunhu singh! ikk bacan hamārā prathamai hamnai jāpu ucārā ...
> pun do caṇḍī caritar banāe ... (p. 50).

12 David R. Kinsley, "The Portrait of the Goddess in the *Devī-māhātmya*," *Journal of the American Academy of Religion* 46: 4 (December 1978).
13 V. S. Agrawala, *Devī-Māhātmyam: The Glorification of the Great Goddess*. (Varanasi: All India Kashiraj Trust, 1963), 149.
14 *Caṇḍī Caritra*, in *Śabdārath: Dasam Granth Sāhib*, vol. 1, p. 92.
15 *Akāl Ustati*, in *Śabdārath: Dasam Granth Sahib*, vol. 1, p. 16.
16 Kapur Singh, *The Baisakhi of Gurū Gobind Singh*, 5.
17 We discussed in Chapter 2 Gurū Nānak's view that the gods and goddesses were the creation of the Ultimate Transcendent.
18 *Vār Durgā Kī*, in *Śabdārath: Dasam Granth Sāhib*, vol. 1, p. 154.
19 See Taran Singh, *Dasam Granth: Rūp te Ras* (Chandigarh: Gurū Gobind Singh Foundation, 1967), 223.
20 Opening of *Caṇḍī Caritra, Śabdārath Dasam Granth Sāhib*, vol. 1, p. 92.
21 *Caṇḍī Caritra*, in *Śabdārath: Dasam Granth Sāhib*, vol. 1, p. 92.
22 Ibid., 127.
23 James L. Jarrett, *The Quest for Beauty* (Englewood Cliffs: Prentice-Hall, Inc., 1957), 74.
24 Max Müller, *Introduction to the Science of Religion* (London: Longman's, Green, 1873), 352.
25 Amos Niven Wilder, *Theopoetic: Theology and the Religious Imagination* (Philadelphia: Fortress Press, 1976), 73–100.
26 Charlene Spretnak, introduction, "Mythic Heras as Models of Strength and Wisdom," to *The Politics of Women's Spirituality* (New York: Anchor/Doubleday, 1982), 90.
27 Cornelia Dimmitt and J. A. B. van Buitenen (eds.), *Classical Hindu Mythology: A Reader in the Sanskrit Purāṇas* (Philadelphia: Temple University Press, 1978), 221.
28 *Mārkaṇḍeya Purāṇa*. The passage has been taken from Agrawala, *Devī-Māhātmyam: The Glorification of the Great Goddess*, 47. In verse 2.15, the original Sanskrit word *angulya* will be rendered more appropriately as "toe," and not as "finger" as in Agrawala's translation.
29 Dimmitt and van Buitenen, *Classical Hindu Mythology*, 221.
30 *Akāl Ustati*, in *Śabdārath: Dasam Granth Sāhib*, vol. 1, p. 16.
31 *Vār Durgā Kī*, in *Śabdārath: Dasam Granth Sāhib*, vol. 1, p. 155.
32 Agrawala, *Devī-Māhātmyam: The Glorification of the Great Goddess*, 98.
33 *Akāl Ustati*, in *Śabdārath: Dasam Granth Sāhib*, vol. 1, pp. 43–44.
34 Ibid., p. 44.
35 Ibid., p. 44.
36 Agrawala, *Devī-Māhātmyam: The Glorification of the Great Goddess*, 83.

37 S. H. Nasr, "What is Metaphysics?," Gifford Lecture, Temple University, Philadelphia, March 18, 1981. In S. H. Nasr's words, the concept of "wholeness" would correspond to her being both Eve and Mary.

38 Miriam Starhawk, in Spretnak (ed.), *The Politics of Women's Spirituality*. She writes, "The importance of the Goddess symbol for women cannot be overstressed. The image of the Goddess inspires women to see ourselves as divine, our bodies as sacred, the changing phases of our lives as holy, our aggression as healthy, our anger as purifying, and our power to nurture and create, but also to limit and destroy when necessary, as the very force that sustains all life. Through the Goddess, we can discover our strength, enlighten our minds, own our bodies, and celebrate our emotions. We can move beyond narrow, constricting roles and become whole" (p. 51). In Gurū Gobind Singh's perception, the goddess would inspire *both* women and men.

39 *Caṇḍī Caritra*, in *Śabdārath: Dasam Granth Sāhib*, vol. 1, p. 127.

40 Spretnak (ed.), *The Politics of Women's Spirituality*, 91–96.

41 Bella Debrida, in Spretnak (ed.), *The Politics of Women's Spirituality*. She further states: "Once we begin to delve into the mythology, we find that it has been perverted. A deliberate selection process has determined who our female models may be, and even those few models have been twisted to serve patriarchal aims" (p. 142).

42 Ananda K. Coomaraswamy, *The Transformation of Nature in Art* (Cambridge, MA: Harvard University Press, 1935), 52.

43 Ananda K. Coomaraswamy, *The Hindu View of Art* (Bombay: Asia Publishing House, 1957), 57.

44 Harbans Singh, *Aspects of Punjabi Literature* (Ferozepore: Bawa Publishing House, 1961), 86. This passage is also found in Harbans Singh, *Guru Gobind Singh*, 24–25.

45 *Caṇḍī Caritra*, in *Śabdārath: Dasam Granth Sāhib*, vol. 1, p. 124.

46 Ibid., 120.

47 Ashta, *The Poetry of the Dasam Granth*, 259.

48 *Caṇḍī Caritra*, in *Śabdārath: Dasam Granth Sāhib*, vol. 1, p. 113.

49 *Vār Durgā Kī*, in *Śabdārath: Dasam Granth Sāhib*, vol. 1, p. 166.

50 *Caṇḍī Caritra*, in *Śabdārath: Dasam Granth Sāhib*, vol. 1, p. 113.

51 *Vār Durgā Kī*, in *Śabdārath: Dasam Granth Sāhib*, vol. 1, p. 168.

52 Ibid., 163.

53 *Caṇḍī Caritra*, in *Śabdārath: Dasam Granth Sāhib*, vol. 1, p. 105.

54 Ibid., 105.

55 Ibid., 119.

56 *Vār Durgā Kī*, in *Śabdārath: Dasam Granth Sāhib*, vol. 1, p. 156.

57 Ibid., 167.

58 Ibid., 156.

59 Harbans Singh, *Aspects of Punjabi Literature*, 86.

60 *Vār Durgā Kī*, in *Śabdārath: Dasam Granth Sāhib*, vol. 1, p. 157.

61 *Caṇḍī Caritra*, in *Śabdārath: Dasam Granth Sāhib*, vol. 1, p. 142.

62 *Vār Durgā Kī*, in *Śabdārath: Dasam Granth Sāhib*, vol. 1, p. 161.
63 *Caṇḍī Caritra*, in *Śabdārath: Dasam Granth Sāhib*, vol. 1, pp. 151–152.
64 Ibid., 140.
65 Ashta, *The Poetry of the Dasam Granth*, 289.
66 *Caṇḍī Caritra*, in *Śabdārath: Dasam Granth Sāhib*, vol. 1, p. 142.
67 *Vār Durgā Kī*, in *Śabdārath: Dasam Granth Sāhib*, vol. 1, p. 167.
68 Ibid., 167.
69 Ibn al'Arabi, *The Bezels of Wisdom*, trans. R. W. J. Austin, *The Classics of Western Spirituality* (NJ: Paulist Press, 1980), 29. Connections are also made in Hebrew between the word *rachum* or *racham*, usually translated "compassion," and the word for womb (*racham* or *rechem*). See Phyllis Trible, *God and the Rhetoric of Sexuality* (Philadelphia: Fortress Press, 1978), 31–59; and Virginia Ramey Mollenkott, *The Divine Feminine: The Biblical Imagery of God as Female* (New York: Crossroad, 1989), 15–19.
70 *Vār Durgā Kī*, in *Śabdārath: Dasam Granth Sāhib*, vol. 1, p. 160.
71 Leo Tolstoy, *What is Art?* (Oxford: Clarendon Press, 1938), 121.
72 Ellen Umansky, "Creating a Jewish Feminist Theology: Possibilities and Problems," in Judith Plaskow and Carol Christ (eds.), *Weaving the Visions: New Patterns in Feminist Spirituality* (New York: Harper & Row, 1989), 187–198.
73 Debrida, in Spretnak (ed.), *The Politics of Women's Spirituality*, 142.
74 Philip Wheelwright, *Metaphor and Reality* (Bloomington: Indiana University Press, 1962), 71.
75 Marcia Falk, "Notes on Composing New Blessings: Toward a Feminist-Jewish Prayer," in Plaskow and Christ (eds.), *Weaving the Visions*, 131–132.
76 *Akāl Ustati*, in *Śabdārath: Dasam Granth Sāhib*, vol. 1, p. 16.
77 *Bacitra Nāṭak*, 1.
78 *Vār Durgā Kī*, in *Śabdārath: Dasam Granth Sāhib*, vol. 1, p. 154.
79 *Śabdārath: Dasam Granth Sāhib*, 5.
80 Marcia Falk, "Notes on Composing New Blessings: Toward a Feminist-Jewish Prayer," in Plaskow and Christ (eds.), *Weaving the Visions*, 131.
81 *Vār Durgā Kī*, in *Śabdārath: Dasam Granth Sāhib*, vol. 1, p. 168.
82 Ibid., 157.
83 *Caṇḍī Caritra*, in *Śabdārath: Dasam Granth Sāhib*, vol. 1, p. 100.
84 *Vār Durgā Kī*, in *Śabdārath: Dasam Granth Sāhib*, vol. 1, p. 155.
85 Agrawala, *Devī-Māhātmyam: The Glorification of the Great Goddess*, 78–82.
86 *Vār Durgā Kī*, in *Śabdārath: Dasam Granth Sāhib*, vol. 1, p. 156.
87 Ibid., 158.
88 Ibid., 158.
89 Ibid., 155.
90 *Bacitra Nāṭak*, 1, 2.

91 Harbans Singh, *Gurū Gobind Singh*, 34.
92 The *Zafar-Nāmah*, or Epistle of Victory, was a letter in Persian verse Gurū Gobind Singh wrote to Emperor Aurangzeb. It consists of 111 verses and is more appropriately a fair-sized poem, impressing upon the Emperor how the moral principle should be the supreme law in matters of state as it should be for private behavior. Two of Gurū Gobind Singh's Sikhs, Dayā Singh and Dharam Singh, were charged with carrying the letter to the south to the Emperor, to whom, it is believed, it was delivered in Aḥmadnagar before he died in 1707. The *Zafar-Nāmah*, written in Gurmukhī characters, forms part of Gurū Gobind Singh's *Dasam Granth*.
93 Kapur Singh, *The Baisakhi of Gurū Gobind Singh*, 139–140.
94 *Caṇḍī Caritra*, in *Śabdārath: Dasam Granth Sāhib*, vol. 1, p. 127.
95 In his *Akāl Ustati*, in *Śabdārath: Dasam Granth Sāhib*, vol. 1, p. 28.
96 Ibid., p. 28.
97 *Jāpu*, in *Śabdārath: Dasam Granth Sāhib*, vol. 1, p. 5.
98 *Akāl Ustati*, in *Śabdārath: Dasam Granth Sāhib*, vol. 1, p. 21.

## 5 THE MAIDEN WEAVES: GARLANDS OF SONGS AND WAVES

1 Nripinder Singh, *The Sikh Moral Tradition: Ethical Perceptions of the Sikhs in the Late Nineteenth/Early Twentieth Century* (New Delhi: Manohar, 1990), 287–319.
2 Dr. Rattan Singh Jaggi (ed.), *Gurbāṇī Ṭīke Anaṅdghana* (Patiala: Punjab Bhāshā Vibhāg, 1970), 139.
3 David Kopf, *The Brahmo Samaj and the Shaping of the Modern Indian Mind* (Princeton: Princeton University Press, 1979); V. S. Naravane, *Modern Indian Thought* (Benares: Hindu University Press, 1944). See also French Hal (ed.), *Religious Fermentation in Modern India* (New York: St. Martin, 1982).
4 Harbans Singh, "A Passage from the Twentieth Century into the Twenty-first," a special address given at the International Conference on Sikhism, New Delhi, January 3, 1992.
5 A note from Giani Ditt Singh, editor of the *Khālsā Akhbār* (Punjabi) Lahore, May 25, 1894. It was brought to my attention by Harbans Singh in his address, "A Passage from the Twentieth Century into the Twenty-first."
6 Harbans Singh, *Bhai Vir Singh* (New Delhi: Sahitya Academy, 1972), 26.
7 Harbans Singh, *The Heritage of the Sikhs* (New Delhi: Manohar, 1983), 225–259.
8 G. S. Talib and Attar Singh (eds.), *Bhai Vir Singh: Life, Times, and Works* (Chandigarh: Publication Bureau, Punjab University, 1973), 15.

9 Harbans Singh, *Aspects of Punjabi Literature* (Ferozepore: Bawa Publishing House, 1961), 30.

10 *Bhāī Vīr Singh Racnāvalī*, vol. I (collection of poetry) (Patiala: Punjab Bhāshā Vibhāg, 1972), 191. (Hereafter referred to as *Bhāī Vīr Singh Racnāvalī*.)

11 Gurū Granth, 1343.

12 Ibid., 397.

13 *Bhāī Vīr Singh Racnāvalī*, 199.

14 Gurū Granth, 118.

15 A relationship that is much desired by western feminists. See, for example, Sallie McFague, "God as Mother," in Judith Plaskow and Carol Christ (eds.), *Weaving the Visions: New Patterns in Feminist Spirituality* (New York: Harper & Row, 1989), 139–150.

16 Gurū Granth, 118.

17 *Bhāī Vīr Singh Racnāvalī*, 193.

18 Gurū Granth, 1331.

19 Ibid., 23.

20 Ibid., 596.

21 *Bhāī Vīr Singh Racnāvalī*, 195.

22 Gurū Granth, 2.

23 *Bhāī Vīr Singh Racnāvalī*, 191–192.

24 Gurū Granth, 448.

25 Ibid., 1095.

26 Ibid., 13.

27 Ibid., 743.

28 Ibid., 287.

29 Ibid., 13.

30 *Bhāī Vīr Singh Racnāvalī*, 195.

31 Gurū Granth, 7–8.

32 *Bhāī Vīr Singh Racnāvalī*, 196.

33 Probably denotes that It is in every material object, for according to the Saṁkhya theory everything is constituted of the three strands – *sattva*, *rajas*, and *tamas*, signifying white, red, and black.

34 *Bhāī Vīr Singh Racnāvalī*, 212.

35 Ibid., 17.

36 Naomi Goldenberg, "Feminist Witchcraft: Controlling Our Own Inner Space," in *The Politics of Women's Spirituality*, ed. Charlene Spretnak (New York: Anchor/Doubleday, 1982), 216.

### 6 THE WOMAN ASKS: "WHAT IS LIFE?"

1 William V. Spanos, *A Casebook on Existentialism* (Thomas Crowell, 1966), 2.

2 Wilfred Cantwell Smith, *The Meaning and End of Religion: A New*

*Approach to the Religious Traditions of Mankind* (New York: Macmillan, 1962), 17.

3 Wilfred Cantwell Smith, *Questions of Religious Truth* (New York: Scribner, 1967), 68.

4 Gurū Arjan in *Rāg Sūhī*:

bed kateb simriti sabhi sāsat inh paṛiā mukti na hoī
Liberation is not attained by reading the Vedas, the Qur'ān and all the varied books. (Gurū Granth, 747)

For a detailed account of Gurū Nānak's rejection of the existing schools of thought, see Sher Singh, *The Philosophy of Sikhism* (Amritsar: Shiromani Gurdwara Parbandhak Committee, 1980), 73–120.

5 Edith Kern, *Existential Thought and Fictional Technique: Kierkegaard, Sartre, Beckett* (New Haven: Yale University Press, 1970), vii.

6 *Bhāī Vīr Singh Racnāvalī*, vol. 1 (collection of poetry) (Patiala: Punjab Bhāshā Vibhāg, 1972), 30–35. Hereafter referred to as *Jīvan kī Hai?* In the original Punjabi, the lake is described as "pāre vāṅg chhaṁb ikk" (p. 30).

7 Martin Heidegger, *Being and Time*, trans. John Macquarrie and Edward Robinson (New York: Harper & Row, 1962).

8 Ibid., 234.

9 Ibid., 231.

10 Ibid., 234.

11 Gurū Granth, 156.

12 Ibid., 1279.

13 *Being and Time*, 232.

14 Gurū Granth, 1273.

15 Ibid., 205.

16 Ibid., 78.

17 Ibid., 432.

18 Michelle Murray (ed.), *A House of Good Proportion: Images of Women in Literature* (Simon & Schuster, 1973), 126.

19 See S. Radhakrishnan, *The Principal Upaniṣads* (London: George Allen & Unwin, 1953), 695–705.

20 Gurū Granth, 8.

21 Elie Wiesel, *Night* (New York: Bantam, 1960), 3.

22 Gurū Granth, 931:

rajan rām ravai hitkāri raṇa mahi lūjhai manūā māri
rāti dinaṅti rahai raṅgi rātā.

23 Guru Granth, 522.

24 For instance, See Gurū Granth, 152; 877.

25 Carol P. Christ and Charlene Spretnak, "Images of Spiritual Power in Women's Fiction," in *The Politics of Women's Spirituality*, ed. Charlene Spretnak (New York: Anchor/Doubleday, 1982), 239.

7 SUṄDARĪ: THE PARADIGM OF SIKH ETHICS

1 Bhāī Vīr Singh, *Suṅdarī* (New Delhi: Bhāī Vīr Singh Sahitya Sadan, 1985), 127–128.
2 Harbans Singh, *Bhai Vir Singh* (New Delhi: Sahitya Academy, 1972), 45.
3 *Bhāī Vīr Singh Racnāvalī*, vol. II (collection of novels) (Patiala: Punjab Bhāshā Vibhāg, 1973). *Suṅdarī* forms pages 5–46 of this volume; hereafter referred to as *Suṅdarī*.
4 *Suṅdarī*, 5.
5 *Laws of Manu*, Ch. IV.
6 Says the Nawāb: "I won't give away this golden bird. Gold, silver, pearls, or diamonds are no price for her," *Suṅdarī*, 6.
7 *Suṅdarī*, 6.
8 Nripinder Singh, *The Sikh Moral Tradition: Ethical Perceptions of the Sikhs in the Late Nineteenth/Early Twentieth Century* (New Delhi: Manohar, 1990), 292.
9 Ibid., 292.
10 *Suṅdarī*, 7.
11 Ibid., 8.
12 See Ursula King, *Women and Spirituality: Voices of Protest and Promise* (London: Macmillan Education, 1989), 82.
13 *Suṅdarī*, 13.
14 Bhāī Vīr Singh (ed.), *Vārāṅ Bhāī Gurdas* I. 29.
15 *Gurū Granth*, 661.
16 Ibid., 931.
17 Ibid., 26.
18 Ibid., 457.
19 Ibid., 457.
20 *Suṅdarī*, 25.
21 Harbans Singh, *The Heritage of the Sikhs* (New Delhi: Manohar, 1983), 99–100.
22 *Suṅdarī*, 34.
23 *Gurū Granth*, 967.
24 Ibid., 33.
25 Ibid., 401.
26 Ibid., 412.
27 *Suṅdarī*, 44.
28 Ibid., 119.
29 Ibid., 44.
30 Ibid., 35.
31 Sheila Mullet writes, "We shift from seeing the world as an individual moral agent to seeing it through the eyes of a 'we.'" See Lorraine Code, Sheila Mullet, and Christine Overall (eds.), *Feminist Perspectives: Philosophical Essays on Method and Morals* (Toronto: University of

Toronto Press, 1988), 116. See also Sandra Lee Bartky, "Toward a Phenomenology of Feminist Consciousness," in *Feminism and Philosophy*, ed. Mary Vetterling-Braggin (Totowa, NJ: Rowman and Littlefield, 1977), 22 37.

32 *Sundarī*, 30.

33 Ibid., 43.

34 Ibid., 106.

35 *Khālsā Advocate*, English (Amritsar, December 15, 1904).

36 *Sundarī*, 40.

37 Ibid., 40.

38 Ibid., 44.

39 Ibid., 35.

40 Gurū Granth, 319.

41 Harbans Singh, *Bhai Vir Singh*, 43.

42 *Sundarī*, 40.

43 Ibid., 44.

44 *Sundarī*, 22.

45 Rachel M. Brownstein, *Becoming a Heroine: Reading about Women in Novels* (New York: Viking Press, 1982), 295.

46 Madonna Kolbenschlag, *Kiss Sleeping Beauty Good-bye: Breaking the Spell of Feminine Myths and Models* (New York: Doubleday, 1979).

## 8 RĀṆĪ RĀJ KAUR: THE MYSTICAL JOURNEY

1 G. S. Talib and Harbans Singh, *Bhāī Vīr Singh: Poet of the Sikhs* (Delhi: Motilal Banarsidass, 1976), 103.

2 Evelyn Underhill, *Mysticism* (New York: Dutton, 1961). First published in 1911.

3 Ibid., 86–87.

4 Steven T. Katz (ed.), *Mysticism and Religious Traditions* (Oxford: Oxford University Press, 1983), 4.

5 Gurū Granth, 4–5.

6 Bhāī Vīr Singh, *Rāṇā Sūrat Singh* (Amritsar: Khālsā Samācār, 1967); hereafter referred to as *RSS*. See also G. S. Talib and Harbans Singh, *Bhāī Vīr Singh*, 103–155, which carries Harbans Singh's lucid introduction to and translation of sections from *Rāṇā Sūrat Singh*.

7 Gurū Granth, 505.

8 *RSS*, 9.

9 Ibid., 83.

10 Mary Daly in *Beyond God the Father: Toward a Philosophy of Women's Liberation* (Boston: Beacon Press, 1978) reflects upon the degradation of the term "witch," which has at its root the term "wit" (p. 66).

11 Rāṇī Rāj Kaur's architectural venture is reminiscent of Shāh Jahān, the Moghul Emperor who had the Tāj Mahal built in memory of his dear wife, Mumtāz Mahal. Indeed, the words used to describe the Tāj,

that it is "a teardrop on the cheek of time" (Rabindranath Tagore), or its white marble "symbolizes the purity of love" (Eleanor Roosevelt), can easily be applied to Rāj Kaur's creation as well. The image of the monument as a "teardrop" is very appropriate; so, too, the white marble which marks the purity of Rāṇī Rāj Kaur's love and the steadfastness of her devotion.

12 *RSS*, 2.
13 Ibid., 7.
14 Ibid., 7.
15 Ibid., 7.
16 Ibid., 12.
17 Ibid., 3.
18 Ibid., 3.
19 Ibid., 8.
20 Ibid., 8.
21 Gurū Granth, 1102.
22 *RSS*, 16.
23 Ibid., 125.
24 Ibid., 10.
25 Ibid., 5.
26 Ibid., 5.
27 Ibid., 11.
28 Ibid., 8.
29 Ibid., 5.
30 Symbol has been defined as a surrogate by Samuel Brandon in *Man and God in Art and Ritual* (New York: Scribner, 1974).
31 *RSS*, 5.
32 Ibid., 6.
33 Taran Singh (ed.), *Gurū Nānak Bānī Prakāś*, vol. II (Patiala: Punjabi University Press, 1969), 749.
34 William James, *The Varieties of Religious Experience* (New York: Collier, 1961), 300.
35 *RSS*, 23.
36 Ibid., 23.
37 Ibid., 23.
38 G. S. Talib, *Guru Nanak: His Personality and Vision* (New Delhi: Gurdas Kapur and Sons, 1969), 186–226. See also Mircea Eliade, *Yoga: Immortality and Freedom* (Princeton: Bollingen, 1969), 47–100.
39 Gurū Granth, 1025.
40 Ibid., 905.
41 Ibid., 1043.
42 *RSS*, 219.
43 Ibid., 24.
44 Ibid., 24.
45 Ibid., 33.

46 Ibid., 36
47 James, *The Varieties of Religious Experience*, 209–300.
48 *RSS*, 23.
49 Ibid., 23.
50 Ibid., 24.
51 Ibid., 24.
52 Ibid., 25.
53 Ibid., 25.
54 Ibid., 26.
55 Ibid., 26.
56 Ibid., 26.
57 Ibid., 27.
58 Ibid., 31.
59 Ibid., 31.
60 Rāṇī Rāj Kaur's flight is reminiscent of the flight expressed by Brancusi in *Stone: Bird in Space*. In "Brancusi and Mythology," Eliade comments that "The symbolism of flight expresses an escape from the universe of everyday experience, and the double intentionality of that escape is obvious; it is at the same time *transcendence* and *freedom* that one obtains by 'flight'" in Diane Apostolos-Cappadona (ed.), *Mircea Eliade: Symbolism, the Sacred, and the Arts* (New York: Crossroad, 1985), 101. During her ascent, Rāṇī Rāj Kaur does experience both *transcendence* and *freedom*.
61 *RSS*, 23.
62 Ibid., 23.
63 Ibid., 25.
64 Ibid., 23.
65 Gurū Granth, 198.
66 *RSS*, 25.
67 Ibid., 31.
68 Ibid., 34.
69 James, *The Varieties of Religious Experience*, 300.
70 *RSS*, 28.
71 Ibid., 28.
72 Ibid., 31.
73 Ibid., 28.
74 Ibid., 28. Putting the scarf around and covering the head signify a posture of humility and reverence.
75 *RSS*, 28.
76 Ibid., 28.
77 Ibid., 31.
78 Ibid., 32.
79 Ibid., 33.
80 Carol Christ, *Diving Deep and Surfacing: Women Writers on Spiritual Quest* (Boston: Beacon Press, 1980), 34. Carol Christ here seems to identify

queen with goddess. Indeed, the ideal society sought under the image of goddess by feminist thealogians comes into being under the rule of Rāṇī Rāj Kaur.

81 James, *The Varieties of Religious Experience*, 300.
82 *RSS*, 32.
83 Ibid., 35.
84 Ibid., 35.
85 Ibid., 36.
86 Ibid., 36.
87 Ibid., 36.
88 Judith Baskin, "The Separation of Women in Rabbinic Judaism," in *Women, Religion and Social Change*, ed. Yvonne Yazbeck Haddad and Ellison Banks Findly (New York: State University of New York Press, 1985), 3.
89 Mariana Alcoforado, quoted by Charlene Spretnak in "Self Images of Strength," in *The Politics of Women's Spirituality* (New York: Anchor/Doubleday, 1982), 247.
90 *RSS*, 34.
91 Ibid., 36.
92 Underhill, *Mysticism*, 81.
93 Ibid., 447.

### CONCLUSION

1 Thomas Aquinas, *Summa of Christian Teaching* 1.32; in Mary T. Clark, *An Aquinas Reader* (New York: Doubleday, 1972), 134–136.
2 Ibid., 34.
3 Gurū Granth, 637.
4 Bhāī Vīr Singh would later retain Gurū Gobind Singh's artistic spirit by comparing the strength and alacrity of his women protagonists with that of the Hindu goddess.
5 David Kinsley, "The Image of the Divine and the Status of Women in the *Devī-Bhāgavat Purāna*," *Anima*, 9/1, 50–53.
6 *The Sri Mad Devi Bhāgavatam*, The Sacred Books of the Hindus, vol. 26, trans. Swami Vijnananda (New York: AMS Press, 1974), 17.
7 Ibid., 53.
8 Ibid., 1192: "Never any woman nor any Śudra is to read this herself or himself, even out of ignorance; rather they should hear this from the mouth of a Brahmana." Now C. MacKenzie Brown, in his study *The Triumph of the Goddess* (New York: State University of New York Press, 1990), tries to downplay the incongruity by stating that "There is occasionally at least a suggestion that the greatness and positive attributes of the divine feminine overflow into the social realm, even if only somewhat tentatively" (p. 200). Unfortunately, such streams of power have never succeeded in affecting the social realm; their

influence has been no more than a tentative suggestion which has never been carried out.

9 Simone de Beauvoir, "Myths: Dreams, Fears, Idols," in *The Second Sex: The Classic Manifesto of the Liberated Woman* (New York: Vintage, 1952), 179.

10 The film is set in the vicinity of Calcutta, during the latter part of the nineteenth century. As Durgā-Kālī, the goddess has been venerated in the entire state of Bengal for centuries. Satyajit Ray, born and brought up in Calcutta, must have been highly conscious of her presence. The writer Prabhat Kumar Mukerjee published a short story on this theme in 1899, but the original inspiration for his story came from Rabindranath Tagore, who was also from Calcutta and had a lot of influence on the young Ray. Most artistically, most poignantly, Ray's *Devī* raises profound questions: why would a household with a female deity at its center be governed by a domineering patriarch? Or in a larger sense, why would a society that has worshiped goddesses from time immemorial be androcentric, misogynist?

Ray's film brings to mind the Bengali saint Ramakrishna (1836–86). He was the temple priest at the Kālī temple at Daksinesvar, north of Calcutta. He is one of the figures who made the cult of the black goddess very popular in the state of Bengal. The extreme homage paid to the black goddess by Kālīkankar, the protagonist of Ray's film, would be by no means unusual in nineteenth-century Bengal. Ramakrishna and his followers adored Kālī as the Supreme Mover, the Mother of the Cosmos. Ramakrishna even dressed up and acted like a woman and immersed himself in the feminine mood. But he looked upon real women as "ferocious, voracious felines coming to devour him." See Carl Olson, *The Mysterious Play of Kālī: An Interpretive Study of Ramakrishna* (Atlanta, GA: American Academy of Religion, Scholars Press, 1990), 39. Olson's study begins with the apt question, "If you encountered someone who assumed the dress and demeanor of a woman yet held a misogynist attitude, would you not wonder about such a person?"

11 Sallie McFague, *Models of God: Theology for an Ecological, Nuclear Age* (Philadelphia: Fortress Press, 1987), 128.

12 Judith Plaskow, *Standing Again at Sinai* (New York: Harper & Row, 1990), 162.

13 Mary Daly, *Beyond God the Father: Toward a Philosophy of Women's Liberation* (Boston: Beacon Press, 1973), 7–8.

14 Plaskow, *Standing Again at Sinai*, 125.

## EPILOGUE

1 G. S. Talib, *Bhai Vir Singh: Life, Times & Works* (Chandigarh: Punjab University Publication Bureau, 1973), 7.

2 Daljeet Singh, "Comparison of Nathism, Vaisnavism and Sikhism," in Gurdev Singh (ed.), *Perspectives on the Sikh Tradition* (Patiala: Siddharth Press, 1986), 133.
3 Upinder Jit Kaur, *Sikh Religion and Economic Development* (New Delhi: National Book Organisation, 1990), 308.
4 Nripinder Singh, *The Sikh Moral Tradition: Ethical Perceptions of the Sikhs in the Late Nineteenth/Early Twentieth Century* (New Delhi: Manohar, 1990), 244–252.
5 Gaston Bachelard, *The Poetics of Reverie: Childhood, Language, and the Cosmos* (Boston: Beacon Press, 1960), 1.
6 Hélène Cixous and Catherine Clément, *The Newly Born Woman*, Theory and History of Literature, vol. 24, trans. Betsy Wing (Minnesota: University of Minnesota Press, 1986), 93.

# *Bibliography*

## NON-PUNJABI SOURCES

Agrawala, V. S. *Devī-Māhātmyam: The Glorification of the Great Goddess* (Varanasi: All India Kashiraj Trust, 1963).

Ahluwalia, Jasbir Singh. *The Sovereignty of the Sikh Doctrine* (New Delhi: Bahri Publishers, 1983).

Apostolos-Cappadona, Diane (ed.). *Mircea Eliade: Symbolism, the Sacred, and the Arts* (New York: Crossroad, 1985).

Arabi, Ibn al'. *The Bezels of Wisdom.* Trans. R. W. J. Austin in *The Classics of Western Spirituality* (NJ: Paulist Press, 1980).

Archer, John Clark. *The Sikhs in Relation to Hindus, Moslems, Christians and Ahmadiyyas* (Princeton: Princeton University Press, 1946).

Arnheim, Rudolph. *Art and Visual Perception* (Berkeley: University of California Press, 1966).

Ashta, D. P. *The Poetry of the Dasam Granth* (New Delhi: Arun Prakashan, 1959).

Aurobindo, Sri. *The Synthesis of Yoga*, vol. 1 (Pondicherry: Sri Aurobindo Ashram, 1965).

Bachelard, Gaston. *The Poetics of Reverie: Childhood, Language, and the Cosmos* (Boston: Beacon Press, 1960).

Banerjee, I. B. *Evolution of the Khalsa*, 2 vols. (Calcutta: A. Mukherjee, 1936).

Bardwick, Judith. *Psychology of Women: A Study of Bio-Cultural Conflicts* (New York: Harper & Row, 1971).

Barrier, N. Gerald. *The Sikhs and their Literature* (New Delhi: Manohar, 1970).

Bartky, Sandra Lee. "Toward a Phenomenology of Feminist Consciousness," in *Feminism and Philosophy*, ed. Mary Vetterling-Braggin (Totowa, NJ: Rowman and Littlefield, 1977), 22–37.

Baskin, Judith. "The Separation of Women in Rabbinic Judaism," in *Women, Religion and Social Change*, ed. Yvonne Yazbeck Haddad and Ellison Banks Findly (New York: State University of New York Press, 1985), 3–18.

Beauvoir, Simone de. *The Second Sex*, trans. H. M. Parshley (New York: Vintage, 1974).

Bhachu, Parminder. *Twice Migrants* (London and New York: Tavistock Publications, 1985).

Bouquet, A. C. *Sacred Books of the World* (Baltimore: Pelican, 1967).

Brown, C. MacKenzie. *The Triumph of the Goddess* (New York: State University of New York Press, 1990).

Brownstein, Rachel M. *Becoming a Heroine: Reading about Women in Novels* (New York: Viking Press, 1982).

Carroll, Theodora Foster. *Women, Religion, and Development in the Third World* (New York: Praeger, 1983).

Christ, Carol. *Diving Deep and Surfacing: Women Writers on Spiritual Quest.* (Boston: Beacon Press, 1980).

"Symbols of Goddess and God in Feminist Theology," in *Book of the Goddess*, ed. Carl Olson (New York: Crossroad, 1985), 231–251.

Christ, Carol and Judith Plaskow. *Womanspirit Rising: A Feminist Reader in Religion* (New York: Harper & Row, 1979).

Cixous, Hélène and Catherine Clément. *The Newly Born Woman.* Theory and History of Literature, vol. 24, trans. Betsy Wing (Minnesota: University of Minnesota Press, 1986).

Coburn, Thomas. *Encountering the Goddess: A Translation of the Devī Māhātmya and a Study of its Interpretation* (New York: State Univesity of New York, 1990).

Code, Lorraine, Sheila Mullet, and Christine Overall (eds.). *Feminist Perspectives: Philosophical Essays on Method and Morals* (Toronto: University of Toronto Press, 1988).

Cole, Owen W. *The Guru in Sikhism* (London: Darton, Longman & Todd, 1982).

*Sikhism and its Indian Context: 1469–1708: The Attitude of Guru Nanak and Early Sikhism to Indian Religious Beliefs and Practices* (New Delhi: D. K. Agencies, 1984).

Cole, Owen W. and Piara Singh Sambhi. *The Sikhs: Their Religious Beliefs and Practices* (New Delhi: Vikas Publishing House, 1978).

Coomaraswamy, Ananda K. *Christian and Oriental Philosophy of Art* (New York: Dover, 1956).

*The Hindu View of Art* (Bombay: Asia Publishing House, 1957).

*The Transformation of Nature in Art* (Cambridge, MA: Harvard University Press, 1935).

Corbin, Henry. *Œuvres philosophiques et mystiques de Shihabaddin Yahya Sorawardi, Opera Metaphysica et Mystica* II (Tehran, 1952).

Courtright, Paul B. "Syncretism and the Formation of the Sikh Tradition," in Harbans Singh (ed.), *Punjab Past and Present: Essays in Honour of Dr. Ganda Singh* (Patiala: Punjabi University, 1976), 417–432.

Daly, Mary. *Beyond God the Father: Toward a Philosophy of Women's Liberation* (Boston: Beacon Press, 1973).

*Gynn-Ecology: The Metaethics of Radical Feminism* (Boston: Beacon Press, 1978).

*Pure Lust: Elemental Feminist Philosophy* (Boston: Beacon Press, 1984).

Delahoutre, Michel. *Les Sikhs* (Belgium: Editions Brepolis, 1989).

Delahoutre, Michel and Harbans Singh. *Le Sikhisme: Anthologie de la poésie religieuse sikh* (Belgium: Louvian-La-Neuve, 1985).

Dimmitt, Cornelia and J. A. B. van Buitenen (eds.). *Classical Hindu Mythology: A Reader in the Sanskrit Purāṇas* (Philadelphia: Temple University Press, 1978).

Downing, Christine. *The Goddess: Mythological Images of the Feminine* (New York: Crossroad, 1981).

Dunning, Stephen. "The Sikh Religion: An Examination of Some of the Western Studies," *Journal of Religious Studies* (Patiala: Punjabi University, autumn 1970): 1–27.

Edgerton, Franklin (trans.). *Bhagavad-Gītā* (Cambridge, MA: Harvard University Press, 1972).

Eliade, Mircea. *The Two and the One* (New York: Harper Torchbooks, 1965).

*Yoga: Immortality and Freedom* (Princeton: Bollingen, 1969).

Faruqi, Ismail al. *Tawhīd: Its Implications for Thought and Life* (Kuala Lumpur: International Institute of Islamic Thought, 1982).

Findly, Ellison Banks. "Gārgī at the King's Court," in *Women, Religion, and Social Change*, ed. Yvonne Yazbeck Haddad and Ellison Banks Findly (New York: State University of New York Press, 1985), 37–58.

Fiorenza, Elisabeth Shüsler. *In Memory of Her: A Feminist Theological Reconstruction of Christian Origins* (New York: Crossroad, 1983).

Fox, Richard G. *Lions of the Punjab: Culture in the Making* (Berkeley: University of California Press, 1985).

Goldenberg, Naomi. "Feminist Witchcraft: Controlling Our Own Inner Space," in *The Politics of Women's Spirituality*, ed. Charlene Spretnak (New York: Anchor/Doubleday, 1982), 213–218.

Grahn, Judy. "From Sacred Blood to the Curse Beyond," in *The Politics of Women's Spirituality*, ed. Charlene Spretnak (New York: Anchor/Doubleday, 1982), 265–279.

Grewal, J. S. *The New Cambridge History of India: The Sikhs of the Punjab* (Cambridge: Cambridge University Press, 1990).

Grimshaw, Jean. *Philosophy and Feminist Thinking* (Minneapolis: University of Minnesota Press, 1986).

Gross, Rita. "Hindu Female Deities as a Resource for the Contemporary Rediscovery of the Goddess," in *The Book of the Goddess Past and Present: An Introduction to Her Religion*, ed. Carl Olson (New York: Crossroad, 1985), 217–230.

Gutman, Joseph (ed.). *The Image and the Word: Confrontations in Judaism, Christianity and Islam* (Atlanta, GA: Scholars Press, 1977).

Haddad, Yvonne Yazbeck and Ellison Banks Findly (eds.). *Women, Religion and Social Change* (New York: State University of New York Press, 1985).

Hall, Robert W. (ed.). *Studies in Religious Philosophy* (New York: American Book Company, 1969).

Heidegger, Martin. *Being and Time*. Trans. John Macquarrie and Edward Robinson (New York: Harper & Row, 1962).

*Poetry, Language, Thought*. Trans. Albert Hofstadter (New York: Harper & Row, 1971).

Holdrege, Barbara A. "The Bride of Israel: The Ontological Status of Scripture in the Rabbinic and Kabbalistic Traditions," in Miriam Levering (ed.), *Rethinking Scripture: Essays from a Comparative Perspective* (New York: State University of New York Press, 1989), 180–261.

Hunt, Mary E. "On Feminist Theology," *Journal of Feminist Studies in Religion* (fall 1985), 85–86.

Ikram, S. M. *Muslim Civilization in India* (New York: Columbia University Press, 1964).

Iqbal, Muhammad. *The Development of Metaphysics in Persia* (Lahore: Bazmi-i-Iqbal).

Jain, Nirmal Kumar. *Sikh Religion and Philosophy* (New Delhi: Sterling, 1979).

James, William. *The Varieties of Religious Experience* (New York: Collier, 1961).

Johnson, Elizabeth A. "The Incomprehensibility of God and the Image of God Male and Female," *Theological Studies* 45 (1984).

Juergensmeyer, Mark and N. Gerald Barrier (eds.). *Sikh Studies: Comparative Perspectives on a Changing Tradition*, Berkeley Religious Studies Series (Berkeley, 1979).

Kang, Kanwarjit Singh. "Art and Architecture of the Golden Temple," *Marg*. 3.3 (June 1977), 23–35.

"Sikh Gurus in the Murals of the 19th Century Punjab," in *Punjab Murals of Sikh Gurus* (Patiala, n.d.).

Katz, Steven T. (ed.). *Mysticism and Religious Traditions* (Oxford: Oxford University Press, 1983).

Kaur, Guninder. *The Gurū Granth Sahib: Its Physics and Metaphysics* (New Delhi: Sterling Publishers, 1981).

Kaur, Gurnam. *Reason and Revelation in Sikhism* (New Delhi: Cosmo Publications, 1990).

Kaur, Madanjit. *The Golden Temple: Past and Present* (Amritsar: Guru Nanak Dev University Press, 1983).

Kern, Edith. *Existential Thought and Fictional Technique: Kierkegaard, Sartre, Beckett* (New Haven: Yale University Press, 1970).

*Khalsa Advocate*, English (December 15, 1904).

King, Ursula. *Women and Spirituality: Voices of Protest and Promise* (London: Macmillan Education, 1989).

Kinsley, David R. "Durgā, Warrior Goddess and Cosmic Queen," in *The Goddesses' Mirror: Visions of the Divine from East and West* (New York: State University of New York Press, 1989).

"The Image of the Divine and the Status of Women in the *Devī-Bhāgavat Purāṇa*," *Anima* 9/1, 50–53.

"The Portrait of the Goddess in the *Devī-māhātmya*," *Journal of the American Academy of Religion* 46:4 (December 1978), 489–506.

Kohli, S. S. *A Critical Study of the Adi Granth* (New Delhi: The Punjabi Writers' Cooperative Industrial Society Ltd., 1961).

Kolbenschlag, Madonna. *Kiss Sleeping Beauty Good-bye: Breaking the Spell of Feminine Myths and Models* (New York: Doubleday, 1979).

Kopf, David. *The Brahmo Samaj and the Shaping of the Modern Indian Mind* (Princeton: Princeton University Press, 1979).

Laeuchli, Samuel. *Religion and Art in Conflict* (Philadelphia: Fortress Press, 1980).

Loehlin, C. H. *The Sikhs and their Scriptures* (Lucknow: Lucknow Publishing House, 1964).

Macauliffe, Max Arthur. *The Sikh Religion, its Gurus, Sacred Writings and Authors*, 6 vols. (Oxford: Clarendon Press, 1909).

McConnell-Ginet, Sally, Ruth Borker, and Nelly Furman (eds.) *Women and Language in Literature and Society* (New York: Praeger, 1980).

McFague, Sallie. *Models of God: Theology for an Ecological, Nuclear Age* (Philadelphia: Fortress Press, 1987).

McLeod, W. H. *Early Sikh Tradition: A Study of the Janam-sakhis* (Oxford: Clarendon Press, 1980).

*Gurū Nānak and the Sikh Religion* (Oxford: Clarendon Press, 1968).

*The B40 Janam-Sakhi* (Amritsar: Guru Nanak Dev University, 1981).

*The Evolution of the Sikh Community* (New Delhi: Oxford University Press, 1975).

*The Sikhs: History, Religion and Society* (New York: Columbia University, Press 1989).

*Who is a Sikh? The Problem of Sikh Identity* (Oxford: Clarendon Press, 1989).

Marenco, Ethne K. *The Transformation of Sikh Society* (Portland, OR: HaPi Press, 1974).

Miles, Margaret. *Image as Insight: Visual Understanding in Western Christian and Secular Culture* (Boston: Beacon Press, 1985).

Mollenkott, Virginia Ramey. *The Divine Feminine: The Biblical Imagery of God as Female* (New York: Crossroad, 1989).

Moltmann-Wendel, Elisabeth. *A Land Flowing with Milk and Honey: Perspectives on Feminist Theology* (New York: Crossroad, 1986).

Müller, Max. *Introduction to the Science of Religion* (London: Longman's, Green, 1873).

Nasr, S. H. *Knowledge and the Sacred* (New York: Crossroad, 1981).

*National Catholic Reporter* (January 31, 1975).

Noss, J. B. *A History of the World's Religions* (New York: Macmillan, 1990). First published under the title *Man's Religions* (Macmillan, 1974).

O'Connell, Joseph T. (ed.). *Sikh History and Religion in the Twentieth Century* (Toronto: University of Toronto, Centre for South Asian Studies, 1988).

O'Flaherty, Wendy. "*Comments*: Mediation in the Sant Tradition," in *Sikh Studies: Comparative Perspectives on a Changing Tradition*, Berkeley Religious Studies Series (Berkeley, 1979), 87–90.

*Women, Androgynes, and Other Mythical Beasts* (Chicago: University of Chicago Press, 1980).

Olson, Carl. *The Mysterious Play of Kālī: An Interpretive Study of Ramakrishna* (Atlanta, GA, Scholars Press, 1990).

Olson, Carl (ed.), *The Book of the Goddess, Past and Present: An Introduction to Her Religion* (New York: Crossroad, 1985).

Otto, Rudolph. *The Idea of the Holy* (New York: Galaxy, 1958).

Pettigrew, Joyce. *Robber Noblemen: A Study of the Political System of the Jat Sikhs* (London: Routledge & Kegan Paul, 1975).

Pinkham, Mildreth. *Woman in the Sacred Scriptures of Hinduism* (New York: AMS, 1967).

Plaskow, Judith. *Standing Again at Sinai* (New York: Harper & Row, 1990).

Plaskow, Judith and Joan Arnold (eds.). *Women and Religion* (Missoula, MT: Scholars Press, 1974).

Plaskow, Judith and Carol Christ (eds.). *Weaving the Visions: New Patterns in Feminist Spirituality* (New York: Harper & Row, 1989).

Preston, James. *Cult of the Goddess: Social and Religious Change in a Hindu Temple* (Illinois: Waveland Press, 1980).

Rabuzzi, Kathryn Allen. *The Sacred and the Feminine: Toward a Theology of Housework* (New York: Seabury Press, 1982).

Radhakrishnan, S. *An Idealist View of Life*, Hibbert Lectures (New York: AMS Press, 1981).

"Gurū Nānak: An Introduction," in *Guru Nanak: His Life, Time and Teachings*, ed. Gurmukh Nihal Singh (New Delhi: Guru Nanak Foundation, 1969).

*The Principal Upanisads* (London: George Allen & Unwin, 1953).

Randhawa, G. S. "Guru Nanak's Vision of Human Society," *Khera: Journal of Religious Understanding* (October–December 1990) (New Delhi: Bhai Vir Singh Sahitya Sadan), 1–11.

Rank, Otto. *The Myth of the Birth of the Hero* (New York: Vintage, 1959).

Ray, Niharranjan. *The Sikh Gurūs and the Sikh Society* (Patiala: Punjabi University Press, 1970).

Ronan, Marion. "The Liturgy of Women's Lives: A Call to Celebration," *Cross Currents* 28: 20, 17–31.

Rosaldo, Michelle Zimbalist and Louise Lamphere (eds.). *Woman, Culture, and Society* (Stanford: Stanford University Press, 1974).

Ruether, Rosemary Radford. *New Woman New Earth: Sexist Ideologies and Human Liberation* (New York: Seabury Press, 1975).

*Sexism and God-Talk: Toward a Feminist Theology* (Boston: Beacon Press, 1983).
"The Future of Feminist Theology," *Journal of the American Academy of Religion* 53 (December 1985), 703–713.
Russell, Letty M. (ed.). *The Liberating Word: A Guide to Nonsexist Interpretation of the Bible* (Philadelphia: Westminster, 1976).
Santayana, George. *The Sense of Beauty: Being the Outline of Aesthetic Theory* (New York: Dover, 1955).
Schimmel, Annemarie. *Mystical Dimensions of Islam* (Chapel Hill: University of North Carolina Press, 1975).
"Women in Mystical Islam," *Women's Studies International Forum* 5/2 (1982), 145–151.
Schomer, Karine and W. H. McLeod (eds.). *The Sants: Studies in a Devotional Tradition of India* (New Delhi: Berkeley Religious Series and Motilal Banarsidass, 1987).
Shange, Ntozake. *for colored girls who have considered suicide when the rainbow is enuf* (New York: Macmillan, 1975).
Shiva, Vandana. *Staying Alive: Women, Ecology and Development* (London: Zed Books, 1989).
Singh, Avtar. *Ethics of the Sikhs* (Patiala: Punjabi University Press, 1970).
*Secularism and Sikh Faith* (Amritsar: Guru Nanak Dev University Press, 1973).
Singh, Bhai Jodh. *The Japji*. (Amritsar, 1956).
Singh, Diwan. *Guru Nanak and the Indian Mystic Tradition* (Ludhiana: Lahore Book Shop, 1981).
Singh, Gopal (trans.). *Sri Guru Granth Sahib*, vols. I–IV (Chandigarh: World Sikh University Press, 1978).
Singh, Gurdev (ed.). *Perspectives on the Sikh Tradition* (Patiala: Siddharth Press, 1986).
Singh, Gurmukh Nihal (ed.). *Guru Nanak: His Life, Time and Teachings* (New Delhi: Guru Nanak Foundation, 1969).
Singh, Harbans. *Aspects of Punjabi Literature* (Ferozepore: Bawa Publishing House, 1961).
*Berkeley Lectures on Sikhism* (New Delhi: Guru Nunak Foundation, 1983).
*Bhai Vir Singh* (New Delhi: Sahitya Academy, 1972).
*Guru Gobind Singh* (New Delhi: Sterling, 1979).
*Guru Nanak and Origins of the Sikh Faith* (Bombay: Asia Publishing House, 1969).
*Guru Tegh Bahadur* (New Delhi: Sterling, 1982).
*The Heritage of the Sikhs* (New Delhi: Manohar, 1983).
Singh, Harbans (ed.). *Perspectives on Guru Nanak* (Patiala: Punjabi University, 1975).
*Punjab Past and Present: Essays in Honour of Dr. Ganda Singh.* (Patiala: Punjabi University, 1976).

Singh, Kapur. *The Baisakhi of Gurū Gobind Singh* (Jullundur: Hind Publishers, 1959).
Singh, Khushwant. *Hymns of Guru Nanak* (Bombay: Orient Longman, 1991).
Singh, Nripinder. "Guru Nanak, Prophecy and the Study of Religion," in *Studies in Sikhism and Comparative Religion* (New Delhi: Guru Nanak Foundation, April 1989), 15–23.
*The Sikh Moral Tradition: Ethical Perceptions of the Sikhs in the Late Nineteenth/Early Twentieth Century* (New Delhi: Manohar, 1990).
Singh, Puran. *The Spirit of Oriental Poetry* (London: Kegan Paul, 1926).
Singh, Sher. *The Philosophy of Sikhism* (Amritsar: Shiromani Gurdwara Parbandhak Committee, 1980).
Singh, Teja. *Essays in Sikhism* (Lahore: Sikh University Press, 1941).
Smith, Margaret. *Rābi'a: The Mystic and her Fellow-Saints in Islam* (Cambridge: Cambridge University Press, 1928).
Smith, Wilfred Cantwell. *Questions of Religious Truth* (New York: Scribner, 1967).
*Religious Diversity*, ed. Willard G. Oxtoby (New York: Harper & Row, 1976).
*The Crystallization of Religious Communities in Mughul India* (Tehran: Intishrat Daneshgah, 1969), 197–220.
*The Meaning and End of Religion: A New Approach to the Religious Traditions of Mankind* (New York: Macmillan, 1962).
Spacks, Patricia M. *The Female Imagination* (New York: Alfred A. Knopf, 1975).
Spretnak, Charlene (ed.). *The Politics of Women's Spirituality* (New York: Anchor/Doubleday, 1982).
Swidler, Leonard. "Is Sexism a Sign of Decadence in Religion?," in *Women and Religion*, ed. Judith Plaskow and Joan Arnold (Atlanta, GA: Scholars Press, 1974).
Tagore, Rabindranath. *The Religion of an Artist* (Calcutta: Visva-Bharati, 1953).
Talib, Gurbachan Singh. *Guru Nanak: His Personality and Vision* (New Delhi: Gurdas Kapur and Sons, 1969).
*Impact of Guru Gobind Singh on Indian Society* (Chandigarh: Guru Gobind Singh Foundation, 1966).
*Japuji: The Immortal Prayer-Chant* (Delhi: Munshiram Manoharlal, 1977).
and Harbans Singh, *Bhāī Vīr Singh: Poet of The Sikhs* (Delhi: Motilal Banarsidass, 1976).
*The Bible Today* 22:5 (September 1984).
*The Sikh Review* (Calcutta, May 1955).
Tillich, Paul. *Systematic Theology*, vol. 1 (Chicago: University of Chicago Press, 1951).

Trible, Phyllis. *God and the Rhetoric of Sexuality* (Philadelphia: Fortress Press, 1978).

*Texts of Terror: Literary Feminist Readings of Biblical Narratives* (Philadelphia: Fortress Press, 1984).

Trumpp, Ernest (trans.). *The Adi Granth or the Holy Scriptures of the Sikhs* (first published 1877; 2nd. edition: New Delhi: Munshiram Manoharlal, 1970).

Ulanov, Ann Belford. *The Feminine in Jungian Psychology and in Christian Theology* (Evanston: Northwestern University Press, 1971).

Underhill, Evelyn. *Mysticism* (New York: Dutton, 1961).

Vaudeville, Charlotte. *Bārahmāsā in Indian Literature* (Delhi: Motilal Banarsidass, 1986).

*Kabir* (Oxford: Clarendon Press, 1974).

Waley, Arthur. *The Way and its Power: A Study of Tao Tê Ching and its Place in Chinese Thought* (New York: Grove Press, 1958).

Washbourn, Penelope. *Becoming Woman: The Quest for Wholeness in Female Experience* (New York: Harper & Row, 1977).

Welch, Holmes. *Taoism: The Parting of the Way* (Boston: Beacon Press, 1965).

Wheelwright, Philip. *Metaphor and Reality* (Bloomington: Indiana University Press, 1962).

Wilder, Amos Niven. *Theopoetic: Theology and the Religious Imagination* (Philadelphia: Fortress Press, 1976).

Woolf, Virginia. *Collected Essays* (London: Hogarth Press, 1966).

Zaehner, R. C. (ed.). *The Concise Encyclopaedia of Living Faiths* (Boston: Beacon Press, 1959).

Zimmer, Heinrich. *Myths and Symbols in Indian Art and Civilization* (Princeton: Bollingen, 1974).

Zuckerkandl, Victor. *Sound and Symbol: Music and the External World* (Princeton: Bollingen, 1956).

## PUNJABI SOURCES

Bālā, Bhāī. *Janamsākhī* (Lahore: Rāī Sāhib Munshī Gulāb Singh).

Bhāī Vīr Singh, *Santhya Srī Gurū Granth Sāhib*, vol. I (Amritsar: Khālsā Samācār, 1958).

*Bhāī Vīr Singh Racnāvalī*, vol. I (collection of poetry) (Patiala: Punjab Bhāshā Vibhāg, 1972).

*Bhāī Vīr Singh Racnāvalī*, vol. II (collection of novels) (Patiala: Punjab Bhāshā Vibhāg, 1973).

Bhāī Vīr Singh. *Japujī Sāhib Santhyā* (Amritsar: Khālsā Samācār, 1981).

*Rāṇā Sūrat Singh* (Amritsar: Khālsā Samācār, 1967).

*Vārān Bhāī Gurdās* (Amritsar: Khālsā Samācār, 1977).

Bhāī Vīr Singh (ed.). *Purātan Janamsākhī Srī Gurū Nānak Dev Jī* (Amritsar: Khālsā Samācār, 1948).

Bhallā, Sarūp Dās. *Mahimā Prakāś* (Patiala: Languages Department, 1971).
*Gurbilās Chevīṅ Pātshāhī* (Patiala: Languages Department, 1970).
Jaggi, Rattan Singh (ed.). *Gurbāṇī Ṭīke Anandghana* (Patiala: Punjab Bhāshā Vibhāg, 1970).
Miharbān. *Janamsākhī Srī Gurū Nānak Dev Jī* (Amritsar: Khālsa College, 1962).
Padam, Piara Singh. *Dasam Granth Darśan* (Patiala: Kala Mandir, Lower Mall, 1990).
*Śabdārath: Dasam Granth Sāhib*, vol. I (Patiala: Punjabi University Press, 1973).
*Śabdārath: Śri Gurū Granth Sāhibjī*, vols. I–IV (Amritsar: Shiromaṇi Gurdwara Prabandhak Committee, 1969).
Sharma, G. L. (ed.). *Caṇḍī dī Vār* (Amritsar: Sundar Dass & Sons, 1979).
Singh, Kartar. *Nitnem Stīk* (Amritsar: Shiromaṇi Gurdwara Prabandhak Committee, 1977).
Singh, Taran (ed.). *Gurū Nānak Bāṇī Prakāś*, vols. I and II (Patiala: Punjabi University Press, 1969).

The translations from the above sources are mine unless otherwise indicated.

# Index

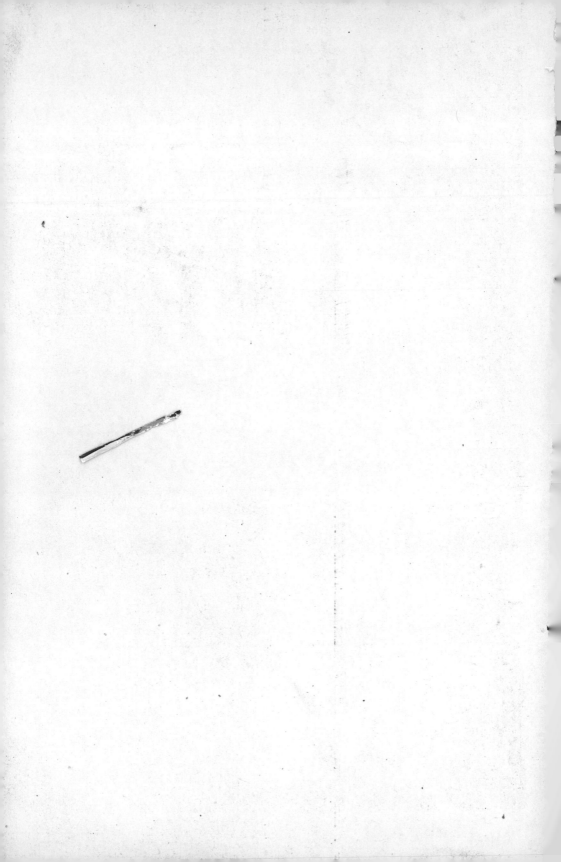